DICTIONARY OF MILITARY TERMS

A GUIDE TO THE LANGUAGE OF WARFARE
AND MILITARY INSTITUTIONS

Other titles from H.W. Wilson

DICTIONARY OF MILITARY TERMS

A GUIDE TO THE LANGUAGE OF WARFARE

AND MILITARY INSTITUTIONS

Second Edition

Compiled by

Trevor N. Dupuy

Curt Johnson

Grace P. Hayes

Priscilla S. Taylor

John M. Taylor

The H.W. Wilson Company
New York ◆ Dublin
2003

Library of Congress Cataloging-in-Publication Data

Dictionary of military terms: a guide to the language of warfare and military institutions / compiled by Trevor N. Dupuy . . . [et al.].— 2nd ed.
     p. cm.
   Includes bibliographical references.
   ISBN 0-8242-1025-5
   1. Military art and science—Dictionaries. 2. Naval art and science—Dictionaries. 3. Military history—Dictionaries. 4. Naval history—Dictionaries. I. Dupuy, Trevor Nevitt,1916–

U24 .D574 2003
355'.003—dc21

2002032960

Editing and design services provided by New England Publishing Associates, Inc.

Printed in the United States of America

The H. W. Wilson Company
950 University Avenue
Bronx, NY 10452

Visit H. W. Wilson's Web site: www.hwwilson.com

Preface

When the first edition of this dictionary of military terms appeared in 1986, it was acclaimed as "an excellently conceived and presented volume. There is really nothing quite like it" (*American Reference Books Annual*). It was also declared to be "useful for its intended audience of military professionals, buffs, and students" and recommended for university, public, and high school libraries (*Booklist*).

It had been five years since the H. W. Wilson Company first approached Trevor N. Dupuy about compiling the dictionary. A World War II combat veteran, Colonel Dupuy was a noted military theorist and historian who had served as a staff planner at Eisenhower's headquarters in Europe and at the Pentagon and had taught military subjects at Harvard and elsewhere. He had become acutely aware that there was no sound, standard reference work satisfactory to both the American military profession and the wider audience of students and historians. With Grace P. Hayes and Curt Johnson as Dupuy's collaborators, the first edition of this dictionary appeared in 1986. In his introduction Dupuy noted, "No one hoping to acquire or maintain an understanding of world events can afford to be unfamiliar with the vocabulary of military affairs. Indeed, the military dimension enters any informed discussion of national and international policy issues, such as the defense of Western Europe or the federal budget."

The original book provided concise definitions of some 2,500 terms related both to modern military affairs and to military history from ancient times to the 1980s. It sought to cover "all aspects of military and naval affairs, including strategy, tactics, weapons, fortifications, organizations, ranks, and administration." It was not an etymological dictionary; it strictly emphasized the military meanings and derivations of words and phrases, accurately conveying the military sense of both widely used and highly technical terms. Unlike many other publications, it also cut through bureaucratese.

Much has changed in the world since 1986, and numerous entries in the original dictionary required updating. Moreover, military terminology has expanded to encompass new concepts in weapon systems, strategy, and intelligence. When we were invited to update this dictionary, we first compared it with the myriad competitors that have flooded the marketplace—on paper and on the Internet. We found that this book still held a niche as the most compact, authoritative, and readable dictionary of military terms available.

In producing the new edition, we have deleted some entries, revised others, and added about one-third more new terms, mostly to encompass developments since the mid-1980s, including the war on terrorism, and to expand coverage of terms relating to the air force, surface navy, submarines, and intelligence. In looking for new terms we have extensively searched the Web as well as more traditionally published references, including government publications. In defining the terms, we have distilled and cross-checked information from multiple sources. Note that we have used SMALL CAPS like these (instead of "q.v.," or "which see") for terms mentioned in one definition but defined elsewhere in the book.

We are grateful to Lynn Messina, general reference editor, and her assistant, Jennifer Peloso, at the H.W. Wilson Company for their production support. We hope that this updated dictionary will continue to meet the needs of a general as well as a military audience for accessible, accurate, authoritative, and interesting explanations of current and historical military terms.

Priscilla S. Taylor
John M. Taylor
McLean, Virginia
March 2003

A-4—See **Skyhawk.**

A-6—See **Intruder**.

A-7—See **Corsair II**.

A-10—See **Thunderbolt II**.

A-12—See **Avenger II**.

A-26—See **Invader**.

AA—Antiaircraft.

AAA—See **antiaircraft artillery**.

abatis—A defensive obstacle formed of trees felled for the purpose, forming a kind of thicket, with butts embedded in the ground and trunks slanted outward so as to present the sharpened ends of their branches to the enemy. See also **plashing** and **zareba**.

ABC warfare — Atomic, biological, and chemical warfare. See also **NBC**.

Able—First letter of the old phonetic alphabet. See also **alphabet, phonetic**.

ABM—Antiballistic missile. See **missile, antiballistic**.

abort—*v.* To call off before completion, especially used of a bombing mission. *n.* The act of such cancellation.

about face—*n.* 1) A complete reversal of stationary position or attitude. 2) The command for such a reversal. *v.* 1) To execute such a reversal, usually in response to a command. 2) In the imperative, the command to do it. See also **face**.

Abrams (M-1)—The 70-ton U.S. Army main battle tank. Introduced in 1980, it is heavily armored, mounts a 120mm gun, can travel at 45 miles per hour, and is capable of destroying enemy tanks from beyond the reach of enemy fire. See also **tank, main battle**.

abreast—Side by side.

abri—A shelter, such as a cave or a dugout.

absent without leave (AWOL) — Away from a place of duty without authorization. If absence is without intention of returning, under U.S. military law it becomes desertion.

Abu Nidal organization—A Muslim terrorist organization that split from the Palestine Liberation Organization in 1974. It has long had close ties with Iraq, Libya, and Syria.

Abu Sayyaf Group—An Islamic fundamentalist group in the Philippines that split from the Moro Liberation Front in 1991. In 2001 the Abu Sayyaf Group kidnapped two American missionaries, one of whom died in a rescue attempt in June 2002.

academies, military—Schools for the training of officers. The establishment of permanent armies and navies in the late 17th century in Europe made it necessary to establish training programs and institutions for officers. In many countries (e.g., Russia) military academies are schools for advanced training, comparable to War Colleges in the United States. Academies in the United States provide the basic training and education for prospective military officers. The U.S.

Military Academy at West Point, N.Y., was founded in 1802; the U.S. Naval Academy at Annapolis, Md., in 1845; the U.S. Coast Guard Academy at New London, Conn., in 1876; and the U.S. Air Force Academy at Colorado Springs, Colo., in 1954.

accolade—Originating in medieval times, a ceremony (often performed by a monarch) conferring knighthood. In England the accolade is still given by a tap of the blade of a sword on the shoulder of a kneeling subject. "Accolade" has come to mean any recognition of special merit.

accountability—In terms of military mores, the practice of holding commanders responsible for the actions of their subordinates. In matters of administration, the obligation imposed for keeping accurate records regarding property, documents, or funds.

accoutrement or accouterment—Equipment (other than weapons and clothes) carried by a soldier, such as badges and emblems.

accoutrement

accuracy of fire—The measure of the deviation of fire from the point of aim, expressed usually in terms of the distance between the point of aim and the mean point of impact. It has two components: the inherent accuracy of the weapon and the proximity of the CENTER OF IMPACT to the point of aim.

ace—A fine flier. During World War I the French decided to recognize fliers who had downed five or more enemy aircraft and used the French word *as*, or "ace." Over time the term came to refer to any outstanding pilot or a standout in any field.

Achilles' heel—The vulnerable part of a person or organization, especially a military organization.

ack-ack—ANTIAIRCRAFT ARTILLERY. The phonetic term originated with British signalmen in World War II to represent the initials AA, standing for "antiaircraft."

acknowledgment—A response to a message informing its originator that the communication has been received and is understood.

acorn—A U.S. Navy unit of administrative personnel, and the requisite material needed to construct, operate, and maintain an advanced landplane and seaplane base. In the Pacific Theater during World War II, the personnel and matériel were assembled and then delivered as a unit to a captured island, where the base could be constructed and put into operation quickly.

acoustic—Activated by sound, as in **acoustic mine** or **acoustic torpedo**. For example, both of these are detonated by the sound of a ship's propeller.

acoustic intelligence — Intelligence derived from the collection and processing of acoustic data, especially the noise "signatures" of surface ships and submarines.

acoustic warfare—The use of sophisticated listening devices to monitor enemy activity under water and to employ countermeasures such as jamming to neutralize the collection of friendly acoustic emissions.

acquire—To locate and define a target for artillery or other weapons. The term has also been applied to radars in two senses: For acquisition radars, "acquire" means to detect the presence and location of a target clearly enough so that it can be identified; for tracking radars, "acquire" means to position a radar beam so as to reveal a target and permit it to be attacked effectively.

acting rank—Temporary rank, generally assigned to an officer or a noncommissioned officer who is performing duties normally performed by someone of higher rank.

action—1) A move on the part of a military force that imposes combat upon, or affects the condition of, an opponent. For example, when artillery "goes into action," it begins to place fire upon the enemy. 2) A minor combat encounter between two hostile forces (see also **battle, engagement, skirmish**). 3) Performance of activity for an administrative or operational purpose, as "remedial action is being taken." See also **conflict levels of intensity.**

action officer—The officer assigned to assure that a specific task is accomplished.

action station—1) An assigned or prescribed position for a vessel in a naval formation or cruising disposition. 2) An assigned position to be taken by a person in case of air attack. 3) An assigned area in an approach, contact, or battle disposition.

activate—1) To establish, or put into existence by official order, a unit, post, camp, station, base, or shore activity that has been previously constituted and designated by name or number or both so that it can be organized to function in its designated capacity. 2) To prepare for active service a naval ship or craft that has been in an inactive or reserve status.

active air defense—Direct defensive action taken to destroy or reduce the effectiveness of an air attack. It includes such measures as the use of aircraft, antiaircraft artillery, surface-to-air guided missiles, and electronic countermeasures. See also **defense.**

active defense—A posture of ground force defense in which limited offensive actions or counterattacks (by either frontline units or mobile reserves) are used to deny a position to the attacker. See also **defense.**

active duty—Full-time duty in active military service. It may be permanent, temporary (especially for training purposes), or extended for the convenience of the government. The active services (Army, Navy, Air Force, Marine Corps, Coast Guard) include career people on permanent active duty, reservists on extended active duty, and reservists on temporary active duty for training.

active list—1) A list of all regular officers on active duty. 2) A list of air units assigned to a major air command for activation, and those that have been activated and are serving in active status.

active sectors—Areas (usually designated by boundaries) where combat is taking place.

act of hostility—An act that is unfriendly or belligerent.

act of war—An action by one nation intended to initiate a war or considered by another nation to be sufficient cause for war.

actual range—In aerial bombardment, the horizontal distance a bomb travels from the moment of release until the moment of impact.

ADC—See **aide-de-camp**.

adjust—To align a weapon, especially artillery, by firing so that its projectiles strike the target or its immediate vicinity. Such firing is often called "adjustment fire." See also **aimed fire**.

adjutant—An officer who serves as administrative assistant to the commanding officer of a military unit or formation below the level of division. The adjutant is principally concerned with correspondence, the issuance of orders, and other nonlogistical administration of the unit or formation.

adjutant-general—1) Adjutant of a unit with a general staff. 2) The officer in charge of a state's contingents in the U.S. National Guard. 3) The chief administrative officer of the U.S. Army, who serves as a principal assistant to the Army Chief of Staff. He is head of the Adjutant General's Corps, which publishes all orders and is responsible for all correspondence, personnel actions, awards, records, publications, and other nonlogistical administrative functions.

administration—1) The management and execution of all military matters not included in tactics and strategy—primarily, office management, logistics, and personnel management. 2) Internal management of units.

administrative control—Exercise of authority in matters not directly related to combat, such as personnel management and services. For example, a unit temporarily under the operational control of another unit or formation often remains under the administrative control of its own higher commander.

administrative order—An order concerning aspects of military performance not directly related to combat operations.

administrative services—Activities essential for the functioning of an organization, such as supply, communications, transportation, finance, personnel management, construction and maintenance, military justice, discipline, and public relations.

administrative troops—Troops in units designed to render supply, maintenance, transportation, evacuation, hospitalization, and other services required by air and ground combat units.

admiral—The highest rank in most navies, including the U.S. Navy and Coast Guard. There are four degrees in the U.S. Navy: a) fleet admiral, a rank given during or just after World War II to William D. Leahy, Ernest J. King, Chester W. Nimitz, and William F. Halsey; b) admiral (equivalent to general); c) vice admiral (equivalent to lieutenant general); and d) rear admiral (equivalent to major general); all are known as flag officers. (The rank of COMMODORE, also a flag officer, is equivalent to brigadier general). The word "admiral" apparently originated before the 12th century with Arabs who combined *amir,* commander, the article *al,* and *bahr,* the sea, in *amir-al-bahr,* which was shortened by the Sicilians to *amiral.* Near the end of the 13th century the English commander of the Cinque Ports was given the Latin title *admirabilis.*

admiral of the red, admiral of the white, admiral of the blue, admiral of the yellow—By 1620 the English commander at sea was known as an admiral. The English fleet at this time comprised three squadrons. Ships of the squadron in the center flew red ensigns, and their commander was known as "admiral of the red." The van squadron ships flew white ensigns, and their commander, a vice admiral, was known as "admiral of the white." The squadron in the rear flew blue ensigns, and their commander, a rear admiral, was known as "admiral of the blue." If a captain was promoted over others senior to him to become admiral of the blue, those passed over were made rear admirals on the retired list. The common expression was "yellowed," and they were called "admirals of the yellow," a fictitious squadron.

admiralty—Office of the British government responsible for managing naval affairs and for commanding the Royal Navy. Prior to 1964, when the administrative offices of the British armed services were merged into the Ministry of Defence, the official title of the admiralty was Board of Admiralty. The 10-man Board of Admiralty (4 civilians and 6 admirals known as SEA LORDS) performed its functions under the chairmanship of the First Lord of the Admiralty, a civilian member of Parliament who was also a cabinet minister. Since 1964 it has been known as the Admiralty Board of the Defence Council.

advance—*v.* 1) To move forward, used particularly in reference to an attacking force. 2) To raise in rank; to promote. *n.* The distance moved forward. See also **advance rate**.

advanced base—A base located in or near a theater of operations, the primary mission of which is to support military operations.

advanced synthetic aperture radar system (ASARS-2)—A high-resolution reconnaissance system carried on U-2 aircraft to locate ground targets and transmit data to a designated command center. ASARS data contributed to damage assessment during Operation DESERT STORM.

advanced targeting forward-looking infrared (ATFLIR)—An infrared targeting system that increases the detection range of aircraft such as the HORNET.

advance force (amphibious) — A temporary organization within an amphibious task force that precedes the main body to the objective area. Its function is to help prepare the objective for the main assault by conducting such operations as reconnaissance, seizure of supporting positions, minesweeping, preliminary bombardment, underwater demolitions, and air support.

advance guard—A portion or detachment of a ground combat force sent ahead of the main body for any of several purposes: to gain information about the location and strength of the enemy's forces, to protect the main body against surprise, to remove obstacles and repair roads and bridges, to cover the deployment or conceal the movements of the main body by occupying the attention of the enemy. In France the term is *avant-garde.* In late medieval and early modern times the advance guard was generally about one third of a field army; in battle formation it was either deployed in front of the main body, to initiate combat, or arrayed on the right flank of the main body.

advance landing field—An airfield, usually having minimal facilities, in or near an objective area.

advance rate—The speed of the advance of a military force, usually expressed as miles or kilometers per 24-hour day.

advance to contact—Move forward in an effort to gain or reestablish contact with the enemy.

adverse weather aerial delivery system (AWADS)—An aircraft instrumentation system that permits the precise delivery of personnel and supplies in adverse weather without requiring ground navigational aids.

AEF — See **American Expeditionary Force**.

Aegis—An integrated shipboard weapon system that combines computers, radars, and missiles to provide a defense umbrella for surface units. Its advanced radar and command elements make it capable of simultaneous operation against air and surface threats.

aerial barrage—See **barrage**.

aerial dart—A metal dart dropped from an aircraft, used in World War I against a target such as a zeppelin. Also called FLÈCHETTE.

aerial gunner—U.S. Army enlisted specialty.

aerial mining—The act or process of laying mines (usually naval mines) from aircraft. See **mine**.

aerographer—U.S. Navy warrant officer with meteorological duties.

aerographer's mate—U.S. Navy enlisted specialty in meteorology.

aeromedical evacuation—The movement of patients to and between medical treatment facilities by air transportation.

aeronautical chart—See **chart**.

aeronautical rating—One of several ratings conferred on a member of the U.S. Air Force (or Army, Navy, or Marine Corps air components) who has completed the requisite training and obtained the requisite competence in a given aspect of flying. In addition to pilots, such persons include bombardiers, navigators, radio and radar personnel, engineers, and gunners with aeronautical specialties. Recipients of such ratings are usually authorized to wear a metallic emblem, in the form of wings, on the chest of the uniform tunic or shirt.

aerospace—The earth's envelope of atmosphere and the space above it, two separate areas often considered a single realm for activity involving vehicles that will travel in both environments.

aerospace defense—Air defense measures designed to destroy or nullify attacking enemy aircraft and missiles and to neutralize hostile space systems.

"Affirmative"—A signal transmission response indicating agreement with, or confirmation of, the previous transmission. See also acknowledgment and "Roger."

National Archives photo

Afrika Korps

Afrika Korps (Deutsches Afrika Korps)—Designation of a renowned force of German troops, commanded by Gen. (later Field Marshal) Erwin Rommel, sent to North Africa in February 1941 to reinforce Italian forces that had been badly defeated by British Commonwealth forces during the winter of 1940–41. Rommel assumed command of all Axis forces in North Africa, and the Afrika Korps became the mainstay of the German-Italian Panzer Army, which fought against the British Eighth Army in Libya and Egypt during 1941 and 1942. Rommel's defeat at El Alamein (23

October–4 November 1942) preceded a long retreat to Tunisia, where, in May 1943, the Axis forces, including the remnants of the Afrika Korps, surrendered to Allied forces.

afterburner—A device on the engine of a jet aircraft that provides extra thrust by burning additional fuel in the hot exhaust gases.

after-trim—A variable ballast tank used to adjust a submarine's depth.

AFV — Armored fighting vehicle. See also **infantry fighting vehicle (IVF)**.

agema—An elite corps of the Macedonian armies of Philip II and Alexander the Great. Composed of HYPASPISTs, this was the infantry bodyguard of the king.

Agent Orange—A powerful herbicide and defoliant containing dioxin, a toxic impurity suspected of causing health problems, including cancer, in some persons exposed to it. It was used by U.S. armed forces during the Vietnam War to defoliate jungles.

agger—Originally a Roman term for a mound, or rampart, thrown up in front of a ditch to protect a camp or other position. The term was also used for a mound built in ancient siege operations to overlook the defenders' walls or to provide a direct approach to their ramparts. Now the term is sometimes used for a military road, particularly one built up above the land it traverses. Typical historical examples were Alexander's agger at the siege of Gaza (332 B.C.) and the Roman agger at the siege of Masada (A.D. 70).

aggression—An unprovoked attack upon the territory or interests of a state by the armed forces of another state, termed "the aggressor."

aggressor force—1) A force that initiates a combat action, particularly by invading the territory of another nation. 2) Euphemism often used by the U.S. Army to designate the enemy in two-sided peacetime maneuvers in field exercises. The U.S. Army now usually uses the term **opposing forces** or **op-for**.

AGM-28B—See **Hound Dog**.

AGM-45—See **Shrike**.

AGM-53—See **Condor**.

AGM-62—See **Walleye**.

AGM-65—See **Maverick**.

AGM-69—See **short-range attack missile (SRAM)**.

AGM-78—See **Standard ARM**.

AGM-88—See **high-speed antiradiation missile (HARM)**.

AGM-114B—See **Hellfire**.

AGM-154—See **joint standoff weapon (JSOW)**.

AH-1J—See **Sea Cobra**.

AH-64A/D—See **Apache**.

aide-de-camp (ADC) — An officer who serves as a personal assistant to a GENERAL or FLAG OFFICER, performing mainly administrative duties. Usually referred to as an "aide."

aid man—A medical corpsman who serves with a combat unit, usually of company size.

aiguille—A tool used to bore for buried land-mines.

aiguillette—A loop of one or more strands, generally of gold braid, worn on the shoulder of a uniform. In the United States aiguillettes are worn by officers serving as aides to high-ranking officers or government officials. In France they are used to identify troops in units that have been awarded unit citations for exceptional or valorous conduct in battle. In Britain they are worn by noncommissioned officers of the Household Cavalry. In some countries they are worn by the gendarmerie. Aiguillettes were originally used to secure armor plates to the shoulder of the leather jerkin worn underneath.

aim—v. To point a weapon so that its effective component (missile, projectile, point, blade) will strike a selected target. n. The direction or line of fire or of sighting thus identified.

AIM-7—See **Sparrow**.

AIM-9—See **Sidewinder**.

AIM-54A—See **Phoenix**.

AIM-120 (AMRAAM)—An advanced, medium-range, air-to-air missile for U.S. Air Force and Navy aircraft designed to replace the SPARROW series. It incorporates active radar with an inertial reference unit that makes the missile less dependent on the fire-control system of the launching aircraft.

aimed fire—Fire that is placed on a target by direct-fire weapons when the target is seen by the individual or crew firing the weapon, and by indirect-fire weapons when the target is seen by an observer who can communicate with personnel using the weapons to adjust the fire. Aimed fire can be directed at both point targets and area targets.

aiming point—A common reference point for the gunners of artillery pieces or mortars of a unit toward which they aim the sights of their weapons. For indirect fire—and most artillery and mortar fire is indirect—all commands for direction or deflection are given in angular measurements (usually MILs, sometimes degrees) with respect to the aiming point. When a field artillery unit (usually a battery) occupies a position, all weapons are immediately laid in a PARALLEL SHEAF in the general direction of fire, usually by the battery executive officer, who then selects the aiming point and orders the gunners to refer to it. If no prominent, readily identifiable fixed object is available for such reference, the cannoneers will set out AIMING POSTS for reference as the aiming point for an individual gun or mortar.

aiming posts—Stakes or poles, two for each weapon, carried with each gun or mortar, and available for use as an AIMING POINT, if needed. The stakes are painted in sharp, contrasting colors, usually red and white, so as to be readily identified by gunners looking through their sights. When the command to refer to aiming posts is given, a cannoneer, carrying the stakes, runs out in the direction indicated by the gunner, who is looking through the sight of the gun. The gunner aligns the aiming posts, which are placed about 100 feet and 50 feet, respectively, from the gun, usually to the rear or flank, by giving directions to the cannoneer, so that only the closer of the two stakes is visible through the sight. All firing commands for direction or deflection are then applied to the gun as angular measurements related to the aiming posts.

air attack—An attack on a surface target by combat aircraft.

air base—See **base**.

airborne—1) In relation to personnel, it refers to troops transported by air to a designated area to debark either by parachute or by actual landing. 2) In relation to equipment, it refers to matériel that has been designed for use by airborne forces. 3) The state of an aircraft, from the instant it is sustained by air until touchdown.

airborne command post — A suitably equipped aircraft used by a commander to command forces.

airborne warning and control systems (AWACS)—Aircraft equipped with search radar, height-finding radar, and communications equipment for controlling weapons, generally other aircraft, especially fighters. AWACS are used for surveillance, early warning, and control.

airburst—The explosion of a bomb or projectile above the surface of the earth, as distinguished from an explosion on impact with the surface or after penetration (ground burst).

airburst fuze—Either a TIME or a PROXIMITY FUZE. See **fuze**.

air-capable ship—A ship other than an aircraft carrier, or other vessel specifically designed as a landing platform, from which aircraft can take off and be recovered.

air cavalry—Units that make use of air mobility (usually by helicopter) to perform missions, such as reconnaissance, screening, and surprise attacks, traditionally performed by horse cavalry before the early 20th century. See also **armored cavalry**.

air chief marshal—See **air marshal**.

air command—A major subdivision of the U.S. Air Force, normally consisting of two or more AIR FORCEs.

air commodore—1) A commissioned rank in the air forces of Britain and other countries corresponding to that of brigadier general in the U.S.A.F. 2) A person holding this rank.

air corridors—Restricted air routes of travel specified for use by friendly aircraft and established to prevent friendly aircraft from being fired on by friendly forces.

air cover—1) Protection against attack, especially air attack, provided to surface or airborne forces by combat aircraft. 2) The aircraft providing such protection.

aircraft—A vehicle capable of traveling through the air. Types of aircraft include heavier-than-air (airplane and helicopter) and lighter-than-air (balloon, blimp, dirigible). Military aircraft are further categorized by their functions (fighter aircraft, bomber aircraft, reconnaissance aircraft), by their means of locomotion (jet, turboprop), and by their configuration (fixed-wing, rotary-wing, helicopter, biplane).

aircraft-arresting barrier—An apparatus or system for slowing, and ultimately stopping, the progress of an aircraft landing on the flight deck of an aircraft carrier. The first such arresting gear was emplaced on the planked-over afterdeck of the U.S. armored cruiser *Pennsylvania* in January 1911, when pioneer naval aviator Eugene B. Ely made the first landing on an "aircraft carrier." Most arresting apparatuses employ the same principles: A steel cable stretched across a carrier's deck catches a hook dropped from the tail section of the aircraft's fuselage.

aircraft-arresting system — A series of components, whether barriers or other gear, used to engage an aircraft and absorb the forward momentum of a routine or emergency landing (or aborted takeoff).

aircraft carrier (CV)—A naval vessel that serves as a floating air base. Modern carriers have an angled flight deck, with the control center, or "island," to one side. Aircraft are brought to the flight deck by great elevators. Most U.S. carriers are nuclear-powered and designated CVN. Today's fleet carriers are the largest man-made moving objects in the world.

aircraftman—Any of the four lower enlisted grades or ranks in the British Royal Air Force: aircraftman second class, aircraftman first class, leading aircraftman, and senior aircraftman.

air crew—The personnel assigned to operate an aircraft.

air defense—Defense against attack from the air by hostile aircraft or missiles; also the system itself. Air defense measures include antiaircraft artillery, surface-to-air missiles, and fighter aircraft. See also **active air defense**, **passive defense**.

air defense area—A specifically defined and established territory (or air space over territory) that includes objectives of possible enemy air attack for which air defense must be provided.

air defense artillery—Crew-served weapons and equipment that provide defense against attack from the air, including hostile aircraft and missiles. Usually applied to ballistic gunpowder weapons, as opposed to SURFACE-TO-AIR MISSILES. See also **antiaircraft artillery**.

air defense direction center—An installation with the capability of performing air surveillance, interception control, and direction of air defense weapons. Some centers have an identification capability.

air defense identification zone (ADIZ)—Air space within which the identification, location, and control of airborne vehicles are required.

U.S. Navy photo
The USS *Saratoga*, Forrestal class, c. 1970.

aircraft carrier

air defense warning conditions— The likelihood of an attack is graded by the following code: **warning yellow**—attack by hostile aircraft or missiles is probable; **warning red**—attack by hostile aircraft or missiles is imminent or in progress; **warning white**—an attack is improbable.

air delivery—Air transport of units, personnel, supplies, and equipment. The term includes AIRDROPs and air landings and covers both tactical and administrative movements.

airdrop—*n.* The act of unloading personnel or matériel from aircraft in flight. This is used as a means of supply in difficult terrain, where land lines of transport are difficult or nonexistent, as in Allied operations in Burma in World War II. An airdrop may be with or without parachute; in the latter case it is sometimes called a "free drop." *v.* To unload from an aircraft in flight.

air echelon—1) The part of an organization that is moved by air, by military transport aircraft or a unit's own aircraft, or both, as distinguished from the elements that are moved by sea or land. 2) The part of an air force organization that is composed of its air crew members. 3) The military force that operates in the air, as distinguished from ground or naval forces.

air force—1) The component of a country's armed forces or of one of its services concerned with military operations in the air; for example, U.S. Air Force, Army Air Force, Naval Air Force. 2) A major organizational unit within a national air force, distinguished by a name or number; for example, Fifth Air Force.

air front—1) The direction from which aircraft attack, especially coming toward a nation's strategic targets. 2) The direction toward which an air attack is made.

air gap—In World War II, the portion of the North Atlantic beyond the range of antisubmarine aircraft based in North America, Iceland, or Britain, and therefore an area in which U-boats could operate with relative impunity. The introduction of escort carriers in 1944 effectively closed the air gap.

air gun—A gun in which the projectile is discharged by compressed air, liquid carbon dioxide, or a combination of compressed air and an ignitable fuel. See also **dynamite gun.**

air gun

airhead—1) A tactical base for an airborne or essentially airmobile operation. Usually seized as the first step in an airborne opera-

tion, an airhead constitutes an operational base of maneuver and a secure logistical base for supporting the operation. 2) A location used for supply and reinforcement and evacuation of wounded in an operations area.

air interdiction—Interdiction fire on, or bombardment of, ground targets by weapons from one or more aircraft. See also **interdict** and **interdiction fire**.

airland battle—1) Combat waged by ground forces with air support. 2) A doctrinal concept of aggressive, mobile, air-supported ground combat introduced by the U.S. Army in the early 1980s.

airlift—*v.* To transport passengers and cargo by use of aircraft. *n.* 1) The transportation of personnel or cargo by air. 2) The total weight of personnel or cargo that is or can be transported by air.

airman—Enlisted grade in the U.S. Air Force, first, second, and third class; corresponds to private in the Army and seaman in the Navy.

air marshal—A commissioned rank in the British Royal Air Force and certain other national air forces (but not the U.S.A.F.). There are usually four grades: a) air vice marshal, equivalent to major general; b) air marshal, equivalent to lieutenant general; c) air chief marshal, equivalent to general; and d) marshal of the air force, equivalent to general of the air force.

airmobile operations—Ground combat in which some of the combat forces move in air vehicles under the command of a ground force commander.

air observation—Visual observation of an enemy's positions, forces, or installations from the air.

air observer—A person whose primary mission is to observe an enemy's positions or other targets, or to take photographs of them from an aircraft in order to adjust artillery fire or obtain military information.

air picket—An airborne early warning aircraft positioned to detect and track approaching enemy aircraft or missiles. See also **airborne warning and control systems.**

air portable—Denotes equipment that can be carried in an aircraft with only such minor dismantling and reassembly as would be within the capabilities of user units. This term is usually qualified to show the extent of air portability in relation to cargo aircraft by weight, size, or specific aircraft designation.

air raid—An attack by aircraft against a surface target. Although air raids generally are thought of as bombing attacks, they include attacks with machine guns or cannon (strafing), rockets, torpedoes, or any other weapon by which aircraft can directly damage or destroy surface targets.

air room—A room or rooms at major U.S. air commands where intelligence on the current situation is given to authorized personnel in the form of briefings, film showings, maps, drawings, charts, written summaries, etc. It corresponds to the Army's war room.

airship—A lighter-than-air craft, such as a blimp or dirigible.

U.S. Air Force photo
The *Macon* over Berkeley, Calif., c. 1932.

airship

airship rigger—U.S. Navy enlisted specialist who maintains lighter-than-air ships.

air sortie—See **sortie**.

airspace reservation—Airspace over which flight of aircraft is prohibited or restricted by appropriate authority.

airspeed—The speed of an aircraft relative to the air mass through which it is flying. **Calibrated airspeed** is airspeed shown on an instrument (**indicated airspeed**), corrected for errors in the installation of the instrument. When corrected for compressibility errors it becomes **equivalent airspeed**. Equivalent airspeed corrected for error due to

air density (i.e., altitude and temperature) is **true airspeed**.

air strike—An offensive attack by one or more aircraft on a specified target or targets.

airstrip—An unimproved or partially improved surface that has been adapted for takeoff or landing of aircraft, usually having minimum facilities.

air superiority — Preponderance in air strength of one force over another to the extent that the weaker force cannot prohibit the other's conduct of air, ground, or sea operations. Although air superiority provides one side with general domination of the air space over surface combat operations, it does not mean total denial of air operations by the weaker side. Such denial, however, is implicit in AIR SUPREMACY.

air supply—The delivery of cargo by airdrop or air landing.

air support—All forms of support, operational or administrative, given by air forces to forces on land or sea. See also **close air support**.

air supremacy—The degree of air superiority wherein the opposing air force is incapable of effective interference with ground, sea, or air operations.

air-to-air missile—See **missile, air-to-air**.

air-to-surface missile—See **missile, air-to-surface**.

air transport—1) The movement of personnel or cargo by aircraft, as distinguished from surface or ground transport. 2) An aircraft used for such movement.

air-transportable units— Ground units, other than airborne, that are trained and whose equipment is adapted for movement and delivery by transport aircraft.

air vice marshal—See **air marshal**.

air wing—An air force unit usually composed of two or more groups with support units, including at least supply, maintenance, and medical.

AK-47 assault rifle — A Soviet-made .30-caliber automatic rifle popular with guerrilla groups and terrorists. Known also as the

"Kalashnikov," it is still used by the Russian army and others.

aketon (hacqueton)—A type of early medieval body armor resembling a padded coat; it was made of buckram, stuffed with cotton, and stitched longitudinally. It was worn as padding under the HAUBERK and covered the body from the neck to the knees.

ala, alae—A Roman cavalry organization consisting of 12 TURMAE. Its modern equivalent would be a cavalry squadron. The ala formed up in two or three lines.

ALCM—See **missile, air-launched cruise**.

alert—A condition in which all members of a unit stand by in a state of readiness for active operations, either because of an anticipated attack or the possibility of such an attack, or because of contemplation of other combat operations. The seriousness of the alert is frequently identified by numbered categories (as **alert status one**) or code designations (as **red alert**); an alert may also be related to the forces affected, such as **air alert** or **ground alert**.

alert force—A force maintained in a state of readiness for immediate operational performance.

Alfa—First letter of NATO phonetic alphabet. See also **alphabet, phonetic**.

al Fatah—Founded in 1957, al Fatah is one of the oldest of the Palestinian liberation groups. "Fatah" is the Arabic word for "conquest." Al Fatah is associated with the PALESTINE LIBERATION ORGANIZATION and the Palestine Authority, and seeks an independent, secular Palestinian state.

alienation—A psychological phenomenon often associated with persons attracted to political violence or terrorism. Such persons may resort to violence when privileges and economic benefits they regard as entitlements are withdrawn or denied.

alignment—1) Relative positions of military forces in tactical operations; can be abreast (usually referred to as "in line"), echeloned, or one behind another (usually referred to as "in column"). 2) The bearing of two or more conspicuous objects (such as lights or beacons) as seen by an observer. 3) Representation of a road, railway, and the like on a map or chart in relation to surrounding topographic details.

all hands — All members of a ship's company or of any naval unit, including the entire Navy.

alliance—1) A formal agreement by two or more nations to support and assist each other. 2) The collective members of such a union.

allotment of pay—A deduction from the paycheck of a member of the armed forces, paid directly to another person or organization.

allowance—1) A payment, the amount of which is usually specified by rank, to a member of the armed services in lieu of provision of quarters, food, or other items or as recognition of performance of special duty, such as sea duty, overseas duty, or submarine duty. 2) Specified quantities of various forms of supply, to include rations, to be provided regularly to a unit or an individual.

allways fuze—An impact fuze designed to function regardless of the part of the fuze or projectile that makes contact with the target.

all-weather fighter—See **fighter aircraft**.

ally—A nation joined with another in an alliance by treaty or by common interests. In both World Wars I and II the nations fighting together against Germany and its cobelligerents were called the Allies.

almain armor—See **armor**.

Alpha 66—An anti-Castro exile group centered in Miami, Fla. It is composed primarily of Cubans of African descent.

alphabet, phonetic—*World War II*: Able, Baker, Charlie, Dog, Easy, Fox, George, How, Item, Jig, King, Love, Mike, Nan, Oboe, Peter, Queen, Roger, Sugar, Tare, Uncle, Victor, William, Xray, Yoke, Zebra. *NATO*: Alfa, Bravo, Charlie, Delta, Echo, Foxtrot, Gold, Hotel, India, Juliet, Kilo, Lima, Mike, November, Oscar, Papa, Quebec, Romeo, Sierra, Tango, Uniform, Victor, Whisky, Xray, Yankee, Zulu.

al Qaeda—The Islamic terrorist organization that carried out, among other acts, the 11 September 2001 attacks on the World Trade Center and the Pentagon. The term translates in Arabic to "the base," presumably a reference to Afghanistan. The origins of al Qaeda are obscure, but it may have been organized about 1989. Financed by the Saudi multimillionaire Osama bin Laden, al Qaeda is believed to have cells in 40 or more countries. See also **terrorism** and **cell**.

Amazon—A mythological female warrior from ancient Scythia.

ambulance—In the Napoleonic Wars, an ambulance (*l'hôpital ambulant*) was a litter fitted with first aid equipment that served as a field medical unit. In time, ambulances became more elaborate; in the American Civil War they were horse-drawn wagons, and by World War I they were motorized.

ambuscade—An ambush.

ambuscader—One who takes part in an ambush.

ambush—*n.* A sudden, carefully prepared, surprise attack by a force whose position had been carefully concealed against an advancing hostile force. *v.* To make such an attack.

American Expeditionary Force (AEF)—The U.S. Army force sent to France in 1917 under the command of Gen. John J. Pershing. It eventually comprised 42 divisions and totaled more than 2 million men.

ammo—Ammunition.

ammunition—Destructive materials intended to damage, destroy, or suppress hostile personnel and matériel, and the ancillary consumable equipment required to make them function. Projectiles fired from a gun are the principal form of modern ammunition. A ROUND of ammunition comprises not only the projectile but a primer, fuze, propellant charge, and a case or jacket that holds the propellant and (usually) connects it with the projectile. Projectiles are usually in the form of bullets or artillery shells. Ammunition also includes missiles, torpedoes, mines, and bombs. Nonexplosive ammunition (generally pregunpowder) includes arrows, bullets, shot, or stones for slings. (Nondestructive materials designed for specialized use in weapons such as blanks, or subcaliber training projectiles, and ancillary items, are considered to be ammunition.) Types of modern ammunition include the following: **fixed ammunition**—The most common kind of ammunition for all types and calibers of guns, in which the projectile (or bullet) is firmly attached to the propellant and primer by means of a cartridge (usually called "cartridge case for artillery weapons"). **semifixed ammunition**—This type is similar to fixed ammunition to the extent that the projectile is assembled with cartridge case, propellant, and primer; but the projectile can be lifted off to permit removal of part of the propellant (powder charge in separate bags) and thereby to permit a variety in charges with consequent differences in muzzle velocity and range. **separate-loading ammunition**—The projectile and propellant are packaged separately. The primer is sometimes assembled with the propellant and sometimes attached just before firing or put into a receptacle in the breech block. This type of ammunition (without cartridge case) is standard for larger calibers of medium and heavy artillery.

ammunition, armor-piercing (AP) — Ammunition designed to penetrate resistant materials; in particular, armor on warships, tanks, and other vehicles, or installations; a characteristic of certain bombs, bullets, shells, and other projectiles. Types of modern armor-piercing ammunition include the following: **armor-piercing discarding sabot (APDS)**—A long, thin, arrow-like projectile encased in a SABOT, which falls away after firing; the projectile obtains its penetration capability from high velocity. **high-explosive antitank (HEAT)**—A projectile using a SHAPED CHARGE detonated on impact by a base fuze to produce a very hot jet of flame that sears its way through armor. **high-explosive squash-head (HESH)**—A round that achieves penetration by a combined action of the collapsible head (to prevent ricochet) and a shaped charge. **hypervelocity armor-piercing (HVAP)**—A projectile with an extremely hard core of tungsten carbide; fired at high velocities, it can penetrate many inches of armor.

ammunition belt—See **belt**.

ammunition chest—A wooden chest used to store ammunition for use in the field. See also **caisson**.

ammunition consumption—1) The process of expending ammunition by firing in combat. 2) The rate (usually daily) of such expenditure.

ammunition dump—A depot for storage of ammunition.

ammunition supply point—Storage location of ammunition close to the front lines, from which the combat units obtain replenishment for ammunition consumed in battle.

amphibious assault—See **amphibious operation**.

amphibious assault ship (LHA/LHD)—Designed to sustain combat operations at sea, these ships employ various combinations of helicopters and specialized aircraft, in addition to conventional landing craft and assault vehicles. They can deliver and support all elements of a marine landing force by air and amphibious craft.

U.S. Navy photo

The USS *Guam.*

amphibious assault ship

amphibious attack—See **attack**.

amphibious command ship—A ship from which a commander exercises control of amphibious operations.

amphibious force — The entire force trained, organized, and equipped to perform amphibious operations, including personnel, vessels, and supporting forces. The naval elements form an organizational unit of a fleet; the ground elements are generally designated as the LANDING FORCE.

amphibious group—A command within an amphibious force under a headquarters designed to exercise operational command of assigned units in the execution of a division-size AMPHIBIOUS OPERATION.

amphibious lift—The total capacity of assault shipping used in an amphibious operation, expressed in terms of personnel, vehicles, and measurement or weight tons of supplies.

amphibious operation—An operation involving the transfer of troops between ships and land. There are several types of amphibious operations: a) an opposed landing on a hostile shore (AMPHIBIOUS ASSAULT) to obtain a BEACHHEAD from which to carry out further combat operations; b) an unopposed landing of forces; c) a withdrawal of land-based forces.

amphibious striking force — A seaborne force capable of projecting military power upon adjacent land areas.

amphibious task force—The task organization formed to conduct an amphibious operation. The amphibious task force always comprises naval forces and a landing force, and, when appropriate, air forces.

amphibious vehicle—A vehicle capable of operating on both land and water.

anchor watch—A detail of personnel on a warship in port that stands deck watches of from 2 to 4 hours, in turn, from 11 P.M. to turn-to in the morning, about 5:30.

angel—1) A type of confusion reflector having the reflecting material suspended from parachutes or balloons to delay the descent. 2) 1,000 feet of altitude.

angles of fire—The placing of artillery or missiles to achieve special firing objectives. Angles of fire include **enfilade fire**, in which weapons are placed at right angles to the enemy, and **plunging fire** from a position above the enemy works (e.g., high-arching fire directed at the decks of an enemy ship rather than at the sides).

annihilate—To take action that causes an enemy force to be totally incapable of further resistance. It is important to note that the military sense of this word is not synonymous with its nonmilitary sense of complete destruction.

antiaircraft artillery (AAA) — Guns used for attacking aerial targets from the ground or shipboard and the radar, searchlights, and other equipment and devices related to them. Antiaircraft artillery weapons are classified as light (20–57mm), medium (58–99mm), and heavy (100mm or larger).

antiair warfare — A U.S. Navy/Marine Corps term used to designate the action required to eliminate an enemy air and missile threat or to reduce it to an acceptable level. The term encompasses interceptors, bombers, antiaircraft guns, missiles, and electronic warfare measures.

antiballistic missile (ABM)—See **missile, antiballistic**.

antipersonnel mine—See **mine**.

antisatellite (ASAT)—A term for systems that are designed to neutralize or destroy enemy satellites. They can be dealt with in a number of ways (e.g., by destroying them or by disrupting their communications).

antisubmarine rocket (ASROC)—A ship-launched, rocket-propelled nuclear depth charge or homing torpedo.

antisubmarine torpedo (ASTOR)—A submarine-launched, wire-guided, deep-diving, wakeless torpedo capable of carrying a nuclear warhead.

antisubmarine warfare (ASW) — Operations conducted against submarines, including detection and attack.

antitank artillery—See **artillery**.

antitank grenade—See **grenade**.

antitank mine—See **mine**.

antitank weapons — Weapons, such as BAZOOKAs, guns, and guided missiles, that may be mounted on tanks or other armored vehicles, the main purpose of which is combat against other tanks and armored vehicles.

ANZAC (Australian and New Zealand Army Corps)—Formed in World War I. Commonly used in both World Wars I and II for a member of the Australian or New Zealand armed forces.

AOP—Air observation post. See **air observation** and **observation post**.

AP — Armor-piercing. See **ammunition, armor-piercing**.

Apache (AH-64A/D)—An all-weather twin-engine army attack helicopter, developed by McDonnell Douglas, with mounted 30mm automatic cannon as well as air-to-surface missiles. Introduced in the 1980s, it first saw combat in the Gulf War.

appreciation—British term for ESTIMATE OF THE SITUATION.

approaches—1) Regions through which an attacker draws close to any enemy position. 2) Trenches or other works erected to protect troops that are laying siege to a fortified position. The classical procedure was to dig a line of trenches parallel to the defenses and outside the artillery range of the defender and then to dig one or more zigzag approach trenches or SAPs leading partway toward the enemy's position, at which point another trench line was dug parallel to the original line. The process was repeated until a line of trenches was dug close enough to the enemy fortification to allow an assault. Thus the word "parallels" is often used—incorrectly—as a synonym. **Counterapproaches** are works erected by defenders to interfere with the besieger's approach works. See also **parallel** and **siege works**.

apron—A paved or otherwise hard-surface area, generally located near airport or airfield hangars, terminals, or control areas, where aircraft stand or park for purposes of loading and unloading, refueling, arming, as well as rearming, and servicing. Aprons are also called "hardstands" and "ramps."

AQM-60—See **Kingfisher**.

arbalest—A medieval missile launcher designed on the crossbow principle. See **ballista, catapult, crossbow**.

arbalest

archer—A person who shoots with a bow and arrow. The origins of the bow, and consequently the archer, are unknown. Evidence of bows, in the form of arrowheads, has been found from Palaeolithic times and in many parts of the world. Archers appear in the paintings and sculpture of many ancient cultures, and mounted archers in those where horses were used. The Persians of the 1st millennium B.C. combined foot archers and horse archers in the opening moves of battle. By the beginning of the Christian era, the horse archer dominated warfare in all of Asia except India. The Mongols were outstanding horse archers. In Roman times mounted soldiers began to carry lance, sword, and shield as well as a bow. In late medieval and early modern times, the term "archer" acquired two new meanings. It was used to refer to personnel in certain bodyguard units who may have been armed with bows and may have been mounted (e.g., the Scottish Archers of the French Royal Household). It was also used to refer to heavy, lance-armed cavalry, which, until the 1540s, were a component of gendarme units, whether LANCE or company. Men usually enlisted as archers in gendarme companies and, after serving a period of military apprenticeship, advanced to the rank of GENDARME, or MAN-AT-ARMS.

architecture, military—1) Class of structures uniquely designed for military purposes. The term is usually applied to castles or other permanent fortifications. 2) The design of such structures.

architecture, naval—The art of designing seagoing vessels to perform military missions.

arc of fire—The segment of a horizontal circle through which fire may be directed from a weapon without shifting its position. This, with the weapon's range, sets the limits of the area it can cover by fire.

area—*n.* A surface section of land or sea (or of a building or ship) that has generally defined boundaries. The term is also applied to intangible entities (e.g., responsibility, study, or power) that can be delimited for a specified purpose. *adj.* Referring to a large space rather than a specific point. An **assembly area** is a place where the units of a military command come together in preparation for an operation; an **area of operations** is where military operations are conducted pursuant to an assigned mission; a **forward area** is the area nearest to and including the front line; a **combat area** is the site of combat; a **rear area** is behind the area of operations, where reserves of men, equipment, and supplies are held. A **bombing area** is an area within which bombing is to take place; **area bombing** is bombing intended to destroy a large area rather than specific targets or types of target. A **command area** is the area assigned to a command (army, division); an

area command in U.S. forces is a command related to a geographical area (North Pacific, Southeastern United States) in which all forces of all services are under a single commander. A **defense area** is an area to be defended; an **area defense** is a defense with units deployed to prevent attacks on a geographical area rather than a specific installation or target. A **target area** is an area designated for attack; an **area target** is a target consisting of an area rather than a single point.

area bombing—See **area**.

area command—See **area**.

area defense—See **area** and **defense**.

area fire—Fire that is directed at a general area, rather than at a precision target. Area fire can be either OBSERVED FIRE or UNOBSERVED FIRE.

area target—See **area**.

Arena—A Russian active defense system for main battle tanks. Its radar is designed to track incoming missiles and to activate a system that fires an explosive charge into the path of the missile.

argoulet—A French light cavalryman of the Renaissance period.

arm—*n.* 1) A weapon of war. Two categories are a) SMALL ARMS—weapons carried and fired by one person; b) SIDE ARMs—weapons, such as revolvers, knives, or swords, that are worn at the side or on a belt (included in small arms). 2) A combatant branch of an army, in a modern army usually including infantry, cavalry, armor, artillery, and air defense, and sometimes engineers. 3) An organized branch of a nation's armed forces, in modern times usually including army, navy, and air force. In addition, the United States has a marine corps, Russia has rocket and missile forces, and Russia and others have air defense forces. *n. pl.* Heraldic device of a family or a government. *v.* 1) To furnish with weapons of offense or defense. 2) To adjust the firing mechanism of a mechanical or explosive device (e.g., a bomb or a mine) so that when triggered, the device will explode.

armada—Any large fleet of warships or aircraft. In 1588 Philip II of Spain sent a fleet, known to history as the Spanish Armada, against England. Although it was considered to be invincible, in fact it was weaker in fire-power than the waiting and defending English vessels and the Armada suffered a disastrous defeat.

Armageddon—1) The site of the final battle between the forces of good and evil, as referred to in the Bible, Rev. 16:16. 2) Any great and crucial conflict.

armament—1) The weapons and other equipment, including defensive equipment and supplies, of a nation's armed forces, or any portion thereof. 2) All of the offensive weapons of a ship. 3) The process of arming.

arme blanche—A blade weapon, usually a sword, saber, or bayonet, used in hand-to-hand combat.

armed conflict—A war, a battle, an engagement, or other meeting between forces of two or more nations or factions in which weapons are used to inflict physical damage.

armed forces—All the military forces of a nation or a group of nations.

armed merchantman—A commercial vessel equipped with guns or other weapons. In World War I, ships were armed as protection against surface raiders and submarines. In World War II, the practice was general, with emphasis on protection by antiaircraft guns against air attacks.

armed neutrality—The condition of maintaining a nation equipped and prepared for war while refraining from taking sides in a conflict. The term was apparently first used in 1780, during the American Revolution, when Empress Catherine the Great of Russia proclaimed a state of "armed neutrality" for the protection of shipping of neutral nations. The belligerents were called on to accept principles of neutrality embodied in a defensive treaty signed by Russia, Denmark, and Sweden. Spain and France accepted; Great Britain disregarded the principles.

armed propaganda—A term used to describe acts of violence that lack a clear tactical objective and are designed to draw attention to the executing group's grievances. It is closely associated with terrorism but may have a military objective as its target. See also **terrorism**.

armed reconnaissance—An air mission flown with the primary purpose of locating and attacking TARGETS OF OPPORTUNITY (i.e., enemy matériel, personnel, and facilities), in assigned general areas or along assigned ground communications routes and not for the purpose of attacking specific briefed targets.

armet—A type of medieval light helmet having a movable visor and protection for the neck.

armiger—An armor-bearer for a knight, generally a squire. One of the many duties of the squire was to assist the knight in donning his armor.

armistice—A suspension of hostilities agreed upon by warring forces; a truce. Terms under which armistices are negotiated vary from complete cessation of all action to temporary halt of battlefield action for a specific length of time. Best known is the Armistice of 11 November 1918, signed by representatives of the Allies and Germany, which ended fighting on the Western Front in World War I.

armistice demarcation line—A line from which disputing or belligerent forces disengage and withdraw to their respective sides after a truce or cease-fire agreement.

armor—1) Material or equipment used to protect personnel, animals, ships, vehicles, aircraft, and other equipment from hostile destructive agents (arrows, swords, bullets, shells, bombs, mines, etc.). Includes a) **body armor**—Some sort of body protection was used by warriors from the earliest times. Increased technological capability permitted the use of more and more durable materials, animal hides, leather, layered or quilted fabrics, bronze, iron, steel, and, in modern times, fiberglass and synthetic materials such as kevlar. Among the major types of body armor are the following: **almain armor**—Light armor for the upper body, consisting of helmet, gorget, breastplate, backplate, and arm splints. This half-armor was common during the 16th century. **bronze armor**—The capability of working bronze permitted the use of this metal for helmets and for body armor. Bronze armor varied greatly from country to country and from age to age. The earliest known whole body armor dates from the 15th century B.C. It covered the wearer from shoulder to knee and had articulated shoulder pieces. Greek armor generally consisted of a

CUIRASS, which covered the chest, with a shirt of various materials, separate leg pieces, GREAVES, and helmets of various designs. **fabric armor**—Various fabrics, usually quilted, have been used for protection. Linen, padded with tow, was commonly used in medieval Europe. Heavy silk shirts were worn under armor by the Mongols in the 13th century to improve protection and by some in Britain at the end of the 17th century. During World War I, silk was tested and found to protect against shell splinters and shrapnel at speeds of up to 1,000 feet per second. The Chinese also made use of fabric armor, sometimes lacquered. Combinations of man-made fibers, including fiberglass and metallic fibers and metals, have been used in modern times. LAMELLAR or **scale armor**—Used from antiquity, it consisted of pieces of metal or other material sewn in overlapping rows like shingles to a garment of cloth or leather. **leather armor**—Hides, and then tanned leather, provided a fairly inexpensive and readily available material that could be shaped to the human form. Leather helmets were cheaper than bronze and worn by the ordinary soldier in ancient and medieval armies. Garments of leather were common, and sometimes used as a base for attaching metal or other protective materials. **mail**—Also called "chain mail," it consisted of interlocking metal rings forming a sort of fabric, normally in the form of a shirt. Used by the Romans, it survived into medieval times, sometimes in combination with plate armor. **plate**—Armor made in a solid piece, as opposed to **mail** or **lamellar**. Plate armor was carried to its ultimate form in the early 16th century, when knights were armored from head to foot in plate and fought on horses that also had their own armor protection. b) **ship's armor**—The armor on ships is usually specially treated case-hardened steel. It is thickest in the most vulnerable areas, particularly gun turrets, the deck, and below the waterline. c) **tank** and **vehicle armor**, including **self-propelled artillery**—Armor is applied to many kinds of vehicles that may be used in areas subject to enemy fire. It may be added as protection to an otherwise regular automobile, truck, construction vehicle, etc.; in addition, the design of the basic combat vehicle, such as the TANK or SELF-PROPELLED ARTILLERY may call for construction with armor protection. Most self-propelled artillery is protected by armor; most towed guns have armor shields. d) **armored fortifications**—Rifled siege guns, as demonstrated in the American Civil War and Franco-Prussian War, made brickwork forts obsolete; therefore, in the latter decades of the 19th century, modern permanent fortifications were constructed of concrete and earth. Cast-steel armor, used in gun turrets and for protection of underground magazines and living quarters, was first used in forts designed by Gen. Séré de Rivière to protect the French frontier with Germany. Construction of this system was begun in 1873. 2) A general term for all combat vehicles, including tanks, that are armored. 3) The general designation given to armored force components of an army or a command.

armor belt—See **belt**.

armored—Equipped with special physical protection, generally made of metal.

armored artillery—See **artillery.**

armored car—A light armored vehicle used primarily for reconnaissance and security missions.

armored cavalry—Motorized units that replaced horse cavalry after World War I. Also called "mechanized cavalry," armored cavalry units have been employed in reconnaissance and screening missions in much the way that horse cavalry had previously been used. See also **air cavalry.**

armored cruiser — A late-19th- and early-20th-century warship with both the armored deck of the protected cruiser—sometimes two decks—and belts of armor on both sides, as well as armored bulkheads fore and aft.

armored division — A combined-arms ground force of DIVISION type and size, the principal combat components usually being tank units.

armored force—A military ground force in which most elements, or a preponderance of the major fighting elements, are ARMORED VEHICLES or are units built around armored vehicles.

armored fortifications—See **armor.**

armored infantry—The infantry in an armored brigade or division. These units generally move into combat in ARMORED

PERSONNEL CARRIERs or INFANTRY FIGHTING VEHICLEs.

armored personnel carrier (APC)—An armored vehicle, usually fully enclosed, used to transport infantry into combat, from which the troops usually debark to fight.

armored vehicles — Armor-protected vehicles, such as TANKS, INFANTRY FIGHTING VEHICLES, many self-propelled artillery weapons, armored cars, personnel carriers, cargo carriers, recovery vehicles, and FIRE DIRECTION CENTERs.

armorer—1) A person who makes or repairs armor or weapons or has the care of them for a particular unit. 2) A person, especially a ground crew member, who repairs, loads, and handles aircraft armaments and bombs.

armor-piercing ammunition (AP) — See **ammunition, armor-piercing**.

armor-piercing   discarding   sabot (APDS)—See **ammunition, armor-piercing**.

armory—1) A place for storing weapons and equipment. The term is often used in the United States for an Army Reserve or National Guard installation, where the principal purpose is drilling and training the part-time military units and where the storage of weapons and equipment is only incidental. 2) A factory for making arms. 3) An arsenal.

arms—See **arm**.

arms control—The concept of restricting, through international agreement, the number, type, or performance of weapons systems, including command and control, logistics support, and related intelligence-gathering mechanisms, or the strength, organization, equipment, deployment, or employment of armed forces. The concept differs from disarmament in its focus on limiting, rather than eliminating, war-making capabilities.

Armstrong gun—A gun invented by Sir William Armstrong in the mid-19th century and commonly used by the British Royal Navy in the 1860s. The Armstrong gun was a rifled breech-loader.

army—1) That element of a nation's defense establishment designed and organized especially for ground combat, including supporting arms. 2) A tactical and administrative element (often called a FIELD ARMY) within a national army. The size and composition of an army vary: In the U.S. Army a field army (normally numbered First, Second, etc.) consists of a headquarters, two or more corps, and auxiliary forces. In the latter half of the 20th century the U.S. Army eliminated field armies from its command hierarchy, with corps commanded directly by ARMY GROUPs. Types of armies include the following: **combined arms**—An army including all major arms and branches of the nation's army (particularly Russian). **field**—Another term for a combined-arms army (particularly in the United States). **standing**—A permanent army of professional, paid soldiers. **consular**—A Roman army commanded by one of the two consuls of Republican Rome. It usually had 18,000 to 20,000 men and a combat front of about a mile and a half. If the two consular armies were joined, the consuls would alternate in command, usually every 24 hours.

army corps—See **corps, army**.

army group—Two or more field armies under a designated commander.

army of occupation — The units of an army stationed in the territory of a defeated enemy.

army reserve—See **reserve**.

army reserve corps—See **Reserve Corps**.

army service area—An administrative region in the rear area of a combat zone, usually behind the rear boundary of the combat corps of an army or army group and in front of the combat zone rear boundary. Most of the administrative establishment and service troops in the combat zone are located in this area, and administered and commanded by an army service area commander.

arquebus—A 15th-century MATCHLOCK GUN, the first handgun to have a stock shaped to fit the shoulder. The arquebus was equipped with an S-shaped clamp (SERPENTINE) that held the match. A trigger would move the serpentine so that the match would ignite the powder in a pan and fire the bullet. The weapon was also called HARQUEBUS or HACK-

BUT. It was first used extensively in the Spanish army and became common in all European armies in the 16th century. See also **caliver**.

arquebus

arquebusier—A foot soldier who carried and fired an arquebus. Arquebusiers wore a variety of dress and armors. In the late 15th and 16th centuries, when arquebuses became a regular part of an army's weaponry, arquebusiers served with pikemen in mixed foot units of "pike and shot." Throughout this period, generally, the proportion of arquebusiers or "shot" to pikemen in infantry units rose gradually. In the mid- to late-16th and early-17th centuries, all European armies replaced the arquebus with the MATCHLOCK MUSKET, and the arquebusier of the earlier period became the musketeer of more recent times.

arquebusier

arquebusier, mounted—An arquebusier mounted on a horse.

array—*n.* 1) A body of soldiers drawn up in battle order. 2) Any deployment of troops or weapons, as a TARGET ARRAY. *v.* To draw up troops in battle order.

arrest—*v.* To seize and hold under authority of the law. *n.* A state of restriction on the movement and freedom of a military person, who is then "under arrest." In this use of the word, it means a restriction less than confinement.

arrow—A straight, thin shaft, usually made of light wood with a pointed head at one end and flight-stabilizing feathers at the other, and propelled from a bow.

arrowhead—The tip of an arrow, usually made of a hard material, like stone or metal, and shaped to facilitate penetration.

arsenal—1) An installation where weapons, ammunition, and other military matériel is made, repaired, or stored. 2) An armory, but without drill facilities. 3) A stock of weapons, from that of a single person to the total weapons holdings of a nation.

Articles for the Government of the Navy—Regulations for the disciplinary governance of the U.S. Navy. For many years the articles were displayed in all ships and stations and were read to the assembled crew regularly. They were superseded on 5 May 1950 by the adoption of the Uniform Code of Military Justice and issuance of combined ARTICLES OF WAR for all services. See also **"Rocks and Shoals."**

Articles of War—A code of regulations governing the conduct of military forces. Those in existence today in the U.S. and British military establishments derive from articles that were in use by the British before the American Revolution. In 1950 the Articles of War of the U.S. Army and U.S. Air Force and the ARTICLES FOR THE GOVERNMENT OF THE NAVY were combined into an all-service code of Articles of War. The articles describe the offenses for which a member of the armed forces may be tried under the UNIFORM CODE OF MILITARY JUSTICE.

artificer—A specialist, dating at least from the 18th century, concerned primarily with the repair of weapons or equipment. The term is also used for an enlisted specialist rating in the military services. In the U.S. Navy artificers repair a range of equipment, from engines to gun sights and optical instruments.

artillery—1) A general term, usually referring collectively to gunpowder weapons (cannon) too large to be hand-carried, although all large, pregunpowder devices for firing missiles may be considered artillery. 2) The branch or arm of an army that is equipped with such weapons.

Artillery may be categorized in many ways, but there are two principal types: **mobile artillery**, which includes **cannon** and comparable weapons that can be shifted from one place to another, and **fixed artillery**, which includes all such weapons permanently emplaced in fortifications or other installations. Types of artillery include the following: **antiaircraft** or **air defense**—Weapons that may be cannon or missiles designed for employment against hostile aircraft. **antitank**—Cannon or other crew-served weapons designed specifically for use against tanks and other armored vehicles. **armored**—Artillery designed to support armored forces. Armored artillery weapons are usually self-propelled, and the crews and weapons are often protected by armor. **field**—1) Cannon and other mobile artillery weapons including armored artillery, designed for use against most surface targets; in some nations this category includes antitank weapons. 2) The branch or arm of an army that is equipped with such weapons. Field artillery is usually categorized by weight (light, medium, and heavy) and by means of mobility. **Light artillery** is intended primarily for direct support of infantry and armor, and includes cannon with calibers up to 105mm; the largest light artillery piece currently in the U.S. Army is the 105mm howitzer. **Medium artillery** refers to weapons in size from 105mm guns to 155mm howitzers. **Heavy artillery** includes guns of at least 155mm. Mobility categories include towed and self-propelled. **Self-propelled artillery** refers to weapons that are permanently mounted on vehicles each with its own means of propulsion; **towed artillery** refers to cannon incapable of independent movement, thus drawn by horses or by a PRIME MOVER.

art of war—The conduct of combat operations by means of imagination, skill, and professionalism.

ASDIC—Anti-Submarine Detection Investigation Committee, commonly written "Asdic." A British name developed before World War II for the undersea echo-sounding submarine detection device also known as SONAR.

as foragers (en fourrageurs)—A command of the late-19th and early-20th centuries for a military unit to deploy from close-order formation to an irregular open-order line.

ASROC—See **antisubmarine rocket**.

assault—*n.* 1) A planned, sharp attack upon a defended position, such as a gun emplacement or a fortified hill. 2) In an amphibious operation, the period from the time the first waves cross the line of departure to the seizure of the initial objectives. 3) In an airborne operation, the period in which the airborne force is delivered to the objective area and attacks the designated objective positions. *v.* To make a violent attack on a local objective.

assault aircraft—Aircraft, including helicopters, which move assault troops and cargo into a combat objective area and provide for their resupply.

assault craft—Small craft and amphibious vehicles employed for landing troops and equipment in the assault waves of an amphibious operation.

assault gun—A cannon mounted on an armored, tracked vehicle, designed for close engagements and direct fire at fortifications. Traverse is usually limited and speed is usually slow. The German *Sturmgeschuetz* of World War II was an assault gun originally designed to provide antitank and close fire support at less cost in money and production time than a tank, because of its relative simplicity. It was often used as a tank by the Germans, particularly late in the war. It was more heavily armored than self-propelled artillery and had a different combat role. See also **tank destroyer**.

assault landing—In amphibious operations, the debarkation of assault troops directly into combat.

assault shipping—Shipping assigned to an amphibious task force to transport assault troops, vehicles, equipment, and supplies to the objective area.

assault troops—Troops assigned to carry out an assault.

assault wave—A formation of forces, including assault troops, landing craft, amphibious vehicles, and assault aircraft, scheduled to arrive at a beach at the same time during an amphibious assault.

assegai (assagai)—A light throwing or stabbing weapon like a javelin or short spear, usually pointed at both ends, used by the

Zulus and other African tribes. A similar weapon was used by the Albanian STRADIOTS in the 16th century.

assembly—A bugle call calling troops to form ranks.

assembly area—1) An area in which a command is assembled preparatory to further action. 2) In a supply installation, the gross area used for collecting and combining components into complete units, kits, or assemblies. See also **area**.

asset (intelligence)—Any resource (person, group, installation, or instrument) at the disposition of an intelligence organization. Often used with a modifier such as "agent asset" or "propaganda asset."

assign—To integrate units or persons into an organization.

assignment—1) The status of being assigned. 2) The process of being placed in an assigned status. Unlike ATTACHMENT, an assignment is considered permanent and is terminated by a new assignment.

Assize of Arms—An important royal decree, given by King Henry II of England in 1181, which reestablished the old Saxon national militia, the *fyrd*, by directing all freeholders to provide themselves with arms and armor according to rank; it was also decreed that all should be ready to answer a summons to arms by the sheriff.

ASTOR—See **antisubmarine torpedo**.

ASW—See **antisubmarine warfare**.

asymmetrical warfare—1) Attacks in which the potential damage to the target area is disproportionately large relative to the risk to the attacker (e.g., the carpet bombing of German cities in World War II). 2) Threats that are outside the range of conventional warfare and difficult to respond to in kind (e.g., a suicide bomber).

"As you were"—The command that cancels a previous order, in effect saying that the previous order was inappropriate.

Atlantic Wall—In World War II, Hitler's string of coastal defenses stretching from the northern tip of Denmark to Brittany and southward to the Franco-Spanish border. It was a line of permanent fortifications at in-

tervals along the coast. In areas where attack was anticipated, it was often laced by strongpoints and field positions, as well as protected by minefields and underwater obstacles.

atom bomb—See **atomic weapon**.

atomic warfare—Warfare involving use of atomic weapons. See also **nuclear warfare**.

atomic weapon—A weapon whose explosive power is derived from atomic fission. However, the term is also loosely applied to all nuclear weapons, including those whose power is based on fusion. Atomic weapons include missiles, rockets, bombs, artillery shells, and land mines.

"at priority call"—A precedence in artillery firing which requires that a given unit assure the availability of fire at an agreed rate.

atrocity — An act of wanton brutality and cruelty, such as the intentional killing of non-combatants.

attach—To place people or units in or under the command of a larger organization on a temporary basis.

attaché, defense—See **attaché, military**.

attaché, military—A military officer attached to a diplomatic office, usually an embassy.

attachment—1) The status of being attached. 2) The process of being placed in an attached status. Attachments are temporary, and upon their conclusion individuals or units return to their regular ASSIGNMENTs.

attack—*n.* The initiation of combat by one force attempting to gain an objective held by another; a strike against a target to seize or destroy it. *v.* To launch such an action. Special types of attack include these: **airborne**—An attack carried out by troops landing by means of parachutes, gliders, or helicopters. **amphibious**—An attack on a beach by forces delivered by landing craft. **deliberate**—An attack characterized by coordinated employment of firepower and maneuver to close with and destroy or capture the enemy. **flank**—An attack delivered against the side or flank of an enemy's forces rather than against his immediate front. **frontal**—An attack directly against the front of an enemy's force. **holding**—An attack designed to pin down a portion of an enemy's forces while a major effort is being made in another sector. **main** or **major**—A principal attack made on a portion of an enemy's forces, while lesser attacks are engaging other portions of those forces in other sectors. **piecemeal**—An attack begun by a limited force, with reinforcements joining the attack as they arrive on the battlefield or otherwise become available. **secondary**—Same as a holding attack.

attack aircraft carrier (CV)—A carrier designed to engage targets afloat or ashore and to engage in sustained operations in support of other forces. If nuclear-powered, it is designated CVN.

attack cargo ship—A naval vessel designed or converted to transport combat-loaded cargo in an ASSAULT LANDING. These ships have greater capability for carrying landing craft, more speed and armament, and larger hatches and booms than comparable cargo ships. Designated as AKA.

attack carrier striking force — A naval force organized around one or more aircraft carriers. Other vessels accompany the carriers primarily to support them and screen against attacks by submarines or aircraft. Carrier-based aircraft are the main offensive weapons.

attack column—See **column**.

attack group—In the U.S. Navy a subordinate task organization of an amphibious task force. It is composed of assault shipping and supporting naval units designated to transport, protect, land, and initially support a landing group.

attack transport—A naval vessel equipped with landing craft and designed to carry a battalion landing team with its equipment and supplies to an offshore point from which an amphibious landing can be made. Designated as APA.

attention—1) The posture assumed by a member of the armed services characterized by the body erect, shoulders square, eyes to the front, arms at the sides, and heels together. 2) The command to assume such a posture.

attenuation—1) The decrease in intensity of a signal, beam, or wave, as a result of absorption of energy. 2) In mine warfare, the reduction in intensity of an influence as the distance from the source increases. 3) In camouflage or concealment, the process of making an object or surface less conspicuous by reducing its contrast to its surroundings.

attitude—See **spin**.

attrition—Reduction of the effectiveness of a force caused by loss of personnel and matériel. Sometimes used synonymously with "loss rate." The ATTRITION RATE is usually expressed in percentages or in casualties or losses per thousand.

attrition rate—A factor, normally expressed as a percentage, reflecting the anticipated losses of personnel or matériel within a specified period of time.

Aum Shinrikyo—The Japanese doomsday cult responsible for the March 1995 nerve-gas attack on the Tokyo subway system. See also **Tokyo Subway Gas Attack**.

authentication—1) Evidence by proper signature or seal that a document is genuine or official. 2) A security measure designed to protect a communication system against fraudulent transmissions.

authenticator—A letter, numeral, or groups of letters or numerals, or both, attesting to the authenticity of a message or transmission.

authority—The power to direct action or to use resources to accomplish assigned missions.

automatic weapons—Firearms that fire continuously upon activation, without the necessity for repeated triggering. They include machine guns, automatic pistols, and automatic rifles. See also **BAR**.

auxiliaries—In the ancient Roman army, soldiers with special capabilities who were not Roman citizens, such as archers from Crete and slingers from the Balearic Islands. These auxiliaries (*auxilia*) served in special units, originally in the frontier areas of the empire from which they came, but later abroad as needed. After 25 years of service, an auxiliary was granted Roman citizenship. 2) Military personnel not regular members of a force or service.

auxiliary force—1) An aggregation of military personnel, weapon systems, vehicles, and necessary support, or a combination thereof. 2) A force set up or established to assist in periods of need, as an auxiliary air force, auxiliary unit, etc.

AV-8—See **Harrier**.

Avenger II (A-12)—Designed to provide the most advanced technology of any carrier-based combat aircraft, the A-12 was jointly produced by McDonnell Douglas and General Dynamics. By 1991 program costs had risen so high that it was cancelled by the Defense Department in what was then the largest contract termination ordered by that department.

aventail—A band of mail attached to the helmet of a 14th- or 15th-century warrior to protect the neck and throat.

aviation—Pertaining to air forces or to aerial activity.

aviation boatswain's mate — U.S. Navy rating.

aviation electrician's mate — U.S. Navy rating.

aviation machinist's mate—U.S. Navy rating.

aviation metalsmith—U.S. Navy rating.

aviation ordnanceman—U.S. Navy rating.

aviation pilot—U.S. Navy rating.

aviation radioman—U.S. Navy rating.

aviation radio technician—U.S. Navy rating.

AWACS—See **airborne warning and control systems**.

AWOL—See **absent without leave**.

ax—A weapon with a broad, bladed head mounted on a handle. From earliest times axes were used as weapons in hand-to-hand fighting, and many types are known. In the 8th century, Vikings used a **bearded ax**, so called for its odd shape, in profile somewhat resembling a truncated adze. The Viking **broadax** of the 10th and 11th centuries flared from a narrow base. The Franks in the 6th century to 8th century used a **throwing ax**, known as the "francisca." The **lochaber ax** was used in Scotland from about the 16th century to the mid-18th century. The blade, attached to the end of a pole, was a semi-ellipse; a hook facing the other way was used by the foot soldier, who carried it for pulling mounted men off horses and for tearing defenses apart. The Danish **battle-ax** was carried by most soldiers in England in the 11th century. It was later combined with a pistol, like the **boarding ax** which, with or without the pistol, was used by seamen or marines in sailing warships to chop masts and rigging off enemy vessels as well as to behead enemy sailors.

axis—A line or route assigned for purposes of control; often a road, or group of roads, or designated series of locations, identifiable both on a map and on the ground.

axis of advance—An axis or a route to be followed in advancing toward the enemy.

axis of communications — An axis or a route designated for coordination of front-to-rear communications or movement during a combat operation. See also **line of communications**.

azabs—Turkish irregular light infantry of the late medieval and early modern period. Azabs were armed with a variety of weapons, including arquebus, or a bow, a spear, or a sword and shield.

azimuth deviation—The lateral angle of deviation of a projectile or bomb from its intended direction, measured in degrees or mils.

Azon—A kind of bomb used in World War II, with movable control surfaces in the tail adjustable by radio signal so that the missile's flight could be controlled.

B

B-1B—See **Lancer**.

B-2—See **Spirit**.

B-17—See **"Flying Fortress."**

B-24—See **Liberator**.

B-25—See **Mitchell**.

B-26—See **Invader** and **Marauder**.

B-40—A shoulder-held, rocket-propelled grenade launcher used by Communist forces in Vietnam and Cambodia.

B-52—See **Stratofortress**.

B-70—See **Valkyrie**.

Baader-Meinhof Gang — A news media term for the German terrorist group RED ARMY FACTION.

backplate—A piece of PLATE ARMOR that covers the back.

back-step—*v.* To march backward, away from the direction in which one is facing. *n.* The command to so march.

backsword—A sword with a broad blade and only one cutting edge. The term is also used for any heavy sword with a basket hilt or shell hilt.

backup force—Any organized force prepared to back up or reinforce units already engaged in, or committed to, an assault.

badges—Devices worn on a uniform, sometimes to indicate rank or membership in a group or office. However, the term is applied primarily to pin-on devices awarded for attainment of proficiency or excellence in marksmanship or other military skills, or for experience in such performance.

baggage—The equipment and supplies, other than weapons, accompanying a military force.

baggage train—The supplies and equipment required by a military force and the vehicles that transport them. Transportation may be by animal, truck, railroad car, or whatever other means are available. A baggage train usually follows the main body and can sometimes stretch for miles behind the advancing combat force.

bail/bailey—Both "bail" and "bailey" were terms for the outer wall of a castle and for the court it enclosed. In the plural, the term "bails" is synonymous with PALISADE.

Bailey bridge—A type of bridge designed by British engineer Sir Donald Coleman Bailey and first used by British and American forces in World War II. Carried to the riverbank in pieces, it is rapidly assembled by fastening prefabricated latticed panels of electrically welded high-tensile steel to form girders or larger panels. The resulting components can be laid side by side or superimposed, the quantity and procedure depending upon the span and the load for which the bridge is needed.

"Baka"—See **"Oka."**

Baker—Letter of old phonetic alphabet. See also **alphabet, phonetic**.

balanced collective force—A force comprising elements from more than one nation and in such variety and strength that the total force will fulfill the mission for which it has been created.

balance of power—An approach to the conduct of international relations that aims at preserving stability by preventing any one nation or alliance of nations from becoming strong enough to dominate or destroy other nations. Under this approach, if one nation threatens to dominate the international system, the threatened powers realign themselves, throwing their combined weight against the threatening power and restoring the balance.

baldric—A shoulder belt for attaching a sword or a bugle. It was usually worn across the shoulder and chest but could simply be slung over one shoulder.

balisage—The marking of a route by a system of dim beacon lights enabling vehicles to be driven at near daytime speed under blackout conditions.

ball—A solid missile, commonly but not always spherical, usually propelled by an explosive device. The term is also used as a collective noun for such missiles. Balls are generally described by the weapon that fires them (e.g., cannonball, musket ball, pistol ball).

ball cartridge or **ball ammunition**—A small-arms bullet and its cartridge (usually brass). The term is carried over from earlier centuries when musket and rifle bullets were spherical in shape.

ballista—One of the many kinds of ancient military machines designed originally to hurl rocks and stones at an enemy. It consisted of a large wooden frame, with two projecting arms, to which were attached the ends of a twisted cord, consisting of skeins of human hair and animal tendons. It operated much like a giant crossbow, in that the cord provided the power to propel missiles toward the enemy. The energy of the cord was derived from torsion rather than tension, as was the case for the catapult or the later crossbow. The cord was pulled back to the end of a trough on which the missile was placed. Re-

lease of the cord by a trigger mechanism propelled the missile with great force along a path delineated by the trough. The ballista was an antipersonnel weapon and commonly weighed about 60 pounds, although some varieties were much larger and were used as siege weapons. A ballista was designed by Vitruvius in about 26 b.c. and seems to have originated in a Greek-speaking area, inasmuch as the name means "thrower" in Greek. Later the ballista, like the catapult, was used to propel large darts or arrows as well as rocks.

ballista

ballistic missile—See **missile, ballistic**.

ballistic missile early warning system (BMEWS)—An electronic system for providing detection and early warning of attack by intercontinental ballistic missiles.

ballistics—The branch of applied physics that studies the motion of missiles or projectiles of all types. **Internal ballistics** is concerned with the action of missiles as they are expelled through and from the tube of the propelling weapon, **external ballistics** with their action in flight, and **terminal ballistics** with their action upon approach to a target.

ballistic trajectory—The path traced by an object after the propulsive force is terminated and the object is acted on only by gravity and aerodynamic drag.

ballistite—See **cordite**.

ball, minié—1) Invented in 1849 by French Capt. Claude Etienne Minié, it was a lead projectile shaped like a blunt-nosed bullet (cylindro-conoidal) and originally used in the

Minié muzzle-loading rifle musket. The original minié ball had three spiral grooves and a conical depression in the base. The grooves were usually filled with tallow, and the depression was an iron cup that was forced farther into the ball by pressure of the gas resulting from the explosion of the powder, causing in turn the lead to expand into the grooves of the rifle. Smaller than the bore of the rifle musket, minié balls could be dropped down the barrel, greatly decreasing the time required for loading the weapon. Most smoothbore muskets could be converted by rifling to use a minié ball. 2) Mid-19th-century U.S. slang for any bullet fired from a rifled musket.

ballock dagger or **ballock knife**—A 14th-century short dagger with two rounded lobes at the end of the handle, carried between the thighs on a low-slung belt. In was used until the 17th century in northern Europe. It was also known as a **dudgeon-dagger,** and in the 19th century it was called a **kidney-dagger**.

balloon—A bag of nonporous material filled with hot air or a gas lighter than air, causing the bag to rise above the earth's surface. Since their invention by the Montgolfier brothers in late-18th-century France, balloons have been used for aerial observation, either floating free or, more usually, anchored, where they could raise the observer high enough to see beyond enemy lines. By World War I most military balloons (or nonrigid airships) were cylindrical in shape. Because of the vulnerability of balloons to modern weapons, their use for reconnaissance and observation was discontinued after World War I. **Barrage balloons** are anchored and float at very high altitudes near vulnerable targets as protection from air attack, mainly because their mooring lines pose a danger to lower-flying aircraft.

ball, red-hot—See **hot shot**.

ball turret—A turret in the shape of a ball, designed to project from the belly of an airplane and to house a machine gunner. The turret rotates as the gunner brings the guns to bear.

ban—1) A medieval lord's summons of vassals to arms. 2) Collectively, those so summoned.

banderole—Derived from the Italian for "small flag," the term specifically applies to a small flag or streamer attached to a knight's lance or flown from a ship's masthead.

bandit—A hostile aircraft.

bandmaster—A warrant officer in the U.S. Navy and the British Royal Navy.

bandolier or **bandoleer**—A belt, usually of webbing, worn by soldiers over one shoulder and across the chest, with loops or small pockets in which cartridges are carried.

bandon—The basic military unit of the Byzantine army. **Banda** (plural) varied in size and organization at different periods and according to whether they were infantry or cavalry. Infantry banda at the beginning of the 10th century had 256 men, and cavalry banda 200 to 400. Also known as **numerus**.

Bangalore torpedo—A device for cutting wire entanglements or for exploding mines. It consists of a long piece of TNT-filled iron pipe with a detonating cap and a long fuze that allows the igniter to leave the vicinity after lighting it. The name comes from the city of Bangalore, India, where a prototype was first used in the British siege of 1799.

banneret—Probably derived from the word for a small banner, the term "banneret" referred to a knight, ranking above a knight bachelor and below a baron, who led men into battle under his own standard.

banquette—A raised platform area along the inner wall of a trench or a parapet where soldiers stand and fire.

banzai attack—A charge by Japanese troops in World War II, so named for the word they shouted as they approached their opponents. Literally translated as "A thousand years," *"Banzai!"* is roughly equivalent to "Hurray!"

BAR—Browning automatic rifle. Invented by John M. Browning (1855–1926), the BAR, used in World War I and (in a slightly improved version) in World War II, was a .30-caliber, air-cooled, gas-operated, magazine-fed rifle. With a firing rate of 200 to 350 rounds per minute and serving the same function as a light machine gun, it was fired by a BAR man, with an assistant BAR man, an infantryman, who dropped his rifle to pick up the BAR if its operator was incapacitated.

barbarian—A savage, uncivilized person. In ancient Rome, the term was applied to all who lived outside the bounds of the Roman Empire.

Barbarossa, Operation—Code name applied to Germany's invasion of the Soviet Union on 22 June 1941. Ordered by Hitler, Operation Barbarossa condemned Germany to a two-front war and, more than any other single action, assured an Allied victory.

barbed wire—Strands of wire with barbs of various types. Such wire was used for delineating boundaries long before its first military use in 1874. Its full military significance was realized in World War I and has been exploited since. Barbed wire placed in rolls or strung on pickets in front of a defended position slows the advance of attackers and holds them in the line of defensive fire.

barbette—A support that raises a gun high enough so that its fire may be directed over the surrounding protective armor or parapet, rather than through an opening in the protecting material. A barbette may be a mound of dirt, a platform, a carriage, or any other supporting device. A gun so mounted is said to be *en barbette*.

barbican—A fortification, such as a tower, guarding the approach to a castle or town, commonly placed at a gate or drawbridge.

barbut—An almost cylindrical helmet with a rounded crown, similar to the classical Greek Corinthian helmet. It protected the cheeks and neck and sometimes had only a narrow T-shaped opening for the eyes and nose.

bardings—Armor, leather, or other material used to protect or decorate a WAR HORSE. Bardings of various types and styles were slung on the forequarters or hindquarters, or both, of the horse.

bare base—A base that includes minimum facilities for air operations but has a runway and aircraft parking areas.

barge—The boat used by an admiral or the commanding officer of a large warship, for transportation to and from the ship or flagship.

barracks—A permanent building used for housing military personnel. The term is often used specifically to designate housing for enlisted personnel, as distinct from separate quarters in which officers and noncommissioned officers live.

barracks bag—See **bag, duffel**.

barrage—1) A temporary means of preventing enemy movement or action, usually consisting of a concentrated, continuous massing of fire by any kind of weapon. 2) Most commonly, a screen or curtain of high-explosive fire placed in front of friendly troops by artillery or mortars. 3) Variations of barrages in type and purpose are as follows: **normal**—Defensive artillery barrage to be placed directly in front of a friendly position in anticipation of a possible enemy attack. It is fired automatically upon call from the supported troops. **box**—A curtain of continuous artillery fire around three or four sides of a position to deny access by the enemy. **rolling**—An offensive barrage placed in front of attacking friendly troops. By periodic adjustments of range and deflection (direction) settings on the weapons, the curtain of fire moves forward into the enemy positions at the same rate as the attacking troops' forward movement. **aerial**—An approximation of an artillery barrage by aerial bombardment, with the curtain effect sustained by sequential flights of bombers over the target area. **balloon**—A screen formed by the mooring wires of barrage balloons (see **balloon**) to inhibit the approach of enemy aircraft to a defended area. **electronic**—Jamming measures put into effect over a wide frequency spectrum to interfere with such enemy electronic devices as radios and radars.

barrel—The tubular part of a weapon through which its projectile travels when the propellant charge has been detonated. See also **bore**.

barrel roll—A maneuver in which an aircraft executes a complete revolution around its longitudinal axis.

barricade—*n*. A structure, usually temporary and constructed of whatever material is at hand, set up to prevent passage of traffic along a means of approach to a defended area. *v*. To erect barriers to deny access to an area.

barrier or **barrier system** — A coordinated series of obstacles designed or employed to canalize, direct, restrict, delay, or stop the movement of an opposing force and to impose additional losses in personnel, time, and equipment upon the opposing force.

barrier forces—Air, surface, or submarine units and their supporting systems positioned along routes that enemy forces are expected to travel. Barrier forces are intended to detect and report enemy movement, block it, and destroy as much of the enemy force as possible.

barrier minefield—A minefield laid as part of a barrier system to block the approach of attacking enemy units, particularly toward the flanks of the defending force, and to channel the attack to selected battle areas.

bar shot—A projectile consisting of two cast-iron balls or hemispheres joined by an iron bar, thus resembling a dumbbell. Because its motion was erratic and it caused more damage than ordinary round shot, bar shot was used particularly in naval cannon for destroying the rigging of enemy ships.

bascinet—A type of helmet, developed by the early 14th century, having a pointed skull and extending below the ears. An AVENTAIL of mail was generally fastened along the bottom to protect the neck. The commonest form of visor was shaped like a snout and hinged at the temples, but later helmets had the visor hinged at the front.

base—*n.* 1) A location or an area from which combat operations are projected and supported. 2) An area or a location consisting largely of logistic, maintenance, and support installations. 3) An installation at which aircraft or naval vessels are assigned and to which they return following any trips or combat or noncombat operations in the air or at sea. *v.* To assign or station military individuals or units or matériel at a location or installation.

base altitude—An altitude maintained during an air mission, especially on the flight to the target or rendezvous.

base cluster—A collection of bases grouped for mutual protection and for ease of command and control.

base command—1) An area containing a military base or a group of such bases organized under one commander. 2) The command organization of a base, as opposed to the command of the units it supports.

base ejection shell—A type of shell that ejects its load from its base.

base exchange—See **post exchange**.

base fuze—See **fuze**.

base line—A surveyed line, established with more than usual care, to which surveys are referred for coordination and correlation, usually to assure accurate artillery fire and military mapping, particularly construction of air photo mosaic maps.

base of operations—An area or a facility from which a military force begins its offensive operations, to which it falls back in case of reverse, and in which supply and support facilities are organized.

base pay—The pay of an officer or enlisted person according to rank and longevity before additional pay or allowances are added for quarters, subsistence, flying status, hazardous duty, sea duty, or other special reasons for awarding extra reimbursement.

base plate—A large, flat piece of metal to which the barrel of a mortar is attached, to provide solid, even footing for the weapon.

base point—A selected registration point for an artillery unit (usually of battalion size), easily identifiable on the ground and, if possible, on a map or firing chart. The base point is selected to be as close as possible to the center of the unit's sector of fire. If the situation permits, one gun from each battery is registered on the base point; otherwise, batteries that do not register must be tied to the registering battery by survey. When in position, a unit may register on several check points, but there is only one base point; all targets and concentrations fired on and marked on the firing chart are related to the base point. The line on the firing chart from the guns of a battery to the base point is the battery's BASE LINE. When, for any reason, it is not possible to register on a base point on the ground, the unit registers on a point in the sky by means of a HIGH-BURST ADJUSTMENT. See also **registration** and **precision fire**.

base section—An area within the communications zone of an area of operations organized to provide logistic support to forward areas.

bashi bazouks—Volunteer irregular troops, both infantry and cavalry, in the Turkish armies from the late 18th to the late 19th century. These soldiers, who provided their own weapons and horses and served under officers attached to but independent of the army, were brutal and undisciplined. They fought in Egypt against Napoleon, in the Crimean War, and in the Russo-Turkish War of 1877–78, after which the Ottoman government was forced to stop using them because of their excessive barbarity. The name comes from *bashi bozuq*, Turkish for "one whose head is turned."

basic intelligence—Fundamental data regarding the general situation, resources, capabilities, and vulnerabilities of a country or a possible area of military operations.

basic load—The quantity of supplies that is required to be on hand and can be moved by a unit or formation.

basic load (ammunition)—The quantity of ammunition, measured in rounds or other units of measure, issued to an organization for all its weapons. Basic load is related to the calculated use per weapon for a period of time. A unit going into or already in combat is generally issued several basic loads. Sometimes called "a day of fire."

basic (military) training—The initial instruction, including drill, given to former civilians immediately after entering a military force; it is designed to provide essential fundamental knowledge of military service and practices. Trainees are then generally assigned to further training in the specialty in which they are expected to serve.

basilard—A short sword or dagger of the late 13th century, named for the city of Basle. It was apparently a forerunner of the Swiss shortsword.

basilica—A huge BOMBARD designed by the Hungarian engineer Urban and used by the Turks in the siege of Constantinople in 1453. Built of wrought-iron bars and hoops, with a bore 36 inches in diameter, it fired stone balls weighing 1,600 pounds. It was designed to fire about seven shots a day and had a range of more than a mile. Two hundred men and 60 oxen were required to move the gigantic weapon. However, after firing only a few shots it blew up.

basilisk—A 16th-century artillery piece weighing about 12,000 pounds, firing a projectile of about 90 pounds, with a bore of 10 inches and a length of 10 feet. Its effective range was 750 yards, with a maximum range of 4,000 yards.

basket hilt—See **hilt**.

basket leave—A kind of contingency leave taken by officers who are away from their authorized post or station on a weekend or holiday. A request for leave is placed in the commander's in-basket before the officer departs and is destroyed in the event the officer returns before expiration of the holiday. It is approved and charged as leave if the officer is delayed in returning.

bastard sword—A weapon developed in the 14th century, with a long blade and a grip so lengthened that two hands could be used to wield it. By the 16th century it had acquired the name "bastard sword" because it was neither a two-handed nor a one-handed sword. It is sometimes called a "hand and a half" sword.

bastille—A defensive tower or fortress. Because the Bastille in Paris, captured by the revolutionaries on 14 July 1789 at the start of the French Revolution, was used as a prison, the name has come to mean a prison or jail.

bastion—A projection, often triangular, from the main walls of a fortification, presenting two faces from which defenders could fire on enemies attacking the main wall or adjacent bastions. It has come to mean any well-fortified or well-defended position. A bastion with only one face and one flank is a demi-bastion.

bateau—A flat-bottomed, shallow-draft boat, tapering toward both ends, used on American rivers. Col. Benedict Arnold used bateaux in the march to Québec, which nearly ended in disaster because they were poorly constructed.

batman—A soldier who acts as a servant to an officer in the British army. See also **orderly**.

baton—An emblematic stick or staff carried by one who holds a high office or rank. Traditionally the emblem of a field marshal.

battalion—1) A tactical unit of one branch of a ground army's combat arms, varying in size and composition but generally in the range of

500 to 1,000 troops and usually commanded by a lieutenant colonel. It normally consists of three to five of the basic combat units of its branch (company for infantry, battery for artillery, company or troop for armor). Three or four battalions are usually combined to form a REGIMENT or BRIGADE. 2) A unit of similar size and composition in one of the supporting branches of an army, such as engineers, signals, and ordnance.

battalion company—See **flank company**.

battalion landing team—In an amphibious operation, an infantry battalion reinforced by combat and service elements; the basic unit for planning an ASSAULT LANDING.

batter—The receding slope of the outer face of a wall, from bottom to top.

battering ram—A device in various forms that was driven with force against a wall or other obstacle in order to break through. The simplest rams—long, heavy beams or poles or tree trunks with metal tips—were carried by troops who ran with them against the wall. Rams could be mounted on wheels or suspended within huge wooden assault towers. The largest tower-enclosed battering rams could be as long as 200 feet and were operated by as many as 1,000 men.

protected battering ram

battery—1) A set of guns, torpedo tubes, searchlights, or missile launchers, usually of the same size or caliber. 2) The guns of a warship. 3) The place where one or more pieces of artillery are installed (hence the Battery in lower Manhattan). 4) The basic firing unit of artillery, usually comprising four to eight guns and administrative and combat personnel to operate the weapons. In the U.S. Army

three batteries, usually of six guns each, constitute an artillery battalion. In the British army the unit comparable to such a U.S. battalion is a field regiment. 5) The piece of steel struck by the flint in a SNAPHANCE LOCK.

battery ship—A vessel designed or modified for the bombardment of shore fortifications from the sea. Also called a FLOATING BATTERY, battery ships were often converted old men-of-war.

battle—A major combat encounter between the military forces of two belligerents, each having opposing aims or objectives (assigned or implicit) and each seeking to impose its will on the opponent by achieving its objective, while preventing the enemy from achieving his. A battle ends when one side has clearly achieved its objective or when one (or sometimes both) has clearly failed to achieve its objective. Modern land battles between large forces usually are made up of several engagements and can last many days. Naval battles tend to be short and, in modern times, decisive.

battle-ax—A medieval hand weapon with a heavy wooden handle 2 to 3 feet long and an ax-like cutting and smashing blade, usually curved. See also **ax** and **halberd**.

battle bill—A list of duties and responsibilities assigned to a ship's crew during battle. See also **battle station**.

battle casualty—A member of a military organization who is killed, wounded, missing, or captured in combat action. See also **casualty**.

battle cruiser—A warship with the main armament of a battleship but less armor, which enables it to reach the speed of a cruiser.

battle cry—A yell uttered by troops about to engage in close combat, particularly by the attackers. It may be a scream, a chant, a word (like the Japanese *"Banzai!"* in World War II), or any other vocal utterance, such as the "rebel yell" of the American Civil War.

battle damage assessment—The estimate of damage resulting from the application of military force against an objective. It is usually an intelligence responsibility.

battle drill—Practice specifically for combat, including close duplication of the sights, sounds, and sensations of battle, in order to accustom troops to performing under actual combat conditions.

battle fatigue—See **fatigue, combat.**

battle force—An operational naval task force including carriers, surface combatants, and submarines, assigned to numbered fleets. A battle force may be subdivided into battle groups.

battle formation — The arrangement or DEPLOYMENT of the elements of a military organization preparatory to entering combat.

battle group—A tactical and administrative infantry or airborne unit of the U.S. Army in use during the late 1950s and early 1960s, consisting of four rifle companies and one mortar company, or five rifle companies. The battle group was larger than a battalion but smaller than a regiment or brigade. See also **pentomic division.**

battle, line of—See **line of battle.**

battle map—A map showing ground features in sufficient detail for tactical use by all forces, usually at a scale between 1:25,000 and 1:100,000.

battlements—The top portion of a fortified wall behind which defenders stood to fight, consisting of high portions for protection (**merlons**) alternating regularly with low portions (**crenels**) through which arrows or other missiles could be fired. Battlements appear in representations and remains of fortifications from earliest times and in many societies throughout the world.

battleship—A major fighting warship, heavily armed with powerful guns and, since about 1860, heavily armored. Modern battleships were the largest naval vessels until the introduction of the fleet carrier in World War II, and were so called because they were included in the LINE OF BATTLE. Battleships have traditionally combined heavy armor and armament with extensive cruising radius at fairly high speeds. Since World War II, most navies have eliminated the battleship because of its high cost and vulnerability to air attack. The United States maintains a few of modified World War II–vintage in its active fleet, with others "IN MOTHBALLS" in its reserve fleet. See also **capital ship** and **ship of the line.**

battle sight—A predetermined sight setting on a weapon that will enable the firer to engage targets effectively at close battle ranges when conditions do not permit exact sight settings.

battle station—The place and duty to which each member of a ship's crew is assigned during a battle. Every person has such a station assigned in the BATTLE BILL.

battle surface—A submarine maneuver in which the boat is made buoyant by blowing tanks but is held down by the bow and stern planes until it leaps upward. A submarine thus handled will surface on an almost horizontal plane so as to permit rapid deployment of gun crews.

battle turn—In naval tactics, a 180-degree turn in which vessels reverse course.

"battlewagon"—Slang for a 20th-century battleship.

bayonet (plug, ring, socket, knife)—A daggerlike weapon designed to be attached to the muzzle end of a rifle for use as a thrusting weapon in close combat. The etymology of the term is in dispute, but the term was probably derived from the French *bayoner*, meaning "to put a spigot in a cask." A plug bayonet, inserted in the muzzle of the musket and widely used toward the end of the 17th century, permitted musketeers to perform as pikemen, who were no longer needed. However, the bayonet rendered the weapon inoperable as a firearm and tended to jam or to fall out. About 1680 the ring bayonet was invented (possibly by French Marshal Sébastien le Prestre de Vauban), which fitted around the muzzle, leaving the bore free for firing. This was soon improved by a socket in the handle that firmly locked the bayonet to a stud on the musket barrel. The bayonet is still used in hand-to-hand fighting.

bazooka—A portable rocket launcher. First used in World War II, the bazooka was designed primarily as an antitank weapon, but it proved effective against other targets as well. It originally consisted of a 2.36-inch tube (later enlarged to 3.5 inches) 4.5 to 5 feet long, open at both ends, with a shoulder rest and sights attached. Electrically fired, it launched a rocket-propelled armor-piercing (hollow-cone) projectile.

BDO—battle dress overgarment.

beach—*n.* In an amphibious operation, that portion of the shoreline suitable for the landing of a tactical organization. *v.* To run a vessel ashore deliberately, either as part of a landing operation or for such other purposes, as preventing a vessel in distress from sinking.

beachhead—A section of a hostile shore that, when seized and held, may ensure the continuous landing of troops and matériel and that provides enough maneuver space to conduct subsequent operations ashore. The primary, initial objective of an amphibious operation is to establish a beachhead that has adequate space and depth for logistical and troop buildup and is suitable as a base for subsequent offensive operations.

U.S. Navy photo

U.S. soldiers establish a beachhead during the invasion of Leyte Island, October 1944.

beachhead

beachmaster—The officer who commands a BEACH PARTY in an amphibious operation.

beach party—The naval component of a SHORE PARTY.

beach support area—The area to the rear of an established landing force, operated by SHORE PARTY units. It contains facilities for unloading troops and equipment and maintaining them ashore, and for evacuating the wounded, prisoners of war, and captured matériel.

beacon—In current military usage, an apparatus that emits signals, electronically or by light, for the determination of location or bearing. **Beacon fires** were used for the same purpose (as well as for the transmission of messages) from earliest times.

beam—The measure of a ship at its widest point.

beam rider—A missile guided by radar, radio, or laser beam.

bear—1) To direct or aim weapons at a target by means of a BEARING, as in "bring to bear." 2) To lie in a certain direction, as in "bears to the southeast."

bearded ax—See **ax**.

bearing—The horizontal angle at a given point measured clockwise from a specific reference datum to a second point, which can be a target or an indication of a navigational direction. Bearings may be measured in MILs or degrees.

bearskin—A tall hat of black fur worn as part of the dress uniforms of certain units of the British and other European armies. Use by the British Guards was authorized in 1768 after the Grenadier Guards had started covering the front of their stiff hats with fur during the Seven Years' War. See also **busby**.

beaten zone—The area on the ground that is hit by the shots fired from a gun or gun battery at a certain combination of range (or elevation) and deflection (or direction) settings. It is the area on the surface of the earth that intercepts the CONE OF FIRE of a gun.

beat to quarters—*n.* A drum beat relaying an order to all hands on a naval vessel to go to their battle stations. *v.* To execute such a beat.

beaver—A movable section of armor attached to a helmet, or sometimes to a breastplate, to protect the lower part of the face and the throat. Its first known use was late in the 13th century. The word was later used for the visor.

beefeaters—A corps, originally serving as the personal bodyguard of the sovereign of England and now performing ceremonial functions as part of the royal household. The corps has been in existence since 1485.

beehive projectile—A direct-fire, defensive antipersonnel artillery round, it was an advance over earlier CANISTER-type ammunition. The beehive projectile of the U.S.

105mm howitzer is a canister filled with 8,500 steel FLÈCHETTES that is fired in a flat trajectory and detonated by a time fuze. At detonation the flèchettes fan out, producing a shotgunlike effect. The first combat use of the beehive round was by U.S. troops in late 1966 during the Vietnam War.

beleaguer—To surround an enemy fortress or other defensive position with troops. Synonymous with BESIEGE and INVEST.

belfry—A movable tower built of wood, used particularly in Roman and medieval times as a watchtower or in the attack and scaling of fortification walls.

belligerence—A state of war or hostilities.

belligerent status—A legal term according a degree of recognition short of diplomatic recognition to a nation or group engaged in hostilities.

belt—A band of a flexible material generally worn around the waist, sometimes over the shoulder, which in military use often serves to carry a sword or other weapon. An **ammunition belt** is a string of cartridges, either linked with metal or plastic or carried in the loops of a fabric belt, to be fed into a machine gun. Ammunition belts can be classified according to the way the cartridge is removed therefrom. The cartridge may be pushed directly from the belt into the chamber or may be withdrawn to the rear and then, by reverse movement, thrust into the chamber or stripped sideways from the link and then fed. An **armor belt** is a strip of armor that is added to the hull of a warship at the waterline. See also **Sam Browne belt**.

beneficiarii—In the Roman army, soldiers with privileges granted by their commanders, including exemption from certain labors, such as digging trenches and fetching wood and water.

berm—A ledge at the base of the exterior wall of a permanent or field fortification, between the vertical or sloping wall and the top of the moat or SCARP.

Berserker—A member of the bodyguard of any of several mythological or ancient Scandinavian heroes; also a type of legendary warrior who fought in a frenzy. The original Berserk was a mythological warrior who fought without armor and with great fury.

berth — In naval terminology 1) A place to sleep. 2) The docking place of a ship. 3) Any recognized personnel position.

besiege—1) To lay siege to. 2) To cut off all access to or egress from a town or fortress for the purpose of capturing it and forcing its defenders to surrender. See also **beleaguer** and **invest**.

bicorne—A hat with the brim turned up on two sides so that two points are formed on opposite sides. Such hats were worn by both army and naval officers, either sideways or fore and aft, in the 18th and 19th centuries and are still used as part of the formal dress uniform in some countries. See also **cocked hat**.

"Big Bertha"—A 420mm German howitzer of World War I. This type of gun battered the forts of Liège into submission in August 1914. The nickname was given the guns by the Germans, for Bertha Krupp von Bohlen und Halbach, a member of the famous German manufacturing family. The term has sometimes been applied, erroneously, to the German long-range guns that bombarded Paris in 1918.

big wing—A tactic proposed by British Squadron Leader Douglas Bader in 1940 to resist attacks by the German Luftwaffe on targets in the British Isles during the Battle of Britain. The proposal was to meet and overwhelm German attacks with from two to five squadrons of aircraft, instead of the single squadron or less that was then being sent to intercept and ascertain the objectives of the raiders in accordance with the doctrine of the Royal Air Force commander, Air Chief Marshal Sir Hugh Dowding. A long and serious controversy developed between supporters of the two tactics. Modern theorists agree that Dowding was right and Bader was wrong under the circumstances of the Battle of Britain.

bill or bill-hook—A HALBERD-like weapon with a long shaft and a head incorporating a single cutting edge, which, at the top, divided into a forward-curving hook and a spike; at the middle of the back of the head was another spike, projecting at a right angle. The bill was common in 16th-century armies, which used it for hacking, grabbing, and ripping in close combat. Soldiers armed with the bill were called **billmen**.

billet—*n.* 1) Housing for troops in military or nonmilitary buildings, most often used with respect to nonmilitary housing. 2) In naval parlance, an assignment or position. *v.* To assign troops to housing, particularly to nonmilitary lodgings.

binnacle—The stand or housing for a ship's compass, located on the bridge.

binnacle list—A list, generally circulated daily in naval commands, of those personnel excused from duty by a medical officer.

biological agent—A microorganism that causes disease in humans, animals, or plants, or causes the deterioration of matériel.

biological defense—The plans and procedures involved in employing defensive measures against attacks by biological agents.

biological warfare—The employment of microorganisms or toxic biological agents to cause disease or death in humans, animals, or plants.

bireme—A galley propelled by two banks of oars on each side. See also **galley**.

bitter end—1) The loose end of any rope. 2) The inboard end of a ship's anchor chain, which is secured to the chain locker.

bivouac—*n.* A temporary assembly or encampment of troops in the field, with temporary shelter or, more often, none. *v.* To so encamp.

Blackbird (SR-71)—A strategic reconnaissance aircraft developed as a successor to the U-2. Whereas the U-2 had been designed for high altitudes and had a relatively slow speed, the SR-71 can fly at 2,000 miles per hour at 85,000 feet and produces a relatively small radar signature. Cameras in an SR-71 can sweep more than 100,000 square miles of the earth each hour.

"black gang"—Navy slang for sailors whose duties were below decks—machinists, engineers, and the like—whereas sailors in the SEAMAN'S BRANCH served above decks.

blacklist—A list of confirmed or suspected enemy collaborators who represent a potential threat to friendly forces.

black powder—A mixture of potassium nitrate, carbon, and sulfur that burns rapidly and, if confined, explosively. It was the original GUNPOWDER, developed in China before it was in Europe. It produces a large amount of whitish smoke and was replaced as a propellant for military use in the late 19th and early 20th centuries by smokeless powder. Black powder is still used for primers, fuzes, and blank-fire charges.

black propaganda—See **propaganda**.

Black September Organization (BSO)—A clandestine group established by AL FATAH in 1971 to avenge the expulsion of its parent organization, the PALESTINE LIBERATION ORGANIZATION, from Jordan. Attempts by the BSO to assassinate Jordan's King Hussein were unsuccessful, but it carried out the attack on the Israeli team at the 1972 summer Olympics in which 11 Israeli hostages were killed.

blank ammunition—Ammunition containing powder but no projectile, used in firing salutes, in signaling, and in training.

blast effect—Destruction of or damage to structures and people caused by the rush of air from the center of an explosion or the point of impact of an explosive projectile.

blast wave—A sharply defined wave of increased pressure from a center of detonation or similar disturbance.

blimp—A lighter-than-air craft consisting of a heavy airbag, shaped like a stubby cigar, with a cabin and two or more motors attached below. The term was first applied to observation balloons in World War I. (Cartoonist David Low later created a cartoon character, a pompous former officer, whom he named Colonel Blimp.) Operating at low altitudes and slow speed, blimps were used by the U.S. Navy in World War II for antisubmarine patrol and convoy escort within short distances from shore and for various photographic and search-and-rescue operations.

blind—A cover to conceal a force in ambush or a covert operation.

blind bombing—A World War II aerial bombardment technique conducted against targets that could not be seen visually or by radar (because of bad weather or successful camouflage or other passive measures). The location of these targets was estimated or calculated by means of navigation.

blind bombing zone—An area established to permit bombing that is unrestricted by concern for friendly forces.

blindside—To attack unexpectedly.

blinker tube or **blinker light**—A light covered with shutters that are opened and closed to signal from one ship to another, using Morse or comparable code.

"Blitz"—German for "lightning." The term applied to the German air bombardment campaign against Britain in World War II, 1940–41, after the German failure in the Battle of Britain. Large numbers of German bombers flew over British cities night after night, causing great destruction, killing 43,000 civilians, and seriously wounding 51,000.

blitzkrieg—In German, "lightning war." Blitzkrieg tactics were developed in the 1930s by the Germans as a result of their experiences in World War I and were first practiced by them in the attack on Poland in 1939. Gen. Heinz Guderian was a major proponent of such tactics. Primarily conceived as the adaptation of armored firepower, mobility, and protection, supported by ground-attack aircraft, to the German tactics developed in World War I, blitzkrieg was characterized by speed, surprise, maneuver, and overwhelming firepower.

blockade—*v.* To isolate a city, region, or country by cutting off communications to or from a city, a harbor, or the entire coastline and frontiers of a nation by the posting of military forces to intercept all traffic. *n.* Such cutting of communications. The most common blockades are naval, imposed by warships, like the blockade imposed by the Union navy on Southern ports during the American Civil War, or the total blockade of German ports in World Wars I and II, but there are also air and ground blockades.

blockade runner—A person, vehicle, or ship that crosses or circumvents a blockade. Maritime blockade runners in the American Civil War, operating mostly at night in coastal waters, took war materials from Europe, usually via the West Indies, into Confederate ports, most notably Wilmington, N.C.

blockbuster—Any bomb considered powerful enough to destroy a city block.

blockhouse—A defensive structure of heavy timbers, concrete, or other substantial material with small openings or loopholes for observation and for the firing of weapons. In North America in the colonial period, blockhouses were often two-story log structures, with the second story overhanging the first on all sides. Blockhouses of reinforced concrete, often partially covered by earth, usually form part of modern fortified defensive systems.

blocking position—A defended position situated so as to thwart enemy penetration between positions or areas, or to cover enemy lines of advance that could otherwise bypass forward defended positions.

blockship—A stationary ship, often sunk, so placed as to deny or limit passage to a harbor or other shore objective.

blowback—1) The escape to the rear of gases under pressure formed during the firing of a gun. 2) A type of weapon operation in which the force of expanding gases acting against the face of the bolt furnishes all the energy required to push it back and to initiate the complete firing cycle of the gun.

bluejacket—A naval enlisted man, so called for the navy blue uniform jumper, coat, shirt, or jacket.

blue water—The open sea.

blunderbuss—A short, wide-bore musket, often flaring at the muzzle. Commonly used in the 17th century, the gun seems to have been known in Holland as early as 1353, for Dutch documents of that period mention a **donrebusse**. Several balls or other small projectiles could be fired simultaneously. Blunderbusses of various calibers, as large as light artillery, were used in both armies and navies of the period. It was the weapon of Miles Standish, among many others.

Smithsonion Institution

blunderbuss

board—*v.* To enter a vehicle, particularly a naval vessel. Commanders of sailing or rowed warships in a battle attempted to get close enough to an enemy vessel to put a **boarding party** of soldiers, sailors, or marines on it. Armed with **boarding pikes, axes,** or **pistols,** the men would attack, attempting to destroy the masts and rigging of the enemy ship. In modern times a boarding party may be sent to examine the papers or cargo of a ship that has been stopped for such inspection. *n.* A group of people, usually officers, under a chairman or president, which has a temporary or permanent mission or function to perform, for instance, a board of investigation.

boarders—Sailors in a boarding party.

boarding ax—See **ax** and **board.**

boarding party—See **board.**

boarding pike—See **board.**

Board of Admiralty—See **admiralty.**

boar's head—A square tactical formation established by Marshal Thomas R. Bugeaud in the French conquest of Algeria, c. 1840.

boat—A small craft, propelled by oars, sail, or motor, small enough to be carried on a ship. Of the larger vessels, the term is applied only to submarines.

"boat people"—Political refugees who escape by sea. The term is most often applied to Vietnamese who escaped by water in the mid-1970s after the Communist takeover.

boatspace—The space and weight factor used by planners to determine the capacity of boats, landing craft, and amphibious vehicles to carry personnel, supplies, and equipment required for an amphibious operation. With respect to landing craft and amphibious vehicles, it is based on the requirements of one person with equipment together assumed to weigh 224 pounds and to occupy 13.5 cubic feet of space.

boatswain (bo's'n)—In the U.S. Navy and the British Royal Navy, a warrant officer in charge of the instruction and performance of the deck crew of the ship in matters related to practical seamanship. The boatswain is also responsible for care of the rigging and gear; the boatswain's insignia is crossed anchors. The origins of the rating antedate the establishment of the Royal Navy.

boatswain's call or **boatswain's pipe**— A small silver whistle carried by a boatswain as a badge of office and used to sound commands to the deck crew. The pipe was known as early as the Crusades in 1248 and was considered a badge of rank by the English in the 15th century, when it was worn by the Lord High Admiral.

boatswain's mate—Naval enlisted ratings (first and second class) concerned with seamanship and related duties. A boatswain's mate third class is called a coxswain in the U.S. Navy.

boattail—A ballistic body whose cross section decreases in diameter toward the tail to reduce aerodynamic drag.

bodkin—1) A small dagger or stiletto. 2) A light arrow with a stiff, straight point, used particularly in the 16th century.

body—A number of troops or units physically assembled together, as a body of troops. The **main body** is the principal portion of a force.

body bag—A zippered, rubberized bag used to carry a dead body from a war zone.

body count—The number of enemy dead counted in the battle area after conclusion of combat. A term widely used in the Vietnam War.

Bofors gun—A 40mm light antiaircraft gun developed by the Swedish firm Bofors in the early 1930s. The Bofors gun, which could fire 80 to 120 rounds per minute over a slant range of 4 miles, was built under license or copied by nearly all the major belligerents of World War II. It was adopted as the standard light antiaircraft gun by the United States, Britain, and Russia, and copied by Japan and (in 37mm) Germany.

bogey—An air contact that is unidentified but assumed to be enemy. Not to be confused with "unknown."

boilermaker—U.S. Navy enlisted specialty rating, chief and first, second, and third class.

bolas—A South American weapon consisting of two stone balls connected by a strong cord or thongs. It was swung around the head and then thrown so as to entangle the legs of enemy soldiers or livestock.

bolo or **bolo knife**—A broad, single-edged knife similar to the MACHETE, used in the Philippines as a weapon.

bolt—1) The missile shot by a CROSSBOW or CATAPULT generally having the form of short, stout, blunt-headed arrow. 2) A device on a breech-loading rifle used to prevent the escape of gas from the breech, to eject a spent cartridge from the rifle, and to insert a fresh cartridge from the magazine into the barrel preparatory to firing the next round.

bolter—A carrier-based aircraft that, in an attempted landing, fails to engage the arresting cable and is obliged to attempt another landing.

bomb—*n.* Originally an explosive shell fired from a cannon but currently a device placed or thrown by hand or dropped from an airplane or a vessel. The shape, the explosive agent, and the purpose of a bomb vary. A **depth bomb** is an antisubmarine weapon exploded under water. A **fragmentation bomb** is designed to explode in the air and scatter sharp pieces of metal over a broad area. An **incendiary bomb** contains chemicals that will start raging fires. A **high-explosive (HE) bomb** is designed to cause damage by the blast and the effect of metal fragments scattered by the explosion. A **time bomb** contains a device that delays explosion until some time after setting. A **propaganda bomb** explodes in the air and scatters propaganda material. *v.* To attempt to destroy a target with a bomb, especially by dropping a bomb from an aircraft.

bombard—*n.* An early form of cannon, with a short, wide barrel. Bombards varied in size from a weapon that could be hand-carried to Henry VIII's massive bronze bombards in the Tower of London, each of which required 24 horses to be moved. *v.* To fire large numbers of missiles, particularly artillery shells or aerial bombs, at a fixed target.

bombardier—1) A person responsible for the delivery of bombs to a target. 2) In American usage, the member of the crew of an aircraft who operates the bombsight and releases the bombs. 3) In British usage, a noncommissioned artillery officer.

bombardment—The act of bombarding.

bomb bay—The compartment in the fuselage of a bomber where the bombs are carried for release through the bomb bay doors.

bomber—An aircraft whose primary mission is the delivery of bombs to a target from the air. Bombers are classified by range or by function. Types of bombers classified by range include the following: **medium range**—Bombers that have a maximum combat radius between 925 and 1,850 kilometers when flying at best speed and altitude and when taking off at maximum gross weight. **intermediate range**—Aircraft that have a maximum combat radius of between 1,850 and 4,600 km when flying at best speed and altitude and when taking off at maximum gross weight. **long range**—Bomber aircraft that have a maximum combat radius of at least 4,600 km when flying at best speed and altitude and when taking off at maximum gross weight. **very long range**—Bomber aircraft designed to have a maximum tactical operating radius of up to 8,050 kilometers when flying at best speed and altitude and when taking off at maximum gross weight. Types of bombers classified by function include the following: **dive bomber**—Aircraft designed to drop steeply from a high altitude, aiming bombs by diving toward the target; bombs are released at low altitude, just before the plane pulls out of the dive. **fighter bomber**—See **fighter aircraft**. **torpedo bomber**—Aircraft, particularly naval aircraft, that fly low enough to release torpedoes at enemy warships.

bombfall—1) The fall of one or more bombs, either simultaneously or successively. 2) The bombs while falling. 3) The points of impact of bombs. 4) The pattern or configuration formed by both the fall of bombs through the air and their impact and explosion.

bomb impact plot—A graphic representation of the target area on which prominent dots are plotted to mark the impact points of bombs dropped.

bombing—The dropping or delivery of bombs, particularly from an aircraft on a target. See also **blind bombing, carpet bombing, dive bombing, horizontal bombing, pattern bombing, precision bombing,** and **skip bombing**.

bombing area—See **area**.

bomb ketch—A small craft used in the early- to mid-19th century. Armed with mortars, it lobbed shells into enemy fortifications. Usually ketch-rigged.

bomb line—An imaginary line following, if possible, well-defined geographical features, prescribed by the ground troop commander and coordinated with the air force commander. Forward of the bomb line, air forces are free to attack targets without reference to the ground forces; behind this line, all attacks must be coordinated with the appropriate troop commander.

bombproof—*adj.* Designed to resist and if possible to survive the explosive force of bombs. *n.* A shelter secure against bombing; DUGOUT shelters in the American Civil War were called "bombproofs."

bomb release point—The point in space at which bombs must be released to reach the desired point of detonation.

bomb run—The flight course of a bombing airplane, from an initial point where the bomb run officially begins to the bomb release point. More generally, the flight course just before the release of bombs; the action of flying this course.

"Bombs away"—1) A phrase used by the bombardier to indicate to the pilot and other members of an airplane crew that the bombs have just been released. 2) The instant when the bombs are released.

bombshell—Archaic expression for SHELL.

bomb ship—See **battery ship**.

bombsight—A device that determines or enables a bombardier to determine the point in space at which a bomb must be released from an aircraft in order to hit a target. U.S. bombers in World War II were equipped with the highly secret NORDEN BOMBSIGHT, the most accurate one then available. Using preset data and manual operation by the bombardier, the Norden bombsight computes the correct dropping angle and, in connection with an automatic pilot or pilot direction indicator, determines the proper course of the aircraft required to maintain the necessary line of sight to the target.

bonnet rouge—A revolutionist. The name derives from the red caps worn in the French Revolution.

booby trap—*n.* An explosive device, especially an apparently ordinary, harmless object, so concealed that it will be triggered by an unsuspecting victim. *v.* To place a device, especially an explosive device, in or near an apparently harmless object or place.

boom—A floating structure, frequently made of logs, sometimes having a metallic net suspended from the floats, which reduces or closes access to a harbor, river, or berth to provide protection for vessels within, particularly protection from submarines.

boondockers—Ankle-high boots.

booster—A high-explosive element of a shell or other explosive device that is activated by a fuze or primer and in turn activates the more powerful main explosive.

boost phase—The portion of the flight of a ballistic missile or space vehicle during which the booster and sustainer engines operate.

boot camp—Where military recruits (usually naval or marine) receive their initial training.

bootlicker—A person who devotes most of his or her energies to cultivating the good opinion of superiors.

boots—1) Heavy footwear, usually of leather, that cover all or most of the lower leg, and in some types the thigh as well. Various types have been worn through the ages. 2) Gaiters, originally khaki but bleached white by frequent washing, worn by naval recruits in BOOT CAMP, by naval personnel on shore patrol or other official duty ashore, and in ceremonial functions, such as parades. 3) Naval recruits.

booty—Material items of value seized or captured from an enemy or in enemy territory either legally (as in prizes captured on sea or on land) or illegally (as loot or plunder).

BOQ—Bachelor officers' quarters.

bore—1) The cylindrical inner chamber of a gun, in modern weapons extending from the breechblock to the muzzle. 2) The inner diameter of a gun barrel; the CALIBER.

boresight—*v.* To check the alignment of the tube of a gun with its sight or aiming device.

boss—A projection from the surface of a shield, generally round and decorative. The boss in the center of some shields provides extra protection for the hand grip inside.

"Bouncing Betty"—A German antipersonnel mine of World War II vintage, so called because when activated it jumped as high as 7 feet into the air before exploding. It was filled with high explosive and about 300 steel or lead balls that, together with fragments of the steel casing, were hurled in all directions by the force of the explosion.

bound—The distance covered in one movement by a unit that is moving from cover to cover.

boundary—The line separating areas of responsibility. In modern armies, boundaries are usually indicated on a map, and they divide the territory that is to be occupied, or for which responsibility is assigned, among units and formations for purposes of command and control. Boundaries frequently follow natural features such as streams or ridges. They normally change as forces advance or withdraw.

bounds, fire by—Sequential changes of artillery firing data to move the center of impact of the rounds from one point to another. Fire by bounds usually is done by changing range, but it can also be done by changing direction of deflection.

bounds, movement by—Advancement in a series of moves, usually from cover to cover, often made by troops under artillery or small arms fire. Also called LEAPFROG.

bounty, enlistment—A bonus paid for signing up for military service.

bounty jumper—A soldier who enlists to receive a bounty, then deserts and enlists elsewhere to get another bounty. The practice was prevalent among soldiers of the Continental Army and state militias in the American Revolution.

bouquet mine—In naval warfare, a device in which a number of buoyant mine cases are attached to the same sinker, so that if the mooring of one mine is cut, another mine rises from the sinker to its set depth.

bow—A weapon consisting of a narrow, curved piece of wood or other material, with a cord stretched between its two ends, by which an arrow is propelled. The bow was a basic

weapon of most armies from earliest times until after the introduction of gunpowder. Bows have been made in many sizes and shapes, and apparently were invented independently in many widely separated cultures. The simplest bow, the **self-bow**, is made of a single stave of wood or other flexible material, including horn, sinew, metal, and, in modern times, plastic, usually thickest in the center and tapering to the two ends. A bow made of two or more strips of the same material bonded together is called a **built bow**. **Composite bows**, made of a combination of materials, were used as early as the 3rd millenium B.C. The earliest ones combined wood, horn, and sometimes sinew, and were particularly popular in the Near East and Asia. Most Asian bows were **reflex bows**; that is, they were naturally curved in shape, but when strung were bent in the opposite direction. The deadly **Mongol bow**, principal weapon of the cavalry armies of Genghis Khan and his successors, was comparable in length and power to the English LONGBOW but, unlike the longbow, was composite and reflex in nature. See also **crossbow**.

Bowie knife—A knife, usually about 15 inches long, with a long single-edged blade, a hilt, and, originally, a handle made of horn. The first Bowie knife is said to have been made in Arkansas in 1825, after a design by the frontiersman James Bowie. The knife was very popular among pioneers, who used it for a variety of purposes, including hunting and hand-to-hand combat. It was adopted as a weapon by the Texas Rangers and, subsequently, by many Confederate troops in the American Civil War. A knife like the Bowie knife was used by British commandos and U.S. Rangers during World War II.

bowman—See **archer**.

bowyer—1) An ARCHER. 2) One who makes bows.

box — Term sometimes applied to a self-contained, all-around defensive position of field fortifications, with strongpoints linked by trenches.

box, ammunition—A box to hold ammunition, particularly one from which linked ammunition can be fed into a machine gun.

box barrage—See **barrage**.

box, cartridge—1) A small pouch, usually made of stiff leather, worn by soldiers on cross belts over their shoulders or attached to their waist belt, in which musket cartridges were carried. 2) In the 19th century a webbed pouch, holding two or more clips of rifle ammunition, usually attached to a webbed waist belt.

box magazine—See **magazine**.

bracket—Successive rounds (or volleys or salvos) of artillery fire aimed so that one falls beyond the target and the next falls short. When a target is thus bracketed, its range can be established and the observer can quickly bring fire for effect directly on the target. The term can be applied to DEFLECTION as well as to RANGE. See also **straddle**.

bracketing—The process of seeking to bracket a target; this is the basis of normal field artillery fire adjustment.

Bradley fighting vehicle (M-2/M-3)— An armored troop carrier, first deployed in 1981, that has become a mainstay of U.S. ground forces. The Bradley brings infantry to the battlefield, provides cover to dismounted troops, and suppresses enemy armor. The M-2 carries a three-person crew and six fully equipped infantrymen. The M-3 is designed for scout missions.

branch—An element of a military service having a specialized function. It can include the combat arms or services (e.g., artillery, infantry, submarines) and the support elements (quartermaster corps, signal corps).

"brass"—A slang term for senior officers.

brassard—1) A strip of cloth worn around the upper arm to indicate affiliation with a particular organization or performance of some specialized function, or otherwise to distinguish the wearer. For example, brassards are worn by personnel who are temporarily or permanently performing the function of MILITARY POLICE or SHORE PATROL. 2) Plate armor that protects the upper arm.

Bravo—Letter of NATO phonetic alphabet. See also **alphabet, phonetic**.

breach—*n*. A gap or rift in a structure such as a fortification wall, an obstacle like a minefield, or an enemy line. *v*. To create such a gap.

"Break away"—The radio call between an aerial tanker and a recipient indicating that immediate separation between the tanker and recipient is required.

break off—To terminate a combat activity unilaterally.

breakout—An operation whereby a force that is surrounded or besieged escapes and regains freedom of action by disrupting the lines of encirclement.

"break ranks"—1) To fall out of formation. 2) To disagree with one's superiors.

breakthrough—An attack in which the attacking force successfully disrupts the lines of the hostile defender and obtains freedom of maneuver in the defender's rear area.

break-up—1) In radar imagery, the separation of one solid return into a number of individual returns that correspond to the various objects or structure groupings. 2) In imagery interpretation, the result of magnification that causes the imaged object to lose its identity and become a random series of impressions.

breastplate—A piece of plate armor that covers the breast.

breastwork—A protective wall, usually one that is hastily constructed of earth or other available materials, roughly high enough to reach the breast area of the typical soldier.

breech—The rear part of a gun, specifically, the opening at the rear where the projectile and charge are inserted.

breechblock—The part of a gun, especially a cannon, that closes the breech. The breechblock usually contains the firing pin; in many types of guns it is also used to set the round firmly in the chamber.

breech-loader—Any firearm in which the ammunition is loaded at the breech. Breechloading weapons had been used before the 18th century but were generally unsatisfactory because imprecisely fitted metal parts left seams in the breech through which gas and flames could leak. The technology of the 19th century remedied this deficiency. By permitting the user to load and reload at a more rapid rate and to lie prone while doing so, the breech-loading rifle of the mid-19th century made the muzzle-loader obsolete. Mass adoption of breech-loading guns came first in the Prussian army in 1848, although the so-called NEEDLE GUN was not unveiled until the Danish War of 1864. Breech-loading cannon, which could fire more rapidly than muzzle-loaders, soon followed.

Bren gun—A light machine gun used as a standard weapon by the British army and others in World War II. Developed in Brno, Czechoslovakia, the gun was manufactured in Enfield, England, and its name was taken from the cities Brno and Enfield. It was a gas-operated, air-cooled, .303-caliber weapon that could fire 120 rounds per minute, effective up to 1,000 yards. It could be fired from the shoulder and a bipod or from a tripod, but was usually mounted on a light vehicle, called a Bren gun carrier, the term often being applied to the gun and carrier together.

brevet — A semihonorary, semitemporary rank, originally in the British service, usually awarded for meritorious conduct. Brevet rank was applicable in some circumstances but not in others, creating confusion in terms of precedence and authority. The practice was adopted in the U.S. Army in the 19th century. The last American officer to hold brevet rank was Gen. Tasker Bliss, who was promoted by President Wilson to four-star general by brevet when he was appointed to the Supreme Allied War Council in 1918.

bricole—1) A type of catapult. 2) A piece of armor protecting the breast of a horse.

bridge—1) A means of crossing a stream, in military context often a temporary bridge. Bridges may be constructed of various materials, depending on what is available and how urgently a bridge needs to be constructed. Temporary **floating bridges** may be put together from a variety of materials and objects—including small boats (Xenophon described the crossing of the Tigris River by the Ten Thousand on a bridge of boats in 401 B.C.), logs, rafts, or gasoline barrels—placed side by side and lashed together, and generally covered with planks or other solid material on which a force can move. See also **Bailey bridge, drawbridge**, and **ponton bridge**. 2) The area of a ship, usually forward and high, from which the vessel and its operations and the operations of other vessels in a naval command are controlled.

bridgehead—A piece of ground on the enemy side of a river or DEFILE that is seized and held by advance troops of an attacking force as a base for further operations.

briefing—1) The act of providing instructions or information about a task or a mission to the person who is to perform it or who has an interest in it. 2) A report, usually oral, on a subject about which the recipient wishes to be informed.

brig—1) The prison on a naval vessel or station. 2) A sailing vessel with two masts, both square-rigged, carrying a quadrilateral gaff sail aft of the mizzenmast and at least two headsails. It is to be distinguished from a **brigantine**, which carries fore and aft sails rather than square ones on the mainmast. Brigs were used as naval vessels (usually sloops of war) and as commercial ships.

brigade—A military unit smaller than a DIVISION, in use since the 18th century, whose composition has varied from time to time and army to army. In World War I, the infantry brigades of most armies were composed of two infantry regiments of three BATTALIONs each. Two brigades, each commanded by a brigadier general, constituted a division. A British division consisted of three brigades of four battalions each. In World War II, a British brigade consisted of three battalions, and was roughly the equivalent of an American regiment. The U.S. Army changed its divisional organization in the late 1930s to three infantry regiments, and eliminated the infantry brigade as a combat formation. In World War II, there were no more than three or four two-regiment brigades in the U.S. Army. Under the combat-arms regimental system, which the U.S. Army adopted in 1961, a new structure was called for: three battalions made up a brigade, and three brigades, in various configurations of armored and mechanized battalions, constituted a division. The entire body of midshipmen at the U.S. Naval Academy is called the Brigade of Midshipmen. At the U.S. Military Academy the Corps of Cadets consists of two brigades.

Brigade 2056 — The Cuban exile unit trained by the CIA for the ill-fated Bay of Pigs invasion in April 1961. The brigade was trained mainly in Guatemala by CIA and paramilitary officers.

brigade combat team—See **combat team, regimental**.

brigade major—A military position in the British army corresponding to brigade or regimental adjutant in the U.S. Army; the principal administrative officer of a British brigade, usually a major in rank.

brigadier—An officer rank between colonel and general. In the British army it is a temporary appointment of an officer who is permanently a colonel. In most armies of other nations that follow British organization it is a rank comparable to brigadier general.

brigadier general—The most junior general officer in the U.S. Army, Air Force, and Marine Corps. The insignia of rank is a single star. See also **general**.

brigandine—A type of armored jacket of the 15th century made of fabric with metal scales riveted to the inside in overlapping rows. In many instances, the heads of the rivets were gilded and thus showed through on the outside of the garment.

brigands—French medieval infantry armed with spears and shields.

brigantine—See **brig**.

"brilliant" munitions—A generic term applied to a proposed new generation of ordnance. Whereas "smart" munitions can be guided directly to their target, the technology of the next generation may allow munitions to make postlaunch decisions as to which may be the target of highest priority.

briquet—A short, curved, cutting sword carried by infantry soldiers in the 18th and 19th centuries. Inscribed briquets, called *briquets d'honneur*, were presented for valor in Napoleonic France.

broach—The act of a submarine rising out of the water and coming to the surface.

broadax—See **ax**.

broadcast controlled interception — See **intercept**.

broadside—1) All the guns on one side of a warship or, in vessels with turrets, all the guns that can be fired on one side. 2) The firing of all the guns at the same time.

broadside gun—1) On a modern naval vessel, any gun of less than 8 inches in caliber (excluding antiaircraft guns and guns for saluting purposes only). 2) On pre–20th-century warships, one of the guns placed for firing on either side of the vessel.

broadsword—Any of various cutting swords with wide blades, particularly those that had a large basket guard.

broken-back war—In nuclear weapons theory, hostilities continuing after an unrestricted nuclear exchange between major powers. Originally, British slang for a conventional phase of global war following the exhaustion of stocks of nuclear weapons.

Bronco (OV-10) — A light, twin-turboprop observation aircraft, sometimes equipped with machine guns and light ordnance for ground support missions.

bronze armor—See **armor**.

"Brown Bess"—British version of the 18th-century FLINTLOCK musket with an offset ring bayonet. The origin of the name is unclear. It seems to have come from a combination of the color of the wooden stock and a corruption of the "buss" in "blunderbuss."

Browning automatic rifle—See **BAR**.

buck and ball—A combat musket load consisting of a musket ball and three or more buckshot commonly used by American troops in the Revolutionary War.

buckler — *n*. 1) A small, round shield that could be carried in the hand or worn on the arm, allowing the hand freedom. 2) A person or thing that defends or protects. *v*. To defend.

BuDocks—Bureau of Yards and Docks. The division of the U.S. Department of the Navy responsible for the administrative and executive aspects of the physical plants of naval shore activities and certain service craft.

buffalo soldiers—A term describing black U.S. soldiers on the western plains after the Civil War. The term is believed to be of Indian origin.

buff coat—A coat made of cowhide or other heavy leather that resisted penetration or cutting by a sword. It was worn in the 17th century, particularly by cavalrymen.

buffer distance—In nuclear warfare, 1) The horizontal distance that, when added to the radius of safety, will assure that a specified degree of risk will not be exceeded. 2) The vertical distance that is added to the fallout-safe height of burst to assure that fallout will not endanger friendly aircraft.

bug—A concealed microphone or listening device.

bugle—A brass wind instrument without keys or valves, blown by a bugler in both armies and navies to transmit orders or announcements in the form of BUGLE CALLS. Calls, composed of different combinations of notes, signal time to get up (reveille) and times to perform the routine duties of a military force. In the modern U.S. services, bugle calls are generally broadcast from recordings.

buildup—*n.* The process of increasing the strength of military units and their supplies and equipment. *v.* (**build up**) To increase the strength of units and their supplies and equipment.

built bow—See **bow**.

built-up area—An urban or semiurban region.

built-up gun—A gun constructed by shrinking an envelope of iron or steel over an iron or steel barrel. Probably invented by a French naval officer, M. Thiery, the built-up technique produced a strong compressive tension on the barrel, so that the expansive force and heat of the exploding powder charge encountered the resistance of this compression from the first instance of the explosion.

bullet—The projectile, spherical or cylindrical with a pointed end, fired from a small arm. The term is often used for the complete round of ammunition—bullet, cartridge case, powder, and primer.

bullet, explosive—A small-arms projectile containing a small charge of explosive that detonates on contact with its target. See also **dum-dum bullet**.

bulwark—A strong, defensive wall.

BuMed—Bureau of Medicine and Surgery. The division of the U.S. Department of the Navy responsible for the health and medical care of all naval and marine corps personnel.

bunker—A small defensive structure covering a gun emplacement or serving another purpose. It may be a permanent structure of steel and concrete with openings through which guns can be fired, sometimes sunk entirely or partially in the ground, and may be one of a series, like those of the SIEGFRIED LINE in World War II. Or it may be a dugout roofed with logs and covered with dirt and various forms of concealment.

"bunker buster"—See **EGBU-27**.

BuPers—Bureau of Naval Personnel. The division of the U.S. Department of the Navy responsible for the administration of all naval personnel. It was formerly known as the Bureau of Navigation.

burgonet—A helmet worn from the 16th into the 19th century, having a visor similar to that on a baseball cap and a covering for the nape of the neck. Most burgonets had a comb and ear pieces. They were used particularly for protection of SAPPERs in a siege operation.

burgs (Frankish forts)—Fortified posts or towns originating in the Frankish system and under Charlemagne, built along the frontier of newly captured territory. Burgs were connected to each other and to what had been the old frontier by roads. Stocked with supplies, these forts became bases for the maneuver of the disciplined Frankish cavalry, to maintain order in the conquered territory or to serve as a base in further operations.

burn (intelligence)—To expose a clandestine operative or group as unreliable.

burst—The explosion of a shell or a bomb, marked by smoke and dust at the point of impact or explosion. The **area of burst** is the area, usually measured in square yards or meters, directly affected by the shell's explosion. A **burst interval** is the distance between the bursts.

BuSandA—Bureau of Supplies and Accounts. That division of the U.S. Department of the Navy responsible for all aspects of procurement of supplies other than ammunition and payments. The Chief of BuSandA is Paymaster General of the Navy.

busby—A tall fur hat worn with the dress uniform by certain units of the British and other armies, principally hussars, artillery-men, and engineers.

BuShips—Bureau of Ships. The division of the U.S. Department of the Navy responsible for all aspects of procuring and maintaining naval vessels and for purchasing ships and smaller craft for the U.S. Army and Air Force.

bushwhacker—1) Specifically, one of a group of Confederate guerrillas in the American Civil War. 2) A GUERRILLA.

butt—1) The end of a hand-held weapon such as a spear, lance, or rifle, opposite the point or muzzle. 2) A mound of earth or other material behind practice targets, to catch projectiles that miss the target. 3) In archery, it is the mound on which the targets are set.

butterfly bomb—A small fragmentation or antipersonnel bomb equipped with two fold-ing wings that rotate and arm the fuze as the bomb descends. It was developed in Germany and adopted by the United States.

butternut—A slang term that referred to Confederate soldiers in the American Civil War because of their homespun brown clothes.

BuWeps—Bureau of Weapons. The division of the U.S. Department of the Navy responsible for administrative and executive aspects of the aeronautic equipment and naval weapons and ammunition. In 1959 BuWeps superseded and combined the functions of the Bureaus of Aeronautics and of Ordnance.

"buy it"—Slang for "to die in combat."

"buzz bomb"—See **V-1**.

byrnie—A coat of mail; HAUBERK. Apparently sometimes used for a type of breastplate.

C-4—See **command, control, communications, and computer systems**.

C-5A—See **Galaxy**.

C-130—See **Hercules**.

C-141—See **Starlifter**.

cabasset—A type of helmet, dating from the 16th century, having a narrow brim and a pointed, keeled crown, and chin straps that were sometimes covered by plates to protect the ears. It was commonly worn by infantry and ceremonial guards.

cab rank — A formation of fighter and fighter-bomber aircraft, usually in line ahead, awaiting call for CLOSE AIR SUPPORT missions, while patrolling in the vicinity of the anticipated area of action. Cab rank was organized by the Royal Air Force's Desert Air Force in the Mediterranean campaigns of World War II.

cache—A prepositioned source of supplies for evasion and recovery operations.

cadence—A rhythmic beat. In military units, a regular measured timing for simultaneous activity, such as marching in step.

cadet—A student in military training to become an officer.

cadre—A disciplined group of trained officers and enlisted personnel whose capabilities include the principal military specialties that will be required in a military unit or formation and thus provide a nucleus for the establishment of such a unit or formation.

caisson—1) A horse-drawn, usually two-wheeled, vehicle used to carry artillery ammunition. Caissons are still used by the U.S. armed forces to carry coffins in military funerals. 2) A large box designed to contain ammunition.

caliber—1) The diameter of a projectile, usually a bullet or a shell, or of the bore of a gun barrel. Caliber is usually expressed either in millimeters or, for some small arms in the United States, in hundreds or thousandths of an inch. Thus, the diameter of the bore of a .50-caliber machine gun is 0.5 inch, that of a .357-caliber Magnum a bit over 0.33 inch. Nations on the metric system almost always express caliber in millimeters. 2) A measure for the length of a cannon bore expressed in multiples of the diameter of the bore. For example, a 5-inch, 38-caliber naval gun has a bore length of 190 inches.

calibrated airspeed—See **airspeed**.

caliver—Another name for an ARQUEBUS. The term is an English corruption of the word CALIBER. Calivers were arquebuses of a standardized caliber. In the mid-16th century the English and the French began to standardize the caliber and lock mechanisms of their arquebuses in order to simplify ammunition supply and training procedures.

call for fire—A request from ground units for support from artillery or aircraft. The call includes the data necessary to identify the target.

call mission—A type of air support mission that has insufficient time to permit detailed planning and briefing of pilots before takeoff.

call sign—Any combination of characters or pronounceable words that identifies a communications facility, a command, an authority, an activity, or a unit; used primarily for establishing and maintaining communications.

caltrop—A small device, dating at least from Roman times, that, when thrown on the ground, presented one or more protruding points to slow the advance of troops or horses. The Roman caltrop was a wooden ball with a number of spikes protruding from it. The medieval caltrop was made by twisting and hammering two strips of iron. Leonardo da Vinci designed machines to throw caltrops. Settlers in Virginia used them against the Indians. Sometimes called "crow's foot" or "crowfoot."

camisade—An unanticipated night attack. The name, dating from at least the 16th century, seems to derive from the Spanish *camisado*, meaning "wearing a shirt," inasmuch as night attackers often wore white shirts over their armor for identification.

camouflage—*v.* To disguise troops, matériel, equipment, or installations by covering them or changing their appearance so as to conceal from the enemy their existence, form, location, or movements. *n.* 1) The art of disguising military objects. 2) Any device that disguises or contributes to a disguise.

camouflet—1) A land mine placed in or near an enemy's mining tunnel so that its explosion causes the tunnel to collapse. 2) The underground cavity resulting from a deep underground explosion.

C. 18th–19th centuries.

cannon

camp—1) A group of tents, huts, or other shelters for temporarily housing troops. A camp is more permanent than a BIVOUAC, and the term is sometimes applied to any military post. 2) Military service, particularly used in World War I and for periods of active duty training.

campaign—A phase or a stage of a war involving a series of related operations aimed at achieving a single specific strategic result or objective. A campaign may consist of a single battle but more often comprises a number of battles conducted over a protracted period of time or considerable distance but within a single specific theater or delimited area. A campaign is usually identified with respect to a region (as the Peninsular Campaign of the American Civil War) or a period of time (as the Campaign of 1806).

campaign medals—Medals awarded for participation in, or service during, a battle, a campaign, or an entire war. Sometimes called SERVICE MEDALS.

camp follower — Any nonmilitary person who follows an army as it moves from place to place. Camp followers have traditionally included merchants, families of soldiers and officers, laundresses, and prostitutes.

canalize—To force a hostile attacker to limit his advance or attack to a narrow sector; achieved by the use of terrain, obstacles, defensive deployments, or some combination of these.

canister—A cylindrical metal container packed with small projectiles (**canister shot** or **case shot**). When fired from a gun, the container bursts, scattering the shot. Canister was used by artillery from the early 15th century to the middle of the 19th century. A modern version of canister is the BEEHIVE PROJECTILE.

cannibalize—1) To remove parts from one piece of equipment for use in repair of another. 2) To take personnel from one unit in order to build up another.

cannon—1) A large gunpowder weapon, too heavy and bulky to be transported by hand, and usually having a caliber of 20mm or more. The term has traditionally been used to distinguish all larger and heavier weapons, usually artillery pieces, from small arms. In modern terminology, there are three types of cannon: GUN, HOWITZER, and MORTAR. In general parlance the term is used interchangeably with "gun" or "artillery piece." Most modern cannon are rifled, but some high-velocity tank cannon are smoothbore. Cannon can be automatic (as in aircraft cannon and in some tank, naval, and air defense cannon). The name is derived from the Latin *canna*, meaning "reed" or "tube." 2) A special type of 16th-century artillery piece, 15 to 28 calibers long and weighing from 1 to 6 tons. Subcategories included quartocannon, demicannon, bastard cannon, cannon serpentine, cannon, cannon royal (the largest of 16th-century cannon, also known as "double cannon" in England), and BASILISK.

cannonade—*n.* Bombardment using cannon only. *v.* To bombard with cannon.

cannoneer—1) One who fires a cannon or is a member of a cannon crew. 2) An artilleryman or gunner.

cannon lock—The part of a cannon that mechanically causes the propelling charge to be detonated.

canteen—1) A bottle or flask in which soldiers carry drinking water. 2) A recreational area for soldiers or sailors, including such services as a clubroom, a recreation hall, and a place to buy refreshments. 3) A POST EXCHANGE. 4) A British club for soldiers. 5) In the 18th and 19th centuries, a chest in which British officers stored food and liquor.

canton—To billet troops.

cantonment—1) A group of temporary structures used for housing troops. 2) The act of assigning troops to such structures. 3) A military post or camp.

cap—See **percussion cap**.

CAP—See **combat air patrol**.

capability—In general terms, the potential of an armed force to achieve certain objectives. A military strategy based on enemy capabilities usually assumes that the enemy will employ his military assets efficiently and postulates the maintenance of sufficient force to counter all contingencies.

capital ship—The largest class of ship in a navy of first rank. In each period of history since the development of multimasted ships, the biggest ships with the most guns have been designated capital ships. From the mid-17th to mid-19th century, a capital ship was called a SHIP OF THE LINE. From the mid-19th century on, ships mounting a battery of a caliber greater than 8 inches were considered capital ships. Since World War II, aircraft carriers have also been designated capital ships.

capitulate—To surrender on terms agreed between the combatants.

capitulation—1) The act of surrendering on agreed terms. 2) The agreement containing the surrender terms. 3) Any formal agreement, such as the several concluded by the Swiss Diet or Swiss cantons separately with France and other European states, from the 16th to the 19th century, specifying the terms of mercenary service by Swiss regiments or corps in foreign armies.

caplock—The mechanism used to ignite a PERCUSSION CAP.

capping the T—See **crossing the T**.

captain—1) In most navies, the senior officer below FLAG RANK, ranking between rear admiral (or commodore) and commander; comparable rank in other services: colonel or group captain. 2) In most navies and some air forces, the commander of a vessel or an aircraft, regardless of rank. 3) In most armies and many air forces, the senior COMPANY-GRADE officer ranking between major and first lieutenant; comparable rank in other services: lieutenant in most navies or flight lieutenant in many air forces.

captain-general—A term used from the 15th to the 18th century for the supreme commander or commander in chief of an army or of a nation's armed forces.

captain's mast—The lowest disciplinary authority in the U.S. Navy. For minor infractions an enlisted man would normally be required to appear before the commanding officer, who has the authority to assign certain types of relatively light punishment, within limits prescribed by the Uniform Code of Military Justice. Captains may also hold mast to give awards and commendations. The term carries over from the days of the sailing navy, when captains performed such functions by the mainmast.

carabinier—1) Term for cavalryman of 16th-century France during the reign of King Henry IV. Carabiniers (or **carbineers**) were so called because they were armed with the **carabin**, a short ARQUEBUS. 2) Elite light infantryman (sometimes called **carabinier à pied**) in 18th- and 19th-century armies.

caracole—A cavalry tactic developed by the Germans in the 16th century for their heavy cavalry, newly armed with WHEELLOCK pistols. The cavalry advanced at a slow trot in dense columns, with two horses' width between files or pairs of files. As they approached a foe, each front-rank horseman emptied his three pistols, then swung away sharply to the rear in a 180-degree turn, falling in behind the last rank in his file. While the first ranks were reloading and joining the rear of their respective files, the succeeding ranks continued the process of deliberate advance, pistol fire, and peeling off. The caracole tactic was often used prior to a general advance. It was a very difficult operation to carry out smoothly.

car, armored—See **armored car**.

carbine—A light, short-barreled shoulder weapon used primarily by cavalrymen from the end of the 16th to the end of the 19th century. The name originated with the **carabin**, a heavy, smoothbore pistol about 3 feet long. The carbine developed through several stages, first becoming a shoulder weapon. Cavalry carbines were often rifled after the 17th century; cavalry carbines were among the first automatic shoulder small arms in the mid-19th century.

carbine

carcass—An iron shell with three to five vents around a fuze hole. Developed in the late 17th century, it became standard incendiary ammunition for smoothbore cannon. The carcass was filled with pitch and ignited before firing, and the flames came out through the vents.

careen—To lay a ship over on its side in order to repair or clean the bottom. Before the invention of the drydock, even large sailing vessels were careened periodically to remove barnacles and other marine growth from the hull, replace caulking, and paint.

careerism—A term to describe the mindset of a military bureaucrat who focuses on his or her own career to the exclusion of creativity or innovation.

carpenter—U.S. Navy warrant officer.

carpenter's mate—U.S. Navy enlisted petty officer specialty rating, first, second, and third class.

carpet—1) Any of a group of airborne electronic devices for radar jamming. 2) Intensive and comprehensive coverage of an area with high-explosive detonations, as in CARPET BOMBING.

carpet bombing—The laying down of bombs by a large number of aircraft on a target area in a close pattern intended to cover the area as with a carpet.

carriage—Term used for a supply train or transport in the 16th and 17th centuries. See also **gun carriage**.

carrier—See **aircraft carrier**.

carrier air group—Two or more aircraft squadrons on a single carrier, organized under one command for administrative and tactical control of operations.

carrier task force—A naval force composed of one or more aircraft carriers and support combatant ships capable of conducting strike operations.

carroballista—A large BALLISTA mounted on wheels. This form of the ballista was in common use in the Roman world after A.D. 200.

carroccio—A medieval wagon, usually drawn by an ox, that carried the standard of an Italian free city, a bell, and usually a crucifix. In battle it served as a rallying force for the city's forces.

carronade—A short, large-bore, relatively thin-walled iron cannon developed in 1776 in the Carron Iron Works in Scotland and used into the 19th century. The carronade fired a very heavy ball and was designed for use at close range. Primarily a naval weapon, it was also used ashore, particularly to guard fortress gates, where it was fired with GRAPE-SHOT or case shot (see **canister**).

"Carry on"—An order to resume prior activity.

cart—A light, two-wheeled vehicle drawn by men, horses, mules, jeeps, or other vehicles. Carts have many uses and have been employed since early times for hauling military equipment and ammunition. In modern armies they are commonly used for a specific weapon, such as a machine gun or light mortar, or for ammunition, in areas not traversable by heavy vehicles.

cartel—In its narrower sense, an agreement entered into by belligerents for the exchange of prisoners of war. In its broader sense, it is any convention concluded between belligerents for the purpose of arranging or regulating kinds of nonhostile intercourse otherwise prohibited by the state of war. Both parties to a cartel are honor-bound to scrupulously observe its provisions, but it is voidable upon proof that one party intentionally violated an important particular.

cartouche—A cartridge case made of heavy paper used from the early 17th to the mid-19th century.

cartridge—A cylindrical case containing the charge, primer, and projectile for use in a firearm. Paper cartridges were invented in the late 17th century; modern cartridges are usually made of brass. The cartridge greatly reduced the time required to load a weapon. See also **ball cartridge**.

U.S. Army photo
.30-cal. cartridges for a U.S. Springfield rifle.

cartridges

casemate—1) A large chamber, usually covered with a vault, built in the thickness of a fortress wall. Such casemates usually had embrasures in the outer wall and housed a gun. They might also be used as barracks or quarters for officers. 2) A protective enclosure for a ship's gun which is attached to or part of the ship's structure, sometimes armored.

caserne—A barracks.

case shot—See **canister**.

cashier—To dismiss with ignominy from military service.

casque—A helmet, particularly one with a pointed crown, sometimes with a nosepiece.

castellum—A small blockhouse-type Roman fortress, often integrated into long walls defending exposed frontiers of the empire.

castle—1) A large fortification, usually composed of a number of fortified buildings within a walled enclosure, most often the residence of a ruler or his noble vassal in the feudal societies of medieval Europe. 2) A small defensive structure built on the deck of a warship in medieval times. 3) A small tower in which several men could ride with some protection, set on the back of a war elephant.

castrametation—The building of a camp. The word derives from the Latin *castrum*, a fortified place. The Romans developed castrametation into an efficient system and an integral element of military doctrine. Whenever a Roman military force halted overnight, each man performed a specific task for which he had been trained, and thus a fortified camp was quickly and efficiently constructed. It then provided the commander with a secure base for offensive or defensive combat.

casual—A military person awaiting duty assignment or transportation from a station at which he or she is not assigned or attached.

casualty—A person lost to his or her organization for reasons other than an ordered transfer. A **battle casualty** is one who, as a result of combat action, is dead, wounded, or missing (whether captured or simply unaccounted for). A **nonbattle casualty** is one who is sick, injured (other than through combat action), or missing in a noncombat situation.

casualty rate—The rate at which casualties are incurred in combat. Although it may be expressed in absolute numbers over time, a casualty rate is more commonly expressed as a percentage of troop strength over time, usually per day.

casualty status—A means of classifying casualties for treatment, evacuation, and reporting. The seven categories are as follows: a) deceased, b) whereabouts unknown, c) missing, d) very seriously ill or injured, e) seriously ill or injured, f) incapacitated by illness or injury, and g) not seriously injured.

casus belli—An action taken by one nation toward another, or an event related to two or more nations, that is interpreted as justifying a declaration of war.

cataphract—A heavily armored horse archer. Introduced in the Roman army in the 2nd century, the cataphract, who rode an armored horse, became the mainstay of the Byzantine army. He combined firepower, discipline, mobility, and shock-action capability. His arms might include bow, quiver of arrows, long lance, broadsword, dagger, and ax. Men and horses were superbly trained and capable of complex tactical evolutions on drill-ground and battlefield.

catapult—1) A machine developed before the 5th century B.C.—apparently in Syria—for hurling arrows to distances of up to 500 meters; constructed like a large crossbow, it used the force of tension to propel the missile. The catapult was distinguished from the later BALLISTA mainly by the nature of the power (the ballista used torsion) and the nature of the missile (the ballista originally hurled rocks), although by the time of the Roman Empire, distinctions between ballista and catapult had become blurred. 2) Any ancient war machine of the catapult or ballista type.

3) A device for launching an airplane without a runway, as from the deck of a ship.

cat-o'-nine-tails—A whip with nine knotted cords at the end of a short handle. This device was used for flogging as punishment for infractions, particularly in navies during the era of sail. The practice was abandoned in the British Royal Navy and the U.S. Navy by the mid-19th century.

cavalier—1) From medieval times, a cavalryman, equivalent to the French chevalier. 2) A tall structure inside a fort or other defensive work, high enough to permit fire over the wall. Because of its visibility it was an easy target, and thus it was abandoned after the introduction of high-explosive shells in the late 19th century.

cavalry—A military force that fights on horseback, or, in modern times, in tanks, armored vehicles, or helicopters. Cavalry has been used since at least 1100 B.C., forming an important element of most armies because of its contribution to speed, mobility, and maneuver. The extreme vulnerability of the horse to high-powered rifles and automatic weapons caused the use of cavalry to diminish by the late 19th century. Its place has been taken by armored units, although some nations retain cavalry units for ceremonial purposes; and at least one, China, maintains saber-wielding cavalry units. Horse cavalry units were sometimes distinguished as **heavy** and **light**. Modern calvary units are generally designated as **mechanized** or **armored cavalry**. The principal cavalry functions are RECONNAISSANCE, SCREENING, raiding, and mobile shock action.

caveat—A designator used with a security classification to further limit the dissemination of restricted information.

CBR—Chemical-biological-radiological. Refers to warfare using gas, germ bombs, and nuclear weapons.

cease-fire—An agreement between belligerents to stop firing. A TRUCE.

cell—A small group of individuals who work together for clandestine or subversive purposes.

center of burst—See **center of impact**.

center of impact—1) In gunnery, the center of a dispersion pattern of projectiles fired from a gun or a group of guns, without change in range or deflection. 2) In bombing, the center of the area of greatest concentration in a bombing pattern.

centurion—The officer in command of a Roman CENTURY. The LEGION, principal formation of the ancient Roman army, was divided into 60 centuries, each of 80 to 100 men. A centurion was generally promoted from the ranks. The senior centurion in a MANIPLE, which contained two centuries, or a COHORT, which contained six centuries, commanded all of the centuries in the units, much as a battalion officer does in modern armies. The senior centurion in each legion participated in councils of war.

century—A unit of the Roman army consisting of approximately 80 to 100 men, of whom two thirds were heavily armed JAVELINEERS and a third were SKIRMISHERS.

CEP—See **circular error probable.**

CH-47SD—See **Chinook.**

CH-53—See **Sea Stallion.**

chaff—Narrow strips of aluminum or other reflective material that are fired from the ground or dropped from aircraft to confuse radio and radar receivers. Chaff was first used in World War II. Also called **window.**

chain mail—See **mail.**

chain of command—The succession of commanding officers from a superior to a subordinate through which command is exercised. An **administrative chain of command** is permanent, and applies in all administrative matters. An **operational chain of command** may be established solely for a specific operation or a series of continuing operations.

chain shot—A type of projectile consisting of two balls or hemispheres joined by a chain. Fired into the rigging of a naval vessel, chain shot was a particularly effective device in naval battles, for the balls would rip through sails and wrap themselves around spars or lines, cutting, tearing, and snapping them.

challenge—Any process of identification carried out by one unit or person to ascertain the friendly or hostile character or identity of another.

chamade—A drumbeat or trumpet call signaling a desire to parley.

chamfron—The armor that protected the head of a warhorse.

chandelier—A solidly built wooden frame that can be filled with FASCINES or other material. Chandeliers can be carried with troops and set up as field fortifications, particularly where it is difficult to dig, as in rocky, swampy, or frozen ground.

Chaparral (MIM-72)—A short-range, low-altitude, surface-to-air air defense artillery system, essentially a SIDEWINDER missile mounted on a vehicle chassis. The system is designed to be self-contained and air transportable.

chaplain—A clergyman, commissioned as an officer, who is responsible for the religious welfare of service-connected personnel and who advises their commander on all matters pertaining to religious life, morals, and morale.

charge—*n.* 1) An accelerated, concentrated attack, such as a cavalry charge. 2) The substance with which a bomb, shell, or mine is filled, such as explosive, thermite, bacteria, or other material. 3) A given quantity of explosive, either by itself or contained in a bomb, shell, or mine, or used as a propellant for a bullet or shell. 4) A cartridge or round of small-arms ammunition. See also **shaped charge.** *v.* 1) To dash rapidly against an opponent or a target. 2) To fill an explosive device—bomb, mine, shell—with a charge. 3) To move a round of ammunition into the firing chamber of a weapon.

charger—A horse used as the mount of a military man, particularly a knight or an officer.

chariot

chariot—A type of ancient horse-drawn battle vehicle, usually with two wheels, sometimes with four, drawn by one to four horses. Chariots are pictured in reliefs and vase paintings from as early as the 3rd millenium B.C. in Mesopotamia, and were used in most armies until the development of CAVALRY. The Gauls, the Britons, and the Picts used them as late as the 3rd century A.D. They usually carried two people, the **charioteer,** who drove the horses, and the warrior, armed with bow, lance, or spear, or some combination of these. In the West, chariots were used primarily for transportation, and the warriors dismounted near the field of battle to fight on foot. In Asian armies, chariots became the principal shock-action weapons, sometimes with scythes attached to the wheels to increase their deadliness.

Charlie—1) Letter of old and NATO phonetic alphabets. See also **alphabet, phonetic**. 2) **"Charlie"** or **"Charley"** is military slang; it was used to refer to the Viet Cong enemy in Vietnam.

chart—A map used for navigation. **Nautical charts** show information about the depth of water and the nature of the sea bottom, aids to navigation, the location of channels, hazards, and other matters required for safe ship handling. **Aeronautical charts** give equivalent information for the use of the aerial navigator. See also **firing chart**.

chase—The portion of a cannon from the TRUNNIONS to the muzzle.

chaser—A cannon placed in the bow or the stern of a vessel, used in pursuit or in defense against pursuit.

Chassepot—A French breech-loading rifle invented by Antoine Chassepot and used by the French army after 1866. This bolt-action needle rifle, whose caliber was 11mm, differed from the earlier Prussian NEEDLE GUN in that the firing pin ignited the primer at the base of the cartridge. After modification to take metallic cartridges in 1874, the weapon was renamed the "Gras rifle."

chasseur—1) A French soldier, lightly armed and equipped, for reconnaissance and screening purposes. The term is now applied to light armor and light infantry units of the French army. 2) **Chasseur à pied** is a light infantry soldier, first so designated in 1743. 3) Infantry troops trained for mountain warfare are called **chasseurs alpins**. 4) **Chasseurs à cheval**, light cavalry troops, were introduced in 1779.

Chatellerault gun—A French machine gun developed in the Chatellerault Arsenal in the 1920s. It had a very high rate of fire, 500 rounds per minute.

chausses—Medieval leg and foot armor made of mail.

checkerboard formation—A formation in which elements of a military force are posi-

tioned in a checkerboard or "quincunx" pattern. Such a formation was used in the Roman legion and has been employed in other tactical formations ever since.

checkpoint—1) A predetermined and clearly identifiable point on the earth's surface used as a means of controlling movement, or as a registration target for fire adjustment, or as a reference for location. 2) Geographical location on land or over water above which the position of an aircraft in flight may be determined by observation or by electronic means. 3) A place where military police check vehicular or pedestrian traffic in order to enforce circulation control measures and other laws, orders, and regulations.

chemical agent—A solid, liquid, or gas that, through its chemical or incendiary properties, produces lethal or damaging effects on humans, animals, plants, or material, or produces a screening or signaling smoke.

chemical, biological, and radiological operations—A combining term used only when referring in the collective sense to the three areas of chemical operations, biological operations, and radiological operations. These are operations that involve nonconventional weapons (e.g., poison gas, biological or bacteriological agents, and the radiation effects of nuclear weapons) and that cause damage through effects other than violent impact or explosive forces.

Chemical Corps—In the U.S. Army, the branch of service charged with furnishing the means for and technical guidance in the employment of and defense against chemical and biological weapons. The functions performed by the Chemical Corps in support of combat operations are twofold: a) operation of smoke-generating equipment and special chemical weapons and b) decontamination of areas and matériel and assistance to other units in carrying out such tasks.

chemical warfare—The employment in warfare of chemical agents other than explosives to kill or disrupt hostile forces, to contaminate areas, or to destroy matériel.

cheval-de-frise—A military obstacle consisting of wooden beams, frames, or barrels from which spears or pointed stakes protrude at intervals, first used in the Dutch War for Independence in the 16th and 17th centuries, primarily as a defense against cavalry. The name derives from "horses of Friesland." Benjamin Franklin devised a submarine version that was placed in the Delaware and Hudson rivers during the Revolution as an obstacle to British warships.

chevron—A mark or insignia in the shape of a caret or a V worn on a uniform sleeve to indicate rank and class of service. Also called "crow."

chicken feed (intelligence)— Information knowingly provided to an enemy intelligence agency through an agent or a double agent. Such information must be of sufficient quality to convince the enemy agency of the usefulness of continuing to operate the agent but not so sensitive as to damage one's own interests.

chief gunner—See **gunner**.

chief officer—Second in command of a vessel.

chief of section—1) The senior noncommissioned officer in a small military subunit, usually part of a platoon. 2) In the U.S. Army Field Artillery, the commander of a gun crew, usually a sergeant.

chief of staff—1) The senior or principal member or head of a staff, usually a general staff (see also **chief of the general staff**). 2) The principal assistant in a staff capacity to a person in a command capacity. 3) The head or controlling member of a staff for purposes of coordinating its work; a position that is without inherent power of command by reason of assignment, except that which is invested in such a position by delegation to exercise command in another's name.

chief of the boat—A petty officer in charge of enlisted personnel on any small vessel or submarine, generally one of the most experienced noncommissioned officers on board.

chief of the general staff—The senior officer of a general staff, from the level of a division up to the level of a major service of a nation (as in the United States for Army and Air Force) or for a nation's armed forces (as in Russia).

chief petty officer—In the U.S. Navy, the highest enlisted rating below warrant officer. A sailor of that rating may be a chief yeoman,

chief boatswain's mate, or chief in any of the other naval specialties.

Chindit—Member of special forces commanded by British Maj. Gen. Orde Wingate in Burma in World War II LONG-RANGE PENTRATION operations in 1943 and 1944. So called because their emblem was a mythical Burmese animal called a *chinthe* and because their operations took place near the Chin Hills. The entire force was often given the collective name of "Chindits."

Chinook (CH-47SD)—A twin-rotor, heavy-lift helicopter manufactured by Boeing, the Chinook can handle loads up to 14 tons. Its military missions include the transport of troops and supplies to the battlefield.

U.S. Army photo

Chinook

chin turret—A turret installed immediately beneath and slightly behind the nose of a bomber.

chivalry—1) The feudal institution of knighthood. 2) Qualities associated with warfare between knights, including courage and loyalty. 3) The concept that warfare should be conducted according to a code of conduct that protects the rights of noncombatants and dictates respect toward a defeated enemy.

chlorine gas — The form of poison gas first used in modern warfare. Introduced by the Germans against the French in World War I during the Second Battle of Ypres, 22 April 1915. See also **chemical warfare; gas, poison; phosgene**.

CHOP or **Chop Line**—From Change of Operational Control, the dividing north-south line in the North and South Atlantic oceans during World War II, where convoy and ship movements changed from American to British control or vice versa.

Christmas truce—A period of approximately 48 hours on 24–26 December 1914 when opposing German, British, and French soldiers initiated a spontaneous cease-fire and a period of fraternization along much of the Western Front.

CIC—1) U.S. Army: Criminal Investigation Corps. 2) U.S. Navy: COMBAT INFORMATION CENTER.

cipher—Any cryptographic system in which arbitrary symbols or groups of symbols represent units of plain text, usually single letters, or in which units of plain text are rearranged in accordance with predetermined rules.

circular error probable (CEP)—An indicator of the accuracy of a missile or projectile, used as a factor in determining probable damage to a target. CEP equals the radius of a circle within which half of the projectiles fired from a single gun or launcher at given settings for range and deflection are expected to fall. Also known as PROBABLE ERROR.

circumvallation—A wall, trench, or other barrier erected during siege operations to protect the besieging forces from the interference of relief forces; thus the barrier faced outward, away from the place or area besieged, in contradistinction to a barrier of CONTRAVALLATION.

citadel—A central fortress, often located on a hill overlooking a city or larger fortification. The term was formerly used to designate the heavily armored central portion of a warship, including the engines, guns, and other vital portions.

citation—1) A specific mention of a person or unit in orders or other documents for commendable or meritorious action. 2) A written narrative statement of a meritorious action or deed for which a decoration is awarded.

civic action (military)—The use of military forces on nonmilitary projects useful to local populations.

civil affairs—Those phases of a commander's activities that embrace the relationship between the military forces and the civilian population, particularly civil authorities, in a friendly or occupied country or area.

Civil Air Patrol—In the United States, a federally chartered, nonprofit corporation that was designated by Congress in 1948 as a volunteer auxiliary of the U.S. Air Force. Its mission is to provide service during local and national emergencies, motivate youth to high ideals of leadership, and generate interest in and support of the Air Force through aerospace education and training.

civil defense—All those activities and measures designed or undertaken to a) minimize the effects on the civilian population of an enemy attack; b) deal with the immediate emergency conditions created by any such attack; and c) facilitate emergency repairs to, or the emergency restoration of, vital utilities and facilities destroyed or damaged by any such attack.

civil-military relations — Relations between military forces and the civilian people and agencies in areas where troops are stationed.

civil war—A war between indigenous factions in a single country.

clandestine operations — Intelligence-gathering activities sponsored or conducted so as to assure secrecy or concealment. Clandestine operations differ from COVERT OPERATIONS in that emphasis is placed on concealment of the operation rather than on concealment of the identity of the sponsor.

classified information—Official information that has been determined to require, in the interests of national defense, protection against disclosure to people with no need to see or know about it.

claymore—1) A Scottish Highland two-handed, double-edged broadsword. 2) The name of a U.S. Army antipersonnel mine that can also be used as short-range, remote-control weapon fired by an operator-observer; particularly useful for final protective fire and against an enemy advancing through a DEFILE.

clear—*v.* 1) To approve, authorize, or obtain approval or authorization for a proposed action or activity. 2) Specifically, to give one or more aircraft a clearance. 3) To give a person a SECURITY CLEARANCE. *adj.* Of military messages not encoded or encrypted.

clear and hold—A military operation with the objective of occupying an area after it is retaken from the enemy.

clip—A device holding several rounds of ammunition to be fired either single-shot or automatically in an automatic pistol or a magazine rifle.

clipeus—A flat, oval Roman shield.

close air support—Air attacks against hostile surface targets that are in close proximity to friendly ground forces. Such air attacks require detailed integration of each mission with the fire and movement of the ground forces. Usually close air support is flown to meet specific requests from ground forces during the course of a battle.

close controlled interception—See **intercept**.

close-in security—The physical security (defensive) measures taken inside a restricted area or national defense area in direct support or protection of the operational resources in the area.

close order—Deploying or positioning of soldiers in a unit with a minimum of space between them. The amount of space is usually regularized and dependent on the requirements or characteristics of the weapons being carried.

close-order drill—Practice of units in formation in administrative or ceremonial movements. See also **drill**.

close station—1) To cease ongoing activities or operations, particularly for an artillery unit, and to withdraw from a signal network. 2) The order to cease activities and withdraw from the net. The usual complete command is, "Close station, march order."

close stick—A stick of bombs released more or less simultaneously.

close support—Supporting action by one force for another at a distance so slight that the supporting action must be integrated or coordinated directly with the action of the supported force. CLOSE AIR SUPPORT is the supporting action by combat aircraft (usually fighter bombers) by which fire from the air (by bombs, strafing, napalm, etc.) is directed at hostile forces immediately in front of supported ground force units.

close supporting fire—Fire placed on enemy troops, weapons, or positions to support a unit that is in close proximity to or even engaged in combat with the enemy. Such supporting fire must be coordinated with the fire and movements of the supported unit to avoid shelling friendly troops.

close train—One after the other, as in, "The bombs were released in close train."

club the musket—To use a musket or a rifle as a club, usually wielding it by the barrel.

cluster—1) Fireworks signal in which a group of stars burn at the same time. 2) Groups of bombs released together. A cluster usually consists of fragmentation or incendiary bombs. 3) Component of a pattern-laid minefield. 4) Two or more engines coupled together to function as one power unit. 5) Use of two or more parachutes for dropping a single load.

cluster bomb—An aerial bomb designed for use against personnel, armor, airfields, and other ground targets. Composed of many small explosive bombs packed into one container, a cluster bomb is designed to open in flight and release its payload, thereby increasing the dispersion and lethality of the weapon's submunitions.

coastal frontier—A geographical division of coastal area, established for organization and command purposes to ensure the effective coordination of military forces engaged in operations within the area.

coast artillery—1) Fixed or mobile artillery weapons emplaced close to harbors, cities, or strategic waterways, in positions from which they can fire on approaching enemy ships. 2) The personnel or units manning such weapons.

coast guard—A maritime force whose functions in peacetime include such duties as the protection of life and property at sea and the enforcement of laws governing customs, immigration, and navigation. In time of war the U.S. Coast Guard functions as part of the U.S. Navy.

coastwatcher—A person inside enemy-held territory who observes coastal shipping and enemy movements and reports by radio. The United States used coastwatchers on Pacific islands in World War II, landing them clan-

destinely or providing equipment for island-
ers to use.

coat of mail—A defensive garment of metal
scales or chain mail.

Cobra (AH-1)—A single-rotor helicopter, the
Cobra was the first U.S. Army helicopter specifically designed for attack purposes; it saw
considerable service in Vietnam.

cock—1) To draw back the hammer, bolt, or
plunger of a firearm to ready it for firing.
2) To set a bomb release mechanism so as to
make ready to drop the bomb load.

cockade—A rosette or knot of ribbon worn
as a badge, especially on the hat.

cocked hat—A hat with a wide brim, turned
up in two or three flaps. When two flaps are
formed, such a hat may be called a BICORNE;
with three it may be a TRICORNE.

codes—1) Any system of communications in
which arbitrary groups of symbols represent
units of plain text of varying length. Codes
may be used for brevity or for security. (See
cipher.) 2) A word or words used to designate a forthcoming operation.

code word—A word that conveys a meaning
other than its conventional one, prearranged
by the correspondents. Its aim is usually to
increase security; it can be used also for convenience because of brevity.

coehorn—A popular small mortar of the
17th and 18th centuries, invented by Menno,
Baron van Coehoorn, in 1673, which threw
shells weighing up to 24 pounds.

cohesion—The quality or characteristic of a
unit whose members work well together and
demonstrate loyalty to one another and to
their unit under all circumstances. Cohesion
is achieved by training together, living together, and having strong leadership. Sometimes called "cohesiveness."

cohort—1) A unit of the Roman army. From
the 2nd century B.C. a cohort consisted of approximately 420 men, organized in six CEN-
TURIES. There were 10 cohorts in a LEGION. In
the 1st century A.D. the size of the first cohort
was increased to about 800 men, organized in
five centuries. Cohorts were also formed in

special military organizations, such as the
PRAETORIAN GUARD, which was not a legion
but was composed of cohorts. 2) The annual
manpower increment of a nation reaching a
given age, usually that for military service.
3) A unit equivalent to a battalion in the
French national guard during the First Empire.

coif, mail—A skullcap, made of fabric, mail,
or leather, worn by a medieval soldier under
a hood of mail.

cold war—A state of tension between two or
more nations or blocs, with each resorting to
measures short of overt military action to
gain ascendancy. The term *guerra fria* was
used by 13th-century Spaniards to describe
their relations with the Muslim nations of
North Africa, but the term "Cold War" generally refers to the decades of friction between
the Soviet Union and its satellites and the
NATO powers from 1946 until the collapse of
the Soviet Union in 1991.

collateral damage—Unintended damage to
nonmilitary persons, structures, and facilities as a result of military operations, most
often air strikes.

collateral mission—A mission other than
the one for which a force is trained and
equipped, which the force can accomplish by
virtue of its inherent capabilities.

collecting point—A point designated for
the assembly of casualties, prisoners of war,
stragglers, disabled matériel, salvage, etc.,
for further movement to collecting stations or
rear installations.

colonel—The highest military field-grade
rank, that between lieutenant colonel and
brigadier or brigadier general. In 1505 King
Ferdinand of Spain created 20 units called
colunelas, or columns. This was the first
clear-cut tactical formation in Western Europe since the time of the Roman legion. This
unit, prototype of the modern battalion, regiment, or brigade, was commanded by a *cabo
de colunela* (chief of column) or colonel. The
French soon copied the COLUNELA concept,
and adopted the military rank. Napoleon is
credited with having said, "There are no bad
regiments; there are only bad colonels."

colonel-commandant—A British term referring to the commander (usually honorary)
of a REGIMENT, which, in British usage, is an

administrative formation as opposed to a combat unit. Sometimes called **colonel in chief**.

colonel-general—This grade is normally identified with the commander of a field army or an army group, and is comparable to a four-star general.

colonel in chief — See **colonel-commandant**.

colonial troops—Troops of colonial powers raised in, or raised for employment in, a colony; colonial units were raised in many of the colonies belonging to Great Britain. Indigenous colonial units were usually commanded by officers from the colonial power.

color bearer—See **standard bearer**.

color guard—A guard assigned to protect the COLORS in a ceremony or on the march.

colors—1) A flag or banner, particularly that of a nation or of a military unit. The term was first used in Elizabethan times. 2) Military service. In this sense it is used in phrases like "called to the colors."

color sergeant/color corporal — A noncommissioned officer selected to carry the national flag and (in the United States) the flag of a unit or to serve as a guard (usually a corporal, called a COLOR GUARD) for the colors.

Colt revolver—A handgun invented by Samuel Colt about the middle of the 19th century. He designed a cylinder that could hold several cartridges and could be rotated by releasing the squeezed trigger, so that a new cartridge was aligned with the barrel to replace one that had been fired. The Colt revolver, a .45-caliber weapon, was first used by the U.S. Army in the Mexican War.

Colt revolver

columbiad — A 19th-century American muzzle-loading cannon, usually used for coastal defense or siegecraft, with a heavy, long, iron barrel, of 8-, 10-, or 12-inch caliber.

The range of these guns, which replaced similar bronze ones, was more than 5,000 yards.

column—1) A military formation in which a number of like units, whether troops, squads, battalions, ships, vehicles, or aircraft, are deployed one behind the other. The **attack column** came into general use in ground combat during the French Revolution. Perfected by Napoleon, it was an adaptation of the linear system, the deployment of a number of linear units (usually battalions) in depth to provide physical and psychological weight to an attack (see **linear tactics**). The individual units could still operate in a linear formation if desired. The great tactical value of the column lay in its flexibility and versatility. It permitted the commander to move large numbers of troops over the battlefield far more rapidly and with better control than had been possible before. 2) Term used for independent Boer forces, also called commandos.

column cover—Protective cover of a ground column furnished by aircraft in radio contact with the column, thereby providing reconnaissance and protection by attacking air or ground targets that threaten the column.

colunela—A unit created in 1505 in the army of Ferdinand of Spain. Consisting of approximately 1,000 to 1,250 men (mixed pikemen, halberdiers, arquebusiers, and SWORD-AND-BUCKLER troops) organized in five companies. For all practical purposes the colunela was the genesis of the modern BATTALION, REGIMENT, or BRIGADE.

combat air crew—The crew assigned to a combat aircraft.

combat air patrol (CAP)—An aircraft patrol flown over an objective area, over a protected force, over the critical area of a combat zone, or over an air defense area for the purpose of intercepting and destroying hostile aircraft before they reach their target.

combatant—*n.* A person who engages in combat. *adj.* 1) Adept at fighting. 2) Serving or ready to serve in combat. 3) Used in fighting. 4) Involving combat.

combat area—1) The area in which combat units, including close support units, are operating. 2) A restricted area (air, land, or sea) established to prevent or minimize mutual interference between friendly forces engaged in combat operations. See also **area**.

combat boot—A high shoe with a leather cuff, often worn outside the trousers.

combat box—A rectangular formation used with certain airplanes during, or when expecting, combat. The term was applied especially to a heavy-bomber formation during World War II.

combat command—A major tactical unit of combined arms within an armored division, corresponding to an infantry regiment or brigade. A combat command consists of a headquarters and headquarters company and a variable number of units or elements attached.

combat control team—A team of specially trained air force personnel who AIRDROP into forward areas to advise the ground force commander on all aspects of landing area requirements and to provide local air control.

combat effectiveness—1) A term used to described the abilities and fighting quality of a unit. 2) The quality of being effective in combat.

combat fatigue—See **fatigue, combat**.

combat forces—Those forces whose primary mission is to participate in combat operations.

combat information center — Area in a ship or an aircraft manned and equipped to collect, display, evaluate, and disseminate tactical information for the use of the COMMANDING OFFICER.

combat intelligence—The knowledge of the enemy, weather, and geographic features that is required by a commander for planning and conducting tactical operations.

combat loading—The stowing of equipment and supplies on an aircraft or land vehicle for an amphibious assault, or follow-up to an amphibious landing, in such a way that each item of cargo can be unloaded in the sequence of anticipated need.

combat, military—A violent, planned form of fighting in which at least one party is an organized force, recognized by government or de facto authority. One or both opposing parties have at least one of the following objectives: to seize control of territory, to prevent the opponent's seizure and control of territory, or to protect one's own territory. The presence of weaponry creates an atmosphere of lethality, danger, and fear in which one party's achievement of objectives may require its opponent to choose among continued resistance (thereby risking destruction), retreat and loss of territories and facilities, or surrender.

combat model—See **model; scenario**.

combat patrol—A detachment of ground, sea, or air forces sent out by a larger unit to gather information or carry out a destructive, harassing, mopping-up, or security mission.

combat power—The total means of destructive or disruptive force that a military unit or formation can apply against an opponent at a given time.

combat radius—The maximum operational capability of an aircraft, measured from its base to its proposed area of operations.

combat readiness—The capability of a military unit or ship to perform its assigned missions. The status of personnel, equipment, supplies, maintenance, facilities, and training is considered in determining this capability.

combat reserve—A fighting force held in reserve for immediate use if needed during a combat operation.

combat service support — The assistance provided to operating forces mainly in the fields of administrative services, chaplain services, civil affairs, finance, legal services, health services, military police, supply, management, maintenance, transportation, construction, acquisitions, engineering, food service, graves registration, laundry, dry cleaning, property disposal, and other logistic services.

combat support — Operational assistance (including direct combat involvement) furnished to combat elements by other designated units.

combat support troops—Those units or organizations whose primary mission is to furnish operational assistance for the combat elements.

combat team, regimental — A reinforced infantry regiment, normally composed of a three-battalion regiment of infantry strengthened by a battalion of field artillery, a company of engineers, and a battery of antiaircraft artillery. This composition may be changed to meet the demands of the tactical situation. In some situations, a combat team may need other attachments, such as an ambulance platoon, a clearing platoon, a signal company, additional tank units, and additional field artillery. A **brigade combat team** consists of a three-battalion infantry brigade similarly strengthened by ATTACHMENTs.

combat theory—See **theory of combat**.

combat troops—The units or organizations whose primary mission is destruction of enemy forces or installations.

combat vehicle—A vehicle, with or without armor, designed for a specific fighting function.

combat zone—1) The area required by combat forces for the conduct of operations. 2) The territory forward of an army's rear area boundary.

combined—Designating the presence or involvement of two or more forces, branches, agencies, or types of arms (e.g., infantry, armor, and air). In World War II the term "combined" was used to designate committees, forces, or operations involving forces of two nations (principally the United States and Britain, and particularly including the COMBINED CHIEFS OF STAFF and all the staff committees). See also **joint**.

combined-arms army—See **army**.

combined-arms force—A major field force that includes elements of various service branches, usually infantry, armor, and artillery, and frequently air support as well.

combined-arms operation—A military operation performed by a combined-arms force.

Combined Bomber Offensive—The round-the-clock bomber offensive conducted by the U.S. Eighth Air Force and the British Bomber Command against targets in Germany in World War II. Bomber Command attacked the economic system and waged psychological warfare against civilian morale by large-scale nighttime saturation bombing; the Eighth Air Force concentrated on daylight precision bombing against aircraft industrial targets and the Luftwaffe itself. Later, both forces concentrated on vital industries to destroy Germany's ability to make war. It was code-named Operation Pointblank.

Combined Chiefs of Staff (CCS) — The World War II high command organization composed of the military service chiefs of the United States and Britain, whose function was to plan and direct global strategy under the two national leaders.

combined operations—1) Operations involving two or more forces, branches, or agencies participating in the same war-related endeavor. 2) In British usage, amphibious operations.

COMINT—See **communications intelligence**.

command—*n.* 1) The authority vested in an individual member of the armed forces for the direction, coordination, control, and administration of military forces. 2) An order given by a person with authority. 3) An organization or area under the direction and control of a duly constituted authority. 4) A U.S. Air Force organization of three or more wings. *v.* 1) To exercise authority over a military unit or larger force. 2) To order. 3) To dominate an area, a hostile position, or a hostile force by a field of weapon fire or by observation from a superior position.

command and control — The exercise of authority and direction by a properly designated commander over assigned forces in the accomplishment of the mission. Command and control functions are performed through an arrangement of personnel, equipment, communications, facilities, and procedures that are employed by a commander in planning, directing, coordinating, and controlling forces and operations in the accomplishment of the mission.

commandant—1) The commanding officer of a military organization or installation other than an operational combat force. The senior officers of the U.S. Marine Corps and the U.S. Coast Guard have the title of commandant. 2) In the French army, a rank equivalent to major.

command area—See **area**.

command, control, communications, and computer systems (C-4)—Integrated procedures involving doctrine, organizational structures, personnel, equipment, and communications designed to support an officer's exercise of command and control.

commandeer—To take for military use without formality (and usually without customary procedures), as a house or a vehicle.

commander—A person who exercises command.

commander in chief—The commander of a major military force, as Commander in Chief, U.S. Army, Europe, or Commander in Chief, U.S. Fleet. In some nations the title is used for the supreme commander of the nation's armed forces.

commander's concept—See **concept of operations**.

commanding ground—Ground that overlooks neighboring terrain.

commanding officer—An officer who commands a unit or an installation.

commanding position—A position, usually on higher ground than that occupied by the enemy in a ground action, or to windward in an action between sailing vessels, from which one force has a visual or tactical advantage over the other.

command net—A communications net that connects headquarters with subordinate units for the issuance of commands and other messages.

commando—1) Any soldier belonging to a specially selected group of combatants, particularly in the British armed services, trained for hand-to-hand fighting, surprise raids, and other shock tactics. The term was originally used for such troops in World War II and apparently derived from Boer War experience [see 3) below]. 2) Often applied to similar troops of any nation; for example, the American equivalent of the generic "commando" is the ranger. 3) A Portuguese word adopted for a unit of the Boer military forces, composed originally of all males of an electoral district between 16 and 60 years of age; later applied to any Boer independent command. Such units fought effectively in the Boer War. See also **ranger**.

command of the sea—The ability to protect the sea routes taken by a nation's shipping, and to deny to the enemy the use of those routes.

command pilot—1) The highest aeronautical rating in the U.S. Air Force and Naval Air Force, based on years of service, flying time, and performance. 2) A pilot qualified by time and experience to hold this rating.

command post (CP) — The headquarters installation and personnel of a military unit or formation under combat conditions. A commander will sometimes maintain a **forward command post** as close as possible to the front line, as well as the **main command post** farther to the rear.

command post exercise (CPX) — An expanded map exercise for commanders and staff to control operations by using tactical communications systems. A CPX is often part of a larger exercise.

command ship—A specially equipped ship carrying the admiral in command of fleet actions or an amphibious operation and the admiral's staff. Command ships, first used in the Pacific in World War II, carried electronic devices for communications, intelligence gathering, and the functions of command and control. In amphibious operations, such a floating command post enables close personal cooperation between the naval commander, responsible for putting the ground forces ashore, and the ground commander, who assumes control once the troops have gained the beach.

command vehicles—Vehicles designed primarily for command and communication; they may be tracked or wheeled and may also be armored vehicles.

commerce raider—A warship, usually fast and well armed, or a submarine that operated against the enemy's merchant ships. Examples are the Confederate cruiser *Alabama* and the German pocket battleships in World War II.

commissariat—An installation or a department supplying food and other supplies, transport, and so on.

commissary—1) In the United States, a market maintained on a military post where authorized service personnel and their families may purchase food and other provisions. 2) In the British and other armies (and the U.S. Army earlier), an officer responsible for providing food and other supplies. In the 17th and 18th centuries, commissaries oversaw the force's expenses and the conduct of officers and men.

commission—*n.* 1) A written order giving a person rank and authority as an officer in the armed forces. 2) The rank and authority given by such an order. *v.* 1) To confer such rank. 2) To put in or make ready for use or service, as "to commission an aircraft or a ship."

commissioned officer—See **officer**.

commissioned warrant officer—See **warrant officer**.

commit—1) To assign, place, or use a military unit in such a way that it inevitably becomes engaged in combat. 2) To put oneself in a position where withdrawal or change in a course of action becomes impossible.

commodore—1) The lowest naval flag rank, between captain and rear admiral. It was abolished in the U.S. Navy in 1899, reactivated for limited use during World War II, and reactivated again in 1982. 2) A designation used unofficially in the British Royal Navy for a captain with temporary command of a fleet division or a squadron.

common item—1) Any item of matériel that is required for use by or in more than one service or activity. 2) Sometimes loosely used to denote any consumable item except repair parts or other technical items.

common servicing—A function performed by one military service in support of another military service for which reimbursement is not required.

common use—Services, materials, or facilities provided by a Department of Defense agency or a military service for two or more Department of Defense agencies.

communal warfare — Conflicts between states or groups based on ethnic and religious differences, as opposed to national rivalries. Communal warfare may occur within the boundaries of a single state or may cross bor-

ders. Examples of communal warfare are the fighting between Serbs and Muslims in the former Yugoslavia and conflicts between Buddhists and Hindus in Sri Lanka.

communications—1) The system for transmitting messages from one point to another. 2) The route connecting one military force with another, in particular, a force in a combat area with its rear headquarters and source of supply. See also **line of communications**.

communications center—A facility responsible for the reception, transmission, and delivery of messages. Its normal elements are a message center section, a cryptographic section, and a sending and receiving section, which uses electronic communications devices.

communications intelligence (COMINT)—A specialized form of INTELLIGENCE whereby technical information is derived from hostile or foreign communications.

communications, lateral—1) The availability of means—by wire, radio, or messenger—for the headquarters or commanders of two adjacent, friendly forces to communicate with each other. 2) The employment of such means.

communications net—1) The various means, mechanical and other, of transmitting information, orders, and reports within an organization. 2) The system formed by the command posts at different levels of an organization and all lines of signal communication linking them.

communications zone—Rear part of theater of operations (behind but contiguous to the combat zone) that contains the line of communications, establishments for supply and evacuation, and other agencies required for the support and maintenance of combat forces. See also **rear area**.

communication trench—See **trench**.

compagnie d'ordonnance — A medieval French mounted organization, commanded by a captain, consisting of 600 men, organized in *lances* of six men each. Each lance consisted of a knight or man-at-arms, a squire, two archers, a valet, and a page. Because the men were well paid and provided with liberal rations they had no need to pillage. Establishment of the compagnies d'ordonnance was the death knell of feudalism as a military and social system, and the beginning of standing armies and professionalism in modern European warfare.

Companions—An elite cavalry unit of the Macedonian army, so called because Philip, and later Alexander, led them personally in battle.

company—A military organization—particularly in the infantry—consisting of a headquarters and two or more PLATOONS. The next higher unit is usually a BATTALION. An infantry company usually consists of 100 to 200 soldiers. **Ship's company** includes all the officers and sailors assigned to a naval vessel (but not, for instance, members of naval air squadrons on an aircraft carrier, who serve on the ship but have their own organization). In medieval armies, before organization was established, the men who accompanied a lord or knight were known as his "company." Soldiers discharged from service, notably in the 14th century, sometimes formed **free companies** primarily for mercenary service, sometimes for plunder. See also **compagnie d'ordonnance**.

company grade—In the U.S. Army and the Marine Corps, the designation for an officer of rank appropriate for service in or command of a company, usually second lieutenant, first lieutenant, and captain. See also **field grade**.

complement—All the crew required to man a ship or a naval station.

complementary angle of site — See **site, angle of**.

composite bow—See **bow**.

compromise—To expose or reveal classified information or clandestine activities to unauthorized persons, whether done intentionally or inadvertently. A code known to be compromised is immediately discarded for another, unless it is kept alive to feed false information to the enemy.

computer model—See **model, computer**.

concealment—1) Protection from observation. 2) The use of cover, blackout measures, darkness, camouflage, or smoke, or any combination of these, to hide personnel, installations, movements, and the like from enemy observation. 3) The removal of organizational insignia or other identifying marks and the protection of records to keep from the enemy the organizational identity of the troops opposing them. 4) An object, phenomenon, activity, or measure that conceals. The term is often and incorrectly used for COVER.

concentrate—To bring all elements of a combat force together, or close to each other, generally in preparation for action.

concentrated fire—See **fire, concentrated**.

concentration—1) A principle of warfare embodying the doctrine that effective offensive action requires the massing of superior combat power or striking force at a decisive point. 2) The action of massing power or striking force at or against a single point or area. 3) An artillery fire mission against a specified target. See also **mass** and **schwerpunkt**.

concentration area—1) A place, usually in the area of operations, where troops are assembled before beginning active operations. 2) A limited area on which a volume of gunfire is placed within a limited time. See also **concentration**.

concentration camp—A prison camp for the housing of political dissidents or minority ethnic groups. Although the term originated in the Boer War (1899–1902), it is most often associated with Hitler's Germany.

concentric advance—An advance on enemy forces from several directions, so as to bring the separately advancing forces into supporting distance of each other at approximately the same time as they engage the enemy. Usually one or more of the advancing forces is performing an enveloping maneuver.

concentric castles—Castles built with one or more outer walls surrounding an inner KEEP or CITADEL.

concept of operations—A verbal or written statement, in broad outline, of a commander's assumptions or intent in regard to an operation or series of operations. The concept of operations frequently is embodied in campaign plans and operation plans, in the latter case particularly when the plan covers a series of connected operations to be carried out simultaneously or in succession. The concept is designed to give an overall picture of the operation. It is intended to provide additional clarity of purpose, and is frequently referred to as the "commander's concept."

concertina wire—A coil of barbed wire that is compressed for carrying but expands when the constraining band is removed.

U.S. Army photo

concertina wire

concussion fuze—A fuze that detonates a bomb in response to the concussion produced by the explosion of another bomb nearby.

Condor (AGM-53)—An air-to-surface guided missile that provides a standoff launch capability for attack aircraft.

condottiere—The leader of a mercenary band, or FREE COMPANY, in 14th- to 16th-century Italy. Composed of as many as several thousand men, most of them heavily armored cavalry, such bands roamed over Italy, fighting for pay in the wars of the Italian states for whichever side would hire them. When not so employed, they often plundered and fought freely on their own. The term is frequently used for the soldiers as well as their leader.

conduct of fire—The procedure of giving commands to the crew of an artillery piece, battery, or larger unit for the purpose of bringing effective fire on targets.

cone of fire—1) The three-dimensional area on and just above the surface of the ground through and into which fall the bullets or other projectiles of a fixed weapon with a given range and deflection setting. The cone effect is created by the range and deflection dispersion of the projectiles. Usually applied to the lethal area covered by a fixed machine gun. 2) The three-dimensional area covered by the fire of two or more fixed weapons converging on a single point.

confidential—A security classification denoting that unauthorized disclosure of the contents of a document or the characteristics of an object would be prejudicial to the defense interests of a nation.

confinement — Physical restraint under guard in a jail, prison, guardhouse, stockade, or other facility for incarceration of prisoners who are either awaiting trial or serving a sentence imposed by a court.

conflict—A war, or a discrete portion of a war.

conflict levels of intensity — The categories or levels of conflict intensity are as follows: major wars, significant local wars, small wars, minor hostilities, contingencies (both major and minor), engagement, action, high-intensity conflict, low-intensity conflict, and insurgency. A **major war** is a high-intensity conflict between two or more great powers, with the possible involvement of their key allies and with significant national interests of the antagonistic powers at stake. A **significant local war** is a high-intensity conflict in which a great power seeks to protect some aspect of its vital national interests, or in which conflict arises among important regional states, with vital national interests at risk. In a **small war** armed hostilities involve a) a great power in a relatively low-intensity conflict in which there is no significant risk to vital national interests; b) an important regional state in a relatively low intensity conflict in which there is no significant risk to vital national interests; c) civil war or prolonged insurgency in a regional state; or d) hostilities between minor regional states. **Minor hostilities** are a form of low-intensity conflict other than a major war, a significant local war, or a small war. Minor hostilities can include a) limited military expeditions or excursions by major powers or important regional states; b) low-intensity insurgencies; or c) any other low-intensity armed hostilities limited in time and space. **Contingency** is a term used in military planning to designate the possible employment of armed forces in hostilities that might break out at unexpected times or places. From the standpoint of the planner or planning agency, contingencies can be major or minor. A **major contingency** is a military operation involving high-intensity, and probably sustained, hostilities against the forces of one or more great powers or major regional states. Thus it is usually a major war or a significant local war. A **minor contingency** is a military operation involving armed hostilities (other than major wars) limited in time (no more than 6 months) and space (a maximum radius of 1,000 kilometers). A minor contingency consists of one or more engagements or actions and can include a) significant local wars (limited in time and space as specified above), or discrete, limited campaigns or operations within such wars; b) small wars (limited as specified above) or discrete, limited campaigns or operations within such wars; or c) any minor hostilities (limited as specified above). (This definition of military planning for a minor contingency does not include peacekeeping or shows of force, inasmuch as these do not involve hostilities.) An **engagement** is a combat encounter between two forces, whose size is neither larger than a DIVISION nor smaller than a COMPANY, in which each has an assigned or perceived mission that begins when the attacking force initiates action to accomplish its mission. An engagement ends when a) the attacker has accomplished its mission, or b) ceases to attempt to accomplish its mission, or c) one or both forces receive significant reinforcements, thus initiating a new engagement. An engagement is often part of a BATTLE between elements of the division-size or larger forces. An engagement may last only a few hours and is rarely longer than 5 days. An **action** is a minor combat encounter between two small hostile forces, neither of which is larger than a BATTALION or smaller than a SQUAD. An action can last from a few minutes to a few hours, but never lasts more than one day; it ends when one force or the other withdraws or both forces terminate significant combat activity. An action is often part of an engagement or battle between elements of larger forces. **High-intensity conflict** is sustained, armed hostilities between organized military forces, or significant components of those forces, involving frequent combat encounters

in which both sides employ a wide variety of weapons and weapons systems is combined-arms operations. **Low-intensity conflict** involves sporadic or limited armed hostilities between military forces, which may or may not be conventionally organized, in which there may be prolonged lulls between combat encounters or in which the weapons or weapons systems of one or both sides are limited in number, type, or sophistication. An **insurgency** involves intrastate hostilities between forces supporting the government and opposition forces that can be organized, irregular (guerrilla), or both. The intensity of an insurgency can range from that of a significant local war (as in the case of a civil war in a major power) to that of a minor hostility. A military manifestation of internal political unrest or turbulence within a state, it can be brief, but more often, because of the conditions that cause political instability, tends to be prolonged over months or years.

Congreve rocket—A type of rocket developed by British Col. William Congreve at the beginning of the 19th century. The Congreve rocket, given thrust by black powder, resembled a skyrocket, with a stick 12 to 16 feet long, and weighed from 25 to 60 pounds. It was launched from a thin copper tube or trough, had a range of almost 3 miles, and carried a warhead of incendiary material or steel balls for antipersonnel use. Rocket corps soon appeared in European armies. Such corps were used by the British in the War of 1812, and it was the "red glare" of Congreve rockets to which Francis Scott Key referred in "The Star Spangled Banner."

conical bullet—See **ball, minié**.

conn—1) The person directing the helmsman. 2) The act of exerting that authority.

conoidal bullet—See **ball, minié.**

conquer—1) To defeat, particularly a large force or an entire nation, in battle. 2) To gain control by force of arms of territory belonging to another nation.

conquest—1) The act of conquering. 2) The gaining of territory through warfare.

conquistadores—Spanish for "conquerors." Used in English for the Spanish soldiers who conquered Mexico and western South America in the 16th century.

conscientious objector—A person who, for reasons of conscience, including religious and moral scruples, refuses to enter military service or (if in service) refuses to enter combat.

conscript—*n.* A person who is drafted for military service; a draftee. *v.* To cause compulsory enrollment of a person in the military service.

conscription—Involuntary drafting of certain sectors of a population into a nation's armed forces; the draft. It was called "selective service" in the United States and administered at various times in the 20th century under a Selective Service Act. In the French Revolutionary Wars, the term was first used for the enlistment of men for the national armies of France. Conscription was used by the major participants in the Franco-Prussian War of 1870 and in the two world wars.

consolidate—To organize or strengthen a force or a position, particularly a position newly gained in combat.

constable—In West European monarchies since the Middle Ages, a high-ranking officer. In the absence of the king, the constable generally served as military commander.

constitute—To provide the legal authority for the existence of a new unit of the armed services. The new unit is designated and listed but has no specific existence until it is activated.

construction battalion—A unit organized by the U.S. Navy in World War II to construct bases on islands recaptured in the advance toward Japan. Known as "Seabees" after the initials CB, such units contained engineers, construction men, technicians, and other specialists, many of whom were over draft age.

consul—The title of the two highest magistrates of the Roman republic, in whom were vested the executive and military authority of the state. Two consuls were elected each year. They shared responsibility for combat operations, usually exercising command on alternate days. In imperial Rome the office became an honorary one.

consular army—See **army**.

contain—To engage an enemy in combat of sufficient intensity to prevent withdrawal of any part of that force for use elsewhere.

containment—A strategic doctrine that provided a rationale for U.S. policy during most of the Cold War. First enunciated by State Department official George Kennan in 1947, it posited a grand strategy in which the West would not attempt to reverse the post–World War II Soviet gains in Eastern Europe but would resist Soviet expansionism elsewhere.

contamination—The deposit or absorption of radioactive material or biological or chemical agents on and near structures, areas, personnel, or objectives.

Continental Army—The army created in June 1775 by the Continental Congress to represent all the American colonies in the rebellion against Great Britain. In contrast to the colonial militias, this new organization was to be a standing army. George Washington was placed in command.

Continental Navy—The navy established by the Continental Congress in November 1775.

contingency—See **conflict levels of intensity**.

contingency plan—A plan for dealing with one or more developments that can reasonably be expected to arise in a command area.

contingent—A quota or a force, such as personnel or bombers.

contingent effects—The effects, both desirable and undesirable, that are in addition to the primary effects associated with a nuclear detonation.

contingent zone of fire—A zone within the area of fire of an artillery unit other than the normal target zone, on which the unit may have to fire in certain contingencies.

continuous fire—See **fire, continuous**.

contour flying—Low-altitude air operations in which the aircraft follow the terrain to minimize exposure to observation or fire from the ground.

contraband—In the American Civil War, a slave who escaped into the Union lines. By defining such persons as contraband, Union authorities were not responsible for returning them to their owners.

contraband of war—Goods, including ordnance supplies, that a neutral nation cannot supply to a belligerent, except at risk of seizure and confiscation.

contravallation—Defensive works erected around a fortification or walled city, to isolate the besieged installation and to protect the besiegers against sallies by the besieged. See also **circumvallation**.

control—Authority exercised by a commander over the activities of subordinate organizations.

controlled-effects nuclear weapons—Nuclear weapons designed to achieve variation in the intensity of specific effects other than normal blast effect.

controlled exercise—An exercise that is characterized by the imposition of certain constraints by planning authorities in order to provoke certain types of interaction.

control point—1) A position along a route of march where information and instructions for the regulation of supply and traffic are issued. 2) A position that is marked by a buoy, boat, aircraft, electronic device, conspicuous terrain feature, or other identifying object, given a name or number, and used as an aid in navigation for ships, boats, aircraft, or vehicles.

convalescent—A military person recovering from wounds or illness and not yet restored to full duty status.

convention—1) An agreement between two or more nations. 2) An agreement between the commanders of two opposing forces in relation to limitations on military operations.

conventional—1) Nonnuclear. This use of the term has become general, referring to all aspects of warfare that do not involve the use of nuclear weapons (although chemical and biological weapons may also be considered unconventional). 2) Unrelated to insurgency. Used to distinguish operations or forces of a normal combat nature, as opposed to operations or forces of an insurgent or in an INSURGENCY.

converged sheaf of fire — See **sheaf of fire**.

convergent lines of operations — Lines originating at different points and converging on a common objective area so that forces following these lines arrive within supporting distance of each other in the battle area.

convoy—1) One or more merchant vessels or naval auxiliaries escorted by warships and sometimes by aircraft for protection against surface and subsurface attack. 2) A group of military vehicles traveling together for the purpose of control and orderly movement, with or without escort.

convoy escort—1) The warships or combat aircraft traveling in or with a convoy to protect noncombat ships. 2) Armed vehicles accompanying a convoy of vehicles.

convoy loading—The loading of troop units with their equipment and supplies in ships of the same movement group, but not necessarily in the same ship.

coordinates—1) Lines drawn on a map to form a grid by which to locate areas or positions. Coordinates may be related to degrees or minutes of latitude and longitude. They are usually evenly spaced and cross at right angles. 2) The grid values for a specific point on a map.

coordinating point—Designated point at which, in all types of combat, adjacent units or formations must make contact for purposes of control and coordination.

coordination—1) The execution of plans and combat actions of several elements of a command so that their interrelation brings the strongest possible advantage to the command as a whole. 2) Planning for such execution.

coordination of fire—See **fire, coordination of**.

cordite—A smokeless propellant or powder containing nitrocellulose and nitroglycerine, used in some rocket, mortar, or small-arms ammunition.

cordon—A line of soldiers, ships, strongpoints, or other elements placed around an area to deny access to it.

cordon defense—The placement of forces along a defensive line with little or no depth and with insufficient forces available for reserve. See also defense and linear defense.

core state—A nation that serves as a base for a broader political movement outside its borders. The Soviet Union served as a core state for the export of Communism until its collapse in 1991.

corned gunpowder—A granulated mixture of sulfur, saltpeter, and charcoal invented in 1420. When the three elements were held in a steady relationship, with an equal distribution of airspaces, corned gunpowder exploded uniformly and nearly instantaneously.

cornet—1) A British cavalry unit commanded by a captain. 2) The rank of the officer in a cavalry troop who carries the standard, which is also called a cornet.

coronel—A blunt object, often crown-shaped, that was fitted to the point of a lance in jousting. The coronel assured that the lance attached to the opponent's armor, but with minimum penetration.

corporal—1) In nonnaval military forces a noncommissioned rating above private first class and below sergeant. The corporal is the lowest noncommissioned officer. 2) In the British Royal Navy a petty officer who is assistant to the master-at-arms.

corps—1) A specialized branch of one of the armed forces of a nation, like the U.S. Marine Corps, Air Corps, Nurse Corps, or Supply Corps. The students at the U.S. Military Academy are known as the Corps of Cadets. 2) Often used for army corps (see **corps, army**).

corps, army—A tactical unit larger than a DIVISION and smaller than a FIELD ARMY, usually consisting of two or more divisions with auxiliary arms and services.

corps, elite—See **elite corps**.

corpsman—An enlisted person (in the navy, usually with the rating of pharmacist's mate) who is trained to give first aid and some nursing or medical treatment.

corps reserve—See **reserve**.

corps troops—Troops assigned or attached to an army corps but not a part of one of the divisions that make up the corps.

correlation of forces—A Soviet concept of calculating the relative combat power of two opposing forces as a basis for military decision making. It is comparable to the American concept of ESTIMATE OF THE SITUATION, but is more comprehensive and entails a quantitative assessment of all considerations that could affect a combat outcome.

corridor—1) An opening in enemy-controlled territory through which forces may pass in reasonable safety. 2) An **air corridor** is a flight passage for aircraft, especially a passage that either leads through a system of antiaircraft defenses or is established by international agreement. 3) A **terrain corridor** is an area like a valley or an isthmus that permits relatively unhampered movement between terrain features that inhibit movement.

Corsair—A World War II fighter airplane built by Chance Vought. It was flown by the U.S. Navy and had the official designation F4U.

Corsair II (A-7)—A single-engine light attack aircraft designed to operate off carriers.

corselet—Armor that covers and protects the upper torso.

corvette—1) Originally a sailing ship smaller than a FRIGATE, usually carrying guns on only one deck. 2) In modern navies, a ship smaller than a DESTROYER, lightly armed and fast. It is used primarily for antisubmarine missions.

corvus—A combined grappling device and gangway used on Roman war galleys. It was a narrow bridge some 18 feet long, mounted on a pivot near the bow, with a hook or a pointed iron stud on its outboard end to hold the structure to the deck of an enemy vessel. When not in use it was held in a near-vertical position by ropes and pulleys and could be swung outward in any direction. When an enemy ship drew near, the corvus was let down with a crash on the ship's deck, where the gangway was held fast by the iron stud. Immediately, a boarding party stormed across the corvus onto the foe's deck.

cost-effectiveness—A comparative evaluation derived from analyses of alternatives (actions, methods, approaches, equipment, weapon systems, support systems, force combinations, etc.) in terms of the interrelated factors of cost and effectiveness in accomplishing a specific mission.

council of war—A meeting of the senior officers of a military force in combat, called by the commander, usually in an emergency, to seek a majority opinion on tactical or strategic questions. Such a council was common in 18th-century warfare but has been little used in modern times.

countdown—The step-by-step process leading to initiation of an action or an operation. One modern use is in missile testing, launching, and firing. A countdown is performed in accordance with a predesignated schedule.

counter—To make a military move intended to offset a hostile action.

counter air—1) Weapons, tactics, or operations designed to be used against aircraft or hostile air operations. 2) Air attacks, operations, or missions directed against an enemy's air force in an effort to achieve control of the air.

counterapproaches—See **approaches**.

counterattack—Attack by all or a part of a defending force against an enemy attacking force, for such specific purposes as regaining ground lost or cutting off or destroying enemy advance units and with the general objective of denying to the enemy the attainment of his attack objectives. In sustained defensive operations it is undertaken to restore the battle position and is directed at limited objectives.

counterbattery fire—Fire intended to destroy or neutralize enemy artillery weapons. Sometimes called COUNTERBOMBARDMENT.

counterbombardment—See **counterbattery fire**.

counterespionage—A category of COUNTERINTELLIGENCE, the objectives of which are the detection and neutralization of hostile ESPIONAGE.

counterfire — Fire intended to destroy or neutralize enemy weapons, including counterbattery, fire, counterbombardment, and countermortar fire.

counterforce—Employment of strategic nuclear weapons (usually in a first strike) against hostile strategic nuclear weapons to prevent or preempt retaliation.

counterinsurgency—Those military, paramilitary, political, economic, psychological,

and civic actions taken by a government to defeat INSURGENCY.

counterintelligence—The aspect of intelligence activity that attempts to destroy the effectiveness of hostile intelligence activities, in order to protect information against espionage and to prevent subversion against individuals and sabotage against installations or material. The character of counterintelligence activity can be both offensive and defensive. In its defensive mode, it addresses the questions, "What does hostile intelligence activity seek to accomplish?" and "How are hostile espionage operations conducted?" In its offensive mode, it undertakes operations aimed at thwarting the endeavors of hostile espionage agents.

countermand—To issue an order canceling or reversing a previous order.

countermarch—*n.* A march back toward the point of origin. *v.* To march back in the direction from which one has come.

countermeasure—A device or technique that operates to impair the operational effectiveness of enemy activity. Countermeasures may include such diverse operations as tactical maneuvers, electronic jamming procedures, and defensive field fortifications.

countermine—*n.* 1) A mine or tunnel dug to intercept and destroy a mine being dug by an opposing force. 2) An explosive device designed to cause an enemy's mines to detonate. *v.* 1) To dig a countermine. 2) To place a countermining device.

counteroffensive—A large-scale offensive undertaken by a defending force to seize the initiative from the attacking force.

counterpreparation fire—Intensive, prearranged fire delivered when it is discovered or assumed that an enemy attack is imminent. It is designed to break up enemy formations; disorganize the enemy's system of command, communications, and observation; decrease the effectiveness of his artillery preparation; and impair his offensive spirit.

counterscarp—The side of a ditch, moat, or trench that faces the enemy or the expected direction of attack.

countersign—The response to a secret sign or challenge given by a sentry. A PASSWORD.

country team—The senior coordinating and supervising body of a U.S. mission in a foreign country. It is headed by the ambassador or other chief of diplomatic mission and is composed of the senior representatives of each department or agency.

coup de main—A sudden, vigorous, and successful attack to seize a hostile position or defended locality.

coup d'état—Vigorous action, usually violent and usually military or involving the use of military force, to overthrow a legal government and replace it with a new governing authority.

coup d'oeil—The capability of a military commander to make a rapid and accurate estimate of a combat situation. See also **estimate of the situation**.

courier—A messenger responsible for the secure physical transmission and delivery of documents, messages, or materials.

course of action—1) Any sequence of acts that an individual or a unit may follow. 2) A possible plan open to an individual or commander that would accomplish or is related to the accomplishment of a mission. 3) The scheme adopted to accomplish a job or mission. 4) A line of conduct in an engagement.

court-martial—1) A body of military personnel designated by the proper authority as a court to conduct the military trial of persons subject to military law. 2) Trial by such a court. There are three types of court-martial, distinguished by the authority empowered to convene them and the punishments they can impose: **general court-martial, special court-martial,** and **summary court-martial**. The **general court-martial** is the highest type of court-martial in the U.S. armed services. It consists of at least five members not including the law officer and has the power to try any offense punishable by the Uniform Code of Military Justice. A **special court-martial** consists of a law officer and at least three members and has jurisdiction over the trial for any crime or offense that is not capital but is punishable by the Uniform Code of Military Justice. A **summary court-martial**, composed of one officer, may impose punishment of confinement for up to one month, hard labor without confinement for up to 45 days, restriction for up to 2 months, and forfeiture for up to two thirds of one month's pay.

cover—*n.* Protection or shelter, whether natural or created by military action, from hostile fire. *v.* 1) To provide protection for a military force through action by land, air, or naval forces, such as artillery fire or close air support. 2) To maintain a continuous radio receiver watch.

covered way—A protected line of communication, such as a communications trench or a concrete-walled trench or tunnel in a permanent or armored fortification system.

covering fire—1) Fire to suppress hostile weapons, used to protect friendly troops when they are within range of enemy small arms. 2) In amphibious usage, fire delivered prior to the landing to cover preparatory operations, such as underwater demolitions or minesweeping.

covering force—1) A force operating apart from the main force for the purpose of intercepting, engaging, delaying, disorganizing, or deceiving the enemy before he can attack the main force. 2) Any body or detachment of troops that provides security for a larger force by observation, reconnaissance, attack, or defense, or by any combination of these methods.

covert operations—Operations so planned and executed as to conceal the identity of, or permit plausible denial by, the sponsor. Covert operations differ from clandestine operations in that emphasis is placed on concealment of the identity of sponsor rather than on concealment of the operation.

coxswain—A naval enlisted rating corresponding to boatswain's mate third class.

CP—See **command post**.

CPX—See **command post exercise**.

cranequin—A form of crossbow winder, used primarily in Germany.

crash dive—An emergency submergence by a submarine.

crater—The pit, depression, or cavity formed in the surface of the earth by an explosion. It may range from saucer-shaped to conical, depending largely on the depth of burst. In the case of a deep underground blast, when no rupture of the surface may occur, the cavity is termed a CAMOUFLET.

C-ration—A U.S. Army meal consisting of several prepared items, usually canned, issued when troops are out of range of field kitchens.

crease—See **kris**.

crenel—See **battlements**.

crest, military—1) A line on the forward slope of a hill or ridge from which maximum observation of the terrain in front can be obtained without the exposure of a standing observer by being outlined against the geographic crest. 2) An emblem, such as a coat of arms, on the hat or helmet of a uniformed or armored soldier.

crew—1) All officers and enlisted personnel assigned to a naval vessel or an aircraft. Sometimes the term refers only to enlisted personnel. 2) A detail or team manning or serving a piece of equipment like an artillery piece or performing specific duties.

crew-served—Operated by two or more soldiers, such as an artillery piece.

critical altitude — The altitude beyond which an aircraft or air-breathing guided missile ceases to perform satisfactorily.

critique—A critical discussion of a mission just performed, emphasizing mistakes and successes.

crocodile—A World War II Allied tank with a flame gun in place of the forward machine gun. The tank towed a two-wheeled armored trailer that contained the flame fuel. Approximately 100 one-second shots of flame were possible before replenishment. Maximum range was 100 yards.

crossbow—A weapon consisting of a bow permanently fixed transversely on a stock, with various devices for drawing back and releasing the cord of string, and a groove that holds and guides an arrow or bolt. The crossbow is known to have been used in China before the Christian era. The oldest surviving examples in the West are from France, dating to the 1st or 2nd century A.D. Crossbows were widely used in the Middle Ages, from the 10th century on. Their use was prohibited against Christians (but not against infidels) by Pope Innocent II in the 12th century, but they continued in use well after the introduction of gunpowder and are still used for hunting. The medieval crossbow had a range of up to 300 yards. The typical arrow was the "quarrel," a short, heavy arrow with a quadrangular pointed tip. In metallic form (usually iron), the quarrel was called a "bolt." The stabilizing fletchings were generally wood, leather, or brass. Fired from a crossbow, an arrow could pierce even fairly heavy armor. See also **bow** and **longbow**.

crossbowman—A soldier armed with a crossbow.

crossbowman

crossfire—Fire from two or more weapons (which may be firing against each other) that crosses in transit to the target or targets.

crossing the T—A naval maneuver from the days of sailing ships in which a fleet sailing in line ahead (single file) crossed at right angles in front of an enemy fleet. The fleet executing the maneuver could bring the full broadside fire of all its ships to bear on the enemy, whereas the enemy could fire only the bow guns of his lead ships. It was a difficult maneuver to accomplish because the fleet under attack could turn away out of range before the attacking fleet crossed the T. The maneuver figured in several modern naval battles between steam-driven battleships, including Tsushima (1905), Jutland (1916), and Leyte Gulf (1944).

cross loading—A system of loading troops so that different units may be disembarked or dropped at two or more landing or drop zones, thereby assuring unit integrity upon delivery.

cross servicing—Any function performed by one military service in support of another military service for which reimbursement is required from the service receiving support.

"crow"—Slang for **chevron**.

crowfoot—See **caltrop**.

cruise missile—See **missile, cruise**.

cruiser—1) A fast warship, larger, heavier, and more heavily armed than a destroyer but smaller, lighter, and with less firepower and armor than a battleship. 2) A privateer of the 18th century. Modern cruisers are generally classed as light or heavy. A **light cruiser** in the U.S. Navy is a warship with 6-inch naval guns or surface-to-air missiles as the main battery. It is designed to operate with strike, antisubmarine, or amphibious forces against air and surface threats. Full-load displacement is approximately 18,000 tons. It is designated by the U.S. Navy as CL. A **heavy cruiser** is a warship designed to operate with strike, antisubmarine warfare, or amphibious forces against air and surface threats. Main battery consists of 8-inch guns, and full load displacement is approximately 21,000 tons. It is designated by the U.S. Navy as CA.

cruiser, battle—See **battle cruiser**.

cruiser, guided missile (CG)—A warship designed to operate with strike and amphibious forces. Its normal armament consists of 5-inch guns, an area defense antiaircraft missile system, and antisubmarine weapons.

crusade—1) Any of several military expeditions launched from the 11th through the 14th century with the objective of recovering the Holy Land from the Moslems. Crusades were undertaken by European Christians with the sanction of several popes. 2) A European Christian military expedition, during the same general period, directed at pagans, infidels, or heretics outside the Holy Land. Examples were the operations of the Teutonic Knights against the Slavs in Prussia and Lithuania (13th and 14th centuries), the Albigensian Crusade (1203–26), and the Crusade of Nicopolis (1396).

Crusader—1) A British light tank used early in World War II. 2) A self-propelled 155mm howitzer designed by the United States in the 1990s for employment against enemy armor. Seen by the U.S. Army as an essential modernization of its artillery, the original Crusader weighed 55 tons exclusive of its ammunition vehicle. The system was deemed too cumbersome for 21st-century threats and was canceled by the Defense Department in 2002.

crusaders—Warriors who were taking part in a crusade.

cryptanalysis—The deciphering of encoded or encrypted messages, particularly those of an enemy or another nation, and the translating of them into plain language.

cryptologic technician—A warrant officer specialist in the U.S. Navy.

cub—1) In World War II, an advanced base unit consisting of all the personnel and material necessary for establishing a medium-size advanced fuel and supply base. 2) Military slang in World War II for light artillery observation aircraft.

cuirass—Armor for protecting the upper torso. Normally the term refers to a piece that covers both front and back, but it is sometimes used for the breastplate alone.

cuirassier—A European mounted soldier equipped with a cuirass. Most cuirassiers were armed with a heavy saber; cuirassiers armed with lances were usually designated as heavy lancers.

cuisse—A thigh-protecting piece of plate armor developed in the 14th century.

culverin—1) An early musket. 2) A long-barreled, thick-walled artillery piece of the 16th and 17th centuries, designed to fire accurately at long range. Measuring about 11 feet long and weighing about 4,800 pounds, with a bore 5.5 inches in diameter, the culverin fired an 18-pound projectile a maximum of about 6,700 yards. Its point-blank range was 1,700 yards.

cupola—A fixed fortress gun emplacement with overhead armored cover, like a naval turret, usually with 360-degree traverse. The Belgian engineer Henri Alexis Brialmont devised a **disappearing cupola** so that the entire gun with its protective casing could be withdrawn. The cupola traverses with the gun, which may be run out through an opening and withdrawn when not in use.

curtail—A short cannon.

curtain—The portion of a RAMPART or PARAPET or wall between two bastions or gates.

curtain of fire—See **barrage**.

cutlass—A short saber or sword with a slightly curved, single-edged broad blade, especially used by sailors, who found it easy to carry while boarding an enemy vessel and effective in fighting at close quarters.

cutout (intelligence)—An intermediary designed to avoid direct contact between members of a clandestine organization.

cutter—1) A small, single-masted sailing vessel. 2) A ship's boat, next in size to the launch, used for general ship duty. 3) A small, lightly armed vessel used by the U.S. Coast Guard for patrolling and other duties.

cyberterrorism/cyberwarfare — Attacks against Internet-connected defense-related computer systems. The information warfare arsenal includes various computer worms, viruses, and logic bombs, which can be placed in the computer networks of an enemy to paralyze his defenses and shut down power and phone service. Cyberweapons are an alternative to conventional weapons that ROGUE STATES or terrorist groups can employ to cause massive damage to a major power without great expenditure. "Cyber-" words derive from "cybernetics."

cyclic rate—Rate of fire of an automatic weapon, usually in rounds per minute.

D

dagger—A thrusting hand weapon, with a short, usually double-edged, blade. The length varies greatly, and there is little distinction between a long dagger and a short sword. Modern equivalents of the military dagger are the BAYONET and the TRENCH-KNIFE.

Dahlgren gun—A cast-iron cannon invented by U.S. naval officer John A. Dahlgren in the mid-19th century, and used by the U.S. Navy and the U.S. Army in coastal defense installations. A SMOOTHBORE gun, it derived its nickname, "Soda Water Bottle," from its shape.

"Daisy Cutter"—A 15,000-pound bomb used in Vietnam and Afghanistan. Set to explode a short distance above the ground, it can clear jungle and foliage over a wide area.

damage assessment—1) A determination of the effect of attacks on targets. 2) A determination of the effect of a compromise of classified information on the national security.

damage control—In naval usage, measures necessary aboard ships to deal with damage caused by accident or hostile action. The objectives are to preserve and reestablish watertight integrity, stability, maneuverability, and offensive power; to control list and trim; to effect rapid repairs of matériel; to limit the spread of, and provide adequate protection from, fire; to limit the spread of, remove the contamination by, and provide adequate protection from toxic and radiological agents; and to provide for the care of wounded personnel.

Damascus steel—Steel of great tensile strength and flexibility that was originally produced in Damascus and highly prized for sword blades. It was first imported to Europe from the Middle East around the 8th century A.D. It is sometimes called damask steel. Similar sword-blade steel was also produced in Toledo, Spain, following the Arab conquest of Iberia.

dart—A small missile with a sharp point and often with tail fins. Darts may be thrown by hand or fired with a blowgun, crossbow, or other device.

date of rank—The date from which an officer or noncommissioned officer (NCO) holds a given rank. This is the basis for determining seniority among officers or NCOs holding the same rank.

date-time group—An item in military messages; the date and time are expressed in six digits followed by the time-zone identification letter, used to identify the time at which a message was prepared for transmission through military communication channels. An example is 011210Z; the first pair of digits denotes the day, the second pair the hour, and the third pair the minutes; the letter is the international time-zone suffix.

datum point—Any reference point of known or assumed coordinates from which measurements may be taken.

day of supply—The quantity of a given supply commodity adopted as a standard of measurement of expected consumption of that commodity by a unit; used for planning purposes in estimating the average daily expenditure under stated conditions. It may also be expressed in terms of a factor (e.g., rounds of ammunition per weapon per day). For ammunition it is sometimes called a "day of fire."

day room—A room in barracks set aside for the use of soldiers or airmen during their leisure.

dazzle—Temporary loss of vision, or a temporary reduction in visual acuity.

D-day—The unnamed day on which an operation is to begin. The best known D-day is 6 June 1944, the beginning of the Allied invasion of northern France in World War II.

National Archives photo
U.S. soldiers leave a Coast Guard landing boat and head for a French beach on 6 June 1944.

D-day

dead angle—An angle from which an air gunner is unable to direct fire. This situation may be due to equipment failure or to a blind spot.

deadline—*v.* To remove a vehicle or piece of equipment from operation or use for one of the following reasons: a) that it is inoperative because of damage or malfunction, b) that it is unsafe, or c) that it would be damaged by further use. (Note: The term may be used in the sense the "vehicle is deadlined.") *n.* The date or hour at which an action or undertaking must be completed.

dead space—1) An area within the maximum range of a weapon, radar, or observer that cannot be covered by fire or observed

from a particular position, usually because of the intervention of a barrier to fire or observation (as a hill mass), or the technical characteristics (usually ballistic) of a weapon. 2) An area or a zone that is within range of a radio transmitter but in which no signal is received. 3) The volume of space above and around a gun or guided missile system into which it cannot fire because of mechanical or electronic limitations.

death march—Any wantonly cruel treatment of prisoners in transit. The term is often associated with the treatment accorded U.S. prisoners by the Japanese in the Philippines in April 1942 during the Bataan Death March.

debouch—To pass into an open area after marching through a narrow passage or DEFILE.

debriefing—The interrogation and extraction of information from a colleague or intelligence asset.

decamp—To break camp and move on.

"decapitation"—Military action aimed at removing the leadership of a government and thus destabilizing it. An example from the 2003 Gulf War was the first-day air strike on a command headquarters on March 20, 2003, designed to kill or incapacitate Saddam Hussein and his senior leaders.

deception—Measures designed to mislead the enemy by manipulation, distortion, or falsification of evidence in order to induce him to react in a manner prejudicial to his interests.

decimation—In ancient Roman armies, a punishment sometimes inflicted for mutiny or other serious misdeeds. It consisted of selecting every 10th man by lot and executing him. The term has more recently come to be used loosely, with varying degrees of acceptance, to describe heavy losses.

deck court—A disciplinary body in the U.S. Navy for the trial of offenses by enlisted men considered too serious for decision at a CAPTAIN'S MAST, but not serious enough for a SUMMARY COURT-MARTIAL. The deck court was abolished when the Uniform Code of Military Justice went into effect in 1951.

declaration of war—The formal announcement by a belligerent that a state of war exists between it and its adversaries. According to the Hague Convention of 1907, hostilities must not begin "without previous and explicit warning in the form of a reasoned declaration of war." Nevertheless, hostilities in the latter half of the 20th century often were initiated without any formal declaration.

decontamination—The process of making any person, object, or area safe by removing, destroying or neutralizing chemical, biological, or radioactive contaminants.

decoration, military — Tangible recognition of extraordinary achievement. Decorations are awarded for extraordinary feats in battle or in noncombat activities and for outstanding accomplishment in line of duty. (Decorations should not be confused with service medals, which testify to participation in certain wars or battles.) In the United States most decorations include a medal on a ribbon of specific design and a separate ribbon of the same design on a pin. On the ordinary uniform the ribbon alone is worn. If the wearer is entitled to wear more than one, the highest-ranking one is placed at the right of the top row, with others following in sequence of rank of decoration, followed by service medals or ribbons in order of chronological award. Miniature medals and ribbons are worn with evening dress. Only with the full-dress uniform is the full-size decoration worn. A few decorations, among them the highest military decoration in the United States, the MEDAL OF HONOR, are worn with full dress on ribbons around the neck. See also **service medal**.

decoy ship—See **Q-ship**.

decrypt—To convert encrypted text into its equivalent plain text by means of a cryptosystem.

decurion—1) In the early Roman army, the officer in command of 10 cavalrymen. 2) In imperial Rome the officer in charge of a TURMA of 30 to 40 cavalrymen.

deep attack—Application of force or firepower deep behind enemy lines by means of air attacks, long-range surface fire, infiltration, or airborne operation. See also **follow-on forces attack**.

deep penetration—The action of a military force in advancing a considerable distance into enemy-held territory either on the ground or in the air on a military mission. A force making a deep penetration may maintain an overland line of communications with the main force from which the penetration was initiated. When overland communications are not maintained, the operation is a kind of RAID. Examples are Grierson's Raid of the American Civil War and the **long-range penetration** operations of the CHINDITS in Burma during World War II.

deep-penetration bomb—A bomb so designed and fuzed as to penetrate a significant distance into a target before exploding.

deep submergence rescue vehicle (DSRV)—A miniature submarine designed to operate at extreme depths to rescue the crew of a disabled submarine. It is 49 feet long and displaces 38 tons.

defeat—Failure in combat, including one or a combination of the following conditions: failing to accomplish an assigned mission, suffering excessive casualties, and losing important terrain or resources. The consequences of defeat are increasingly serious at higher levels of combat. Thus, defeat in an engagement need not necessarily affect the outcome of a conflict, but defeat in a war could cause the collapse of a national government and irreparably damage a nation's social, political, and economic systems.

defeat in detail—*n.* The overcoming of the various parts or elements of a force one at a time, particularly when the parts are not close together. *v.* To overcome the separate parts of a force in turn.

defense—1) Resistance to attack; the opposite of offense. 2) Structures, tactics, or maneuvers whose purpose is to protect against attack. 3) Barring the way to the enemy or breaking his attack by the use of fire while taking advantage of the terrain in order to stop or delay him. The most important kinds of defense are as follows: **active air defense**—Direct defensive action taken to destroy attacking enemy aircraft or missiles or to nullify or reduce the effectiveness of such attack. **active defense**—The employment of limited offensive action and counterattacks to deny a contested area or position to the enemy. **area defense**—Defense of a general area, in contrast to defense of critically important points, as in "point defense." **cordon defense**—The siting of forces over the front line that have little or no depth and have insufficient reserve forces on hand. **deliberate defense**—A defense normally organized when out of contact with the enemy or when contact with the enemy is not imminent and there is time for organization. It normally includes an extensive fortified zone incorporating pillboxes, forts, and communications systems. **defense in depth**—The siting of mutually supporting defense positions in a zone extending back from the front line of contact with the enemy. It is designed to absorb and weaken progressively the force of attack, to prevent immediate observation of the defender's whole position by the enemy, and to allow the commander to maneuver his reserve. **fortified defense**—A comprehensive, coordinated defense system prepared by a defender having sufficient time to complete planned entrenchments, field fortifications, and obstacles in such a manner as to permit the most effective possible employment of defensive firepower. **hasty defense**—A defense organized while in contact with the enemy or when contact is imminent and there is little time to execute the organization. It is characterized by improvement of the natural defensive strength of the terrain by use of foxholes, emplacements, and obstacles; if occupied for a protracted period, the hasty defense position can be improved to the status of prepared or fortified defense. **mobile defense**— That defense in which minimum forces are deployed forward to find out when an attack is impending and warn the main forces of it, to canalize the attacking forces into less favorable terrain, and to impede and harass them so as to cause their disorganization. The preponderance of the combat power of the main, defending force is held conveniently in the rear and employed in vigorous offensive action to destroy the enemy at a decisive time and place. The mobile defense is a special case of the defense in depth. **passive defense**—Nonviolent or noncombat means of defense, such as the use of camouflage or the burying of telephone lines to protect them from hostile fire. **prepared defense**—A defense system prepared by a defender who has had sufficient time to organize the defensive position but, because of a lack of time or resources, with less than the strength of a fortified position.

Defense Advanced Research Projects Agency (DARPA)—The U.S. defense agency responsible for developing the technology for future weapon systems. It was created in 1958 in reaction to the success of *Sputnik*, the first Soviet space satellite.

defense area—See **area**.

defense attaché—See **attaché, military**.

defense classification—See **security classification**.

defense in depth—See **defense**.

Defense Intelligence Agency (DIA) — An agency of the U.S. Defense Department and a member of the U.S. intelligence community. It specializes in monitoring the defense establishments of foreign powers.

defense readiness conditions (DEF-CON)—A series of progressive alert postures for use within the U.S. Department of Defense. Defense readiness conditions are graduated in consideration of international conditions, with DEFCON 1 the highest state of readiness and DEFCON 5 the lowest.

defensive-offensive—A planned operation in which a military force in defensive posture is prepared to assume the offensive in a counterattack or counteroffensive. The occasion for such a change in posture might be anticipated fatigue on the part of the attacker, the exposed position of his forces or lines of communication, or the disruption of his offensive by an ambush.

defensive position—1) Any area occupied and organized for defense. 2) A battle position. 3) A system of mutually supporting defensive areas or tactical localities of varying size, each having a definite assignment of troops and a mission. A defensive position may be fortified and otherwise organized to the extent that the situation requires or time allows.

defilade—*n.* Protection from hostile observation and fire provided by an obstacle such as a hill, ridge, or bank. *v.* To shield from enemy fire or observation by using natural or artificial obstacles.

defile—*n.* 1) A natural or an artificial terrain feature that canalizes movement. Defiles frequently occur in mountain passes, woods, jungles, towns, river crossings, lake regions, and swamp areas. 2) A march in single file or a column of files. *v.* To march in single file or a column of files.

deflection—1) The turning aside of a moving object from its course by reason of an outside force being exerted upon it (e.g., the force of a crosswind on the trajectory of an artillery shell or a falling bomb). 2) A setting on a bombsight that allows for deflection and permits sighting on the target or on an offset of the target. 3) In gunnery, the horizontal angle between the aiming point and the target. 4) The lead given a projectile from a weapon aimed at a moving target. 5) The direction in which a weapon is fired or is firing.

deflection error—The angle or distance measured between an imaginary line from the gun, drawn through the target or expected point of impact and an imaginary line drawn through the actual point of impact.

deflection pattern—Naval equivalent of a SHEAF OF FIRE.

defoliate—To remove, or cause the removal of, the leaves of a tree or other plant, especially by the use of a chemical or biological spray or dust, known as a **defoliant**. The process and the result are **defoliation**.

degauss—To surround a ship with an electric coil through which a current can be passed that effectively neutralizes the ship's induced magnetic field and prevents it from detonating a magnetic mine. Degaussing was highly effective in reducing losses to mines in World War II. The name derives from the unit used to measure magnetic induction, the gauss, which had been named for Carl Friedrich Gauss, the German scientist who developed it. See also **deperm**.

degradation—A reduction in strength, rank, value, or capability.

delayed-action fuze—See **fuze**.

delaying action — A RETROGRADE MOVEMENT in which the defender inflicts maximum damage on an advancing enemy and delays him in order to gain time for his own withdrawal, but without becoming decisively

engaged in combat or being outflanked. Also known simply as **delay.**

delaying operation—A tactic by which a force under pressure trades space for time by slowing down the enemy's momentum by forcing him to deploy and maneuver, and inflicting maximum damage on him without becoming decisively engaged. The operation is usually undertaken by covering forces and other security attachments, and it is executed most effectively by highly mobile troops. Obstacles covered by fire are generally used to reinforce the delaying capability. Delaying operations are usually marked by deliberate, sequential withdrawal of the defender from one position to another, defending each successive position only long enough to force the attacker to deploy and prepare his forces for a major attack, and then withdrawing to the next position before the defending forces are pinned down. A classic example is the German delay of Allied offensives in Italy in 1943 and 1944 in World War II.

deliberate attack—See **attack**.

deliberate defense—See **defense**.

delivery error—The inaccuracy of a weapon system that results in a dispersion of shot outside the aiming point.

Delta—Letter of NATO phonetic alphabet. See also **alphabet, phonetic**.

demibrigade—A military unit devised in 1793 by Gen. Lazare Carnot for the French army of the revolutionary period (1792–80), the demibrigade was a grouping of three BATTALIONs, two of volunteers or conscripts and one of regular soldiers from the old Royal Army. The intention was to stiffen the untrained conscripts by the addition and example of professional soldiers. Ten years later, demibrigades were designated as regiments, two of them being combined to form a brigade.

demiculverin—An artillery piece of the 16th and 17th centuries constructed to the same general design as a CULVERIN. Its length was 8.5 feet, its weight 3,400 pounds; it had a 4.2-inch bore, a point-blank range of 850 yards, and a maximum range of 5,000 yards. Its projectile weighed 10 pounds.

demilitarized zone (DMZ)—A defined area in which the stationing or concentrating of military forces, or the retention or establishment of military installations of any description, is prohibited.

demilune — A crescent-shaped defensive structure, usually built at the entrance to a fort. The name, meaning "half moon," came to be applied to any structure designed to defend an entrance.

demisaker—See **minion**.

demobilization—The reversion of a person or a force from military to civilian status. "Demobilization" may also be used to mean the reversion of all sectors of a nation's economy from a wartime to a peacetime basis.

demolition—The destruction of structures, facilities, or material by use of fire, water, explosives, mechanical, or other means.

demonstration—1) An attack or show of force on a front where a decision is not sought, made with the aim of deceiving the enemy. 2) In an amphibious operation, an exhibition of force that may be a feint or a minor attack.

demotion—Reduction in rank or rating.

denial operation—Action to hinder or deny an enemy the use of space, personnel, or facilities. It may include destruction, removal, contamination, or erection of obstructions.

denied area—An area under enemy or unfriendly control in which friendly forces cannot expect to operate successfully within existing operational constraints.

dependent—A person, usually a spouse, parent, or child, recognized by military regulations as having a claim upon an officer or an enlisted man or woman for support. The term is often used as an adjective, as in "dependent housing," "dependent travel."

deperm—Action to reduce the permanent magnetic field of a ship. Deperming is done during construction and before installation of degaussing gear. See also **degauss**.

deploy—1) In a strategic or tactical sense, to place forces in desired positions or areas of operations. 2) To change from an approach march, or a cruising approach, to a battle formation. 3) To extend the front of a unit, as in changing from column to line. 4) To extend a unit both laterally and in depth, or to increase intervals or distances, or both. The act of deploying is **deployment.**

depot—A facility for the receipt, classification, storage, accounting, issuance, maintenance, procurement, manufacture, assembly, or salvage of supplies, or for the reception, processing, training, assignment, and forwarding of personnel replacements. It may be an installation or activity of the ZONE OF THE INTERIOR or **area of operations**.

depth bomb — See **bomb** and **depth charge**.

depth charge—Any charge designed for explosion under water, especially such a charge dropped or catapulted from a ship's deck.

deputy—An assistant or aide with authority to make decisions in the absence of the officer whose deputy he or she is.

desert—To leave one's post or ship without permission or orders, and without intention of returning. (Differs from ABSENT WITHOUT LEAVE in terms of intent.) The person who so leaves is a **deserter.**

Desert Shield, Operation—The initial response of the United States and its allies to Iraq's invasion of Kuwait on 2 August 1990. Operation Desert Shield became the largest U.S. military deployment since the Vietnam War. On 17 January 1991, when it became clear that Iraq would not withdraw from Kuwait, Desert Shield became DESERT STORM.

Desert Storm, Operation — The U.S.-led response to Iraq's 1990 invasion of Kuwait. In Operation Desert Storm (February 1991), a U.S.-led coalition expelled the Iraqis from Kuwait and decisively defeated the Iraqi armed forces but failed to oust Iraqi leader Saddam Hussein.

destroy—To damage a person, a force, or an object to the extent that it can no longer function in its normal or intended purpose and cannot be readily restored to its previous condition. See also **destruction** and **annihilate**.

destroyer—A fast warship smaller than a CRUISER, generally armed with 3-inch or 5-inch guns, surface-to-surface missiles, torpedoes, and antisubmarine weapons. The destroyer is a versatile craft that can operate offensively—with strike forces, hunter-killer groups, and in support of amphibious assault operations—or defensively as escort for convoys and larger naval vessels. In order to perform these and other missions, destroyers are built and armed in many different configurations. The U.S. Navy's designation for a destroyer is DD. The first destroyers, introduced in the 1890s to combat the threat of the motor torpedo boat, were called **torpedo boat destroyers**, hence the modern name.

destroyer-escort—A fast warship similar to but smaller than a destroyer. Like the destroyer, the destroyer-escort is versatile but particularly useful for convoy protection. The U.S. Navy's designation is DE.

destroyer, guided-missile (DDG)—A type of destroyer equipped with Standard guided missiles, naval guns, long-range sonar, and antisubmarine weapons.

destruction—1) The action of so damaging a person, a force, or an object that it can no longer function in its normal or intended purpose and cannot be readily restored to its previous condition. 2) The action considered as a military objective or as a capability of a military force.

destruction fire—1) Fire delivered for the sole purpose of destroying objects not enemy troops. 2) The field artillery technique for placing the center of impact of a gun on a target. See also **precision fire**.

detach—To separate a person or unit from the organization to which one is regularly assigned. In the U.S. Army and Air Force this is a temporary separation. See also **detached duty**.

detached duty—A temporary duty assignment for a military person.

detached unit—A unit serving away from the higher organization to which it is assigned.

detachment—1) A part of a military unit separated from its main organization for duty elsewhere. 2) A temporary military or naval unit formed from other units or parts of units. 3) The act of forming such a unit.

detail—*n.* 1) A duty, normally noncombat, to which one or more troops or sailors are assigned, such as kitchen detail or clean-up detail. 2) The selection of people for such duty. 3) The people so selected. *v.* To assign to a specific duty.

detection—The act or action of discovering and locating that which is hidden or obscure, especially an enemy's equipment, installations, and the like, or his electronic signals, as of radar or radio.

deter—To restrain an opponent, or potential opponent, from a course of action by displaying the harmful or disastrous consequences of retaliation that would be inflicted if he undertook that course of action. In a military sense, "deter" usually means to restrain from initiating a war or a major escalation of a war.

deterrence—The situation or action that deters an opponent or potential opponent from a course of action. Deterrence is used especially with respect to the restraints that prevent a nation from using nuclear weapons as a result of the fear of receiving a nuclear attack in response.

detonate—1) To cause the instantaneous combustion of an explosive material. 2) To explode.

detonator—A device that causes the explosion of the active ingredient in a round of ammunition. Basic to the development of effective detonators was an invention of Alfred Nobel, which used gunpowder or a fulminate to detonate a high explosive.

device—An insignia that identifies military personnel by service, unit, rank, specialty, experience, distinction, or the like—for instance, cap devices, shoulder patches, combat badges.

DEW—See **Distant Early Warning line**.

diamond—A formation in which four units or aircraft proceed with one unit in advance, followed by a unit each to the left and the right, with the fourth unit farther to the rear, directly behind the leader. When applied to aircraft, it is generally called a **diamond box**.

diekplus—An ancient Greek naval maneuver in which a vessel, when about to ram an enemy galley, would suddenly back water on one side, causing its bow to sweep across and break the enemy's oars and his steering paddle, then turn forward again and proceed to ram.

digital topographic support system (DTSS)—A mobile terrain analysis system for use on the battlefield. It combines digital maps with ancillary data from a number of sources to display real-time map updates and other topographical products.

diphosgene—A type of poison gas used in warfare.

direct action—Short-duration strikes and other small-scale offensive operations designed to inflict damage in enemy-held areas.

direct fire—Gunfire delivered directly on a target that is visible to the person who aims the gun.

directing staff—In British usage, a group of officers who are members of the faculty of a military school or college or who are responsible for conducting and controlling a field exercise.

directive—Any oral or written communication that initiates, orders, or governs action, conduct, or procedure or that provides a plan of action in certain contingencies. Various kinds of orders and other publications when directive in nature are often called directives, including general orders, special orders, and court-martial orders.

direct laying—The act of aligning the sight of a weapon with a target in DIRECT FIRE.

director—A calculating machine or computer designed to convert commands, radar reports, and sensings into commands that will place fire accurately on a target. Usually used for naval and antiaircraft gunfire.

director fire—In naval gunfire and antiaircraft artillery fire, the method of training and elevating the guns in a battery in accordance with signals transmitted by a DIRECTOR or master gun to the guns.

direct support—An action in which one force, especially artillery (**direct fire support**) or an air unit (**direct air support**), uses its weapons to provide assistance to another. An artillery unit in direct support of an infantry or armor maneuver unit is not usually attached to that unit but is expected to dedicate all of its fire support capability to the directly supported unit, unless given other orders by a higher commander. See also **general support**.

dirigible—A lighter-than-air craft with a rigid metal frame inside to strengthen and shape the gas bag. Dirigibles, called zeppelins (after their designer), were used by Germany in World War I to bomb England. The dramatic burning of the *Hindenburg* (1937), which was used for commercial transport, was one of several disasters that led to abandonment of the zeppelin as a military aircraft. See also **blimp**.

dirk—A short Scottish dagger, also used as a knife, carried by Scottish Highlanders and by British naval officers and midshipmen with nondress uniforms.

dirty bomb—A device in which radioactive materials are packed around a core of conventional explosives. Iraq and some Islamic terrorist organizations are believed to have experimented with such devices. The long-term health effects of exposure to the radiation from a dirty bomb are unknown.

disappearing cupola—See **cupola**.

disappearing gun—An emplaced gun that emerges from cover and concealment, fires, and then, utilizing the force of recoil, is automatically or mechanically withdrawn from sight, usually behind a parapet. This was a typical coastal-defense weapon of the early 20th century.

disarm—1) To remove or disassemble the detonating mechanism of an explosive device. 2) To relieve an armed person of all weapons.

disarmament—1) The voluntary or compulsory laying down of arms by a force or a nation. 2) The elimination of all weapons and war-making capability of a nation or group of nations by treaty or by compulsion. See also **arms control**.

disaster assistance response team (DART)—The U.S. Agency for International Development provides this rapidly deployable team to respond to international disasters. It may include specialists drawn from the military services.

disband—To disperse the members of an established unit or a force that could be of any size and formed for any purpose.

discharge—*v.* 1) To fire a weapon. 2) To release from active duty. *n.* 1) Release from active duty, and the document that proclaims it. In the U.S. armed forces there are several types of discharge, including honorable discharge for one who has contributed to the good of the service; less than honorable; dishonorable; and various others, established by the Code of Military Justice.

discipline—*n.* The maintenance of order and esprit in a unit or formation by the adherence to rules and regulations of conduct. *v.* To impose punishment on a person or a unit for an infraction of prescribed rules or regulations.

disengage—To break off combat with the enemy.

disinformation (intelligence)—1) False information deliberately announced or leaked by a government in order to influence actions by another country. 2) The act of disseminating such information.

dispatch—*n.* An official message, generally brief, sent by radio or other electronic means of communication by a military officer. *v.* To send a person to perform a task.

dispensary—A medical or dental facility for treating minor ailments and giving preliminary diagnoses. A dispensary may have some beds for patients not sick enough to be transported to a hospital, especially if there is no service hospital close by.

dispersion—1) The spreading or separating of troops, matériel, establishments, or activities usually concentrated in limited areas, with the purpose of reducing vulnerability to enemy action. 2) A scattered pattern of hits by bombs dropped under identical conditions or by projectiles fired from the same gun or group of guns with the same firing data. 3) In antiaircraft gunnery, the scattering of shots in range and deflection around the mean point of impact. As used in FLAK analysis, the term includes scattering due to all causes, with the mean point of impact assumed to be the target.

dispersion, cone of—The cone outlined by the flight paths of projectiles fired from a fixed installation.

dispersion error—The distance from the actual point of impact or burst of a round to the mean point of impact or burst. See also **probable error**.

displacement—1) In air intercept (by aircraft, not missiles), separation between target and interceptor tracks—that is, the path taken by an interceptor en route to target—established to position the interceptor so that sufficient maneuvering and acquisition space is provided. 2) The movement of artillery from one position to another. 3) The amount of water that a vessel displaces, expressed in displacement tons.

disposition—1) Distribution of elements of a command within an area. 2) A prescribed arrangement of the stations to be occupied by the several formations and single ships of a fleet (or major subdivisions of a fleet) for any purpose, such as cruising approach, maintenance of contact, or battle. 3) A prescribed arrangement of all tactical units composing a flight or group of aircraft. 4) The removal of a patient from a medical treatment facility by reason of return to duty, transfer to another treatment facility, death, or other termination of medical care. 5) The measures necessary to complete an assigned mission or staff action.

Distant Early Warning line (DEW) — A line of radar stations close to the 70th parallel, financed by the U.S. government and operated in cooperation with the Canadian government for the purpose of detecting hostile aircraft or missiles en route to targets on the North American continent.

distributing point—A place or point at which supplies are distributed to troops in the field and to combat trains. See also **dump**.

distribution—1) The arrangement of troops for any purpose, such as a battle, march, or maneuver. 2) A planned pattern of projectiles about a targeted point. 3) A planned spread of fire to cover a desired frontage or depth. 4) An official delivery of anything, such as orders or supplies. 5) The functional phase of military logistics that embraces the act of dispensing matériel, facilities, and services. 6) The process of assigning military personnel to activities, units, or billets. The list of people or offices to which an order or a document is distributed.

district, military—Any of the several districts established throughout the United States for administering and coordinating military reserve activity (like that of the Air

National Guard), each district's boundaries usually being coincident with, or within, those of the state or District of Columbia with which they are identified.

district, naval—An administrative organization, including all of the U.S. Navy's shore stations and activities, within one of the geographic areas into which the United States is divided by the Navy for administrative control of such installations.

dive-bomber—See **bomber**.

dive-bombing—The bombing of a target from a diving airplane, especially an airplane diving steeply.

diversion—1) An action, such as an attack (**diversionary attack**) or increased activity, intended to occupy the attention of an enemy in an area other than the one in which a primary operation is planned. 2) A change in plans, especially a change in a planned route of march.

divided fire—Fire by a single ship at two or more targets at the same time.

division—1) An administrative and tactical ground formation containing units of the various combat branches of an army and large enough to operate independently. A modern division usually consists of three BRIGADEs or REGIMENTs, each usually containing three BATTALIONs. The division dates from 1759, when the Duc de Broglie introduced a permanent formation of mixed bodies of infantry and artillery. In 1794 Lazare Carnot, the French minister of war, introduced a division of infantry, cavalry, and artillery; and the French army adopted the formation as a standard. The British did not form divisions until 1807, and they did not become a standard organization of the U.S. Army until 1917 (although divisions had been established in previous wars). 2) In the U.S. Navy, a tactical unit consisting of two or more vessels of the same or similar type.   3) In the U.S. Air Force, a tactical unit of two or more combat wings plus their service units. 4) An organizational part of an army headquarters that handles military matters of a particular nature, such as personnel, intelligence, plans and training, or supply and evacuation. 5) A number of personnel of a ship's complement grouped together for operational and administrative command.

divisional troops—Troops assigned to the headquarters staff of a division rather than to any of the combat or support components.

division artillery—Artillery that permanently forms an integral part of a division. For tactical purposes, all artillery placed under the command of a division commander is considered division artillery.

division slice—See **slice**.

division, square—A DIVISION in which the principal combat units are four infantry regiments or brigades. This was the standard division in most armies at the outset of World War I. By World War II, most national armies had followed the German example and converted to triangular divisions. See also **division, triangular**.

division, triangular—The standard modern division, introduced by Germany in World War I, in which the principal combat maneuver units are three brigades or regiments.

DMZ—See **demilitarized zone**.

Do-17—One of a series of twin-engine light bombers manufactured by Dornier and employed by Germany in World War II.

doctrine—Fundamental principles and operational concepts by which the military forces or elements thereof guide their actions in military operations in support of national objectives.

Dog—Letter of old phonetic alphabet. See also **alphabet, phonetic**.

dogfight—An aerial battle, especially between two fighter aircraft, involving considerable maneuvering and acrobatics.

doglock—An English variation of the Dutch snaphance gun. On the outside of the lock of the weapon, a dog catch, a device that caused ignition of the powder charge, was pivoted. It engaged the tail of the cock as a safety. The doglock and the snaphance were replaced by the FLINTLOCK in the second half of the 17th century. See also **snaphance lock**.

"dog tag"—Slang expression for one of two metal identification tags with the name, service number, blood type, religious preference, and tetanus record stamped on it, usually worn about the neck of a person in the military service.

dog watch—See **watch**.

dolman—A jacket, usually elaborately decorated, often worn like a cape as part of a hussar's uniform.

domestic intelligence—Information relating to activities or conditions within a country that, according to its government, may threaten its well-being.

domino theory—A strategic axiom that the collapse of one country in a geographic region must lead to the collapse of its neighbors. The analogy was posited by President Harry Truman in connection with the Truman Doctrine, but is best known for having been invoked by President Dwight Eisenhower in warning about the dangers of a Communist victory in Vietnam.

donjon—French term for the keep, or fortified citadel, or main tower of a castle.

donrebusse—See **blunderbuss**.

"doodlebug"—See **V-1**.

dose rate—The rate at which a person receives nuclear radiation per unit of time, a measure of radiation intensity.

dosimetry—The measurement of radiation doses. It applies to both the devices used (dosimeters) and to the techniques.

double concentration—Two ships firing at the same target.

double envelopment—An attack directed around both of the enemy's flanks. The classic double envelopment was achieved by Hannibal at the Battle of Cannae (216 B.C.), when he drew the Romans into the center of his line, enabling the wings of his army to close on the Roman flanks.

double firing—A 16th-century method of firing explosive bombs or shells with wooden fuze plugs, in which the bomb or shell was inserted in the artillery piece with the fuze on the opposite side from the powder charge. The gunner lit the fuze with one hand and the touchhole of the gun or mortar with the other. This dangerous procedure required precise timing and sometimes resulted in disaster.

double redan—See **redan**.

double sap—See **sap**.

double shot—The firing of two projectiles (balls, canister, grapeshot) at a time, instead of one, from a muzzle-loading piece.

double time—*n*. 1) A rate of march (while running) of 180 steps per minute, each step 3 feet in length. 2) The command to march at that rate. *v*. To run.

doughboy—A nickname applied to U.S. soldiers, particularly infantrymen, in World War I.

Douhet theory—A thesis advanced by Italian Army Gen. Giulio Douhet, in his book *Command of the Air* (1921), that future wars would be won by air forces, striking far behind national boundaries and fighting fronts on the ground. Air power would destroy the war-making capabilities of industrialized nations and so terrorize their populations that the will to continue the war would be eradicated long before a decision could be reached by embattled ground armies. Douhet envisaged the air forces as first among a nation's armed forces, with armies and navies providing supporting elements.

"dove"—A term applied to anyone opposed to the use of force in a given international dispute. It came into general usage during the Vietnam War. See also **"hawk."**

downgrade—To assign a lower defense classification to an item of classified matter.

draft—The compulsory induction of persons into military service. See also **conscription**.

draft board—A group of civilians responsible for local administration of Selective Service or other laws respecting compulsory military service.

draft dodger—A person who seeks to evade the requirement for compulsory military service.

dragon (dragoon)—1) A short musket that could be hooked to a soldier's belt. It was carried by DRAGOONs, who probably took their name from it. 2) A standard, or square flag, derived from *draco,* which was a late Roman and Carolingian standard with a metal dragon's head and a trailing body of fabric.

Dragon (M-47)—A man-portable antitank assault missile.

dragon's teeth—Tank obstacles in the form of reinforced concrete structural barriers or individual tetrapods used as part of the German West Wall constructed before World War II. Long lines of dragon's teeth, four or five rows deep, stretched across all types of terrain and even through towns, and presented an effective delaying device against tanks when U.S. troops approached the West Wall in 1944.

dragoon—A cavalryman, or mounted infantryman, beginning in the 16th century, who usually rode into battle, then dismounted to fight. The principal weapon of the dragoon was originally a short musket, or carbine. Beginning in the American Civil War, all U.S. cavalrymen were dragoons, equipped with carbines; after that war they were usually equipped with the standard infantry rifle. The derivation of the term is in some dispute, but may have come from the short musket called a DRAGON, or sometimes dragoon, carried by early dragoons.

drake—Name of certain light artillery weapons of the 17th and 18th centuries, mobile 3-pounders.

D-ration — A U.S. emergency ration with three 4-ounce bars, each providing concentrated food—mostly chocolate—of 600 calories.

drawbridge—A bridge that can be raised or drawn aside either to prevent access to a castle surrounded by a moat or to permit passage through a channel for vessels too high to pass underneath it.

dreadnought—The largest class of battleships, carrying at least eight large-caliber guns. Named for Britain's HMS *Dreadnought,* which was completed in 1906, these ships revolutionized naval warfare and caused all major navies to build comparable "all big gun" vessels. The *Dreadnought* dis-

placed 21,845 tons and carried ten 12-inch .45-caliber guns, two to a turret. With four turbine-driven propellers, it could make 21 knots.

dress—In formation, to straighten alignment, applied to a line of troops or sailors. On the command "Dress right, dress!" each person turns the head and eyes to the right and extends the left arm to touch the shoulder of the person to the left, while aligning the body to the right. Dress is usually to the right.

dressing station—A place on or near a field of combat where medical personnel can give assistance to the wounded. Also called "aid station."

dress regulations—The rules in any military organization that indicate the times and places for wearing various types of uniform (dress, informal, work, etc.) and the specific components of those uniforms.

dress uniform—A military uniform worn on formal occasions. The dress uniform may differ, in small details or completely, from the regular uniform. In many nations, including the United States, it is the only uniform on which full-size medals and decorations are worn.

Dreyse needle gun—See **needle gun**.

drill—1) Practice of military activities during training. 2) Practice specifically for combat (battle drill), including replication to the greatest possible extent of the sights, sounds, and sensations of battle, in order to accustom the troops to performing their duties under actual combat conditions. 3) Practice in administrative or ceremonial military movements (often called CLOSE-ORDER DRILL).

drill sergeant—A sergeant responsible for drilling the troops.

dromon—A fast, light galley used for coast guard duties in the ancient and medieval Byzantine navy. The name means "the runner."

drone—*n.* 1) A pilotless aircraft of conventional design, or of a modified conventional design, guided by remote control and directed by a mother aircraft or by a controller on the ground. 2) Any land, air, or sea vehicle that is controlled from a distance. *adj.* Subject to remote control.

U.S. Army photo

drone

drop zone—A specified area where airborne troops, equipment, and supplies are dropped by parachute, or upon which supplies and equipment may be delivered by free fall (without parachutes). The NATO term is "drop" or "dropping zone."

drum magazine—See **magazine**.

drum major—An early British or U.S. army noncommissioned officer whose responsibility was to train the regimental drummers. He usually led the field music (drums, bugles, and fifes) of the regimental band and often served as bandmaster.

drummer—1) A person playing a drum in a military field music unit or band. 2) A person beating a drum to relay orders aboard ship or to members of a military force by beating certain patterns on the drum. Many drummers aboard ship were boys too young to serve as gunners.

drungarios—A senior Byzantine army officer, equivalent of modern lieutenant colonel, who commanded a unit of 300 to 400 men.

dual-capable forces—Forces capable of employing dual-capable weapons (such as conventional and nuclear) or of performing two different military functions.

dual- or **multipurpose weapon**—A weapon that can be effectively applied in two or more basically different military functions or levels of conflict. The German 88mm gun of World War II is an example of a multipurpose weap-

on because it served antiaircraft, antitank, and field artillery functions.

dud—Explosive munition that fails to explode as intended.

duel—A formal or informal combat encounter between two individuals, usually fought with matched or closely similar weapons. A duel can also take place between two self-contained weapon systems, as in a tank duel, an aircraft duel, or a warship duel. The emphases in a duel are on the attack (although simultaneous defensive maneuvers may be involved) and on the duality of the fight, in contrast to team or combined-unit efforts at all other levels of military conflict.

duffel bag—A large cylindrical bag, generally of canvas or denim, although the name is applicable to bags of any material, with a drawstring closure, used for carrying personal belongings.

dugout—An underground shelter constructed to protect troops, ammunition, and matériel from gunfire, particularly from the effects of mid- or high-trajectory howitzer and mortar fire. In the American Civil War, dugouts were called BOMBPROOFS.

dum-dum bullet—A bullet that flattens excessively on impact, thereby causing extensive damage to flesh and bones. The use of this type of bullet is forbidden under international law. It is named for a 19th-century British cartridge factory near Calcutta. Standard bullets can sometimes be modified to have a dum-dum effect.

dump—A temporary stock of supplies or a place of storage established in the field or afloat where military supplies are held temporarily. When supplies are issued from dumps, the latter are called DISTRIBUTING POINTS.

Duster (M-42) — A self-propelled, twin-40mm antiaircraft weapon for use against low-flying aircraft. In Vietnam it was used against ground targets as well.

duty—The requirement of military personnel to perform in accordance with law and with the legal commands of lawfully appointed superiors.

U.S. Army photo

Duster

duty officer—1) An officer on duty, or ready for duty, during periods when other personnel are off duty. 2) An officer charged with being personally present to take care of certain matters requiring instant and continuous attention. In the first sense, a duty officer in certain situations may simply be designated for duty if and when the occasion demands. In the second sense, a duty officer is one who looks after dispatches. The person is said to "have the duty." This is also a naval term for being on watch and not free to leave a ship or station. See also **officer of the day**.

duty roster—A listing of the times at which people are scheduled for various duties.

duty station—The station or base to which a person is assigned for regular duty.

dynamite gun—A small cannon hurling a dynamite charge by means of compressed air, adopted briefly by the U.S. Navy in the late 19th century. A dynamite field gun was used by U.S. Army troops at the Siege of Santiago, Cuba, in 1898.

E

E-2C—See **Sentry**.

E-3—See **Hawkeye**.

EA-6B—See **Prowler**.

Eagle (F-15) — A twin-engine, supersonic, turbofan, all-weather tactical fighter plane, capable of employing a variety of weapons against enemy aircraft.

eagle (Roman, Napoleonic) — The national emblem of the Roman republic (and later the Empire). A gold or gilded eagle on a pole was carried by a senior soldier wherever the cohort went—in garrison, in the field, and in battle. Loss of the eagle in battle was considered a disgrace to the cohort. In the French Napoleonic army, the national flag, the tricolor, was flown on a staff surmounted by a gilded eagle, much like that of the Roman cohort.

Eagle boat—A 200-foot, 615-ton craft built by the Ford Motor Company for convoy escort and similar service in World War I. Twelve of these vessels—the first ships to be built on an assembly line—saw service in the war, primarily as submarine chasers. The cost was approximately one-quarter that of a destroyer. The design was less than successful, however; and the Eagle boat was phased out of service by the 1930s.

Eagle Claw, Operation—The unsuccessful attempt, mounted in April 1980, to free Americans held hostage in Iran. The collision between a C-130 transport and a Sea Stallion helicopter resulted in eight American deaths. See also **Iranian hostage crisis**.

Early Spring—An antireconnaissance satellite weapon system.

early warning system—An electronic or visual system of surveillance whose purpose is to detect and report the approach of airborne enemy weapons or weapons carriers as much in advance as possible of their arrival on target. See also **Distant Early Warning line**.

earmarked for assignment—North Atlantic Treaty Organization (NATO) designation for forces assigned to the operational command or control of a commander (NATO, SEATO, CENTO) at some future date, either in peaceful circumstances or in the event of war.

earnest gun—A BREECH-LOADER rifle with a fixed chamber closed by a movable breech-block on the left side of the gun.

earthworks—Any field fortification constructed primarily of earth, including trenches, walls, barriers, or DUGOUTS. See also **entrench.**

Easy—Letter of old phonetic alphabet. See also **alphabet, phonetic**.

E-boat—See **motor torpedo boat**.

E-bomb—A warhead that, on exploding, emits a high-energy pulse to fuze any electrical equipment within range.

echelon—An arrangement of troop units, ships, or aircraft that suggests sequence, steps, or a scale. "Echelon" may refer to any of the following: 1) A subdivision of a head-

89

quarters, as the forward and the rear echelons. 2) A level of command (e.g., a battalion is a lower echelon than a regiment, and a division a higher echelon than a regiment). 3) A portion of a command with a principal combat mission (i.e., the attack echelon, the support echelon, and the rear echelon). 4) A division of forces, used primarily by Russia, with a first echelon, consisting of half to two thirds of a unit or formation, and a second echelon, which will attack behind or through the first. See also **first echelon** and **second echelon**. 5) Positioning of forces, usually in the advance to attack, in such a way that elements of a laterally distributed force are also staged sequentially to the rear, from either the right or the left. This was the kind of echelonment employed by Epaminondas, most notably at Leuctra (371 B.C.), and by Frederick the Great, particularly at Leuthen (1757). The effect of such echelonment is a refusal of the flank that is echeloned to the rear. See also **refuse a flank**.

Echo—Letter of NATO phonetic alphabet. See also **alphabet, phonetic**.

ECM—See **electronic countermeasures**.

economic potential—The total capacity of a nation to produce goods and services, particularly in relation to the national capability to wage war.

economic warfare—Aggressive use of economic leverage to achieve national objectives in peacetime or wartime.

economy of force—A principle of war embodying the thesis that in order to be able to employ adequate forces in the most important portions of an operational area, forces employed elsewhere should be kept at minimum strengths. Thus, to achieve mass, or concentration, at the decisive point or points, economy of force—sometimes called "economy of forces"—should be employed elsewhere.

EDC—See **European Defense Community**.

EEI—See **essential elements of information**.

effective—*adj.* Of troops, fit for service; of fire, accomplishing its purpose. *n.* A soldier fit for service.

effectiveness—See **combat effectiveness**.

effective range—The maximum distance at which a weapon may be expected to fire accurately.

effective U.S. control — Merchant ships that are majority U.S.-owned but operated under flags of convenience. They are considered to be subject to requisition in times of national emergency.

EGBU-27—A guided bomb, weighing approximately 2,200 pounds, that employs GPS guidance for extreme accuracy. Nicknamed the "bunker buster," it can penetrate more than 6 feet of reinforced concrete before exploding. It was launched from F-117A fighters during the 2003 Gulf War.

eighty-eight (88)—A gun of 88mm (3.5-inch) caliber used by the German military in World War II. Initially designed by the Krupp Munitions Works as an antiaircraft weapon, the 88 was also used as an antitank weapon and as a field artillery piece. With its long range—as an antiaircraft weapon its effective range was 34,770 feet; as an antitank or artillery gun its maximum range was about 50,000 feet—the 88 was equally effective against Allied bombers and Allied tanks because its high muzzle velocity enabled the Germans to place the weapon in a commanding position at a considerable distance from its targets.

ejection—Escape from an aircraft by means of an independently propelled seat or capsule.

élan—High-spirited morale usually associated with exceptionally self-confident and elite units.

elbow-gauntlet—A gauntlet of plate armor, reaching to the elbow. Developed in Asia, it was adopted in the West in the 16th century.

electrician—U.S. Navy warrant officer.

electrician's mate—U.S. Navy enlisted specialty rating, first, second, and third class.

electromagnetic deception—The employment of electromagnetic energy in a manner so as to convey misleading information to an enemy's electromagnetic weapons.

electronic barrage—See **barrage**.

electronic countermeasures (ECM) — A major subdivision of electronic warfare involving actions taken to prevent or reduce the effectiveness of enemy equipment and tactics that employ or are affected by electromagnetic radiation. Also, to exploit through electronic means the enemy's use of such radiation.

electronic deception—The deliberate radiation, reradiation, alteration, absorption, or reflection of electromagnetic radiation so as to mislead an enemy in the interpretation of data received by means of electronic equipment.

electronic intelligence (ELINT) — The technical and intelligence information gleaned from monitoring the electronic transmissions of an enemy or potential enemy.

electronic jamming—The deliberate radiation, reradiation, or reflection of electromagnetic signals with the objective of preventing or impairing the use of electronic devices by the enemy. See also **jam**.

electronic security—Measures designed to deny to unauthorized persons data from electromagnetic transmissions such as radar.

electronic warfare (EW) — The military employment of electronics to prevent or reduce an enemy's effective use of radiated electromagnetic energy and to ensure one's own effective use of radiated electromagnetic energy.

element—1) Any subdivision of a military organization that may function apart from the whole or be considered a separate entity. 2) A component of an organization, as in "command element" or "service element."

elephant dugout—A large DUGOUT that is protected by steel ribs or girders. The large semicylindrical, corrugated pieces of thin steel sheeting so used for this purpose in World War I, sometimes in dugouts, sometimes for surface protection, were called **elephant iron**.

elevate—To raise the muzzle of a weapon, or the aim of the gunner, in order to deliver the projectile on or near a target.

elevating arc—1) The portion of the elevating mechanism of a gun in the shape of a segment of a circle, with ratchets along the circumference that are engaged by a worn screw, which rotates when the gunner turns the elevating handle or wheel to raise or lower the muzzle of the gun. 2) An arc attached to the base of the breech of some 19th-century cannon, parallel to the ratchets and graduated in degrees and parts of a degree, to measure elevation. See also **gunner's quadrant**.

elevation—In gunnery, the inclination or angle of the axis of the cannon or gun above ground level to counteract the effect of the force of gravity. The higher the elevation or angle of the gun (up to 45 degrees), the longer the projectile's range. If the gun can be elevated above 45 degrees, the range decreases as the elevation increases above 45 degrees. See also **site, angle of** and **quadrant elevation**.

ELINT—See **electronic intelligence**.

elite corps—A body of troops designated or regarded as elite (see **elite troops**). Examples include the Roman Praetorian Guard, Napoleon's "OLD GUARD," the Confederate Stonewall Brigade, and the Union Iron Brigade of the American Civil War.

elite troops—Troops that, because of special training or some other distinctive and above-average quality, are used for special missions or as a nucleus for troops of lesser quality. In some nations, elite troops have been considered socially superior to the rest of the armed forces.

embarkation—The loading of troops with their supplies and equipment into ships or aircraft.

embattle—1) To become engaged in battle. 2) To arrange in order of battle; to draw up, as troops for battle; to prepare or arm for battle. 3) To furnish with battlements.

"embed"—To integrate journalists into military units to report on military operations. The term emerged just prior to the 2003 Gulf War, when 600 journalists were "embedded" in the coalition's armed forces in Kuwait and given some training in the handling of protective gear before the attack on Iraq.

embrasure—An opening built into a wall or a parapet through which guns can be fired with minimum exposure of the gunners.

emplacement—A prepared position (usually in a field fortification) for housing and operating one or more weapons or pieces of equipment, offering protection against hostile fire or bombardment.

U.S. Army photo

emplacement

encamp—To settle down in a spot or locality and prepare for the shelter and subsistence of a force, generally on a temporary basis.

encampment—A place, usually temporary, where a military force resides. It is generally a collection of temporary structures, often tents, with portable facilities that provide for the subsistence of the people and the administration of the force.

enceinte—A wall that surrounds a fortress. An enceinte may be a single, solid wall or a series of more or less concentric defensive works.

encipher—To convert, by means of a cipher system, a plain-text message into language unintelligible to anyone not possessing the key in order to prevent an enemy from understanding the message if intercepted.

encircle—To surround. The process of surrounding with a military force is **encirclement**. The purpose of an encirclement is to cut off the encircled force from sources of supply and support and thereby encourage it to surrender. Encirclement is often achieved by two or more units approaching the enemy from different directions.

encounter—*n.* A minor battle. *v.* To come against, meet; to engage in conflict with.

encounter battle — A battle that occurs when two hostile forces meet unexpectedly, without preparation or reconnaissance. See also **meeting engagement**.

encrypt—To convert a plain-text message into unintelligible form (a cryptogram) by means of a cryptosystem. See also **encipher**.

endurance—The time an aircraft can continue flying or a ground vehicle or a ship can continue operating under specified conditions, such as without refueling.

enemy—One who is hostile to another. A foe, adversary, antagonist.

enemy capabilities—Those courses of action of which the enemy is capable and which, if adopted, will affect the accomplishment of one's own mission. The term includes not only the general courses of action open to the enemy, such as attack, defense, and withdrawal, but also particular courses of action. In an assessment of enemy capabilities, all known factors affecting military operations, including time, space, weather, terrain, and the strength and disposition of enemy forces, are considered. In strategic thinking, the capabilities of a nation represent the courses of action, in peace or war, that a nation has the power to undertake in order to accomplish its national objectives.

Enfield rifle—Any of a number of rifles, or earlier rifle-muskets, originally manufactured at the royal small-arms factory in Enfield, England. Enfield rifles were used by British soldiers in World Wars I and II. An American-manufactured modification was used by U.S. troops in World War I. The magazine held six cartridges, the barrel was 26 inches long, and the weapon's total length was 46 inches. The Enfield rifle-musket was a mid-19th-century weapon.

enfilade—1) A position, usually on a flank, that permits a force to fire down the length of a hostile line, thus increasing the possibility of hitting a target because range dispersion will not matter. 2) Firing of a gun or guns along the entire line of men or works, from one end to the other, equivalent to RAKE in naval battle.

enfilade fire—See **angles of fire**.

engage—To enter into conflict, or join battle; to fight.

engagement—A battle, or a subdivision of a battle, between elements of larger forces. See also **conflict levels of intensity.**

engagement, naval—A battle or an engagement fought at sea.

engineer, military—A person in military service whose duties involve the construction, repair, operation, or maintenance of structures, defensive positions, and equipment required for combat and noncombat purposes. In the U.S. Army, the Corps of Engineers performs these duties, which range from the construction of fortification, the building of roads, and the laying and removal of mines to the maintenance of inland waterways and harbors. The Civil Engineer Corps of the U.S. Navy performs similar functions and is also charged with the operation and maintenance of the propulsion machinery of U.S. naval vessels.

engineers, amphibious—A subbranch of the U.S. Army Corps of Engineers, established in World War II and active in all Allied landings. Amphibious engineers were specially trained in the techniques of amphibious operations, including the operation of landing craft and the organization and control of beach activities. In the Pacific theater, all these tasks were performed by naval personnel.

engineman—U.S. Navy specialist rating, chief and first, second, and third class.

English lock—A type of FLINTLOCK.

Enigma—The electrical enciphering machine used by the German armed forces during World War II. See also **Ultra**.

enlist—1) To enroll oneself voluntarily in military service. 2) To enroll another person in military service.

enlisted personnel—Personnel in the lower ranks of the armed services who do not hold rank by either commission or warrant. Includes privates, corporals, and sergeants (E1–E8), and equivalent ranks in other services. The British equivalent term is "other ranks."

enlistment—1) A voluntary entrance into military service, as distinguished from induction through conscription. 2) A period of time, contractual or prescribed by law, that an enlisted person serves between enrollment and discharge. 3) The act of enrolling in military service.

ensign—1) In the U.S. and British navies, the lowest commissioned rank, corresponding to second lieutenant in the other services. 2) A flag, especially the national flag, displayed on ships or at naval stations.

entrench—To dig trenches and construct hastily thrown-up fieldworks in order to strengthen a force in position. The fieldworks so constructed are **entrenchments**.

entrenching tool—A small spade or pick, often collapsible, that is normally carried in the pack of infantrymen or other soldiers for use in digging trenches or building earthworks.

U.S. Army photo

entrenching tool

envelop—The act of maneuvering all or part of a military force in such a manner as to attack the enemy's flank, or pass around the enemy's flank, for the purpose of attacking lines of communication or the enemy rear.

envelope — The three-dimensional space that is within range, altitude, and deflection reach of a weapon, particularly an air defense weapon.

envelopment—A maneuver in which the main attack is directed against the flank (close-in envelopment) or in the rear (wide envelopment) of the enemy's main forces. A wide envelopment is often called a TURNING MOVEMENT. The term VERTICAL ENVELOPMENT is often used to describe an airborne operation in the enemy's rear area.

environmental terrorism—To commit an action that degrades the environment without directly affecting the enemy. The term has been applied to Iraq's deliberate spilling of oil into the Persian Gulf during the Gulf War.

epaulement—A wall or other fortification built out from a bastion to protect the flank. The term comes from the French word for shoulder, *épaule*.

epaulet—A decorative device worn on the shoulder, now usually with dress uniforms. At one time commonly worn by both army and naval officers, epaulets derived from the knot of ribbons that was used to hold a baldric at the shoulder. They consist of a strap fastened near the neck, widening and usually ending in a circular piece at the end of the shoulder, to which gold fringe is attached. Devices indicating rank or service are attached to the top. The shoulder board worn by U.S. and other naval officers is a derivation.

epibatae—Greek soldiers who fought aboard ship, like modern marines.

epitagma—A Greek cavalry formation of 4,096 men, usually deployed in battle with one half on each wing of the line of battle.

equerry—An officer in a royal or noble household who primarily manages the care of horses but who may have other duties as well.

equipage—All the equipment, including transportation means but not weapons, required by a military unit or a ship to support the life and operations of its personnel.

equipment—All articles needed to outfit an individual or organization. The term refers to clothing, tools, utensils, vehicles, and similar items, and may include weapons. The specific details of the equipment authorized for a unit in the U.S. Army are prescribed by tables of allowances and by TABLES OF ORGANIZATION AND EQUIPMENT—a type of authorization in which weapons are included.

equites—The collective name for the knights or noble horsemen who made up the cavalry arm in Roman armies before the military reforms initiated by Consul Marius in 105 B.C. As a result of the Marian reforms, the equites disappeared, replaced for the most part by allied and mercenary cavalry, recruited mainly from Thrace and Africa.

escalade—The climbing of a wall or rampart with ladders, especially by an attacking force.

escalation—An increase in the scope or violence of a conflict, deliberate or unpremeditated. It is usually a sequential process of two or more steps of increasing volatility in which one side responds to a step just taken by the opponent.

escarp—In fortification, the surface of a moat or ditch next to a rampart, the surface toward the enemy being called the COUNTERSCARP.

escarpment—1) A steep slope created by cutting away ground about a fortified position, in order to render it less accessible to the enemy. 2) A natural terrain feature that, because of precipitous cliffs or bluffs, imposes similar limitations on an attacker.

escort—1) A naval combatant assigned to accompany and protect another force or convoy. 2) Aircraft assigned to protect other aircraft. 3) Armed personnel accompanying prisoners from one location to another. 4) An armed guard accompanying persons as a mark of distinction. 5) A person assigned to accompany and assist an individual or a group.

esmeril—A 2.5-foot-long artillery piece of the 16th century, with a 1-inch bore and a weight of 200 pounds. It had a maximum range of 750 yards and a point-blank range of 200 yards.

espadon—1) A gigantic two-handed, double-edged sword used by Swiss and German foot soldiers in the 15th century. With a blade over 50 inches long, the espadon, or *zweihander* (which means two-handed), hung from a scabbard down the back like the two-handed samurai sword. In order to avoid slicing the shoulder when the sword was drawn, part of the blade, near the hilt, was usually covered with leather. 2) Any double-edged weapon.

espignole—A kind of BLUNDERBUSS that was loaded with several balls.

espionage—Actions directed toward the acquisition of information through clandestine activity by individual agents and networks.

espontoon—A 17th-century half-pike, about 3 feet in length. Also called SPONTOON.

espringal—A war engine used in pregunpowder times to throw arrows, bolts, rocks, or other missiles. The espringal derived its propulsive force from the principle of tension. Also called "springal." See also **catapult** and **ballista.**

esprit de corps—A feeling of pride in a unit and of pervasive enthusiasm and confidence among its members. See also **élan.**

essedarius—An ancient Roman gladiator who fought in a heavy chariot called an **esseda.** The esseda, used by the Gauls, the Belgae, and the Britons, was open in front instead of behind. The warrior could run forward along the pole to which the horses were harnessed to seek an advantageous position or angle for the discharge of his missiles.

essential elements of friendly information—The information that a commander would wish to know about his own and allied forces in a given situation.

essential elements of information (EEI)—The critical items of information about the enemy and his situation required by a commander in order to reach a logical command decision.

establishment—1) An organization or installation, together with its personnel and equipment, that forms an operating entity. 2) The table setting out the authorized numbers of personnel and major items of equipment in a unit or formation.

estacade—A barricade of piles driven into a sea, river, or morass to halt an enemy's advance.

estec—A long, narrow, thrusting sword, called a "tuck" in Elizabethan times.

estimate, intelligence—A systematic appraisal of available intelligence relating to a specific military situation or condition. The capabilities, limitations, vulnerabilities, and probable intentions (or probable reactions) of an enemy or a potential enemy in a given situation must be evaluated in order to determine the courses of action an enemy might take and the probable order of their adoption.

estimate of the situation — A comprehensive review of the circumstances bearing on a military situation. From such an estimate, a commander decides the course of action to take to accomplish the mission. Sometimes called an APPRECIATION.

estos—A German-Bohemian thrusting sword with a long, thin, rigid blade designed to penetrate the joints of armor. It was a forerunner of the RAPIER.

estramaeon—1) A two-edged sword used in the 16th and 17th centuries. 2) A blow with the edge of a sword.

estrivals—Protection, usually made of mail, for the lower legs of war horses.

ETA (Euzkadi Ta Askatasuna)—A Basque separatist group that has undertaken terrorist acts in pursuit of independence for the Basque provinces of northern Spain.

ethnic cleansing—Political persecution, often accompanied by military action, directed against one or more minority groups in a given area. The most vivid example of ethnic cleansing was Hitler's campaign against the Jews, but the term has also been applied more recently (e.g., to actions by the Serb majority against ethnic Albanians in Kosovo in the late 1990s). See also **genocide**.

European Defense Community (EDC)—French proposal of the early 1950s to create an integrated European army with a single defense ministry and logistical system.

euthytonon—A light, portable BALLISTA. Alexander the Great had 150 euthytonons and 25 PALINTONONs in his army, which he used as field artillery.

evacuate—1) To remove all people from a position, a town, or a locality. 2) To move ill or injured people, generally from a medical facility near a combat area to a facility in a noncombat zone.

evacuation, axis of—A route or series of routes along which sick or wounded troops, prisoners of war, captured equipment, and civilian refugees (and in some instances unneeded troops and equipment) may be transported away from the area of active combat. Such a route is particularly important in a planned withdrawal or DELAYING ACTION.

evacuation point—Medical treatment facilities behind the combat front from which the sick and wounded are evacuated.

evaluation—Appraisal of an item of intelligence for its credibility, reliability, pertinence, and accuracy.

evasion and recovery—Actions carried out by evaders, recovery planners, and recovery forces to evacuate personnel isolated in hostile territory.

evolutions—The movements of troops as they change position. All such movements as marching, countermarching, changing front, forming line, and defiling are evolutions.

EW—See **electronic warfare**.

exchange of prisoners—The trading of one or more prisoners captured by one side in a conflict for prisoners taken by the other. In ancient times, prisoners commonly were retained by the victors as slaves. Before the Christian era, however, the exchange of prisoners and the payment of ransom had become a customary practice. Enslavement for captured soldiers, however, was not eradicated until the 17th century.

executive officer—1) The officer second in command of a military unit. 2) An assistant or deputy to a commanding officer responsible for seeing that command policies as applied to the details of day-to-day operations are carried out. The executive officer in the lower echelons of a military organization combines the equivalent duties of the deputy and the chief of staff in higher echelons.

exercise—Any practice operation, large or small, for the purpose of increasing the proficiency of military personnel and of units in the performance of their tasks. In an exercise, simulated enemy action is used as a training device. An exercise may involve a unit or an entire military force of any branch, and may be conducted at sea or in the field. Exercises may also be simulated on a map, computer, or other device. Those conducted in the field, as opposed to in garrison, are usually called **field exercises**. See also **command post exercise**.

exfiltration—The surreptitious movement of personnel from an enemy-controlled area.

expedition—1) A journey made by a military force from its base to an area where combat is anticipated. 2) A force making such a trip, including all its equipment and means of transportation.

expeditionary force—An armed force organized to accomplish a specific objective in a foreign country. Examples are the British Ex-

peditionary Force (BEF) and the American Expeditionary Force (AEF) in World War I.

expendable property — Matériel that is consumed in use or loses its identity in use and may be dropped from stock records when issued.

exploitation—1) Taking full advantage of success in battle by following up initial gains. 2) Taking full advantage of any information that has come to hand for tactical or strategic purposes. 3) An offensive operation, usually one following a successful attack that is designed to disorganize the enemy in depth.

explosive—A solid, liquid, or gaseous substance capable of an instantaneous chemical or nuclear reaction releasing great heat and force.

exposure dose—A measurement of radiation in relation to its ability to produce ionization. The unit of measurement of the exposure dose is the roentgen.

expugnable—Capable of being conquered or taken by assault; susceptible to the use of force.

extend—To widen the space between files of a formation or units on a front in order to occupy a greater area of ground.

extended order—The deployment of troops in a tactical formation with more than the minimum of space needed for their weapons between ranks and files.

exterior lines—A situation of a military force or group of military forces that are divided into two or more widely separated elements facing a more centrally disposed force, which is said to operate on INTERIOR LINES. Operations by the divided forces are convergent and are said to be on "exterior lines."

external ballistics—See **ballistics**.

F-4—See **Phantom II.**

F4F—See **Wildcat.**

F-5—See **Freedom Fighter/Tiger.**

F6F—See **Hellcat.**

F7F—See **Tigercat.**

F-14—See **Tomcat.**

F-15—See **Eagle.**

F-16—See **Fighting Falcon.**

F-22—See **Raptor.**

F-100—See **Super Sabre.**

F-105—See **Thunderchief.**

F-111—Manufactured by General Dynamics, the F-111 is a twin-engine, swing-wing, supersonic, fighter-bomber, capable of carrying either nuclear or conventional weapons. Its excellent terrain-following capability allows it to fly beneath enemy radar. In the Gulf War the F-111 proved extremely effective in carrying out deep strikes against Iraqi airfields and fuel depots.

F-117—See **Stealth.**

F/A-18—See **Hornet.**

Fabian tactics—A type of warfare in which combat is avoided and, instead, a policy of delay and harassment is directed at the enemy. The name derives from Quintus Fabius Maximus, who defended Rome against Hannibal with such a campaign in 217 B.C., never joining battle and thereby earning for himself the name *Cunctator* (Delayer).

fabric armor—See **armor.**

fabricator (intelligence)—An individual or group who, absent genuine intelligence, invents intelligence or embroiders existing information for purposes of reward or deception.

face—*n.* One side of a formation of troops or a fortified position. *v.* To present the front of a formation or an object in a given direction. See also **about face, left face, right face.**

U.S. Navy photo

F-111

facility—A part or the whole of a building, base, or other structure or group of structures, including associated attachments or equipment, that houses and supports any agency or operating entity related to the armed forces. The entity itself may be considered a facility, independent of, or in combination with, its quarters.

facings—1) The collar, cuffs, and trimmings of a uniform coat. 2) Changes in direction or front of a military unit. 3) The movements of troops by turning on their heels to the right, left, right about, and so on. See also **face**.

fail-safe—A device that disarms a weapon or munition in the event of a malfunction, thus preventing an accidental launch or detonation.

falarica—An incendiary defensive weapon of classical times. It consisted of a long iron javelin with a wooden shaft, bound with tow and smeared with inflammable pitch or resin. The falarica was set on fire and thrown against an attacker's siegeworks.

falarique—A combustible dart or arrow about 3 feet long, used in the Middle Ages for setting fire to a ship or a wooden structure.

falarira—Medieval weapon, similar to a BALLISTA, that threw darts wrapped with inflammable materials.

falchion—A sword with a short, broad, thick, heavy blade that widened toward the point and had a single convex cutting edge. It was used in Western Europe in the 12th and 13th centuries, primarily as a slicing weapon.

falcon (falconet)—An iron or brass cannon used on ships and ashore from the 15th through the 17th century. Weighing about 800 pounds, the falcon was 6 feet long, with a bore of about 2.5 inches, and fired a 3-pound ball. Its maximum range was about 2,500 yards, its point-blank range about 400. A smaller version, the falconet, was 3.7 feet long and weighed 500 pounds. With a bore of 2 inches, it could fire a 1-pound ball as far as 1,500 yards, and had a point-blank range of about 280 yards.

fall in—*v.* To assume an assigned position in a rank or formation. *n.* The command to assume such a position.

fall out—*v.* To break ranks on command. *n.* The command to break ranks.

fallout—The falling to earth of radioactive particles from a nuclear cloud; also applied to the particles themselves.

fallout-safe height of burst—The height of burst at or above which no militarily significant fallout will be produced as a result of a nuclear-weapon detonation.

false flag (intelligence)—An operation in which agents or informers are recruited in the belief that they will be working for a country other than that of their recruiter. Such an operation is undertaken when individuals are perceived as unwilling to work for the agency that needs their services.

fan—A spread of torpedoes.

fantail—The after end of the main deck on a ship.

FARC—See **Revolutionary Armed Forces of Colombia**.

fascines—A tied bundle of wooden sticks or branches, carried with a unit or gathered up in an area, and used to build fortifications, strengthen earthworks, fill ditches, and so on.

fatigue—Noncombat work, generally of a manual or menial kind, such as cleaning barracks. **Fatigue duty** is any labor other than use of arms performed by a soldier and is assigned to troops both to accomplish the job and to keep them occupied.

fatigue, combat — Intense weariness or mental illness caused by continued exposure to hostile fire sufficiently severe to render a soldier incapable of continuing in active combat. Also called **battle fatigue**. In World War I it was called "shell shock."

fatigue duty—See **fatigue**.

fatigue party—A detachment of soldiers detailed on non-combat-related duty.

fatigues (fatigue uniform) — Outer clothing, usually made of denim or another coarse, durable material, worn by soldiers on **fatigue duty**. Slang for work clothes.

fauchard — A 16th-century weapon that looked like a very large razor blade attached to the end of a staff.

FBS—See **forward-based systems**.

FDC—See **fire direction center**.

FEBA — See **forward edge of the battle area**.

fedayeen—A term applied to various anti-Israel Moslem guerrillas, most often consisting of Palestinian refugees displaced by the Israelis.

Fedayeen Saddam — Iraqi paramilitary group considered intensely loyal to Saddam Hussein, who fought against U.S.-led coalition forces in the 2003 Gulf War. Fedayeen Saddam, which roughly translates to "men who sacrifice themselves for Saddam," was reportedly formed in the mid-1990s by Saddam's son Uday.

feint—A mock attack designed to distract, divert, or deceive the enemy, particularly to focus his attention on a place or an area distant from the site where decisive action is planned.

fencible—A soldier enlisted for the defense of the country and not liable to be sent abroad.

fender—Any device hung over a ship's side to prevent rubbing against a pier or another vessel.

Ferguson rifle—A rifled infantry firearm with a screw-plug breech action invented by Maj. Patrick Ferguson, a Scottish officer, during the American Revolution. The Ferguson rifle, probably the most effective military firearm of the period, could fire six shots a minute to an extreme range of 300 yards. Ferguson was killed in the Battle of King's Mountain (9 October 1780), and his rifle was never adopted by the British army.

ferret—An aircraft, a ship, or a vehicle specially equipped for detecting, locating, recording, and analyzing electromagnetic radiation.

feu de joie—French phrase meaning "fire of joy," describing a firing of muskets one after another, closely timed to make a continuous noise, in celebration. The term was also used for a bonfire.

field—1) A place where a battle is fought. 2) Away from garrison or home, usually for combat, training, or field exercises. As in "in the field."

field army—An administrative and tactical organization composed of a headquarters, certain organic, or permanently assigned, army troops, service support troops, two or more corps and independent divisions, and other units. See also **army**.

field artillery—The mobile cannon (guns and howitzers), rockets, and surface-to-surface missiles that are usually employed to provide indirect fire support to maneuver

forces (infantry and armor). This includes most mobile artillery pieces, although coast artillery did include some large mobile weapons. It does not include air defense weapons. In some armies heavy mortars are field artillery. See also **artillery**.

U.S. Army photo
U.S. 105mm howitzer.

field artillery

field duty—Service or duty performed away from garrison, in training, or in operations against an actual or potential enemy.

field exercise—See **exercise**.

field force—1) A combined-arms ground force operating under actual or assumed combat circumstances. 2) The units, general headquarters, installations, and equipment that make up, or are intended to make up, the forces in a theater of operation.

field fortifications — Emplacements and shelters of temporary construction built during combat, as opposed to more elaborate PERMANENT FORTIFICATIONS built prior to hostilities. Field fortifications can be simple, and can be constructed with reasonable ease by units requiring no more than minor engineer supervision and equipment; or they can be built by engineers and can approximate the strength and complexity of permanent fortifications.

field glasses—A small, compact binocular telescope. Military field glasses are usually 4 to 7 power in magnification.

field grade—The officer ranks of major, lieutenant colonel, and colonel.

field kitchen—See **field ration**.

field marshal—In some armies, a senior rank, usually held only by the head of large military organizations such as a group of armies or the entire national army. In the

U.S. Army the equivalent rank is general of the army.

field music—A small group of fifes, drums, trumpets, bugles, bagpipes, or other instruments and their players who play for marching, regimental calls, or certain ceremonies.

field officer—A senior army or marine corps officer with the rank of major, lieutenant colonel, or colonel.

field of fire—The area that a weapon or a group of weapons may cover effectively with fire from its position.

fieldpiece—A mobile cannon, towed or self-propelled.

field radio—A sending and receiving set for communications between elements of a military force in the field. With power supplied by a hand-cranked generator, radio was first used by combat forces in World War I. By the end of World War II, radio had largely replaced the FIELD TELEPHONE as a means of communication in mobile warfare when security was not of primary importance and laying of telephone lines was difficult.

field ration—Food required for one person for one day of field operations. The meals are either prepared in advance and carried by a soldier, usually in prepackaged form, or prepared in a central FIELD KITCHEN and delivered to the troops in containers.

field staff—A staff carried by gunners in the field to hold lighted matches for discharging cannon.

field telephone—A portable, battery-powered telephone designed for field or combat use. The field telephone became the common means of communication and control early in the 20th century.

field training—Training conducted under field conditions, as opposed to in GARRISON.

fieldwork—A temporary construction built for defense by an army in the field. Most often referred to in the plural, **fieldworks** are entrenchments and other temporary fortifications thrown up by an army in the field, either to defend against attack or to cover an attack. All nonpermanent fortifications are fieldworks. See also **earthworks**.

fife—A high-pitched flutelike instrument, about 14 inches long, with no keys but six fingerholes. In military music it is used primarily with drums. It was used in Switzerland in the 16th century and adopted by English military units later. A FIFER is a person who plays a fife.

fifth column—A subversive organization that secretly operates inside a nation prior to or in conjunction with a military attack from without. Its members work by infiltrating legitimate organizations and agencies and by exploiting all opportunities to weaken the legal government politically and militarily. The expression was first used in 1936, during the Spanish Civil War, by Gen. Emilio Mola, commander of four columns of Nationalist forces that were attacking Madrid. Mola referred to the Nationalist underground within the city as his "fifth column."

fifty-mission cap—A service cap worn without the spring stiffener and GROMMET. Wearing caps in this manner was customary in World War II among flying officers of the U.S. Army and Navy, originally because of the need to wear earphones over the cap.

fight—To engage an enemy in COMBAT.

fighter aircraft—Highly maneuverable aircraft that are relatively light in weight, have a crew of one or two, and are designed primarily for air-to-air combat. Also called "fighter-interceptors." **fighter-bomber**—Fighter aircraft designed both for air-to-air combat and for close support of ground forces. They are likely to be assigned to units that have air defense and ground attack roles. **all-weather fighter**—A fighter aircraft equipped with radar devices and other special equipment that enable it to intercept its target when visibility is reduced by darkness or weather conditions.

fighter-bomber—See **fighter aircraft** and **bomber**.

fighter cover—The maintenance of a number of fighter aircraft over a specified area or military force for the purpose of repelling hostile air activities.

fighter sweep—An offensive mission by fighter aircraft to seek out and destroy enemy aircraft or targets of opportunity in an allotted area of operations.

Fighting Falcon (F-16) — A single-engine, supersonic, turbofan, multipurpose, tactical fighter-bomber. It is capable of employing either nuclear or conventional weapons; its primary mission is air superiority.

U.S. Department of Defense photo

Fighting Falcon

fighting load—Items of individual clothing, equipment, weapons, and ammunition essential to a soldier's combat effectiveness.

fighting patrol—See **patrol, fighting**.

file—A column of individual troops or of vehicles traveling one behind the other.

file closer—In 18th- and 19th-century land warfare, file closers were veteran noncommissioned officers who ware stationed behind advancing formations to close ranks when casualties occurred and to intimidate any soldiers who might be inclined to bolt.

file off—To leave a formation, generally consisting of several files, by marching away in single file.

FIM-43—See **Redeye**.

FIM-92A—See **Stinger**.

final protective fire—See **fire, final protective**.

fire—*n.* 1) The discharge of one or more firearms. Often used collectively, as in, "The fire came from the left." 2) The command to discharge one's weapon. The earliest guns, in the 14th and 15th centuries, were discharged by applying fire to a primary charge connected to the propellant in the gun. Thus the origin of the term "fire" for discharge of hand guns and cannon. *v.* To discharge a weapon.

"fire and forget"—Slang for a weapon that includes a self-correcting guidance system (e.g., the STINGER surface-to-air missile).

fire and maneuver—The concept of combining movement with firepower to attack an enemy force in position under the most favorable conditions. Movement or maneuver cannot be effectively performed in combat without FIRE SUPERIORITY.

firearm—An individual weapon, such as a musket, rifle, or pistol, using gunpowder to propel a projectile.

fire arrow—A small iron dart to which was attached a match impregnated with powder and sulfur, used to set fire to the sails of ships.

fireball—1) The luminous sphere of hot gases that forms a few millionths of a second after detonation of a nuclear weapon and immediately starts expanding and cooling. 2) Before the era of nuclear weapons, a ball filled with powder or other combustibles to be thrown among enemy troops.

fire base—The weapons available to a unit commander to achieve fire superiority and to maintain such superiority while the unit's maneuvering elements are closing with the enemy.

Firebee—A remotely controlled target drone powered by a turbojet engine, employed to test and evaluate weapon systems.

fire, concentrated—Fire from a number of weapons directed at a single point or small area.

fire, continuous—1) Fire conducted at a normal rate without interruption. 2) In artillery and naval gunfire support, loading and firing as rapidly as possible, consistent with accuracy, within the prescribed rate of fire for the weapon.

fire control—Control over the direction, range, volume, and time of fire of guns or rockets by a systematic process that may include the use of certain electrical, electronic, optical, or mechanical systems; a fire-control system.

fire controlman—A U.S. Navy enlisted specialty, chief and first, second, and third class.

fire, coordination of—The planning and execution of fire so that targets are adequately covered by a suitable weapon or group of weapons.

fire cross—A signal in ancient Scotland indicating that the people should take up arms.

fire direction—The process of controlling the fire of an artillery unit primarily at the battalion and group levels, although fire direction can be conducted at the battery level. This involves fire control as well as the calculation and transmission of data necessary for placing effective fire on targets.

fire direction center (FDC) — That element of an artillery command post, consisting of gunnery and communication personnel and equipment, by means of which the commander exercises FIRE DIRECTION and FIRE CONTROL. Receiving target intelligence and requests for fire, the fire direction center translates them into appropriate firing data and fire commands.

fire discipline—Control over the firepower resources of a unit to assure that ammunition is not wasted and that information is not given to the enemy.

fire fight—The exchange of fire between two opposing units, usually at platoon or company level.

fire, final protective—A prearranged barrier of fire designed to impede enemy movement across defensive lines or areas. See also **barrage**.

fire for effect—1) Fire delivered after the center of impact or burst is within the desired distance of the target or adjusting/ranging point. 2) Term in a fire message to indicate that the adjustment (or ranging) is satisfactory and fire for effect is desired.

fire for record—The process of formally testing an individual or unit for proficiency in the use of a weapon. Depending on the score achieved, an individual firing a small arm in the U.S. Army is qualified as marksman, sharpshooter, or expert.

firelock—A term formerly used to describe a FLINTLOCK musket.

fire, massed—The process of bringing to bear in a relatively small target area the concentrated fire of a number of artillery batteries or battalions simultaneously or in a short period of time.

fire mission—1) A specific target assignment given to a fire unit, such as an artillery battery. 2) An order used to alert personnel at the guns that the message to follow is a call for fire.

fire pan—The receptacle that held the primer in early gunpowder weapons.

fire plan—A tactical plan for coordinating the use of the weapons of a unit or formation so that their fire will be effective.

fire position—A position from which fire is opened.

firepower—1) The capability of delivering fire. 2) The fire itself, or the quantity or effectiveness of fire delivered. 3) Any explosive or missile that wreaks damage upon the target against which directed. 4) The amount of fire that may be delivered by a position, unit, or weapon system measured in various units (of firepower), including volume and weight.

firepower score—A quantitative measure of the effectiveness of a weapon in comparison with other weapons.

fire, prearranged—Gunfire delivered on known or suspected targets in accordance with a planned schedule on either a time or an on-call basis. Such a schedule is usually prepared with an attack plan. See also **scheduled fire**.

fire, searching—Fire distributed by successive changes in the elevation and deflection settings of a gun. The purpose of such fire is essentially for harassment and interdiction.

fireship—A vessel loaded with combustible material designed to be set afire and let drift so as to destroy docked or anchored enemy ships.

fire storm—A windstorm induced by an immense fire, generally in an urban area, which causes warm air to rise above the burning area in such volume that cooler air is rapidly drawn in toward the burning area from all directions, increasing the intensity and destructiveness of the fire. Often the result of an intensive aerial bombardment.

fire superiority—The battle application of a greater amount of effective firepower than is applied by the opponent. The side with fire superiority has enhanced maneuver capability.

fire support—In U.S. Army usage, the assistance or protection given ground forces in direct contact with the enemy by the firepower of ground or naval guns or by aircraft engaging in close air support.

fire support coordination—The planning and executing of the application of firepower to targets in such a way as to use available weapons most efficiently.

fire support coordination line—A line established by the appropriate ground commander to ensure coordination of fire that is not under the ground commander's control but may affect tactical operations. The establishment of the fire support coordination line is normally coordinated with the appropriate tactical air commander and other supporting elements. The fire support coordination line should follow well-defined terrain features.

fire support ship—A ship whose mission is to support amphibious operations or land operations with weapon fire.

fire support team (FIST)—In the U.S. Army, a small group of artillery personnel, under a lieutenant, one of whom is attached to each company-level maneuver unit (infantry and armor) for the purpose of locating targets, adjusting indirect fire of supporting artillery and mortars, and coordinating these and all other forms of fire support (including naval gunfire and air support), as well as planning for such support with the supported commander. The FIST includes forward observers, communications personnel, and one or more drivers for the FIST vehicle or vehicles. See also **forward observer**.

firing chart—Map, photo map, or grid sheet showing the relative horizontal and vertical positions of batteries, base points, base-point lines, checkpoints, targets, and other details needed in preparing artillery firing data.

firing line—The line on which troops or weapons systems are placed to deliver fire against a target.

firing range—See **range**.

firing squad—1) A detachment of troops assigned to execute a condemned person by gunfire. 2) A detachment that fires the final salute at a military funeral.

firing step—In trench warfare, a small step, board, or ledge about a foot from the bottom of a trench on which men could stand to fire or look out.

firing tables—A compilation of detailed data on the firing characteristics of a type of weapon, based on exhaustive firing tests at a proving ground (e.g., "Firing Tables for Howitzer 105mm, M2 and M2A1, Firing Shell H.E. M1"); typically includes such information as the range in yards or meters for every mil or fraction of a degree of elevation, the FORK, and PROBABLE ERROR for range, and deflection.

first call—A bugle call alerting troops for roll call, ceremonies, or drill.

first echelon—Under the Soviet concept of committing forces by ECHELON during the Cold War, the leading element of a Soviet or Warsaw Pact unit or formation when advancing to combat. In World War II, first echelons of Soviet forces were usually about one-half to two-thirds the strength of a command. The remainder was in the SECOND ECHELON, although it could sometimes be in a reserve. (On rare occasions, in a narrow sector, there were three echelons.) Complicating this doctrine, from the standpoint of both the Soviet army and its possible opponents, was the fact that there could be echelonment of the units or formations within each level of command; that is, a regiment could have a first and a second echelon, and both could be in the first echelon of a division. Similarly, a division could have both a first and a second echelon, and both could be in the first echelon of an army, and so on up through front (or army group) and theater. There is some evidence that the Soviet army made less use of the echelonment concept later in the 20th century than it did in World War II.

first graze—The point where a bullet following a ballistic trajectory will, if not deflected, first strike the ground. See also **point blank**.

first lieutenant—1) A commissioned rank or person immediately above second lieutenant in the U.S. Air Force, Army, or Marine Corps. 2) In the Navy, an officer in the complement of a ship or naval station who is responsible for maintenance and repair.

first line—1) In a formation of troops, vehicles, or units composed of two or more lines, the line most forward or closest to the enemy, not including SKIRMISH LINES, screens, or covering forces. 2) A slang expression that, when qualified, denotes the weapon, weapon system, technique, or capability that will best serve a given purpose or at a given time (e.g., "The F-16 Falcon is a first-line fighter aircraft").

first strike—The first offensive move of a war, generally associated with use of nuclear weapons.

FIST—See **fire support team**.

"Fix bayonets"—An order to attach bayonets to rifles.

fixed gun—A machine gun attached rigidly to the fuselage of an aircraft and aimed by moving the aircraft.

fixed-wing aircraft—A conventional jet or propeller aircraft, as distinguished from a rotary-wing aircraft or HELICOPTER.

flag—A banner of distinctive size, color, or design that serves as a symbol, a marker, or a decoration.

flag bag—The chest or locker aboard ship in which signal flags are kept.

flag bridge—The bridge on a warship where the admiral observes or directs a battle. On an aircraft carrier it is the first bridge above the flight deck.

flag captain—The officer of whatever rank in command of a FLAGSHIP.

flag country—The area of a FLAGSHIP that is used as quarters and for other purposes by the FLAG OFFICER.

flag lieutenant—An aide to an admiral.

flag mast—A disciplinary procedure in the U.S. Navy corresponding for officers to the CAPTAIN'S MAST for enlisted men.

flag officer—1) An officer holding the rank of commodore or admiral in the Navy or the Coast Guard and entitled to fly a navy blue flag showing rank by means of the number of stars on the flag, from one to five. 2) An officer holding any of the grades of general in the Army or the Marines.

flag of truce—A white flag carried or displayed to an enemy, as an invitation to conference or parley. A white flag can also be a signal of surrender.

flag plot—On a flagship, the room where the admiral has the equipment and information for controlling the command.

flag rank—The ranks of naval officers above the rank of captain.

flags—Naval slang for a signalman, referring to the device of crossed flags worn on the rating badge.

flagship—A ship carrying the admiral or other senior officer in command of a fleet, squadron, or other naval organization and flying the commander's flag. A flagship is usually, but not always, the largest of the ships.

flag signals—Signals representing information or orders that are transmitted by flags flown from a staff or mast; the flags' number, shape, or color has a meaning known to both sender and recipients. The only means of communicating in the days of sail and before the invention of the wireless, flag signals have now largely been replaced by short-range radio and are used only when visibility is very good, secrecy is paramount, and there is danger of being overheard on radio. Flag signals may also be flown to indicate unclassified information as to the status or operation of a vessel.

flak—1) Antiaircraft fire directed at enemy aircraft. 2) The shell bursts from such fire. Originating in World War I, the word was adopted from the German acronym for *Flieger Abwehr Kanone*, meaning aircraft defense gun.

flak jacket—A jacket or vest of heavy fabric containing metal or other bulletproof plates, designed especially for protection against flak. The usual type of flak jacket covers the chest, abdomen, back, and genital area, leaving the arms and legs free.

flak tower—A towerlike structure erected as many as 10 stories high in German cities (to provide a field of fire unobstructed by buildings), in which one or more antiaircraft weapons are mounted. Such a tower may also house the crew and store ammunition.

flame thrower—A weapon that projects and ignites incendiary fuel. First used in modern warfare in 1915 during World War I. See also **Greek fire**.

flanchards—Medieval defensive armor to protect the flanks of a horse in combat. The word first appears in a French text of 1302 as *flanchières*.

flange—The extended diameter base of an artillery shell that seats it properly in the firing chamber.

flank—*n*. One of the sides—right or left—of a military formation or position. *v*. To place one's force in position to threaten or attack the opponent's flank. An **open flank** is a flank without adequate protection. A **protected flank** is one resting on an obstacle not easily attacked by an enemy. When a force has one flank open and one protected, the open flank is the **tactical flank**. A **strategic flank** is one that, if enveloped, would permit an enemy to threaten a force's line of communications.

flank attack—An attack directed at the flank of an operational force. See also **attack**.

flank company—In the British army of the American Revolutionary period, the light infantry and grenadier companies in each battalion that were composed of the battalion's best soldiers. The other companies were called "battalion companies." Flank companies from the various battalions were often combined to fight in special units.

flanker—1) A detachment of troops assigned to guard the flank of a marching column. 2) *pl*. Troops belonging to a FLANK COMPANY. 3) *pl*. Formerly, riflemen and all light troops because of their position on the flanks of a force. 4) A fortification jutting out so as to command the flank of an attacking body.

flank guard—A security element deployed to protect the flank of a moving or stationary force.

flanking position—A position that threatens the security of an advancing enemy by attacking on the advancing force's flank.

flare—1) A pyrotechnic device that burns with a brilliant, in some cases colored, light, either stationary or shot into the air, used to signal, to illuminate a target or an area, or to identify persons who fire the device. 2) The nose-up landing attitude favored by land-based fighter aircraft. Carrier pilots normally forgo flare in favor of slam-down landings.

flare gun—A VERY PISTOL or other type of small gun used for shooting flares. Used particularly to indicate the position of a ship or unit in distress.

flash—The flame that issues from the muzzle of any firearm or piece of ordnance when it is fired.

flash hider—A device on the muzzle of a gun that hides the flame or flash when the gun is fired. Also known as a **flash suppressor**.

flash in the pan—A firing of the primer of a flintlock firearm without igniting the main charge.

flash message—A category of precedences reserved for initial enemy contact messages or operational messages of extreme urgency. Brevity is mandatory.

flash ranging—Finding the position of an enemy gun by observing its flash.

flash suppressor—See **flash hider**.

flask, powder—A bottle or similar vessel in which gunpowder or shot was carried before the introduction of the cartridge.

flattop—Slang for an aircraft carrier. The name was coined by Lieut. Comdr. Robert E. Dixon on 8 May 1942, when, after U.S. naval aircraft sank the Japanese carrier *Shoho*, he radioed back to his carrier, "Scratch one flattop!"

flèche—From the French word for "arrow," a fortification of earth shaped like a V, with the point toward the potential attacker.

flèchette—A small metal device shaped like a dart; flèchettes are clustered and fired in a shell that explodes above a target to scatter the projectiles broadly. Larger dartlike steel missiles called *flèchettes de guerre* were dropped from airplanes in World War I.

fleet—1) An organization of ships, aircraft, marine forces, and shore-based naval activities under the command of an officer who may exercise operational as well as administrative control. 2) A less formal organization of a group of warships under a single command. 3) All the naval ships belonging to a nation.

Fleet Air Arm—1) The air arm of the British Royal Navy, separated from the Royal Air Force in 1939. 2) Generically, any naval air arm.

fleet ballistic missile—A ballistic missile carried on and launched from naval vessels.

fleet ballistic missile submarine — A nuclear-powered submarine designed to deliver ballistic missile attacks against either submerged or surfaced targets. Designated in the U.S. Navy as SSBN.

fleet in being—A naval force that avoids action but is large enough and so positioned that an opposing naval force must station a considerable number of ships to watch it and be prepared for sudden movements.

Fleet Marine Force—A U.S. Marine Corps organization serving as an integral part of a U.S. fleet. It was originally set up in December 1933 as a brigade-size unit and a part of the U.S. fleet. A balanced force with land, air, and support elements, the Fleet Marine Force has the primary mission of capturing bases for the U.S. Navy.

Fleet Reserve—In the U.S. Navy the reserve organization composed of retired officers and enlisted personnel.

fleet satellite communications system (FLTSATCOM)—A U.S. Navy communications system, via satellite, between shore commands and units at sea.

fletcher—A person who makes arrows. An arrow is said to be fletched when it has been fitted with feathers to stabilize it in flight.

flexible response—A strategic concept that emphasizes the desirability of applying only that force necessary to accomplishing a given military goal, without resort to nuclear weapons or other draconian measures.

flight—1) In U.S. Navy and Marine Corps usage, a specified group of aircraft usually engaged in a common mission. 2) The basic tactical unit in the U.S. Air Force, consisting of four or more aircraft in two or more elements or flight subunits. 3) A single aircraft airborne on a nonoperational mission. 4) A trip by air from one point to another.

flight cap—Same as OVERSEAS CAP. See also **fifty-mission cap**.

flight deck—1) The upper deck of an aircraft carrier from which aircraft take off and on which they land. 2) An elevated compartment in some aircraft where the crew operates the aircraft.

flight leader—A pilot in command of a FLIGHT of aircraft.

flight lieutenant—A commissioned rank in the British Royal Air Force and the Royal Canadian Air Force, corresponding to that of captain in the U.S. Air Force.

flight nurse—An air force nurse who cares for patients aboard a medical air evacuation aircraft.

flight officer—In the U.S. Army Air Forces in World War II, a rank corresponding to warrant officer, junior grade.

flight sergeant—An enlisted rank or person in the British Royal Air Force or Royal Canadian Air Force, corresponding to master sergeant in the U.S. Air Force.

flint—A very hard, fine-grained quartz. Because it produces sparks when struck with steel, it was used in early firearms to ignite gunpowder. See also **flintlock**.

flintlock—A small-arms ignition system invented by the French gunsmith Le Bourgeoys in 1615. It consisted of a flint held in a vise at the end of a cock. When the trigger was released, the flint struck against a piece of steel, creating sparks. The priming powder was ignited, and it in turn ignited the powder that fired the weapon. Flintlock muskets apparently were first issued to two companies of Cromwell's New Model Army in 1645. The flintlock musket was less accurate and had a slower rate of fire than the model with the improved matchlock but was more reliable and less affected by weather. It was standard in European armies by 1699. The SNAPHANCE LOCK was generally considered a type of flintlock, as were the English lock, the doglock, the Scandinavian snaplock, and the miquelet lock.

flissa—An oriental sword with a straight handle that, with the blade, forms a Latin cross.

floating battery—A group of guns placed on any floating platform, usually protected with plate armor. Such batteries were used by the Allies against the Russian forts on the Black Sea in the Crimean War and in the American Civil War.

floating bridge—See **bridge**.

floating reserves—In an amphibious operation, reserve troops that remain embarked until needed.

FLOT—See **forward line of own troops**.

flotilla—1) An administrative or tactical organization consisting of two or more squadrons of destroyers or smaller ships, together with such additional ships as may be assigned. (Flotillas are not currently used by the U.S. Navy.) 2) A group of ships, usually small ones, more or less formally operating together.

flying army—In the 19th century, a large body of cavalry and infantry capable of rapid movement, and sometimes kept in motion because their mission was to cover the approaches to an area or to protect a frontier. Also called a FLYING CAMP.

flying artillery—In the 19th century, artillery trained to move rapidly. This was usually horse artillery in which each man had his own horse, but it could be horsedrawn artillery with the men mounted on CAISSONs and LIMBERs.

flying camp—1) In the 19th century, a body of troops prepared for rapid movement from one place to another. 2) A term used in the period of the American Revolution for a mobile, strategic reserve.

flying column—A term frequently used in the 19th century for a rapidly moving force, usually cavalry, operating behind enemy lines or sent to seize a key objective.

"Flying Fortress" (B-17)—Nickname for a four-engine World War II bomber of very long range. The most advanced model, B-17G, had

a top speed of 280 miles per hour and a range of 1,100 miles with a 6,000-pound bomb load. The Navy designation was PB-1W.

U.S. Air Force photo

"Flying Fortress"

flying officer—1) A commissioned rank in the British Royal Air Force and the Royal Canadian Air Force corresponding to first lieutenant in the U.S. Air Force. 2) In a general sense, an officer who flies or who holds an aeronautical rating.

"flying pig"—In World War I, a large projectile fired by a German trench mortar.

flying sap—See **sap**.

"Flying Squadron"—A force of fast U.S. Navy armored cruisers and smaller vessels, under the command of Commodore W. S. Schley, held in place off the U.S. Atlantic Coast early in the Spanish-American War in fear of a possible attack against coastal cities by a Spanish naval squadron under Adm. Pascual Cervera.

FO—See **forward observer**.

fodder—Coarse food, such as hay, for cattle, horses, and sheep. A sufficient supply of fodder was always a logistical challenge for armies dependent on horse-drawn transportation.

fog of war—The situation reflecting the inherent inability of commanders and staffs to know and understand everything they want to know about the activities, organization, and plans of the enemy and about the details of combat activities of their own forces. The fog of war can be reduced, but not eliminated, by good intelligence information about the enemy, by good communications between commanders and subordinates, as well as between adjacent commanders, and by close staff surveillance of subordinate activities. The concept was first articulated by Carl von Clausewitz, author of the classic *On War.*

fogy (fogey, fogie)—An allowance paid to a military person for a specified period of service. Because such allowances are given periodically, a career serviceman or -woman may have several fogies. If, for example, a lieutenant gets a $10 per month fogy for every 5 years of service, after he or she has served 10 years at the rank of lieutenant, the monthly base pay will be increased by $20.

follow-on-forces—During the Cold War, a NATO term for Warsaw Pact forces expected, in the event of war, to arrive on the battlefield to reinforce Pact FIRST-ECHELON FORCES already engaged against NATO FORWARD DEFENSE forces. See also **second echelon**.

follow-on-forces attack (FOFA) — A Cold War NATO concept for employing long-range weapons (aircraft and highly accurate surface-to-surface missiles) to disrupt the planned and anticipated arrival of Warsaw Pact FOLLOW-ON-FORCES. See also **deep attack**.

follow-up, amphibious—The landing of reinforcements and stores after the assault and assault follow-on echelons have been landed.

foot—A term once commonly used for infantry or foot soldiers; that is, troops who do not fight mounted on horses, tanks, or other means of transportation.

foot guards—An elite infantry unit with a mission of providing security for a sovereign.

forage—To seek and take food and other necessary items from civilian sources in the area where a military force is stationed or operating.

forage cap—A uniform cap with a low, flat crown and a visor. Usually softer and with a lower crown than a KEPI. Forage caps were common in the 19th century and were worn by both sides in the American Civil War.

foray—*n.* A raid, usually by a portion of a combat force, on a target other than the main objective. *v.* To make such a raid.

force—*n.* 1) An aggregation of military personnel, weapon systems, vehicles, ships, and necessary support. 2) Superior strength applied in order to overcome resistance. *v.* To apply superior strength, mental or physical, in order to overcome resistance.

force de frappe — The independent air striking force with nuclear capability established by Gen. Charles de Gaulle when he was president of France.

forced march—A march performed at an unusually fast pace, generally for a long distance, in order to reach an objective in less time than usual. See also **march**.

force multiplier—A factor, tangible or intangible, that increases the combat value of a force. Clausewitz's famous statement that "defense is the stronger form of combat" indicates that he considered defensive posture such a multiplying factor. In the U.S. Army, force multipliers are considered to include (in addition to defensive posture) such factors as terrain, training, leadership, and morale.

force ratio—The ratio of the strengths of two opposing forces. Strength is indicated by such measures as number of personnel and firepower score.

forecastle/foc'sle—The forward section of a ship's deck on which anchor-handling equipment is located.

forefoot—The forward part of a vessel where the stern and the keel meet.

Foreign Broadcast Intelligence Service (FBIS)—A CIA unit that monitors foreign radio and television stations. The FBIS dates back to 1941, when the U.S. government established a radio-monitoring service at the request of the State Department.

forage cap

Foreign Legion, French—A French military organization of mercenaries of many nationalities who serve under French officers. The Foreign Legion was established in 1832 and served primarily in the French colonies in North Africa but also in France's possessions in Indochina. After most French colonies became independent, the Legion is based in Corsica, though it has overseas units in former colonies.

Foreign Legion, Spanish—A Spanish military organization, similar to the French Foreign Legion, established early in the 20th century. It served mainly in the Spanish colonies of North Africa.

fork—Technical artillery term signifying, for a given elevation setting, the angle in elevation that will move the center of impact four PROBABLE ERRORs on the ground.

form—To assemble in any formation of ranks and files.

formation—1) An ordered arrangement of troops, ships, vehicles, or aircraft for a specific purpose. 2) In U.S. military terminology, a combat organization of division size or larger.

formers—Round pieces of wood of slightly less than the diameter of the bore of a gun around which could be rolled the paper or other material of a cartridge in SEPARATE-LOADING AMMUNITION.

form on—To connect one or several individuals to an object or a formation so as to lengthen a line.

fort—1) A permanent defensive structure often including living quarters for a sizable force. 2) A FORTIFICATION. 3) The term used to designate a permanent U.S. Army installation or garrison, such as Fort Myer and Fort Leavenworth.

fortification—1) The military art of strengthening a place, a position, or an area in order to increase the defensive power of troops against attack. 2) A military defensive work. 3) The act of fortifying. Fortifications are generally classified as PERMANENT FORTIFICATIONS or FIELD FORTIFICATIONS. Throughout the ages, fortifications have been an important, frequently employed asset in warfare. Modern developments, especially since the Industrial Revolution, radically changed the conduct of warfare by making possible new weapons of greatly increased power, requiring troops and armies to resort more frequently than ever before to fortifications. In World War I, machine guns, shrapnel, and high-explosive shells drove the armies into extensive trench systems. For the first time in history (although this develop-

ment had been presaged to some extent in the American Civil War), armies fought a war in which there were no flanks. Victory could be gained only by making costly frontal attacks or by exhausting the enemy's ability or will to make war. The appearance of the first tanks in 1916, and later the introduction of HUTIER TACTICS by the Germans, restored a measure of mobility to the battlefield; but combat in World War I was characteristically a combat of trenches and artillery. During the interwar years, many Europen nations, having analyzed the military experience of World War I, erected permanent fortifications along their frontiers, primarily for strategic purposes. The best-remembered of these works are the French MAGINOT LINE and the German WEST WALL (or SIEGFRIED LINE). Both PERMANENT FORTIFICATIONS and FIELD FORTIFICATIONS were important factors in all World War II land campaigns and in all major wars since World War II.

fortified defense—See **defense**.

fortified line—A series of permanent defensive positions of great depth and hardness, as in the French MAGINOT LINE or the German SIEGFRIED LINEs. Such a line employs concrete or steel-protected gun emplacements, planned supporting fire coverage, heavily protected troops and supplies, and a coordinated series of obstacles to stop combat vehicles. Also called a **fortified zone** because of its depth.

fortify—To strengthen a position by means of forts, entrenchments, batteries, or constructions of any kind that improve the possibility of defense against attack.

Fortitude, Operation—A complex deception operation in World War II designed to convince Hitler and his commanders that the Normandy landings on D-day were merely a feint and that the main attack would be in the area of Pas de Calais. The success of Operation Fortitude was a major factor in the success of the Allied invasion.

fortress—A fortified place, especially a large and permanent military stronghold, often including a town. A fort.

Forty Committee—A group within the National Security Council responsible for approving covert intelligence operations during the 1950s. Its formal name was changed several times, but it is best remembered as the Forty Committee.

forward air controller—An air officer, stationed in an advance ground position or airborne, who directs the activities of aircraft engaged in close air support of ground troops.

forward area—An area at or near the front, in or near a combat area, or near the enemy. See also **area**.

forward-based systems (FBS) — Short-range nuclear weapon systems that can reach targets by virtue of their location in forward areas. During the Cold War, U.S. quick-reaction alert aircraft in Western Europe could have quickly struck at targets in Eastern Europe and the Soviet Union.

forward command post — See **command post.**

forward defense—A Cold War NATO concept that, in the event of an invasion of Western Europe by the WARSAW PACT, NATO forces would defend close to the "Iron Curtain" (the frontier between East and West Germany). This required a high level of readiness and of defensive effectiveness on the part of NATO forces. The reasoning behind this concept was partly political, partly military. Politically, it was important that the West German government and people be assured that NATO would endeavor to save as much of West Germany as possible from invasion. Militarily, West Germany was so narrow that some military theorists believed there was not enough space for traditional defense in depth. Other theorists believed that the forward defense concept had the weaknesses of a LINEAR DEFENSE or CORDON DEFENSE.

forward echelon—The echelon of a headquarters or of a unit that is located in or sent ahead to a forward area, distinguished especially from a rear echelon.

forward edge of the battle area (FEBA)— The line or zone where the forward elements of two opposing armies are engaged in direct combat. Virtually synonymous with FLOT.

forward line of own troops (FLOT)—The front line of a force engaged in combat. See also **FEBA.**

forward observer (FO)—A person located at or near the front line whose mission is to adjust the fire of heavy weapons on hostile targets, using telephone or radio to communicate with the weapons, which are usually to the rear in DEFILADE. A forward observer is usually an artillery officer attached to an infantry or armor unit for the purpose of adjusting supporting artillery fire to help the supported unit accomplish its mission. See also **fire support team**.

foss (fosse)—A moat or a ditch, particularly a moat around a fort.

fougasse—A crude type of antipersonnel mine that projects a charge of broken stone or scrap metal or both. This weapon has been employed since the early days of gunpowder.

4-F—A military draft classification assigned to persons deemed physically unfit for military service.

fourragère—A unit decoration given by France and Belgium, consisting of braided cords of distinctive color and design, usually worn on the right shoulder, as opposed to the AIGUILLETTE, which is worn on the left.

fox—A pre-19th-century term for "sword."

Fox— Letter of old phonetic alphabet. See also **alphabet, phonetic**.

foxer—A World War II device for counteracting the German acoustic torpedo, which could be detonated by the noise of a ship's propelers. The foxer was towed behind a ship and made a noise louder than the propellers so that it would detonate the acoustic torpedo at a safe distance astern.

foxhole—A hole in the earth, shallow or deep, for a single soldier, usually dug hastily for protection against enemy fire.

Foxtrot—Letter of NATO phonetic alphabet. See also **alphabet, phonetic**.

frag—Slang for a fragmentation grenade. In Vietnam, U.S. personnel used the term as a verb, referring to an alienated soldier's attempt to kill his superior with a grenade.

fragmentary order—An abbreviated form of an operation order, usually issued on a day-to-day basis, which eliminates the need for restating information contained in a basic operation order. It may be issued in sections. Sometimes called **frag order**.

fragmentation—The scattering of pieces of metal casing from a grenade, bomb, or shell, generally by explosion above a target area. See also **shell fragment**.

fragmentation bomb—See **bomb**.

fragmentation grenade—See **grenade**.

fraise—From the French word meaning "ruff" or "ruffle." A fraise is a barrier consisting of a series of pointed stakes stuck into the ground at an angle, or a similar construction of barbed wire.

francisca—A single-bladed ax with a particularly heavy head set on the haft at an angle. Used by the Franks from the 6th to the 8th century as a throwing ax, as well as in hand-to-hand combat, it disappeared when the Franks changed to mounted combat. See also **ax**.

franc-tireur—A French guerrilla, particularly of the period of the Franco-Prussian War.

free company—A group of medieval mercenaries, notably English, who hired themselves out to any European ruler who needed tough, skilled, fighting men. See also **company**.

Freedom Fighter/Tiger (F-5)—A two-man tactical fighter built by the Northrop Corporation, the F-5 first flew in 1963. Its weaponry included SIDEWINDER missiles and 20mm guns in the nose. Although handicapped by a short combat radius, the F-5 was acclaimed for its simplicity and ease of maintenance and many foreign air forces purchased it.

free-fire area—An area into which any weapon system may fire without additional coordination with headquarters.

free war game—A war game in which there is no predetermined scenario and in which the controller freely applies personal judgment and military experience or insight to make assessments. See also **war game**.

French 75—A 75mm field gun developed in France in 1897 and widely used during and after World War I. The finest field gun of its time, it was adopted by armies throughout the world. It was the principal light artillery piece of the American Expeditionary Force in World War I. In France the weapon was called a *soixante-quinze*.

friction—Interactions among individuals, units, and formations, manifested by delays, confusion, misunderstandings, and generally reduced tempo of operations in comparison with the ideal. The larger the force, the greater the friction and the performance degradation resulting therefrom. Friction can be reduced, but not entirely eliminated, by intensive training, careful planning, and close surveillance of operations by commanders and staffs. The concept was elucidated by Clausewitz in *On War*.

friendly fire—A category of casualty mistakenly caused by fire from friendly forces engaged with the enemy.

frigate—A class of fast, light warships. The name in ancient times was used for a variety of light, open craft, with oars or sails, in the Mediterranean. Various types of fast ships were called frigates by the Spanish, the Portuguese, and the French in the 16th, 17th, and 18th centuries. At the time of the Seven Years' War (1756–63) the frigate was standardized as a three-masted, fully rigged (square-rigged) vessel with 24 to 50 guns, most of them on one deck but with some on the poop and forecastle. In the 19th century, steam frigates were developed, and they usually carried fewer guns than frigates under sail. The designation has been used by the U.S. Navy since World War II for a class of fast ships weighing 5,000 to 7,000 tons that can operate independently or with others to counter submarine, air, and surface threats. U.S. frigates normally carry 3-inch or 5-inch dual-purpose guns or surface-to-surface missiles, as well as advanced antisubmarine warfare weapons. The U.S. designation is DL.

frill—An ornamental appendage to the shirt usually worn with REGIMENTALS, attached by a hook and eye to the uniform coat. Enlisted men wore frills not attached to the coat.

"Fritz" — World War I slang for a German, particularly a German soldier. See also **"Jerry."**

frizzen—The piece of steel arched over the priming pan of a SNAPHANCE against which the flint was struck to ignite the powder. Also called BATTERY.

frogman—U.S. Navy World War II swimmer equipped with only swim fins and goggles, who performed a variety of underwater tasks. See also **SEAL**.

front—1) In general, the combat area. 2) The line of contact between two opposite forces. 3) The side of a force or a position facing the enemy. 4) Translation of a Russian term for army group.

frontal attack—1) An attack that strikes the enemy along his front. 2) In air interception, an attack by an interceptor aircraft in which the attacker crosses the heading of the other aircraft at an angle greater than 135 degrees. See also **attack**.

front line—1) The line formed by the foremost units in a combat situation. 2) In a more general sense, the line or the area of contact with the enemy, the FRONT. See also **forward edge of the battle area** and **forward line of own troops**.

full charge—The maximum charge when the two or more propelling charges are available for guns with SEMIFIXED AMMUNITION or SEPARATE-LOADING AMMUNITION.

fuller—A groove cut into the face of a sword blade to make it lighter while retaining its stiffness.

functional bombing—Bombing of a special class of key targets, like dams or marshaling yards, within an industrial complex or transportation system, as opposed to bombing the entire system.

funda—1) A Roman sling. See also **funditor**. 2) A crude catapult, used by Visigoths and Franks in sieges after the fall of Rome.

funditor—In the ancient Roman army, a lightly armed skirmisher who carried a sling rather than a bow and arrow or a javelin. See also **veles**.

furlough—An authorized absence of enlisted personnel from a duty station, usually for a period longer than a weekend. Now officially called "leave."

fuze—An instrument for detonating an explosive device. Originally, fuzes were strings of hemp or other slow-burning combustible material that were lit at the end farther from the powder. Mechanical or electrical mechanisms have replaced the older type of fuze and are of a number of types, including **impact**, which triggers the explosion when the projectile hits the ground or the target; **proximity**, which detonates at a set distance from the target; **delayed action**, which detonates at a set time after impact; **time**, a clocklike mechanism that causes a projectile to explode after a period of time to produce an air burst over the target; and **base**, a fuze located in the base of a projectile or a bomb.

fusil—1) A 17th-century light FLINTLOCK musket. 2) A steel that strikes fire out of a flint. 3) A tinderbox. 4) The piece of steel that covered the pan in early firearms.

fusilier—Originally, a soldier armed with the FUSIL. Fusiliers were originally used as artillery guards. Fusilier units, armed with modern weapons, still exist in the British army (e.g., the Royal Welch Fusiliers).

fusillade—*n.* The simultaneous or near-simultaneous discharge of many firearms in combat or in a military exercise. *v.* To shoot down by a simultaneous discharge of firearms.

fustibal—A sling on the end of a 4-foot-long staff. Fustibals were used during the Hussite campaigns as auxiliary weapons and in the 17th century to hurl grenades.

fyrd—The militia in England before the Norman Conquest.

G

G-1, G-2, G-3, G-4—The four main sections of an army staff in the U.S. Army; the organization was adopted in 1917 from the French example. G-1 is concerned with personnel; G-2 with intelligence; G-3 with plans, training, and operations; G-4 with supply. There is sometimes a G-5, which has had such diverse assignments as war plans and civil affairs.

gabion—A cylinder of wicker or other material, sometimes closed at one end. It was filled with dirt or rocks and used for building fortifications. The gabion has been to some extent superseded by the sandbag. A work made with gabions is called a "gabionade."

Galaxy (C-5A)—A cargo transport aircraft powered by four turbofan engines, it is the largest transport aircraft in the U.S. inventory.

Lockhead Aircraft Corporation photo

Galaxy (C-5A)

gallease—A heavily armed three-masted galley used in the Mediterranean in the 16th and 17th centuries.

galleon—A large, three-masted sailing vessel with two or more decks. Numerous countries, but most notably Spain, built galleons in the 15th and 16th centuries for use as both warships and merchantmen.

gallery—1) In a fort, a passageway that is covered overhead and protected by walls or parti-walls on the sides. 2) A mine tunnel or shaft. 3) A portable Roman structure covered with hides and used to conceal and protect men moving forward to attack a besieged fortification.

galley—1) A long, open, or partially decked vessel propelled by oars and sometimes by one or more sails, used particularly in the Mediterranean for centuries. The ancient galleys were often rowed by slaves and had as many as five banks of oars (QUINQUIREME). They were used militarily both for fighting naval battles and for carrying troops for land battles. In medieval times, galleys became much larger. They were gradually abandoned after the development of bigger ships propelled entirely by sail. See also **bireme** and **trireme**. 2) A place aboard ship where food is prepared.

galliot—A light, fast war galley, equipped with both sails and oars, that was used in the Mediterranean region.

galloper—A mounted messenger.

game, war—See **war game**.

113

gaming—A training technique in which players are presented with military situations involving choice and risk.

gantlet—1) A military punishment in which the culprit ran between two rows of men who hit him with sticks, clubs, or other devices as he passed. 2) Variant spelling of GAUNTLET.

gap marker—A device used to mark a minefield gap, an area (usually a lane) cleared of mines. Because gap markers must describe a line or a path, they are referenced to a landmark or an intermediate marker to indicate the boundary of the gap.

Garand rifle—A semiautomatic rifle designed by the American small-arms designer John C. Garand. Adopted in 1936, the Garand served as the basic U.S. infantry weapon in World War II and the Korean War. Officially designated the M-1, it is a .30-caliber gas-operated weapon, weighing about 9.5 pounds and firing an eight-round clip from a 24-inch barrel with four rifled grooves.

Gardner gun—A .45-caliber machine gun named for its designer, William Gardner of Toledo, Ohio. The 1879 model had twin air- or water-cooled barrels. A hand crank on the right side of the action loaded first one barrel and then the other; it also fired and ejected the shell case with one revolution.

Gardner gun

garnishing—The application of material to an object to achieve or enhance camouflage.

garrison—*n.* 1) All units assigned to a base or area for defense, development, operation, and maintenance of facilities. 2) A military post. *v.* To assign troops or units to, or move troops into, a post.

garrison cap—See **overseas cap**.

garrison ration—In the U.S. Army, the standard peacetime ration for all persons entitled to it. See also **ration**.

gas grenade—See **grenade**.

gas mask—A mask worn over the face to protect the eyes from toxic gases and to remove gases from the air as it is inhaled.

U.S. Army photo

gas mask

gas, nerve—Any chemical agent whose physiological effect is a paralysis or derangement of the nerve centers.

gas, poison—Any chemical substance that can produce toxic or irritant effects. Gas was first used in modern warfare during World War I, on the Western Front on 22 April 1915, when the German forces released chlorine against the Allied positions in the Ypres salient, with lethal results. Subsequently, both sides made widespread use of a variety of poison gases. The use of chemical weapons was banned by international agreement in Article 171 of the Versailles Treaty and by similar prohibitions in other treaties signed at the end of World War I. These prohibitions were reinforced by the Treaty of Washington (1922) and by a protocol of 1925 that was signed by more than 40 nations. See also **chemical warfare; Lewisite; mustard gas; phosgene**.

gas, war—See **gas, poison**.

Gatling gun—A multibarreled machine gun designed by Richard J. Gatling. Patented in 1862, it was the first effective machine gun and was adopted by the Union army in the Civil War. It was fired by turning a hand crank but had automatic loading and ejection of cartridges.

Gatling gun

gauntlet—A glove, particularly a medieval armor glove, with a wide wrist to give extra protection. See also **gantlet**.

gear—1) The personal belongings of a sailor, corresponding to the soldier's KIT. 2) The equipment required for a particular job, such as **degaussing gear, flight gear**.

gendarme—1) A member of a national organization of military police, called the **gendarmerie**, responsible for internal law enforcement and security. 2) A member of a royal French cavalry corps that existed in various forms from the 15th century to 1789.

general—1) A senior rank in most national ground and air forces. A **general officer** is one holding a rank above colonel, and entitled to display a flag (red in the U.S. Army) with from one to four stars, depending on whether the rank is **brigadier general** (one star), **major general** (two stars), **lieutenant general** (three stars), or **general** (four stars). The rank of four-star general with title of **General of the Army** has been conferred three times in the United States since the Civil War: in 1866 when it was given to Ulysses S. Grant, in 1869 to William T. Sherman, and 1888 to Philip H. Sheridan. In 1944, during World War II, the title **General of the Army of the United States** (five stars) was given to Henry H. "Hap" Arnold (his title was changed to **General of the Air Force** when an independent air force was established in 1946), Dwight D. Eisenhower, Douglas MacArthur, and George C. Marshall; and in 1950 it was conferred on Omar Bradley. This rank is the equivalent of field marshal in other armies. From 1799 to 1802 the U.S. Army had an official rank of **General of the Armies** (presumably four stars), which was also the equivalent of field marshal but was never awarded. Reestablished in 1919, this rank was conferred on John J. Pershing, who wore four stars.

general court-martial — See **court-martial**.

generalissimo—1) Commander in chief of all of a nation's armed forces. The rank, which is the Italian superlative of "general," has long been used but was first used in its modern sense by Benito Mussolini and subsequently adopted by some others, notably by Joseph Stalin of the Soviet Union and Chiang Kai-shek of China. 2) Commander of a combined force of allied military forces.

general mobilization—See **mobilization**.

general officer—See **general**.

General of the Armies—See **general**.

general orders—1) Permanent instructions, issued in order form, that apply to all members of a command, as compared with special orders, which affect only individuals or small groups. General orders are usually concerned with matters of policy or administration and include such things as citations of units, awards, important appointments, and other matters involving information or orders that are general in application and permanent in character. 2) A series of permanent guard orders that govern the duties of a sentry or post.

general quarters—A condition of readiness of a warship's crew when action is imminent. All battle stations are fully manned and alert; ammunition is ready for instant loading; guns and guided-missile launchers may be loaded.

general reserve—A reserve of troops and units under the control of the commander of a force for use when and where the commander decides.

general staff—A select group of military generalists whose function is to assist a nation's military leadership—or a general commanding a field force of combined-arms elements—in planning, controlling, directing, coordinating, and supervising the activities of all subordinate military elements to achieve an assigned objective. The leader or leadership makes decisions and gives commands; the general staff's responsibility is to provide all possible support to assure that the decisions and commands are timely, sound, and effective.

general support—Support that is given to a whole force rather than to any particular subdivision thereof. It differs from DIRECT SUPPORT, which is provided to a single, specified unit.

general support artillery — Artillery that executes the fire directed by the commander of the unit to which it organically belongs or is attached. It fires in support of the operation as a whole, rather than in support of a particular subordinate unit.

general support-reinforcing — A tactical artillery mission. General support-reinforcing artillery has the primary mission of supporting the force as a whole and a secondary mission of providing reinforcing fire for another designated artillery unit.

general war—Armed conflict between major powers in which the belligerents' total resources are employed and the national survival of a principal belligerent is in jeopardy.

Geneva Convention—One of a series of international agreements signed at Geneva, Switzerland, in 1864, 1906, 1909, 1929, and 1949, establishing rules for the treatment of prisoners of war and of wartime sick or wounded.

Geneva Cross—The symbol used by the Red Cross and by medical services of armed forces of most nations to indicate their neutrality. The red cross, reversing the national heraldic emblem of Switzerland, was adopted at the 1864 Geneva Convention that established rules for the treatment of prisoners and the sick and wounded.

genitors—Spanish light cavalry, armed with light LANCE or JAVELIN, introduced in the wars with the Moors about the 11th century. The genitors continued to serve in Spanish armies through the Italian wars of the 16th century. In weapons and tactics they imitated the Moorish light cavalry.

genocide—The deliberate and systematic extermination of a national, racial, political, or cultural group. Examples are Hitler's campaign against the Jews during World War II,

the campaign against opposition elements in Cambodia in the 1970s, and the massacre of the Tutsis by the Hutus in Rwanda in the 1990s.

George—Letter of old phonetic alphabet. See also **alphabet, phonetic**.

GI—From "Government Issue"; the nickname "GI" was given to U.S. soldiers in World War II because all of their equipment was provided by the government.

GI Bill—The Veterans' Benefit Act of 1944, which provided for federal funding of education for veterans, among other entitlements.

gig—1) The small boat used by the commander of a vessel for transport to and from the main ship, called the "captain's gig." 2) The record of an infraction or shortcoming.

glacis—From French *glace*, meaning "ice," it is a cleared slope extending outward from the base of a fortification so that attacking enemy troops are within sight of the defenders.

gladius—A 2-foot sword with a 2-inch-wide blade adopted by Roman armies about 250 B.C. The HASTATI and PRINCIPES wielded the gladius at close quarters after throwing their javelins. It was primarily a thrusting weapon but could also be used as a hand ax.

glide bomb—*v.* 1) To bomb a target by releasing one or more bombs when the bombing plane is gliding. 2) In a less exact sense, to dive-bomb at a shallow angle. *n.* A bomb fitted with airfoils to provide lift, carried and released in the direction of a target by an airplane.

glide path—1) The flight path of an aircraft or a winged missile as it glides downward, the line of which forms an angle with the longitudinal axis of the aircraft or missile. 2) The line to be followed by an aircraft as it descends for landing. Also called **glide slope**.

glider—A fixed-wing airplane having no internal source of power and constructed so as to glide and soar. Military gliders, used to carry troops or supplies, are normally towed aloft by a powered airplane. Released from the tow, they have limited range but are given lift by their airfoils and thrust by the force of gravity combined with momentum and the reaction of aerodynamic forces upon the lifting surfaces.

Waco CG-4.

glider

global command and control system (GCCS)—The U.S. Defense Department's computerized system for strategic command and control functions. With GCCS, joint commanders can coordinate widely dispersed units, receive accurate feedback, and execute fast-moving operations.

Global Hawk—An unmanned U.S. reconnaissance aircraft manufactured by Northrop Grumman and designed to replace the U-2. See also **unmanned aerial vehicle (UAV)**.

Gold—Letter of NATO phonetic alphabet. See also **alphabet, phonetic**.

gorget—A piece of armor developed in the 15th century consisting of several articulated plates hinged to fit around the neck and fastened with a clasp. Gorgets were worn with buff coats after armor fell into disuse. The term was later used for a badge of rank worn at the throat.

Grande Armée—The name applied to the principal field army of Emperor Napoleon Bonaparte of France. Formed in 1804, when Napoleon was contemplating an invasion of England, it was first employed as the Imperial Army in the Ulm-Austerlitz Campaign (1805). The Grande Armée of 1805–06 numbered some 200,000 men, two thirds of them veterans; it was the best-trained, -equipped, and -led of Napoleon's armies and was the instrument of his greatest victories, including Austerlitz, Jena, Auerstadt, and Friedland. The nucleus of the Grande Armée was largely destroyed in the 1812 Russian Campaign.

grande batterie—A concept devised by Napoleon for massing artillery to support his main attack. Hitting the enemy's front line with concentrated artillery fire would cut a breach and permit the infantry to advance.

Grand Fleet—The designation of the British battle fleet that had the mission of protecting the British Isles against the German High Seas Fleet during World War I. The great fleet, which in 1914 included the 24 battleships and battle cruisers of the First, Second, and Third Home Fleets, was commanded by Adm. Sir John Rushworth Jellicoe from 1914 to 1916 and defeated the German fleet in the Battle of Jutland (31 May 1916), the greatest naval battle of the war. Following Jutland, Jellicoe was appointed First Sea Lord of the Admiralty; he was succeeded in command of the Grand Fleet by Adm. Sir David Beatty, who had commanded the British battle cruisers at Jutland.

"grand slam"—All enemy aircraft in sight have been destroyed.

grand strategy—An imprecise term, used by many military theorists of the late 19th and early 20th centuries, generally signifying strategic concepts at a level above single-theater and campaign strategy and comprising a mixture of military strategy and national strategy. See also **strategy; strategy, military; strategy, national**.

grand tactics—An imprecise term used by many military theorists of the late 19th and early 20th centuries in a largely unsuccessful effort to make a clear distinction between BATTLEFIELD TACTICS and MILITARY STRATEGY. Akin to the more modern CONCEPT OF OPERATIONS.

grapeshot—A type of ammunition composed of a number of iron balls about twice the size of a musket ball or of CANISTER shot, placed in layers—usually three separated by metal plates—inside a shell and fired from cannon. Generally used at short range against attacking troops. Also known as **hailshot**. Grapeshot, or grape, was used in both land and naval warfare in the 18th and 19th centuries.

Gras rifle—See **Chassepot**.

graves registration—Supervision and execution of matters pertaining to the identification, removal, and burial of the dead and the collection and processing of their effects.

gravity drop—The vertical deflection of a bomb or projectile caused by the action of gravity. See also **trajectory**.

gray propaganda—Propaganda that does not specifically identify its source or its origins. See also **propaganda**.

graze—1) Ricochet. 2) As an artillery sensing in time fire, it is the term used to indicate a burst on impact and not in the air.

grazing fire—Fire that is approximately parallel to the ground and does not rise above the height of a person standing.

"grease gun"—Slang for the U.S. Army's .45-caliber M-3A1 World War II submachine gun. Rugged and durable, it acquired its name from its resemblance to a common garage tool.

U.S. Army photo

"grease gun"

Great White Fleet—The 16-battleship battle fleet of the United States which, at the direction of President Theodore Roosevelt, made a round-the-world cruise in 1907–09. It was called the Great White Fleet because all of the warships were painted white.

greaves—Armor for the lower leg, ranging from a shin guard to a type that covered the leg from the knee to the bottom of the heel.

Greek fire—An incendiary mixture, probably including sulfur, pitch, niter, and petroleum with other substances, used by the Byzantine Greeks from at least the 7th century A.D. in both land and naval warfare. "Greek fire" is the Crusader term for what the Byzantines called "liquid fire." Although it is alleged that liquid fire was invented by an engineer named Kallinokos, it seems likely that he merely refined an existing weapon.

grenade—A hollow, explosive-filled projectile hurled at the enemy by hand or by some mechanical device—launcher, gun, or mortar—designed and fuzed to explode on impact or when triggered by a self-contained timer. Until the end of the 13th century, crude pots of clay filled with wet quicklime and other combustible substances were flung at an enemy. In the 16th century, containers filled with gunpowder were used in siege operations. In 1591 Maurice of Nassau invented a cast-iron grenade. In 1667 grenades became a permanent part of the equipment of the French army. They fell into disfavor, although not entirely out of use, but became popular again in the Crimean War. Grenades of various kinds are in modern arsenals. Grenades are classified by means of delivery or propulsion and by their effects. Types of grenades classified by means of delivery or propulsion include **hand grenades** and **rifle grenades** (See also grenade launcher). Types of grenades classified by effects include the following: **antitank grenade**—Designed for use against tanks and armored vehicles. The high-explosive, antitank (HEAT) rifle grenade consists of a body assembly, stabilizer, and fin assembly. The body contains about 12 ounces of high explosive in the form of a shaped charge and a base detonator. A point-initiating fuze is attached to the nose of the grenade. Upon impact, this fuze, which has a small shaped charge, initiates the base detonator, which, in turn, explodes the main charge. At right angles, the jet from this grenade will penetrate upwards of 8 inches of armor plate and is effective up to 65 degrees obliquity. **fragmentation grenade**—The typical hand grenade, used by the U.S. Army in World Wars I and II, weighing about 22 ounces. Its serrated cast-iron body originally contained 2 ounces of black powder. However, in 1943 the powder was replaced by TNT, which shattered the case more effectively and scattered fragments over a circular area of about 10 yards. **gas grenade**—Filled with tear gas or other disabling chemicals and

U.S. Army photo

grenade

used primarily by police agencies for riot control. **illuminating grenade**—Fired by a rifle, this consists of a cylindrical body and a stabilizer assembly. The body contains 0.5 pound of illuminant, a base-igniting fuze, and a quickmatch. Upon impact, the illuminant burns for 55 seconds with 80,000 candlepower, illuminating an area 240 yards in diameter. **incendiary grenade**—Contains thermite, (TH) which burns for 30 seconds at 4,300° F. and is used to set fire to enemy matériel. **offensive grenade**—A cardboard cylinder with metal ends, containing 6 or 7 ounces of TNT. It creates an explosive blast and is most effective in a confined area like a trench or a pillbox. It gets its effect from blast rather than fragmentation. **smoke grenade**—Produces smoke in various colors, which is used for concealing troop movements, for signaling, or for other purposes. See also grenade, "jam pot," and grenade, "potato masher."

grenade, "jam-pot"—An early form of the FRAGMENTATION GRENADE, the "jam-pot" was a tin can containing an explosive and scraps of iron used as a makeshift grenade by the British army in World War I.

grenade launcher—Any of several devices for projecting grenades. In World War II, a launching device that could be fitted to the muzzles of standard rifles fired hand grenades from 100 to 200 yards. One of the best-known types was the Japanese KNEE MORTAR of World War II.

grenade, "potato masher"—A German antipersonnel grenade used in both world wars, so called because it was shaped like an old-fashioned potato masher, with a long handle attached to a cylinder containing the explosive.

grenadier—Originally a soldier whose primary function was to throw grenades. At the defense of Ratisbon in 1632, the name was first used for soldiers who threw grenades from the walls, for which they received extra pay. By the mid-17th century, special companies were being formed of especially strong men who were employed to throw grenades. Although the use of grenades declined during the 18th century, elite units of grenadiers remained in many armies and, as in the British army, often became elite attack troops.

Grey Funnel Line — An in-house British term for the seagoing portion of the Royal Navy.

grid (military grid)—Two sets of parallel lines, labeled by consecutive letters or numbers, intersecting at right angles and forming squares. The grid is superimposed on maps, charts, and other representations of the earth's surface in an accurate and consistent manner to permit precise identification of ground locations, facilitating the computation of direction and distance to other points.

grog—Watered rum, issued generally twice a day in the British Royal Navy from about 1740 until late in the 19th century. "Grog" was the nickname of Adm. Edward Vernon, who first ordered that watered rum rather than pure whiskey be provided to British sailors. The U.S. Navy followed the British example until 1862, when the grog ration was abolished by Secretary of the Navy Gideon Welles.

grommet—1) Small reinforcing metal ring, sewn or crimped into sails or other fabric. 2) A ring of metal or other stiff material placed inside a visored cap to keep it taut.

ground alert—A status in which aircraft on the ground are fully serviced and armed with combat crews in readiness to take off within a specified short period of time after receipt of a mission order.

ground control—1) The guidance given an aircraft or missile in flight by a person on the ground. 2) The electronic equipment or network used in exercising this control. 3) A system of accurate measurements used to determine the distances and directions or

grenadier

differences in elevation between points on the Earth. The system provides a basis for map-making.

ground crew—A team of mechanics and technicians who maintain and service aircraft and aircraft armament.

ground fire—Small-arms ground-to-air fire directed against aircraft.

ground force—1) A force made up of ground troop units as opposed to air or naval units. 2) A force belonging to the ground echelon of an air organization.

ground troops—Troops that are generally employed in ground warfare, such as infantry and artillery (or U.S. Marines), as opposed to air or naval forces.

ground zero—That point on the surface of the earth directly below the center of a nuclear detonation or other cataclysmic event. Since 11 September 2001, the term has been capitalized and applied particularly to the site of the destroyed World Trade Center. See **World Trade Center and Pentagon attacks, 2001.**

group—1) A flexible administrative and tactical unit composed of two or more battalions, two or more squadrons, or two or more ships. 2) A number of ships or aircraft, normally a subdivision of a force, assigned for a specific purpose. See also **groupment**.

group captain—A commissioned rank, title, or person in the British Royal Air Force, equivalent to that of colonel in the U.S. Air Force.

groupment—A temporary task force, usually of artillery units, consisting of two or more battalions under the command of the senior commander or—if a direct-support groupment—of the organic direct-support battalion commander.

"grunt"—U.S. military slang for an infantryman.

G-suit—Nylon trousers that wrap around the legs and waist of an aircraft crewman and automatically fill with air in gravity-intensive maneuvers to retain blood pressure and function.

guard—*n.* 1) A military person, usually but not always enlisted, who is assigned the duty of protecting a place or its occupants against intruders. 2) A body of persons detailed to escort a person, people, or material items requiring safeguard; such guards may perform exhibition drills or carry out other ceremonial functions. 3) Member of an elite body of troops assigned permanently to the protection of a monarch or other national leader. 4) A person who supervises and controls prisoners. *v.* 1) To perform protective functions. 2) To monitor (usually a radio frequency). An **honor guard** is detailed to greet or accompany distinguished persons at a ceremony or, at a funeral, to accompany the coffins of military personnel. Also known as **guard of honor.**

Guardia Civil—Elite gendarmerie of Spain.

guard mail—Mail that is carried by or accompanied by an armed guard.

guard-mount—A ceremony, usually held daily, at which the assigned guard for an installation, garrison, or unit—typically a temporary unit with personnel from other permanent units—is relieved by a new guard. In anachronistic terminology, though still occasionally used, it was called "guard-mounting."

guard of honor—See **guard**.

guardship—A ship detailed for a specific duty for the purpose of enabling other ships in company to assume a lower degree of readiness. For example, a guardship may monitor various radio frequencies on which communications for the company may be sent, in order that the other ships may maintain radio silence.

guardsman—1) One who acts as a guard. 2) A member of the U.S. National Guard. 3) A soldier in a national unit of guards; for example, in the British army, a member of a regiment of the royal household guards.

guarrel—See **crossbow** and **quarrel**.

guerre de course—The interruption of an enemy's seaborne commerce by the destruction of its merchant shipping. Such naval warfare is usually carried on by fast cruisers capable of fighting small enemy warships but able to avoid enemy capital ships by speed, maneuver, or stealth (as in a submarine).

guerrilla—Spanish for "little war." *adj.* Pertaining to irregular warfare. *n.* A participant in fighting not directly connected with a formal military organization or operation. See also **partisan**.

guerrilla warfare—Military and paramilitary operations, including sabotage and harassment, conducted in enemy-held or hostile territory by small bands of irregular, predominantly indigenous forces. Clausewitz specified five preconditions for successful guerrilla operations: a) they must be conducted in the enemy's interior; b) battles must be decided by single blows; c) the operational area must be sufficiently large to allow the guerrillas to move about; d) the terrain must not be easily traversed by conventional forces; and e) the national character of the guerrillas must be such as to find this type of warfare appealing.

guidance—1) The action of pointing out a course to be followed. 2) The action of providing information and advice required by another to carry out an operation. 3) The action of guiding a moving object along a course.

guide—1) A local person, usually civilian, attached to an army to provide information and assistance in respect to local areas. 2) A soldier (or other military person) at the extreme right-front or left-front of a unit marching in close order, whose duty is to set the direction of the unit, in accordance with orders given by the commander.

guided missile—An unmanned missile that moves above the surface of the earth, whose trajectory or flight plan is capable of being altered either by a preset or self-reacting device within the missile or by radio command outside the missile. Guided missiles are divided by their ranges into **long-range** (more than 5,500 kilometers), **midrange** (601 to 5,500 km), and **short-range** (less than 601 km).

guided-missile destroyer (DDG) — See **destroyer, guided-missile**.

guidon—A small flag or pennant, originally carried by a GUIDE to mark the end of a line along which a unit was to form. Guidons are used to identify company-size units in the U.S. Army; different branches of the service have different colors.

Gulf War—In August 1990, Kuwait was invaded and occupied by Iraq. In February 1991, Iraqi forces were routed, and Kuwait freed, by a coalition of Western and Arab nations led by the United States. See also **Desert Storm, Operation**.

gun—1) A mechanism consisting essentially of a barrel, receiver, breech mechanism, and carriage (or stock or handle, depending on the type of gun), using controlled explosives to shoot projectiles or signal flares. 2) A cannon, as distinguished from a small arm. 3) In precise technical definition, a gun is a cannon with a relatively long barrel (usually .25 calibers or more), high velocity, and a consequent flat trajectory, as distinguished from a howitzer or a mortar.

gun, assault—See **assault gun**.

gunboat—Any of a number of types of small craft carrying mounted cannon. Gunboats are normally used in shallow coastal waters or rivers.

gunboat diplomacy — An attempt to achieve a diplomatic objective by a show of force.

gun camera—1) A camera mounted on a gun stock. 2) A camera that is operated by the same mechanism that fires the guns of an aircraft and is used to record the effect of fire on the target.

gun captain—A petty officer, normally a gunner's mate, in charge of a gun crew on a warship.

gun carriage—A platform, fixed or mobile, that provides a secure base for a gun, including towed or immobile framework, truck, tank, or other vehicle. Carriages usually are considered to include the elevating and traversing mechanisms of the gun.

guncotton—A cellulose nitrate used in smokeless powder.

gun crew—Personnel who load and fire an artillery piece or a naval gun.

gun deck—The deck of a wooden warship on which most of the vessel's guns were placed, or where the GUNROOM was.

"gundecking"—Navy slang for fabricating a document or report.

gun, evening—The ritual firing of a gun on army posts at sunset. See also **retreat**.

gun-howitzer—A cannon that has characteristics of both a GUN and a HOWITZER.

gunlaying—The aiming of a large gun at a target by setting azimuth, range, and elevation. The person who does this may be called a gunlayer, or, more often, a GUNNER.

gunnage—The number of guns on a warship.

gunner—1) The person who aims or fires a gun. 2) In a U.S. Field Artillery gun crew, the second in command and the one responsible for aiming the piece in deflection by means of the gun sight. Usually peformed by a corporal. 3) In British parlance, any artilleryman.

4) In the U.S. Navy, a warrant officer concerned with maintenance and firing of a ship's guns. The commissioned officer senior to the warrant officer is a **chief gunner**. Enlisted personnel junior to the warrant officer are the several ranks of GUNNER'S MATEs, who are commonly dubbed "guns."

gunner, master—See **master gunner**.

gunner's mate—A petty officer rank in the U.S. Navy for those specializing in ordnance.

gunner's quadrant—See **quadrant, gunner's**.

gunnery—The science concerned with the use and performance of guns and projectiles. It overlaps the science of ORDNANCE.

gunnery officer—A naval officer in charge of the ship's guns, their operation and maintenance, and the crews that maintain and fire them.

gunnery sergeant—In the Marine Corps, a noncommissioned rating between staff sergeant and first sergeant.

gun pit—An excavation in which a fieldpiece is placed for protection and, sometimes, concealment.

gunpointer—A naval enlisted person who aims and fires a manually operated ship's gun.

gunport—An opening in the side of a ship, the wing of an airplane, a pillbox, or other structure, through which a gun can be fired.

gunpowder—1) Originally, an explosive combination of sulfur, saltpeter, and charcoal. 2) Any explosive mixture used as a propelling charge in a gun. Gunpowder was apparently used in some form in China as early as the 12th century. It seems to have been independently developed in Western Europe in the 14th century, and its introduction as a generally employed weapon propellant revolutionized warfare. It is widely accepted that the first use of gunpowder weapons in battle was by the English at the Battle of Crécy in 1346. See also **corned gunpowder**.

gunpower—The total weight of metal fired by a warship's major battery in a single broadside.

gunroom—An apartment at the after-end of the lower gun deck occupied by the gunner, or, in the British Royal Navy, used as a mess room by the lieutenants.

gun shield—See **shield**.

gunship—An aircraft (usually a helicopter) used as a weapons platform.

gunsight lamp—An optical device that enables a gunner to take aim at an aircraft flying out of the sun.

gunsmith—One who makes or repairs firearms.

gunster—An early term for "gunner."

gunstone—A stone chipped to spherical shape, used as cannon shot during the 15th and 16th centuries. After the invention of iron balls, stones became less frequently used.

gun tackle—The blocks and tackle attached to the inside of a ship's sides, during the period from about 1650 to about 1850, to haul a gun to and from the gunport.

Gurkha—A soldier from Nepal in the British or Indian army. Gurkhas are renowned for their courage and battlefield tenacity.

H

H-2—See **Sea Sprite**.

H-3—See **Sea King**.

H-46—See **Sea Knight**.

hackbut (hackenbusch)—British name for a 15th-century MATCHLOCK gun, known in England as **harquebus**, in France as ARQUE-BUS, in Germany as **hackenbusch**, and by variations of all these terms.

Hague Conventions — Seventeen conventions establishing laws for land and naval warfare, peace, and neutrality, adopted as the result of international conferences held at The Hague, Netherlands, in 1899 and 1907.

hailshot—See **grapeshot**.

halberd (halbert)—A long-handled ax used as an infantry weapon during the late Middle Ages. The halberd is a pike to which a broad-ax blade is affixed just below the point. Halberds in various forms were used from at least the 14th century, and the long weapon enabled a foot soldier to cleave the armor of either mounted or foot warriors. With the abandonment of armor, the halberd became a ceremonial weapon or a badge of rank.

Hale rocket—A stickless rocket developed by William Hale in 1840. Hale controlled the flight of his rockets by placing three metal vanes in the exhaust nozzle, which caused the rocket to rotate in flight. The Hale rocket was adopted by the United States, Great Britain, Austria, and Russia; and a similar one was manufactured in France. Some types of Hale rockets were used into the 1890s.

half-armor—Armor covering the torso and arms only, used mainly by cavalrymen during the 16th and 17th centuries, when armor was disappearing from the battlefield.

half face—To turn half the distance between one's position and a right or left face; such a facing by troops in line makes the line oblique.

half-life—The time required for a radioactive substance to decrease to half its initial value as a result of radioactive decay.

half-moon (demi-lune)—An outwork in the shape of a half-moon, built to protect the entrance to a fort.

half pike—A short PIKE used from the 16th century on; it was used by naval boarding parties and carried by infantry officers as a badge of rank.

half stripe—Quarter-inch braid, usually of gold, that in combination with one or more full stripes on uniform sleeves or shoulder boards indicates ranks of certain naval officers. For instance, in the U.S. Navy one full stripe and one half stripe designate a lieutenant, junior grade; two full stripes and one half stripe designate a lieutenant commander.

half-track—A vehicle with front wheels and reticulated tracks like a tank instead of rear wheels. Half-tracks were developed in the 1930s and are used both as personnel carriers (usually armored) and as weapons platforms.

World War II era half-track.

half-track

Hall rifle—A FLINTLOCK weapon, the Hall rifle was the first breech-loading rifle formally adopted for military use. It was invented by John H. Hall in 1811 and adopted by the U.S. Army 6 years later. The lock mechanism and chamber were in a pivoted breech-lock that could be rotated up for loading and closed and locked in position for firing. The first military weapon in America with standardized parts, the Hall rifle remained the Army's primary infantry weapon and (as a carbine) cavalry weapon for about 35 years. About 1840 it was modified as a percussion weapon.

Hamas—An Islamic group dedicated to the destruction of Israel and the creation of an Islamic Palestinian state. In cooperation with other Palestinian groups, it initiated the first *intifada* uprising on the West Bank in December 1987. Hamas rejects the concept of a secular Palestinian state.

hand grenade—See **grenade**.

handgun—A firearm that is held and fired with one hand; synonymous with PISTOL.

handover—The passing of authority over an aircraft or organization from one control agency to another.

hangar—A building used to house aircraft.

hanger—1) A short cutting sword, with a curved blade and a knuckleguard, carried by infantrymen of European armies during the 18th and 19th centuries. The naval cutlass was developed from it. 2) A device for attaching a sword or dagger to a belt.

hang fire—A delay in the discharge of a round of ammunition after it has been struck by the firing pin or subjected to other igniting action. See also **misfire**.

harass—To disturb an opponent by any of a variety of means, such as artillery fire, raids, patrols.

harassing fire—See **harassment**.

harassment—A function in which the primary objective is to disrupt the activities of a unit, of installations, or of a ship, rather than to inflict serious casualties or damage. **Harassing fire** is fire designed to disturb the enemy's troops, to curtail movement, and, by threat of losses, to lower morale. Harassment can also be carried out by air attacks, usually called **air harassment**.

harbor defense—The defense of a harbor or anchorage and its water approaches against naval surface or submarine attack, enemy mine-laying operations, and sabotage. However, the defense of a harbor against guided or dropped missiles while such missiles are airborne is considered a part of air defense.

hard beach—A portion of beach provided with a sufficiently hard surface extending into the water to facilitate loading and unloading.

hardened site—An installation (which may be a fortification) constructed to withstand the blast and associated effects of a nuclear attack and likely to be protected against a chemical, biological, or radiological attack.

hardstand—See **apron**.

hardtack—A hard biscuit, usually made of flour and water, without salt, formerly a staple of army field rations and shipboard fare in the navy. Also called sea biscuit or sea bread.

HARM—See **high-speed antiradiation missile (AGM-88)**.

harpago—An innovation in naval warfare introduced by Octavian's admiral, Agrippa, it was a pole with a hook on the end that was shot from a catapult into the side of an opposing ship, where the hook would hold it fast. Attached to the end of the harpago was a rope that could be winched in to bring the two vessels together and facilitate boarding. This, the precursor of the whaling harpoon, was first used effectively by Agrippa at the Battle of Naulochos (36 B.C.) and again at Actium (31 B.C.).

Harpoon (AGM-84D)—An all-weather anti-ship cruise missile capable of being mounted on ships, aircraft, or submarines. It normally carries a 500-pound conventional warhead. The Harpoon's low-level trajectory makes it difficult to defend against.

harquebus—See **arquebus**.

harquebusier—See **arquebusier**.

Harrier (AV-8)—A single-engine vertical or short-takeoff-and-landing light attack aircraft designed to operate from either land or ships in a close support role.

hash mark—See **service stripe**.

hastatus—From the Latin, meaning "one armed with a spear or javelin"; the hastati were young but experienced soldiers who carried two javelins (PILUM) about 7 feet long, a shield, and a short broadbladed sword (GLADIUS). They were the principal manpower component of the Roman LEGION. After throwing their javelins, the hastati would close and fight with their swords.

hasty defense—See **defense**.

haubergeon—A short COAT OF MAIL, generally sleeveless. Also known as the "lesser hauberk," it was a shortened version of the HAUBERK.

hauberk—A tunic or shirt or coat of mail. Although HAUBERGEON was sometimes used for short tunics, "hauberk" seems to have included all types.

havelock—A covering of cloth that fits over a cap and has a flap to protect the back of the neck from the sun. The havelock is named for Sir Henry Havelock, a British general who served in India in the mid-18th century. The name was adopted by the U.S. Navy for a rain cover for the WAVES uniform hat.

haversack—A one-strap canvas bag worn over a shoulder to carry supplies on a hike or a march.

havildar—A noncommissioned rank in the Indian army corresponding to sergeant. The most senior holders of this rank were **havildar-majors.**

"hawk"—A term applied to anyone in favor of the use of military force to resolve a given international dispute. The term came into vogue during the Vietnam War. See also **"dove."**

Hawk (MIM-23) — A mobile surface-to-air missile system for low- to medium-altitude air defense. Introduced in the 1960s, it has gone through extensive upgrades. Kuwaiti air defense units equipped with Hawk missiles were credited with destroying 22 Iraqi aircraft during the Gulf War.

Hawkeye (E-2C) — A twin-turboprop, airborne, early warning, and interceptor control aircraft designed to operate from carriers. It carries a long-range radar system and specialist crew for the detection and tracking of airborne targets. The Hawkeye became operational in 1973; and an upgraded version, with improved engine power and radar, entered service in 1992.

U.S. Department of Defense photo

Hawkeye

He-111—A twin-engine German medium bomber manufactured by Heinkel and used extensively in World War II.

headquarters—1) The command echelon of a unit or other organization consisting of a commander and his or her staff. 2) The geographical center of authority of any organization; that is, the building, base, or other place where the commander and the staff are located.

headquarters company—A military unit that supports the headquarters of a battalion or larger unit. In the U.S. Army all enlisted members of a headquarters are assigned for administration, food, and housing to a headquarters company (**headquarters battery**

for an artillery unit, **headquarters troop** for a cavalry unit).

heads up — A warning of forthcoming activity.

head-up display—An arrangement of navigation, attack, or other information in a pilot's forward field of vision.

heavier-than-air (HTA) — Designation of airplanes and helicopters to distinguish them from blimps and other lighter-than-air craft.

heavy—Used to denote a large weapon, ship, tank, or unit. For instance, infantry is normally categorized as light or heavy; artillery as light, medium, and heavy (and sometimes superheavy).

heavy force — A military organization equipped with weighty and cumbersome weapons and other matériel that provide powerful combat capability but limit mobility and transportability.

heavy weapons—U.S. Army infantry term for such crew-served ordnance as mortars, infantry cannon, heavy machine guns, and recoilless rifles.

hedgehog—1) A portable obstacle, made of crossed poles laced with barbed wire, in the general shape of an hourglass. 2) A beach obstacle, usually made of steel bars or channel iron, embedded in concrete and used to interfere with beach landings. 3) An antisubmarine device with 16 charges that could be fired simultaneously. 4) A close formation of pikemen with their long spears that pointed out in all directions like the spines of a hedgehog and were used against attacking cavalry. 5) In World War II, a fortified strongpoint or grouping of fortifications capable of all-around defense.

Hedgehog—Antisubmarine weapon that fires ahead of a ship with a pattern of 16 charges that discharge only upon contact with the target (to avoid disruption of sonar).

hedron—U.S. Navy designation of the headquarters of an air squadron, including administration and support activities.

height of burst — The vertical distance of an exploding projectile from the earth's surface or from a target. For a nuclear weapon, the optimum height of burst is that at which

it will produce destruction over the maximum possible area.

helicopter—An aircraft that derives lift over an approximately vertical axis from revolving engine-driven wings or blades. A helicopter possesses the capability of taking off and landing without a run, and of hovering at a fixed altitude above a given point on the ground or water surface. Helicopters are used for transportation of airborne units in landing operations, for submarine search-and-strike purposes, for reconnaissance, for artillery spotting, for liaison, for evacuation of the wounded, and as weapons platforms.

heliograph—A device with a movable mirror that flashes the light of the sun in order to send messages in a code of long and short flashes (as in the Morse code).

Hellcat (FGF) — Single-engine U.S. Navy World War II fighter, manufactured by Grumman.

Hellfire (AGM-114B)—A laser-guided subsonic missile that can be used in an air-to-air mode against slow-moving aircraft or in an air-to-ground mode against tanks and fortifications. The primary carrier is the Apache helicopter.

helm—1) The device that steers a ship; thus the word also denotes command of a ship or an organization. 2) A steel helmet introduced about 1200 to wear over the steel or iron skullcap. The helm was cylindrical, or nearly so, and evolved from a flat-topped piece to a rounded helmet long enough to attach to the breastplate. It was particularly popular for wearing in tournaments.

Helmet of a soldier in the Roman army.

helmet

helmet—Any special piece of headgear designed to protect the wearer from such hazards as blows, shell fragments, crash injury, and cold. Helmets are usually made of steel, leather, or some other form of armor, and are lined or padded. **Henry rifle**—A breech-loading repeating rifle designed by B. Tyler Henry of the New Haven Arms Co. in the mid-19th century. It had a tubular magazine that held 15 rimfire .44-caliber (11.2 mm) cartridges. A toggle-link lever action moved the cartridges into the firing chamber seriatim, and they could be fired quite rapidly—about 15 shots in 11 seconds with a sustained rate of fire of about 20 rounds per minute, including reloading, over a period of 6 minutes. The Henry rifle was a forerunner of the WINCHESTER RIFLE.

herald, military—An official in a feudal army whose function was to issue proclamations by the commander and carry important messages.

heraldry, military use of—The design and granting of a right to wear a device or coat-of-arms, which indicates the origin or ancestry of a unit or organization and identifies membership in that unit or organization. Heraldry was developed to identify noble and royal families and thus feudal armies and their commanders. It survives in modern military organizations in flags and pennants, badges, shoulder patches, and the like.

Heraldry samples, l. to r.—Order of Alcantara, Star of the Portuguese Order of Christ, Star of the Order of the Annunciation.

heraldry

Hercules (C-130)—A medium-range troop and cargo transport plane, powered by four turboprop engines and designed for airdrop or conventional delivery.

Lockheed Aircraft Corporation photo

Hercules (C-130)

hersillon—A strong beam with spikes protruding from all sides, thrown across a breach in a fortification to prevent attackers from passing through.

Hezbollah ("Party of God")—The name for several groups of Islamic fundamentalist radicals. Iran founded the original organization in Lebanon in 1982 in an effort to expel Israeli forces. Using the name ISLAMIC JIHAD, the organization engaged in suicide bombings against American, French, and Israeli service personnel in Lebanon before switching to kidnapping and killing foreign hostages. Groups claiming to be Hezbollah have also operated in Bahrain, Palestine, and Saudi Arabia.

H-hour—A term customarily used to refer to the precise time at which some specified operation—an attack, an amphibious assault, or a movement—will begin. See also **D-day.**

Higgins boat—A landing craft designed by Andrew J. Higgins in 1939 and used in amphibious landings in World War II. Its principal features were shallow draft and a bow ramp by means of which troops and vehicles could be disembarked rapidly on a beach or in shallow water close to the beach. It was the prototype for most subsequent landing craft.

high-altitude bombing—Horizontal bombing from an aircraft flying at an altitude over 15,000 feet.

high-angle fire—Fire delivered at elevations greater than the elevation of maximum range. In high-angle fire, the range decreases as the angle of elevation is increased. Should not be confused with INDIRECT FIRE, which is entirely different. See also **elevation** and **low-angle fire.**

high-burst adjustment—A registration of an artillery piece on an arbitrary point in the sky when, for any reason, it is not possible to register on a BASE POINT. A single gun is registered by time fire at an elevation and time fuze setting that will assure that the rounds (all at the same settings) will burst in the air and in the field of view of observers with survey instruments at positions precisely located with respect to the guns by survey. Each observed burst is then plotted by triangulation; the center of impact is located on the firing chart, and this becomes the base point until there is an opportunity to register on an identifiable point on the ground. The range elevation for the guns to hit this arbitrary base point is calculated by deducting algebraically the value of the angle of site and complementary angle of site from the QUADRANT ELEVATION.

high explosive—Any powerful, nonnuclear explosive that is characterized by extremely rapid detonation and has a powerful disruptive or shattering effect. Distinguished from a low explosive like gunpowder or nitrocellulose propellant, which was used for exploding or detonating shells or devices before the pre-World War I adaptation of TNT as the standard military explosive.

high-explosive antitank (HEAT) — See **ammunition, armor-piercing**.

high-explosive (HE) bomb—See **bomb**.

high-frequency direction finder (HF/DF)—A radio receiver that is equipped to indicate the direction from which a broadcast is being sent. The point at which the direction lines from two or more receivers in different locations intersect identifies, within a reasonable degree of accuracy, the location of the transmitting radio. **"Huff Duff,"** as HF/DF was commonly called, was extremely important in World War II in directing antisubmarine units to the areas where German U-boats were operating.

high-intensity conflict—See **conflict levels of intensity**.

High Seas Fleet (Hochseeflotte) — The German counterpart to Britain's Grand Fleet in World War I, the High Seas Fleet was ordered by Kaiser Wilhelm II to harass the blockading Grand Fleet to the greatest extent possible and to give battle if favorable circumstances presented themselves. The resulting Battle of Jutland (31 May–1 June 1916) was a limited tactical victory for the High Seas Fleet, but one that convinced Germany that the Grand Fleet was too strong to be challenged again.

high-speed antiradiation missile (HARM)(AGM-88)—A high-speed air-to-surface tactical missile designed to seek out and destroy enemy radar-equipped air defense systems.

hilt—The end of a sword by which it is held. Hilts have been designed in many shapes and sizes. Most distinctive is the **basket hilt**, which includes a guard, more or less in the shape of a basket, that provides cover and protection for the hand.

Hindenburg Line—A highly organized defensive zone prepared by the German army in northern France in early 1917 to shorten the front line and permit it to be held by fewer troops. Behind a lightly held outpost line heavily sown with machine guns lay two successive defensive positions, heavily fortified. Behind these again lay the German reserves concentrated and prepared for counterattack. Each successive defensive line was so spaced in depth that, should one be taken, the attacker's artillery would have to move to another, more forward, fire position before taking action against the next zone. Between the original line and the new zone, the countryside was devastated: Towns and villages were razed, forests leveled, water sources contaminated, and roads destroyed. See also **Siegfried Line**.

hipparch—A commander of cavalry in ancient Greek armies.

hit—*n.* A blow or an impact on a target by a projectile or hand-held weapon. *v.* To strike with a hand-held weapon or a projectile.

hitch—In the U.S. armed forces, a term popularly used for a period of voluntary enlistment.

hoarding (fortification)—Wooden fencing, generally used to support the sides of trenches.

hobelier—A light horseman of the Middle Ages who was used for conducting reconnaissance, carrying intelligence, harassing troops on a march, intercepting convoys, and pursuing a routed enemy.

hoistman—The member of a ship's gun crew who directs the supply of ammunition from a magazine below decks to the gun compartment.

holding attack—A limited attack designed to keep the enemy in position, to deceive him as to the focus of the main attack, and to discourage him from sending reinforcements.

hollow charge—An explosive charge designed to penetrate armor or concrete. It uses the MUNROE EFFECT, whereby a cavity in a high-explosive charge focuses the effect of the detonation in a narrow cone of highly penetrating flame and blast. Hollow charges were first used extensively in armor-piercing projectiles in World War II. Also called a SHAPED CHARGE.

hollow square—See **square**.

holster (saddle, belt) — A leather case shaped to hold a pistol. An item of uniform for all military persons armed with pistols.

holy-water sprinkler—A mace with protruding spikes and a long handle used in the 16th and 17th centuries. Such a mace was sometimes called a MORNING STAR.

home defense—See **home guard**.

home guard—An organization of volunteers or militia set up to provide defense for an area or a nation from which regular military forces have been sent away or are hard-pressed and diverted by battle engagement. In World Wars I and II, for example, many states of the United States, particularly those on the coasts, formed home guards to replace National Guard units that had been called to active military service.

"honey trap" (intelligence)—Use of sex as a means of compromising a potential source and gaining control over the targeted individual.

honor guard—See **guard**.

honors—Recognition, in the form of an award, a ceremony, a written commendation, or other device, of an outstanding achievement or performance or of the presence or arrival of a person of particular distinction.

honors of war—A measure taken by a victor in recognition of merit in a vanquished enemy, such as permitting him to march out of a town or position he has surrendered, armed and with colors flying. Because British Gen. Sir Henry Clinton denied honors of war to the army of Gen. Benjamin Lincoln that surrendered at Charleston in 1779, Gen. George Washington denied honors of war to Gen. Charles Cornwallis's army when it surrendered at Yorktown in 1781.

hoplite—A well-disciplined Greek infantryman who fought in the PHALANX formation. The hoplite carried an 8- to 10-foot pike and a short sword. He wore a helmet, breastplate, and GREAVES; and he carried a round shield, called a **hoplon**. In the Macedonian armies of Phillip II and Alexander the Great, most hoplites were armed with a longer spear, the SARISSA, and a larger shield than were the Greek hoplites. **hoplon**—See **hoplite**.

horizontal bombing—Bombing from an aircraft flying at a constant altitude above a target.

horizontal error—The error—in range or deflection, or the error that is expressed in radius of distance from target—that a weapon may be normally expected to exceed. The horizontal error of weapons making a nearly vertical approach to the target is often described in terms of CIRCULAR ERROR PROBABLE (CEP) in radius distance. The horizontal error of weapons producing an elliptical dispersion pattern (i.e., the dispersion pattern of shell fragments as they strike a target area) is expressed in terms of PROBABLE ERROR, which can be expressed as an angle (degrees or mils) or as a distance at different ranges.

hornbow—See **bow**.

Hornet (F/A-18)—A twin-engine, supersonic fighter-attack aircraft manufactured by McDonnell Douglas. It can mount both air-to-air and air-to-surface weapons and is designed to operate from either land or carriers. In the 1991 Gulf War, Hornets flew some 4,600 sorties without combat loss.

hornwork—A small outwork protruding from a major defensive work or wall, consisting of two half bastions, or demi-bastions, joined by a curtain. Hornworks were designed to protect the approach to a gate or postern entrance in the major work.

horse—Collectively, cavalry or mounted foot soldiers.

horse artillery—Artillery designed to support cavalry, distinguished from horse-drawn artillery by the fact that all personnel were mounted on horses to enhance mobility.

horse guards—1) A mounted formation of GUARDs. 2) Designation of a formation of mounted guards in the British army.

horse holder—1) A soldier designated to hold the horses of a small unit of DRAGOONS or CAVALRY who have dismounted to fight on foot. 2) A member of the staff of a senior officer. The term derives from prints of early generals in which the background showed the subject's aide holding his horse.

horsetail—A Turkish standard, denoting a pasha's rank. Commanders were distinguished by the number of horsetails carried before them.

hospital—A medical facility fully equipped for treatment of the sick and wounded. The U.S. Army maintains both general hospitals, comparable to civilian hospitals, and field hospitals, which are set up temporarily in or near a combat zone.

hospital apprentice—See **hospital corpsman**.

hospital corpsman—In the U.S. armed forces, enlisted personnel in a medical unit, including, in the Navy, **hospital apprentices** (unrated personnel, corresponding to apprentice seamen) and the various pharmacists' mates and other medical ratings.

Hospitaler—A member of a military religious order, the Knights Hospitalers (Knights of St. John), founded among European Crusaders in 12th-century Palestine. Later, the Hospitalers were the defenders of Rhodes and then Malta against Turkish attacks.

hospital ship—A ship equipped as a hospital, completely unarmed, usually painted white and marked with prominent red crosses or other indications of its function and illuminated at night for ready identification. Hospital ships are used particularly during amphibious operations and for evacuating casualties to medical facilities farther away from combat areas.

hostage—A person seized by a belligerent, or sometimes given by one belligerent to another, and held to ensure that certain terms or agreements will be kept.

hostilities—1) Acts of battle or of fighting; acts of warfare. 2) The state or situation under which armed conflict takes place or can be expected to occur. Hostilities may begin or cease without causing the beginning or end of a war.

Hotchkiss gun — Originally a five-barrel, 37mm, revolving cannon designed in 1871 by an American, B. B. Hotchkiss, and used by the British Royal Navy. Later, any gun made by the Hotchkiss Company. Also, a small, single-barreled (8mm) machine gun made by the Hotchkiss Company early in the 19th century and used as a British cavalry weapon into the 1930s.

Hotel—Letter of NATO phonetic alphabet. See also **alphabet, phonetic**.

hot shot—Ammunition, especially cannon balls, heated before firing and generally used against combustible ships or structures. In order to avoid detonation of the propelling charge by the heat of the ball, wet clay or straw was inserted between the powder and the shot. The first use is unknown, but hot shot appears to have been used at the siege of Cherbourg in 1418. Incendiary shells replaced hot shot in the 19th century.

houfnice—The basic Hussite field gun of the 15th century, with a caliber of 150mm to 250mm and a chamber of smaller diameter. The important, innovative feature of this gun was that it was mounted in a two-wheeled carriage with a trail, which made laying the

U.S. Navy photo

U.S. Navy hospital ship *Haven*.

hospital ship

guns much easier for both range and direction. The name comes from the Czech term *houf,* meaning a group of men.

Hound Dog (AGM-28B) — A turbojet-propelled air-to-surface missile designed to be carried externally on the B-52 Stratofortress. It is equipped with a nuclear warhead and can be launched from high or low altitude.

house carls—A member of the bodyguard or household troops of a Danish or early English king or noble.

household cavalry—Mounted units of royal guards.

household troops—Troops whose duty is to guard the security of a sovereign and his or her domestic establishment. See also **guard**.

How—Letter of old phonetic alphabet. See also **alphabet, phonetic**.

howitzer—1) A cannon that combines certain characteristics of guns and mortars. The howitzer is lighter than a gun of comparable caliber and heavier than a mortar and delivers projectiles with medium velocities by low or high trajectories. 2) A cannon with a tube length 20 to 30 calibers. See also **gun** and **cannon**.

U.S. Army photo

World War II–era 240mm howitzer.

howitzer

Huey (UH-1)—A light, single-rotor helicopter used for cargo/personnel transport and for attack support. Sometimes called **Iroquois**.

"Huff Duff"—See **high-frequency direction finder (HF/DF)**.

human resources intelligence (HUMINT)—Intelligence information gathered by collection agents or other nontechnical means.

Humvee (HMMWV) — A hybrid-electric Army all-terrain vehicle. It is capable of speeds up to 80 miles per hour and has a rated payload of 1,700 pounds.

U.S. Department of Defense photo

Humvee

hung bomb — A bomb that accidentally clings to the bomb rack after the releasing action has been taken.

hunter-killer operations/group — Offensive antisubmarine operations combining searching, tracking, and attacking capabilities of air, surface, and subsurface forces in coordinated action to locate and destroy submarines at sea. Hunter-killer operations involve groups of ships consisting of one or more antisubmarine carriers and a number of escort vessels.

hurdles—Obstacles, usually movable and made of lumber or logs, that can be readily emplaced to block roads and DEFILEs.

Hurricane—The first modern, low-wing fighter of the British Royal Air Force in World War II, the Hawker Hurricane had a top speed of approximately 315 miles an hour and played a key role in the defeat of German bombers in the Battle of Britain.

hussar—A light-cavalry soldier with special uniforms and traditions. The original hussars were formed by King Matthias Corvinus of Hungary in 1458, and they performed with considerable success against the Turks. Similar units, generally uniformed in Hungarian-type uniforms with bright color and frogging, were formed and named hussars in other European armies. Like other cavalry units, hussars have been converted from horse cavalry to tank units.

hut—A temporary building, usually small, for housing troops or storing arms. A collection of such buildings is a **hutment.**

Hutier tactics—The name given by the Allies to German infantry tactics that were characterized by a short, sharp concentration of artillery fire, followed immediately by infantry assaults, both guns and troops being brought into position at the last possible moment to ensure surprise. Heavy concentrations of smoke shells fired on enemy strongpoints permitted the attacking infantry and light guns to bypass them. The term "Hutier tactics" was given to this type of offensive because it was first employed on the Russian front in 1917 by a German army un-

der Gen. Oscar von Hutier, who later commanded an army employing these tactics in the German Somme offensive of 1918. The Germans used the term "infiltration tactics."

hypaspist—An ancient Macedonian infantryman. Hypaspists originally carried the shield or weapons of a heavily armed HOPLITE. Philip of Macedon reduced the weight of their equipment and trained them as highly mobile troops. He used them skillfully, notably at the Battle of Chaeronea in 338 B.C., when they attacked on his army's right, then withdrew, pursued by the Athenians, who thus created a gap through which Philip's son, Alexander, drove, to strike the Thebans in the rear.

hypervelocity armor-piercing (HVAP)—See **ammunition, armor-piercing.**

ICBM — See **intercontinental ballistic missile**.

identification friend or foe (IFF)—1) A system using electronic transmissions to which transponder equipment carried by friendly forces automatically responds (e.g., by emitting pulses). It is a method of determining the friendly or unfriendly character of aircraft and ships using electronic detection equipment and associated IFF systems. 2) A general term applied to electronic equipment used to identify hostile or friendly aircraft or ships; any of several systems used in such identification. Before and during much of World War II, identification depended on the use of predesignated signals for challenge and reply.

IFF—See **identification friend or foe**.

IFV—See **infantry fighting vehicle**.

illuminating shell—A shell designed to become a flare when exploded well above a target area, so as to light it for bombing or identification. The flare can be made more effective if combined with a parachute that is released upon explosion. Also called a STAR SHELL.

imagery intelligence (IMINT)— Information derived from photography, infrared sensors, lasers, and other technical means in which objects are reproduced on film, display devices, or other means.

immediate air support—Air support in response to specific requests that arise in the course of a battle and cannot be programmed in advance.

immediate message—See **message precedence**.

Immortals—An elite corps of bodyguards in the ancient Persian armies of Achaemenian Persia, the dynasty that ruled ancient Persia from 559 to 330 B.C.

"Immunes"—A brigade of 10,000 enlisted U.S. volunteers in the Spanish-American War whose immunity to tropical diseases (particularly malaria) allowed them to be used in Cuba, where large numbers of non-battle casualties had been sustained because of communicable diseases of local origin. The "Immunes" were organized into 10 infantry regiments, the 1st through the 10th Volunteer Infantry, six of white troops and four of black.

impact action fuze—A fuze that is activated by the contact of its projectile with a hard object or surface.

impact area—An area having designated boundaries within the limits of which it is intended that all ordnance, including projectiles, bombs, or other missiles fired by artillery or launched from aircraft, will hit the ground.

impact, mean point of—The point whose coordinates are the arithmetic means of the coordinates of the separate points of impact of a finite number of projectiles fired or released at the same aiming point under a given set of conditions. In bombing, it is the mean, or geometrical, center of a bombfall pattern, excluding gross errors. See also **center of impact**.

impedimenta — Supply train; the term comes from the Latin word for "baggage."

impi—A Zulu military regiment, usually consisting of several thousand men.

implosion weapon—A weapon in which a quantity of fissionable material, less than a critical mass at ordinary pressure, has its volume suddenly reduced by compression—a step accomplished by using normal chemical explosives around the fissionable material—so that it becomes supercritical, producing a nuclear explosion.

impressment—The forcing of service in an army or navy through kidnapping or seizing men and transporting them against their will to an army unit or a ship. This practice was common in Great Britain, France, Prussia, and other nations into the 19th century, to the extent that some units were composed predominantly of impressed men who usually fought without enthusiasm. Press gangs roamed seedy, poorly lit areas, kidnapping drunks and other unsuspecting men; others were sent from jails to military units. One of the causes of the War of 1812 was the British practice of sending boarding parties aboard U.S. vessels and impressing men they claimed were British—U.S. citizens among them—to fight in the Napoleonic Wars.

inactive status—The opposite of active duty. A reservist who is not performing full-time military duty with an organized, fully commissioned unit is in an inactive status. An installation or organization that is not actively functioning or not in use by a military organization is in inactive status.

in being — Organized, manned, equipped (though not necessarily at full strength), and ready to operate. Used in reference to any military force.

incapacitating agent—A substance that renders individuals temporarily incapable of performing their normal duties.

incendiary — n. Any chemical compound that causes fire. adj. Causing fire (incendiary attack, incendiary bomb).

incendiary bomb—See **bomb**.

incendiary grenade—See **grenade**.

independent unit or formation — A military organization that is not an organic part of a larger unit or formation. An independent unit may be temporarily attached to another, usually larger, unit but is available for transfer from one to another as the senior commander considers desirable or necessary.

India—Letter of NATO phonetic alphabet. See also **alphabet, phonetic**.

indicated airspeed—See **airspeed**.

indications and warning (intelligence)—Intelligence activities intended to detect and report time-sensitive information on foreign developments that could involve a threat to the United States or its interests.

indirect fire—Fire delivered on a target that cannot be seen by the aimer. It should not be confused with HIGH-ANGLE FIRE, which has a totally different meaning.

induct—To conscript, or to take a person into an armed service without voluntary action on the individual's part. In the United States this has been performed through the Selective Service System.

industrial espionage—Spying in order to obtain commercial information not available through open channels. Because of its leading position in high-tech industries, the United States has long been a target for industrial espionage.

industrial mobilization—The transformation of industry from peacetime activities to the industrial program that supports national military objectives. It includes the mobilization of materials, labor, capital, production facilities, and contributory items and services essential to the wartime program.

inertial guidance—A system designed to project a missile on a predetermined track, in which the track of the missile is adjusted after launching by devices within the missile.

infantry—A branch of an army in which soldiers are organized, trained, and equipped to fight on foot. Infantry units are designated **light** or **heavy** according to the equipment they carry and the speed with which they can move. In modern armies, many if not most infantry units are **mechanized**—that is, they move in vehicles and sometimes fight from them. Light infantry became a standard part of armies in the 17th century. Predecessors were the PSILOI of the Greek and Macedonian armies and SKIRMISHERS in Roman armies and those of the Middle Ages.

infantry division — A combined-arms ground force of DIVISION type and size, the principal combat components usually being three infantry regiments or brigades. It may be motorized.

infantry fighting vehicle (IFV) — An armored vehicle, tracked or wheeled, primarily designed to transport infantry into combat and permit a majority of the transported personnel to engage the enemy from the fully enclosed vehicle.

infiltrate—To carry out INFILTRATION.

infiltration—1) The movement of an individual or a unit into enemy-occupied territory. 2) In intelligence usage, placement of an agent in a target area in hostile territory. It usually involves crossing a frontier or other guarded line.

infiltration tactics—See **Hutier tactics**.

infirmary—A medical facility that is smaller and has less equipment than a hospital. Patients may be given emergency treatment and kept for minor problems or brief periods of recuperation and treatment.

influence fuze—See **proximity fuze**.

information officer—An officer whose duty is to provide authorized information about a command to the nonmilitary public.

information warfare — See **cyberterrorism/cyberwarfare**.

infrastructure—A term used in NATO that is generally applicable to all fixed and permanent installations, fabrications, or facilities for the support and control of military forces. Derived from a French railroad term.

initial issue—First combat supply, placed at the disposal of units of all arms of all services in peacetime. In principle, it enables these units to fulfill their first mission without further supply. It can be transported by the organic transport of the unit.

initial point—1) Any designated place at which a column or an element thereof is formed by the successive arrival of its various subdivisions and comes under the control of the commander ordering the move. 2) A well-defined point, easily distinguished visibly or electronically, used as a starting point for the bomb run on a target. The first point at which a moving target is located on a plotting board.

inshore patrol—A naval defense patrol operating generally within a defensive coastal area and comprising all elements of harbor defenses, the coastal lookout system, patrol craft, supporting bases, aircraft, and coast guard stations.

insignia—Any distinctive device that identifies a person or an object as to nationality, organization, office, rank, or branch of service. Examples of insignia are badges of rank, badges designating branch of service, shoulder patches, chevrons, aircraft and vehicle markings.

inspection—The examination of personnel, organizations, activities, or installations to determine their effectiveness and economy of operation, adequacy of facilities, readiness to perform assigned missions, or compliance with directives; also, the examination of matériel to determine quality, quantity, or compliance with standards. An inspection of personnel or an installation by a visiting dignitary is often a mark of respect and is included in HONORS.

inspection party—See **party**.

inspector general—1) An officer whose duty is to investigate and report on the condition and noncombat performance of a military organization. 2) In some armies (e.g., the German) the senior officer.

installation—A military facility in a fixed or relatively fixed location, together with its buildings, building equipment, and subsidiary facilities such as piers, spurs, access roads, and beacons. See also **base, camp, post, station**.

instrument bombing—Bombing by the use of radar or other instruments to locate the target and direct and release the bombs, without visual reference to the ground.

insurgency—A condition resulting from a revolt or insurrection against a constituted government that falls short of civil war. See also **conflict levels of intensity**.

intelligence — The product resulting from thecoollection, evaluation, analysis, integration, and interpretation of all available information that concerns one or more aspects of foreign nations, their areas of operations, and their military establishments and that is immediately or potentially significant to military and diplomatic planning and operations.

U.S. Air Force photo

intercontinental ballistic missile (ICBM)

intelligence estimate — See **estimate, intelligence**.

intention — An aim or a design (as distinct from a capability) to execute a specific course of action.

intercept—*v.* 1) To interfere with, and if possible prevent, the arrival of a hostile military force at its destination. 2) To overhear, without permission, communications between hostile or potentially hostile electronic stations. 3) To make contact, visually or by radar, of a friendly aircraft with an unidentified one. This includes **close controlled interception**, in which the interceptor is continuously controlled by a surface or air station, and **broadcast controlled interception**, in which the interceptor is given the area of interception by a surface or air station but effects interception without further control.

interceptor—A manned aircraft used for identification and engagement of airborne objects. Usually an interceptor is characterized by a high rate of climb, high speed, high ceiling, effective armament, and relatively short endurance.

interchangeability—A condition in which two or more items of equipment have such functional and physical characteristics as to be equivalent in performance and capable of being exchanged for each other.

intercontinental ballistic missile (ICBM)—A ballistic missile with a range over 3,000 nautical miles. See also **missile, ballistic**.

interdict—To prevent or hinder enemy use of an area or route for supply, communications, or movement. Interdiction may be accomplished by gunfire, by aerial bombing, or by otherwise destroying significant parts of the enemy's route or attacking his combat or support forces on the route.

interdiction fire—Fire placed on an area or point for interdiction purposes. See also **interdict**.

interior guards — The guards who police the entrances of, and key points or areas in, a base or other installation.

interior lines—Advantageous lines of communication resulting from a situation wherein a force, owing to its position with respect to the enemy forces or because of superior lateral communications, enjoys advantages of time and space in the employment of its units against the enemy. Offensive operations on interior lines are usually conducted from a central locality against enemy forces advancing along convergent lines.

intermediate-range ballistic missile (IRBM)—A ballistic missile with a range of up to 1,500 nautical miles. See also **missile, ballistic.**

U.S. Army photo

intermediate-range ballistic missile (IRBM)

internal security—The state of law and order prevailing within a nation that protects it from subversion by a hostile force.

International Security Assistance Force (ISAF)—The peacekeeping force in Afghanistan authorized by the U.N. Security Council in December 2001.

interoperability—The capability of different national forces in an alliance to work together in a combat situation. This is in part a function of weapons and equipment stan-dardization and in part a function of common or compatible doctrines. Used particularly with respect to NATO.

interrogation—The procedure or activity of questioning prisoners of war.

interrupted screw — Construction of breechblock and breech receiver of a gun so that the breechblock can be swung into position and can achieve, by a one-quarter or one-eighth turn of the mechanism, full obturation through the close fit of breechblock and receiver.

interval—1) The space between adjacent groups of ships or boats measured in any direction between the corresponding ships or boats in each group. 2) The space between adjacent individuals, vehicles, or units in a formation that are placed side by side, measured abreast. 3) The space between adjacent aircraft measured from front to rear in units of time or in-flight distance.

intervisibility—The existence of a visually unimpeded, direct line of sight between two geographically identifiable points.

in the clear—A message transmitted in the language in which it was written, as opposed to being sent in code.

intifada—A campaign of politically motivated street violence against Israeli-occupied Palestine, endorsed by and at times directed by the PALESTINE LIBERATION ORGANIZATION. The first phase took place between 1989 and 1992, and resulted in the deaths of some 25 Israelis and 1,000 Palestinians, and thousands of injuries. After a lull during which the PLO called for an end to violence, a second intifada, marked by suicide bombings, began in September 2000.

intruder—1) A hostile or unidentified aircraft that appears in a defended airspace. 2) An aircraft sent on an intruder mission.

Intruder (A-6)—A twin-jet, carrier-based, attack aircraft equipped with a computer system to track and destroy targets. The U.S. Navy began phasing it out of service in the 1990s.

intruder operation—An offensive operation by day or night over enemy territory with the primary objective of destroying enemy aircraft in the vicinity of their bases.

invade—To cross the borders of a nation by force or with a military force for the purpose of seizing territory.

Invader—A U.S. Army Air Corps twin-engine World War II light bomber manufactured by Douglas. Its first designation (A-26) was changed after the war to B-26.

U.S. Air Force photo

Invader

invalid—A soldier who for physical reasons, particularly as the result of enemy action, is assigned to limited, noncombat duty.

invasion—An intrusion of military forces into the territory of another nation.

invest—To deploy troops or ships around an enemy objective in such a fashion as to cut all lines of communication. To BESIEGE.

investment—The deployment of troops or ships around an enemy objective, cutting it off from communication with its own forces.

Iranian hostage crisis—On 4 November 1979 some 3,000 Iranian militants, encouraged by their government, stormed the U.S. Embassy in Tehran and took 66 Americans hostage. The hostages were released on 20 January 1981, after 445 days in captivity. See also **Eagle Claw, Operation**.

Iraqi Freedom, Operation—A military operation against Saddam Hussein's regime in Iraq. Air strikes by a U.S.-led coalition began on March 20, 2003, and were followed by ground operations mounted from Kuwait. See also **"shock and awe"** and **"decapitation."**

IRBM—See **intermediate-range ballistic missile**.

Irish Republican Army (IRA) — An umbrella term for several militant Irish organizations that seek to unify Northern Ireland, which has a Protestant majority, with the Catholic republic to the south by force. The

faction charged with most terrorist activity in the late 20th century was the Provisional Irish Republican Army ("Provos"). The Good Friday Agreement of 10 April 1998 established the basis for a peaceful settlement of the conflict.

ironclad—A naval vessel, usually built of wood and covered with plates of iron (up to 4.5 inches thick) for protection against enemy shot and shell. Ironclad floating batteries were used by French and British forces in the Crimean War. The most famous ironclads were the *Monitor* and the *Merrimack*, which fought each other in the Chesapeake Bay in March 1862, in the Battle of Hampton Roads during the American Civil War. A number of other ironclads were built before the end of the 19th century, when iron plates gave way to hulls built of steel.

Iron Cross—A German military decoration in the shape of a Maltese Cross made of cast iron edged with silver. The *Eisernes Kreuz* was instituted in 1813 as a reward for distinguished service in the War of Liberation against Napoleon, was revived at the time of the Franco-Prussian War (1870–71), and was issued again for service in World Wars I and II.

iron ration—An emergency ration consisting of concentrated food.

"Ironsides"—Nickname for highly disciplined cavalry units of the Parliamentary Army during the English Civil War. The Ironsides were CUIRASSIERS, first recruited and trained by Oliver Cromwell, beginning in late 1642. Cromwell stressed training, unit cohesion, and morale; he would have only "honest and religious" men in his units, and saw to it that they were paid regularly, well equipped, and adequately clothed. These troopers were more than a match for the excellent but undisciplined cavalry of the Royalist Army and became the cavalry backbone of the New Model Army with which the Parliament won the war. See also **"Old Ironsides."**

Iroquois—See **Huey**.

irregular troops—Armed individuals or groups who are not members of regular forces. They are also known simply as **irregulars**.

irregular warfare—Warfare conducted by armed groups of guerrillas, partisans, or other nonregulars usually within enemy-held territory.

Islamic Jihad—This nom de guerre, which translates to "Islamic holy struggle," has been adopted at different times by terrorist groups in Lebanon, Egypt, and the West Bank. Despite the anti-Israel orientation of the Palestinian faction, it has clashed on numerous occasions with Yasser Arafat's Palestinian Authority.

island—The superstructure on an aircraft carrier on the side of the flight deck.

Item—Letter of old phonetic alphabet. See also **alphabet, phonetic**.

J

jack—1) A type of body armor worn by common soldiers and sailors until it was replaced by the buff coat at the end of the 16th century. It consisted of two layers of linen or canvas with pieces of iron or horn sewn between them. 2) A small flag, usually flown on the bow of a naval vessel, indicating its nationality, or used otherwise as a signal flag. The jack used by the U.S. Navy is flown from a small staff called a **jack staff** when a naval vessel is at anchor or moored. 3) A generic term for "sailor," especially in the British Royal Navy. 4) The **Union Jack** is the British national flag.

jack boots—Cavalry boots of thick, firm leather, specially hardened, sometimes lined with plates of iron.

jacket—1) British term for the outer casing of a shell or a bullet. 2) Old British military slang expression for promotion to the rank of senior captain of artillery, because of the distinctive uniform jacket worn by artillery officers of that rank.

jack man—One wearing a JACK; a horse soldier.

jack staff—See **jack**.

jaculator—In the Roman army, a lightly armed soldier whose weapon was the javelin. Derived from the Latin word for "throw." See also **veles**.

jaeger or **jäger**—Rifleman. The first jaegers (literally, huntsmen) were light infantrymen, organized during the Seven Years' War by Frederick the Great from foresters and gamekeepers. They were expert marksmen but armed with hunting rifles whose slow rate of fire put them at a disadvantage against regular troops. The term "jaeger" persisted in the German and Austrian armies, designating both lightly armed and hunter-type units of various kinds; for example, the Panzer Jaeger (or tank destroyer) units and the Jaeger division, or light division, of World War II.

jaeger rifle—A FLINTLOCK hunting rifle, with a grooved barrel, developed in Germany in the 17th century. (Also known as a **jäger**, the German term for "hunter"). The spin thus given to the bullet gave it a great advantage in accuracy and range over the smoothbore muskets that were then the standard infantry weapon. It was, however, much heavier and more cumbersome than the musket and took longer to reload after firing. This heavy weapon was modified in North America, mainly by German craftsmen in Pennsylvania, becoming a lighter, longer-barreled weapon in the 18th century, and thus was the forerunner of the grooved, or rifled, weapons that gradually replaced the SMOOTHBORES in the early decades of the 19th century. See also **Kentucky rifle** and **rifle**.

jam—1) To make the transmission of a radio unintelligible; to make a radar or radio set ineffective, either by use of counter-transmissions or by the use of a confusion reflector. 2) Of a firearm, to stick or become inoperative because of improper loading, ejection, or the like.

janissary—1) A Turkish guard, one of an elite body organized in the 14th century and maintained until 1826 as the permanent element of the army of the Ottoman Empire. The first janissaries were former Christians who had been captured in childhood and brought up to become fanatical Moslems. They were highly disciplined infantry that evolved into a formidable military and political force and a privileged social class but then deteriorated. In June 1826 the janissaries revolted against Sultan Mahmud, whose attempt to modernize and Westernize the army was correctly seen by the janissaries as a threat to their existence. They were massacred by loyal troops and the mobs of Istanbul. 2) Term for a loyal follower, generally used in the plural.

javelin—A light spear—soldiers often carried two or more—that was common in ancient armies. Javelins were usually thrown simultaneously by a massed or formed group against a similar enemy group, although individuals achieved considerable skill at hitting individual targets. After the PHALANX appeared, javelins were used by lightly armed auxiliary troops to shake the enemy's morale, open gaps, and harass flanks.

jeep—1) A rugged four-wheel-drive quarter-ton-capacity vehicle first widely used by the U.S. Army in World War II. The name derives from the pronunciation of the initial letters of "general purpose," GP. 2) In the U.S. armored forces of World War II, the term was applied to the half-ton command-car vehicle; in those units and forces the quarter-ton vehicle was called a "peep." 3) A smaller version of other military items, including a small airplane used for reconnaissance and liaison, an amphibious truck, and an escort carrier.

U.S. Army photo

jeep

jemadar—A rank for native officers in the Indian army corresponding to lieutenant in the U.S. Army.

"Jerry"—Slang for the generic German soldier, used especially in the British army in World Wars I and II.

Jig—Letter of old phonetic alphabet. See also **alphabet, phonetic**.

jihad—A holy war waged on behalf of Islam against infidels as a religious duty.

jinking—An air maneuver designed to change the flight path of an aircraft in all planes at random intervals.

joint—In the U.S. armed forces connoting participation by two or more services, as "joint operation" or "joint command." See also **combined**.

Joint Chiefs of Staff (JCS)—The Chiefs of Staff of the U.S. Army and Air Force, together with the Chief of Naval Operations and the Commandant of the Marine Corps, chaired by an officer from one of these services. Since the establishment of the JCS in 1947, it has served as the principal military advisory body to the President and the Secretary of Defense. The Defense Reorganization Act of 1986 greatly enhanced the authority of the chairman of the JCS and gave additional authority to commanders of regional unified commands.

joint direct-attack munition (JDAM)—A kit used to convert conventional gravity bombs into laser-guided "smart" bombs. The United States employed more than 6,000 JDAMs in Afghanistan, where they proved to be highly accurate.

joint force commander — The combatant commander authorized to exercise command authority over a force drawn from two or more of the armed services.

joint servicing—An administrative function performed by a jointly staffed and financed group whose activity is in support of two or more military services.

joint staff—1) The staff of a specified or unified command or of a joint task force, which includes members from the several U.S. armed services that constitute the force. A joint staff is created to ensure that the commander understands the tactics, techniques, capabilities, needs, and limitations of the force's component parts. Positions on the staff may be divided so that service representation and influence generally reflect the composition of the force. 2) The staff of the Joint Chiefs of Staff as provided for under the National Security Act of 1947 and as amended by later legislation.

joint standoff weapon (JSOW) — A joint Navy–Air Force program designed to provide a variety of precision-guided weapons that will allow aircraft to attack targets from beyond the range of enemy air defenses.

Joint Strategic Objectives Plan (JSOP)—A midrange-objectives plan of the U.S. Department of Defense, prepared by the JCS, that translates U.S. national objectives and policies for a time frame of from 5 to 8 years in the future into terms of military objectives and strategic concepts. The plan also defines basic undertakings for COLD WAR, LIMITED WAR, and GENERAL WAR that may be accomplished with the objective force levels.

joint strike fighter (JSF) — A multipurpose attack/fighter aircraft, the Lockheed Martin JSF is designed to operate from ground bases or from carriers. In a break with past procedure, the United States is encouraging investment in the project by friendly nations with an interest in the final product. The first aircraft is expected to be delivered to the U.S. military in 2008.

joint surveillance and target acquisition radar systems (JSTARS)—A surveillance, targeting, and battle management system in which an aircraft is employed as a command and control platform. The system, employed during the Gulf War, can simultaneously locate and track thousands of mobile and fixed ground targets.

jointure of command—A U.S. Navy term for the transfer of command of an amphibious landing force from the Navy commander to the ground force commander at a certain point in the landing operation.

joust—1) A peacetime competition, usually among knights in medieval times, in the form of serious but nonlethal combat, with lances when the opponents were mounted; a tilting match; a tournament. 2) Any combat suggestive of such a competition.

Ju-52—German twin-engine medium bomber manufactured by Junkers. It was used extensively during World War II, primarily as a bomber but occasionally for troop and cargo transport.

Ju-87/Ju-88—See **Stuka**.

judge advocate general—1) The senior legal officer in one of the U.S. military services who supervises the administration of military justice and such other legal duties as may be required within the service. 2) The legal officer on the staff of a high-level military command. An officer serving as prosecutor in a court-martial, or as legal adviser to a commander, is a **judge advocate.**

Judge Advocate General's Corps — A corps of qualified attorneys who are also military officers and who serve under the judge advocate general of their service, assisting in the supervision of military justice. Most assignments as staff judge advocates or judge advocate generals in higher-level commands are held by members of this corps.

Juliet—Letter of NATO phonetic alphabet. See also **alphabet, phonetic.**

jumpmaster — An officer or noncommissioned officer who commands parachute troops in an aircraft and controls their jumping and the dropping of their equipment from an aircraft.

jump of a gun—1) The motion of a small-arms weapon during the firing period, caused by the force of recoil (also known as "kick"). 2) Any jerky movement of a land or naval cannon, or their carriages, due to play in the mechanism, nonuniform application of moving power, or the like.

junction point—See **coordinating point.**

jungle warfare—Warfare in an environment of dense, intermingled growth that is distinguished from combat in other environments only by those special considerations relating to visibility, mobility, supply, climate, and so on.

junior officer—1) An officer junior to another by virtue of rank or date of rank. 2) In general, an officer of the rank of captain and below in the army, air force, or marine corps, and the rank of lieutenant senior grade and below in the navy. In the U.S. Army those who hold this rank are also generally called COMPANY-GRADE officers.

junta—A council or a board, usually composed of a group of military officers who govern a country, particularly a group that has taken power in a coup d'état.

jus belli—Law of war or the body of doctrine handed down by tradition that specifies the circumstances under which war may be resorted to (**jus ad bellum**) and the practices that should not be engaged in during war (**jus in bello**). The last-mentioned are often called LAWS OF WAR or RULES OF WAR.

justice, military—The legal system governing the military forces of a nation.

just war—A concept developed by Christian thinkers in the Middle Ages which affirms that war can be considered just only under specified conditions. These conditions, as generally stated, are as follows: a) that the war have a just cause; that is, that it be intended to remedy or prevent an injustice; b) that no peaceful means can adequately accomplish the same end; c) that the suffering likely to result from the war not outweigh the injustices it is intended to remedy; d) that a legitimate political authority has authorized the war after giving proper consideration to the requirements of a just war; and e) that the political authority sanctions the war for just motives only.

K

K-9 Corps—The organization established in the U.S. services in World War II for the purpose of using dogs for various tasks, such as guard and patrol. The name is a play on "canine."

Kalashnikov—See **AK-47 assault rifle**.

kamikaze—A specially trained Japanese pilot in World War II; also, his airplane when filled with explosives. The pilot's mission was to fly his plane suicidally into an Allied target, usually a warship. The pilots were given minimal training in the handling of the aircraft and prepared ritualistically for the sacrifice before takeoff. Their sudden appearance in the last months of the war was an act of Japanese desperation. Although many flights were shot down and others aborted, a number succeeded in evading antiaircraft protection and causing considerable damage to U.S. vessels. In Japanese the name means "divine wind."

kampfgruppe—German designation of a combat team or a TASK FORCE.

K-day—1) In World War II, the day set for a strike by a U.S. Navy carrier's aircraft. It corresponds to the land forces' designation of D-day, with which it may or may not coincide. 2) The date for introduction of a convoy system on any particular convoy lane.

Kashmiri secessionists — Islamic fundamentalists seeking to impose Muslim control over the part of Kashmir that has been under Indian administration since the first Indian-Pakistani war in 1947.

KC-135—See **Stratotanker**.

keelhauling—A punishment used in sailing navies, in some cases into the 19th century. The offender, weighted with iron or lead and with ropes attached, was dropped from one yardarm of a vessel, hauled beneath the keel of the vessel, and then hoisted to the opposite yardarm. The punishment was usually fatal.

keep—The strongest area of a fortification or a castle, designed to be held in the final stages of a siege or an attack. The keep, also called a "donjon," was usually centrally located in the fortification. See also **citadel**.

Kentucky rifle — A long-barreled muzzle-loading rifle first developed in Pennsylvania in the 18th century by German immigrants and used for hunting, particularly in the wilderness areas of western Pennsylvania, Virginia, Ohio, Kentucky, and Tennessee. The Kentucky rifle proved an effective weapon in the French and Indian War, the American Revolution, and the War of 1812. Kentucky rifles were frequently elaborately decorated with maplewood stocks, and the barrels were sometimes octagonal, like the JAEGER RIFLE upon which they were modeled. See also **Pennsylvania rifle** and **rifle**.

kepi—A uniform cap worn particularly by French soldiers. The kepi has a visor and rises directly from the head to a circular, flat top, sometimes higher in back than in front. Such caps were worn by soldiers of both sides in the American Civil War. See also **forage cap**.

khaki—Often in the plural, a uniform of tan cotton khaki cloth worn by U.S. service personnel and others in warm seasons and warm climates. The original khaki, from the Persian word for "dust," is a cotton cloth of a light yellowish brown. Khaki has come to mean the color, and modern uniforms are made in a variety of materials of that color.

Khmer Rouge—The popular name for the Cambodian Communist Party, founded in about 1951, which sought to create a Communist society in Cambodia modeled after Mao's China. After achieving power in 1975, the Khmer Rouge depopulated the cities of Cambodia, overworked and starved the people, and brought about the deaths of an estimated 3 million Cambodians. The Khmer Rouge were ousted from power in 1989.

kick—See **jump of a gun**.

killed in action (KIA) — A battle casualty who is killed outright or who dies as a result of wounds or other injuries before reaching any medical treatment facility.

killing area/zone—An area in which a commander plans to force the enemy to concentrate so as to destroy him with conventional or nuclear weapons.

kill potential—The potential of a weapon for killing people or for destroying aircraft or weapons.

kill probability (kp)—The probability of a given percentage of deaths resulting from a shell, bomb, warhead, or the like exploding under a set of given conditions.

Kilo—Letter of NATO phonetic alphabet. See also **alphabet, phonetic**.

King—Letter of old phonetic alphabet. See also **alphabet, phonetic**.

Kingfisher (AQM-60)—An antiship cruise missile.

kit—1) The personal belongings of a soldier. 2) The parts and instructions for use with a piece of equipment for performing some function, as in "repair kit," "mess kit."

kit bag—A small bag used by soldiers for carrying personal articles.

kiwi—1) A nonflying air officer. 2) A student pilot who has not flown solo. The name is taken from the New Zealand flightless bird.

klibanion—A corselet of LAMELLAR ARMOR worn by Byzantine soldiers, generally waist length with short sleeves or sleeveless.

knapsack—A case or bag, usually of canvas or leather, worn on the back to carry supplies and equipment, especially on a hike or march. In the U.S. Army, a knapsack is generally called a "pack."

knee mortar—A 50mm Japanese mortar used in World War II for firing grenades and flares. The name was given to it by U.S. forces because of the mistaken belief that the base plate was concave in shape so that the mortar could rest on and be fired from the knee. American efforts to test this theory with captured mortars resulted in a number of broken legs. Actually, the concavity facilitated rapid use of the mortar from a solid base on the ground or on a fallen tree trunk.

knight—An aristocrat or nobleman of medieval times who served in warfare as a mounted man-at-arms, usually as a leader or officer of a feudal contingent in the service of his liege landlord. A knight was trained from youth as a page and a squire and attained a privileged position in service to his lord.

knot (symbol of rank)—1) An epaulet in the form of a braided knot, usually gold braid in the ceremonial uniform of an officer. 2) A tassel of knotted leather or gold braid on an officer's sword or saber guard.

kontos—A Byzantine lance, originating with the Sarmatians and the Alans. Cavalrymen carried a 12-foot kontos, or kontarion, and infantrymen one of the same length or longer.

Krag/Krag-Jorgensen rifle—A rifle, invented by two Norwegians, Krag and Jorgensen, that was used by the armies of Denmark and Norway and, in a modified version, as the standard rifle of the U.S. Army from 1892 to 1903. It was a .30-caliber, single-shot, bolt-action weapon with a five-round magazine.

K-ration—A packaged emergency ration for use under combat conditions developed for U.S. forces in World War II. Each ration contained three concentrated meals, separately packaged, including bread or biscuits, canned meat, a powdered beverage, and a confection.

Kriegsakademie—Literally war academy, this school was founded by Gen. Gerhard von Scharnhorst in 1810 for the instruction of selected officers of the Prussian army for duties with the General Staff. Originally called the School for Young Officers, it was renamed Kriegsakademie in 1859. It continued as the senior military educational institution of the German army after the unification of Germany in 1871.

kriegspiel — Literally, war game, a game used for instruction and planning, employing a large map or a contoured model and markers or small figures to represent the opposing forces. Introduced into the Prussian army about 1821.

kris—A Malayan sword with a straight handle and a wavy, double-edged blade.

Krupp gun—Any cannon produced by the factories of the Krupp family, including most of the weapons of the Prussian and German armies in the 19th and 20th centuries.

kukri—A short, heavy-bladed sword of Nepal; the hand weapon of Britain's and India's GURKHA troops.

kyklos—A defensive naval tactic in ancient warfare in which fleets formed a circle with all rams pointing outward. It was used by the Greeks in fighting the Persian fleet at Artemisium (480 B.C.), and by the Peloponnesians against the Athenians at Rhium.

A late-19th-century Krupp gun.

Krupp gun

L

Laager—*n.* An encampment for defense, with wagons or armored vehicles encircling it for protection. *v.* To form such an encampment. *Laager* is an Afrikaaner word.

ladle—A long spoonlike instrument that was used to load powder into a muzzle-loading cannon before the advent of cartridges.

Lafayette Escadrille—1) A volunteer squadron made up principally of American fliers who fought for France in World War I before the United States entered the war in 1917. In 1918 it was transferred to the American service and became the 103rd Pursuit Squadron. 2) In World War II, a fighter squadron of French pilots that fought in North Africa under American command and equipped with American aircraft.

lamellar armor — Armor originally developed in eastern Asia, composed of small plates of stiff, laminated fabric laced together. By the end of the 14th century such armor was being worn in Scandinavia, where it seems to have been introduced from Russia. See also **armor.**

Lancaster — The most successful British heavy bomber of World War II, the four-engine Lancaster could carry bomb loads of up to 10 tons.

Lancaster rifle—A naval gun invented by the Englishman Charles William Lancaster. The first rifle cannon to be used in naval warfare, it was introduced by the British in the Crimean War. It had a smooth, elliptical bore that was slightly twisted and fired a projectile that was also slightly elliptical in cross section.

lance—A long, metal-tipped spear used primarily by mounted soldiers. Used by many ancient peoples, including the Assyrians, Egyptians, Greeks, and Romans, lances remained common weapons until the introduction of gunpowder.

Lance—A mobile, liquid-propellant, surface-to-surface missile mounting either a nuclear or a conventional warhead. Designed to provide long-range fire support at the corps level.

lance corporal—1) An enlisted rank in the U.S. Marine Corps above a private and below a corporal; comparable to private first class in the U.S. Army. 2) A British army private acting as a corporal. A British corporal acting as a sergeant is a LANCE SERGEANT.

lancer—A cavalryman armed with a lance.

U.S. Department of Defense photo

Lancer (B-1B)

149

Lancer (B-1B)—The result of a long search for a successor to the B-52, the Lancer was designed for low-level penetration missions with protection derived from a low radar profile and extensive electronic countermeasures. Approximately 100 aircraft were authorized for the SAC inventory in the mid-1980s.

lance rest—A bracket on the right side of an armor breastplate, or a leather pocket on the saddle, into which the butt end of a lance fitted when the rider charged, preventing the lance from being driven backward when the tip hit a target.

lance sergeant—See **lance corporal**.

Lanchester Equations (also known as **Lanchester Laws** or **Lanchester's Equations** or **Lanchester's Laws**)—A concept of military combat power and attrition developed by British aeronautical engineer Frederick William Lanchester in 1914 to show the relationship between force strengths and combat outcomes, particularly combat losses, in standard circumstances. Lanchester Equations have been used since World War II as the basis for the calculation of attrition or casualties in most ground COMBAT MODELs and SIMULATIONs. Lanchester's **Linear Law** applies when the location of the hostile force or forces is known only generally. Lanchester's **Square Law** applies when the location of the hostile force is known precisely.

landing area—1) The part of the objective area within which an amphibious force initiates a landing operation. It includes the beach, approaches to the beach, transport areas, fire support areas, air occupied by close supporting aircraft, and the land through which an advance inland to the primary objective is made. 2) An **airborne landing area** is the general area used for landing troops and matériel by air delivery or air landing. This area includes one or more drop zones or landing strips. 3) Any specially prepared or selected surface of land, water, or deck designated or used for the takeoff and landing of aircraft.

landing attack—An attack against enemy defenses by troops landed from ships, aircraft, boats, or amphibious vehicles. See also **amphibious operation**.

landing beach—A beach on which a landing force disembarks (usually in an assault landing).

landing craft—Any of various craft employed in amphibious operations, specifically designed for carrying troops, supplies, and equipment and for beaching, unloading, and withdrawing. See also **Higgins boat**.

U.S. Navy photo

landing craft

landing force—A task organization of troop units, aviation, and ground assigned to an amphibious assault. It is the highest command echelon in the amphibious operation.

landing-force support party — The forward element of a combat service support element formed to facilitate a landing.

landing operation—See **amphibious operation**.

landing ship—Any of various types of assault ship designed for long sea voyages and for rapid unloading over and onto a beach. It includes various special types, including landing ship, dock (LSD); landing ship, tank (LST); and landing ship, infantry (LSI).

landing site—A continuous segment of coastline over which troops, equipment, and supplies can be landed by surface means. It includes one or more landing beaches.

landing team, regimental—See **regimental landing team**.

landing vehicle, tracked — A lightly armored amphibious vehicle designed for amphibious assaults and operations inland.

land mine—An explosive device placed on or slightly beneath the surface of the ground and usually designed to explode when pressure, particularly that of a passing person or vehicle, is applied. They were first employed in the American Civil War, and even then they were criticized as indiscriminate and inappropriate; Confederate Gen. James Longstreet prohibited their use, calling them "not a proper or effective means of war." More recently, the difficulty of locating and removing land mines at the conclusion of hostilities has led to civilian casualties in countries such as Cambodia and Korea and has encouraged a movement to ban their use entirely. See also **mine**.

Landsknecht—One of a body of mercenary foot soldiers formed by Emperor Maximilian I at the end of the 15th century as a counter to the Swiss infantry. Organized, equipped, and trained as spearmen, just like the Swiss, they were nearly as sought after by European monarchs for the armies of the 16th century as the Swiss themselves. The name means "man of the plains" in German.

Landsturm—A German army reserve category of men who are relatively old or not fully fit. The term, meaning literally "territorial assault force," was originally applied to a general levy of militia. Composition of the *Landsturm* as part of reserve organizations has differed in different historical times.

Landwehr—The army reserve category in Germany and Austria, and some other countries, consisting of people who have relatively recently completed compulsory service. Meaning literally "territorial defense force," *Landwehr* originally referred to the entire militia.

lane marker—A marker used to mark a minefield lane.

lanyard—1) A short piece of line used for fastening items on ships. 2) The cord or line on which a sailor carries a boatswain's pipe, a knife, or similar object. 3) A cord or thong attached to a pistol butt for looping about the neck to prevent loss of the pistol. 4) A cord, a wire, or a cable for firing certain cannon, pyrotechnics, and the like. 5) Any of certain foreign decorations worn over the shoulder.

LAPES—See **low-altitude parachute extraction system**.

laser-guided weapon—A weapon that employs a seeker to detect laser energy from a target and is guided to the target by reflected laser energy.

laser target-designating system — A means of directing laser energy at a target. The system includes a target marker to acquire the target and direct a laser beam against it.

late-medieval concentric castles — See **concentric castles**.

lateral communications—See **communications, lateral**.

latrine—A communal toilet in use by a barracks, a camp, or the like.

launch—*n.* 1) A small boat, powered by sail or motor, used as a tender. 2) The largest boat belonging to and carried on a warship. 3) The transition of a missile from static repose to dynamic flight. *v.* To set in motion an attack, an aircraft, a ship, a torpedo, a rocket, a missile, or other item that, once released or given an impulse, will proceed by momentum or under its own power.

launcher—1) A structural device, erected on a **launch pad** or carried on a truck, designed to support and hold a missile in position for firing. 2) The catapult that launches an aircraft from the deck of a warship.

law, military—The laws governing the operation of the military establishment and the conduct of its members. See also **justice, military**.

laws of war—Rules of behavior for states and individuals engaged in war. These rules have become "laws" by virtue of having been codified and agreed on by treaties and by the general conventions and declarations of Paris (1856), Geneva (1864, 1906, 1909, 1929, 1949), St. Petersburg (1868), The Hague (1899, 1907, 1923), and London (1909, 1930). The first important codification of the laws of war was in *Instructions for the Government of the Armies of the United States in the Field*, prepared by Francis Lieber and issued in 1863 during the American Civil War by the U.S. Army Adjutant General as *General Orders 100*. Laws of war are generally designed to prevent loss and suffering to neutrals and noncombatants and to prevent unnecessary suffering to combatants and prisoners; that is, to prevent suffering that does not directly further the military objectives of the damage-inflicting side.

lay—1) To direct or adjust the aim of a weapon. 2) To drop bombs or aerial mines from an aircraft. 3) To spread, as with a smoke screen. 4) To calculate or project a course.

lay on—To plan and schedule a mission.

leadership—The art of influencing and directing people to an assigned goal in such a manner as to command their obedience, confidence, respect, and loyalty.

leapfrog—Form of movement in which like supporting elements are moved successively through or past one another along the axis of movement of supported forces. Leapfrog movements can be made either forward or to the rear.

leather armor—See **armor**.

leather gun—A cannon developed by a Swedish colonel named Wurmbrandt for Gustavus Adolphus in 1625 and first used by the Swedes in Poland in 1627. Designed to be lighter than the cast iron or bronze guns of the time, the leather gun, of which 14 are known to have been made, consisted of a copper-lined iron barrel wrapped in layers of canvas held by three wooden rings, with an external covering of leather nailed on. The guns weighed about 90 pounds and could be transported more easily than conventional guns. However, after repeated discharges leather guns became so hot that a new charge would sometimes ignite prematurely in the barrel before the cannoneer had ignited the primer.

leatherneck—Term used for a U.S. Marine. The term derives from the leather neckband on the early marine uniforms.

leave—See **furlough**.

Lee-Enfield rifle—See **Enfield rifle**.

lee gage—The naval battle position downwind from an opponent's fleet. See also **weather gage**.

left face—*n.* 1) A 90-degree change of stationary position to the left while at attention. 2) The command to make this change. *v.* 1) To execute such a change in position. 2) In the imperative, the command to do it. See also **face**.

legion—1) A formation of 4,000 to 6,000 men in the Roman army. The size of the legion varied, but it was always the basic Roman military organization. In early republican Rome there were normally four legions, formed into two armies, each under the command of one of the two consuls who were the chief officials of Rome. The men who composed the legions, the legionaries (sometimes called legionnaires in English), were selected at the beginning of each year by the TRIBUNES. They served only when needed and were discharged when an emergency was over. They were divided according to age among HASTATI, PRINCIPES, TRIARII, and VELITES. Each legion was composed of 60 CENTURIES. In the 2nd century B.C. the consul Marius opened the ranks to any citizen who would volunteer, and this action laid the foundation for a permanent professional army. Pay was raised, the lightly armed velites were discontinued, and other organizational changes were made as well. By that time many more legions had been organized, and even more were established in the empire. Roman citizenship remained a requirement of a legionary, but the extension of citizenship to conquered territories resulted in legions with large numbers of non-Roman legionaries. 2) Designation of mixed units of infantry and cavalry (and sometimes artillery) formed in several European and in the U.S. armies during the 18th and early 19th centuries. Typical was the United States Legion, with which Gen. Anthony Wayne defeated the Maumee Indians in the Battle of Fallen Timbers (20 August 1794). See also **Foreign Legion, French** and **Foreign Legion, Spanish**.

legionary or **legionnaire** — A soldier belonging to a LEGION.

letter of marque and reprisal—A commission issued to the owner of a private vessel, authorizing its captain to operate against enemy ships as a PRIVATEER.

levée en masse or **levy en masse**—Universal conscription. In August 1793, during the French Revolution, the Committee of Public Safety decreed conscription of the entire male population of France, thus enabling the nation to put 14 armies into the field very quickly. Previously, most armies had had to depend on the hiring of MERCENARIES when military expansion was required.

level—1) To aim a weapon horizontally. 2) To maneuver an aircraft into flight that is parallel to the surface of the earth after gaining or losing altitude.

level, gunner's—A spirit level used to lay a gun for elevation, or range. Usually called a gunner's QUADRANT.

levy, feudal—A mustering or a calling of troops into service during the medieval era. In feudal times it was the responsibility of vassal lords or landowners to raise a force of agreed size and composition upon the call to arms of the suzerain.

levy, military—*n.* 1) The calling of militia into service. 2) The calling of a segment of a nation's population to service. 3) The troops so levied. 4) The selective calling by an army of troops from one division or other unit to provide cadre for a new organization or to fill out one in existence *v.* 1) To call troops into service. 2) To call on one organization to supply troops for another.

Lewis gun—A gas-operated, air-cooled machine gun with a horizontal drum magazine invented by U.S. Col. Isaac M. Lewis about 1911. It was used as an infantry weapon from the beginning of World War I and widely adopted thereafter in various modifications by ground, naval, and air forces.

Lewisite—A volatile liquid developed during World War I as a lethal, persistent, blistering poison gas, recognizable by its faint, geraniumlike odor. Similar to MUSTARD GAS.

LGM-30—See **Minuteman**.

liaison — The contact or communication maintained between parts of the armed forces to ensure mutual understanding and unity of purpose and action. It is often aided by an exchange of personnel to facilitate the exchange of information. Liaison is lateral when maintained between two adjacent units, whether or not they are under the same commander. Command liaison is that established between echelons in the chain of command.

Liberator—In different configurations, the four-engine U.S. Navy patrol bomber and transport, PB4Y, and the U.S. Army Air Force's B-24, a long-range bomber. The *Liberator* was one of the most important bombers of World War II.

liberty—In the U.S. Navy, authorized absence from duty for less than 48 hours. See **pass**.

Liberty ship—A mass-produced cargo vessel, assembled from offsite components, that played a key role in moving supplies from the United States to Britain and to the Pacific theater during World War II. Liberty ships displaced about 10,000 tons and had a top speed of 11 knots. A later version, called "Victory ship," was capable of 17 knots.

liburnian—A Roman naval vessel.

lieutenant—In French, literally, "holding the place." 1) An assistant or deputy. (This was the original significance of lieutenant commander, lieutenant colonel, lieutenant general.) 2) In most armies and some other services, the lowest officer rank or ranks. In the U.S. Army, Air Force, and Marine Corps, the lowest rank is second lieutenant, the rank next above is first lieutenant. 3) In the U.S. Navy and Coast Guard, the two ranks above ensign. The lower of these is lieutenant, junior grade; senior to this is lieutenant, sometimes called lieutenant, senior grade. 4) In other navies a junior rank at various levels.

lieutenant colonel—In most armies, including the U.S. Army, Air Force, and Marine Corps, a rank above major and below colonel.

lieutenant commander—In most navies, including the U.S. Navy and Coast Guard, a rank above lieutenant and below commander.

lieutenant general—In most armies including the U.S. Army, Air Force, and Marine Corps, a rank above major general and below general. See also **general**.

lifeguard submarine — A submarine employed for aircrew rescue in areas inadequately covered by air or surface rescue facilities.

U.S. Air Force photo

Liberator

lift—See **amphibious lift**.

light artillery—Artillery, other than anti-aircraft artillery, consisting in most armies of howitzers and longer-barreled cannon of 105mm caliber or smaller. See also **artillery**.

light attack fighter—See **fighter aircraft**.

light cavalry—See **cavalry**.

light cruiser—See **cruiser**.

light division—A combined-arms unit of DI-VISION type, usually smaller and more lightly and austerely equipped than standard divisions. The principal reason for establishing "light" divisions is to achieve greater transportability or tactical mobility without greatly sacrificing the striking and holding power of a standard division. An airborne division can be considered a kind of light division.

lighter than air (LTA)—Designation of an airship—blimp, balloon, or dirigible—for which lift is provided by a gas-filled bag rather than by speed and the aerodynamic effects of wings and body surface. The gases most commonly used are helium (used exclusively by the United States) and hydrogen (not used by the United States because of its extreme flammability). Military uses in the United States of aircraft lighter than air are concentrated in a branch of the Naval Air Force.

light force—A military organization that is equipped with light weapons and matériel, to facilitate mobility and transportability, but has more limited combat power and sustainability than more heavily equipped forces have.

light horse—Light cavalry; lightly armed or armored soldiers who fight on horseback.

light infantry—See **infantry**.

Lima—Letter of NATO phonetic alphabet. See also **alphabet, phonetic**.

limber—*n.* The forward, detachable portion of a horse-drawn gun carriage, comprising an axle, two wheels, and a pole for harnessing the horses. Now frequently called "caisson" for the ammunition box that it carries mounted on the axle; the box also serves as a seat for one or two cannoneers. *v.* To attach the horses and forward section (the limber) to a gun carriage, or to a caisson.

limited duty—The duty status of a person who is physically disqualified from performing certain types of military functions.

limited objective—A political or military objective for which a nation or commander commits, or is willing to commit, only part of available resources or effort.

limited war—1) A war looked upon by one or more of its contestants as not involving its own sovereignty or most vital interests, and as being limited in at least one respect, as, for example, to a particular geographic area, to the employment of certain resources, or to the number of contestants. 2) A war considered by a detached observer as relatively limited in some key respect, especially with regard to political objectives.

line—1) A deployment of troops, tanks, ships, forts, or other elements one beside the other. In the U.S. Navy, generally called **line abreast**. 2) The front of the combat area, usually **the line**, or **front line**. 3) The troops in the line; thus, combat troops as opposed to auxiliaries. 4) In most military services, officers who are in the chain of command, as opposed to staff (supply engineers, etc.). 5) Naval term for "rope," particularly when used as part of a ship's working gear, like a halyard or a hawser.

line ahead—The formation of ships one behind the other.

linear defense—The deployment of defensive forces evenly distributed in a line along the entire front, with all or most of the units of the defending force on the line. Such a distribution, sometimes called CORDON DEFENSE, has often provided attacking forces with opportunities to make decisive breakthroughs. The preferred defensive deployment, because of its greater chance for success, is **defense in depth**. See also **defense**.

Linear Law—See **Lanchester Equations**.

linear tactics—A tactical system introduced to ground combat in western Europe by Swedish King Gustavus Adolphus in 1630. Thanks to increased firepower and rate of fire, he was able to form his musketeers and pikemen in lines six deep—half the prevailing depth. Later armies formed as few as three or two lines deep. Units were deployed abreast, along the front, with intervals between units to permit tactical flexibility.

Gustavus and his successors usually used two such lines, with a third in reserve. Although much modified in detail over the centuries, linear tactics are essentially the basis of modern ground combat doctrine.

line company—In the British army of the 18th and 19th centuries, each infantry regiment included several (usually three or four) standard infantry companies and one company each of GRENADIERS and LIGHT INFANTRY. The standard companies were called "line" companies because they usually formed the regiment's line, with the other two companies on the flanks or, more often, detached.

line crosser—A combatant who surrenders to the enemy while not in immediate danger.

line division officer—A U.S. Navy term for an officer in charge of a ship's deck or engineer division. The officer is responsible for the care and upkeep of that part of the ship assigned to his or her division and for training the crew.

line of authority — See **chain of command**.

line of battle—The deployment of forces in a generally linear formation for battle. In land warfare, troops along the two opposing parallel lines face each other. In naval warfare, warships usually form a single-file line of battle so as to bring their broadside fire to bear on the enemy line of battle.

line of communications (LOC) — All the routes—land, air, and water—that connect an operating military force with a base of operations and along which supplies and reinforcements move.

line of departure—1) A line designated to coordinate the departure of attack or scouting elements; a jump-off line. 2) A suitably marked offshore coordinating line to assist the on-schedule landing of assault craft on designated beaches in an amphibious operation. 3) A line tangent to the trajectory of a projectile at the instant of its being fired.

line of direction—A line indicated on early guns by a short point on the muzzle (the front sight) and a slight incision in the base ring (near sight) to direct the eye in pointing the gun.

line of duty—1) The performance of required military duty. 2) Any activity legitimately associated with military duty or service.

line officer—1) An officer in the line of command of combat units or vessels, with command precedence and seniority usually determined by date of rank. 2) An officer assigned to troop duty, as opposed to staff duty; a distinction often recognized in the expression "line and staff." 3) An officer belonging to one of the U.S. Army's combat branches, such as the infantry or artillery.

line of fire—The flight path or paths followed by projectiles or bullets fired from one or more guns.

line of march—1) Direction in which a military force proceeds. 2) The roads taken in a march.

line of sight—The straight line between two points. This line is in the plane of the great circle (that is, a circle on the surface of a sphere whose plane passes through the center of a sphere, such as the terrestrial sphere) but does not follow the curvature of the earth.

line regiments—Standard regiments as opposed to special, elite, or guards regiments.

lines of operation—See **exterior lines** and **interior lines**.

linked ammunition—Cartridges that are fastened side by side by means of metal links to form a belt for continuous feeding into a machine gun.

Link trainer—A trainer for airplane pilots, named for its developer, Edwin A. Link. The Link trainer was a simulation or mock-up of the cockpit of an actual airplane, including the controls and instrument dials. Persons using the trainer could replicate the effects, other than forward motion, of their manipulation of the controls. It was widely used for pilot training during World War II and was the forerunner of modern, more complicated flight simulators.

linstock—A long, forked stick used before 1800 so that the cannoneer could hold the slow match close enough to a cannon's touchhole to ignite the charge while he stood far enough away to avoid the cannon's recoil.

lion—A packaged, or preformed, unit consisting of all personnel and matériel necessary for the establishment of a major, all-purpose naval base. Used in World War II, a lion included the functional components for setting up an advanced base that could repair minor battle damage to a major portion of a fleet. Such bases were delivered in units that could be assembled and functioning in a very short time.

liquid fire—See **Greek fire**.

live ammunition—Ammunition that is ready to use for lethal effect, as distinguished from inert or drill or BLANK AMMUNITION.

Livens projector—A mortarlike device invented by U.S. Capt. William H. Livens in World War I for delivering a toxic agent. Detonated electrically, a boxed propellant charge fired 30 pounds of the agent nearly a mile in a bomb almost 8 inches in diameter and 20 inches long.

loadmaster—An Air Force technician qualified to plan aircraft loading, operate handling equipment, and supervise the loading and unloading of aircraft.

LOC—See **line of communications**.

lochaber ax—A pole with an ax at the end, a weapon formerly used by Scottish highlanders. See also **ax**.

lock—The device in a firearm that causes the charge to explode. See also **flintlock, matchlock, snaphance lock, wheellock.**

locket—A metal band near the mouth of a sword scabbard, which served both as a reinforcement for the scabbard and as a point of attachment for hanging straps.

lodgment—An area gained and held in territory otherwise held by the enemy or a neutral nation. See also **beachhead, bridgehead**.

loft bombing—See **toss bombing**.

log—1) An instrument used to measure a ship's speed, widely employed until the 20th century. The log, tossed overboard, kept its position while unreeling a line that indicated the ship's movement over a given period of time. 2) The record of a ship or an aircraft mission, noting details of weather, navigation, and problems encountered.

logistics—1) That aspect of military activity providing for the buildup and support of a military force so that it will be efficient and effective in both combat and noncombat operations. Logistics includes supplies, equipment, transportation, maintenance, construction, and operation of facilities; provision, movement, and evacuation of personnel; and similar services. 2) The furnishing of supplies and equipment. See also **administration**.

logistics support—The support given by a command or other organization to a person, activity, unit, or force, by means of which all or any part of its supplies, equipment, combat matériel, maintenance, transportation, administration, or any similar service is furnished. Thus, the person, activity, unit, or force can carry out its own operations more expeditiously.

longbow—A bow approximately 6 feet long, developed in Britain (probably in Wales) before the 13th century. Made of elm, hazel, basil, and finally of yew imported from Italy or Spain, the bow, which was curved in the front and flat on the back, tapered from 1.5 inches wide in the middle, where the hand grasped it, to its horn-capped ends. A skilled English archer could fire 10 to 12 of its 3-foot arrows a minute for a maximum of 400 yards, and with considerable accuracy for almost 250 yards. Its one drawback was that the strength and skill necessary for its successful use could be acquired only after years of training. Because it was more accurate, lighter, more easily handled, and more adaptable than the crossbow, either for skirmishing or for volley fire, it ultimately caused the abandonment of the crossbow and hastened the downfall of cavalry as the dominant arm of medieval warfare. See also **bow** and **crossbow.**

Longbow—Mounted on an Apache helicopter, this targeting system allows the helicopter to target 16 enemy tanks at once.

long-range bomber—See **bomber**.

long-range penetration—A concept developed by British Brigadier Orde Wingate and demonstrated in two long-range penetrations behind Japanese lines in Burma in World War II. The principle was that small British ground forces, with logistic support by airdrop, could operate for extended periods deep behind enemy lines, cutting communications, destroying supplies, creating general confusion, and thereby beating the Japanese at their own game of infiltration and encirclement. See also **Chindit**.

lookout posts—Positions occupied by a small number of troops, so placed that the position and movement of an enemy may be observed.

loophole—A slit or small opening of some other shape in a wall, through which small arms may be fired with minimum exposure to the persons firing them.

loot—Any items seized from their owners in a war zone.

looting—Robbery in hostile territory in wartime. The word derives from the Indian word *lootie*, meaning gang of robbers. Looting may result from a breakdown in discipline or it may be condoned by higher authority. At the close of the Boxer Rebellion in 1900, French and British officers permitted and participated in the looting of the Winter Palace in Beijing.

LORAN—A long-range electronic navigation system that uses the time divergence of pulse-type transmission from two or more fixed stations. (This term is derived from "LOng-RAnge electronic Navigation.")

loss rate—The rate at which weapons or equipment are destroyed in combat. Although the rate may be expressed in absolute numbers, it is normally expressed as a daily percentage of the original strength. See also **attrition**.

Love—Letter of old phonetic alphabet. See also **alphabet, phonetic**.

low-altitude bombing—Horizontal bombing with the height of release between 900 and 8,000 feet.

low-altitude parachute extraction system (LAPES)—A system for delivering supplies from an altitude of 5 to 10 feet into areas where neither landing nor parachute resupply is feasible.

low-angle fire—Gunfire delivered at angles of elevation below the elevation that corresponds to the maximum range of the gun. See also **high-angle fire**.

low-intensity conflict—See **conflict levels of intensity**.

lozenge—See **mascle**.

lucky bag—A U.S. Navy term for a place aboard ship or in a naval installation in which articles that are found adrift (i.e., without any obvious owner) are placed to be claimed when the lucky bag is opened.

lunette—1) A type of fieldwork open in the rear, in which the face is in the form of a half-moon or, more usually, in which parallel flanks are connected by two outward projecting faces meeting at the front in an angle. 2) A ring set in a plate at the back end of a gun carriage, with which the PINTLE of the LIMBER or truck is engaged.

M

M-1—See **tank, main battle**.

M-2/M-3—See **Bradley fighting vehicle**.

M-4—See **Sherman**.

M-14—1) The standard U.S. Navy submarine torpedo in the first 2 years of World War II. Until mid-1943 it was plagued with technical problems, including defective exploders. 2) A 7.62mm, lightweight, air-cooled, gas-operated, magazine-fed, semiautomatic shoulder rifle.

M-16 rifle—The most widely used infantry weapon in the world, the rapid-fire M-16 was adopted by the U.S. Army as its basic infantry weapon in 1967.

M-18—See **Hellcat**.

M-42—See **Duster**.

M-47—See **Dragon**.

M-60 machine gun—The M-60 can be used to defend fixed positions, but its light weight—approximately 23 pounds—makes it the first truly portable machine gun in the U.S. inventory. It can fire 600 rounds per minute with a maximum effective range of 3,500 yards.

M-72—A light antitank weapon, the M-72 fires a high-explosive rocket. In Vietnam it proved effective against defensive bunkers.

M-79—A breech-loaded, shoulder-fired grenade launcher with an effective range of 400 meters. It fires a 40mm round with various warheads, including antipersonnel and anti-

armor ordnance, and in Vietnam proved effective against both personnel and fixed positions.

M-88—A tracked vehicle able to recover and tow disabled tanks.

M-106—An armored personnel carrier fitted with an 81mm mortar. Other personnel carriers may be equipped with a 106mm mortar or with special communications equipment.

M-109—See **Paladin**.

MAAG—See **military assistance advisory group**.

macana—A war club used by certain South American Indians.

mace—A heavy club whose large head with protruding spikes or flanges could crush or penetrate armor. Warrior clergymen usually carried maces because they were forbidden by canon law to shed blood. In the late 16th century its use as a weapon was abandoned, and it became a ceremonial instrument or sign of rank. See also **holy-water sprinkler** and **morning star**.

Mace (MGM-13)—An improved version of the MGM-1C Matador missile, differing primarily in having an improved guidance system, a longer-range low-level attack capability, and a more powerful warhead.

Mach—A figure used to describe the speed of aircraft relative to the speed of sound in the air at that altitude. At Mach 2, an aircraft is flying at twice the speed of sound, which at

40,000 feet is 660 miles per hour. The term is named after August Mach, an Austrian physicist.

machete—A long, heavy, broad-bladed swordlike knife, used in the West Indies and Latin America not only for cutting sugarcane and heavy vegetation but also as a weapon.

machicolation—1) A projecting parapet or gallery at the top of a castle wall with holes or openings in the floor through which defenders could drop hot liquids or rocks or fire arrows on attackers at the base of the wall. 2) One of the holes in the gallery.

machine gun—A small, fully automatic weapon of various designs. It fires small-caliber ammunition in rapid successive shots using any of a variety of mechanisms. The first such weapons, invented in the mid-19th century, were the Gatling and Lowell guns, which were multibarreled weapons fired by crank-operated mechanisms. Their first important use was in the American Civil War. The first fully automatic machine gun was a recoil-operated gun built by Hiram Maxim in 1884. The modern machine gun is belt-fed and driven by recoil or ejected gunpowder gas. Machine guns are usually classified as light, medium, or heavy. A light machine gun is usually air-cooled, bipod mounted, portable, and 5mm to 7mm in caliber. A medium machine gun is usually tripod mounted, water-cooled, and of about 7mm caliber. A heavy machine gun is usually air-cooled or water-cooled and 7mm to 13mm in caliber.

machine pistol—1) A pistol capable of fully automatic fire. 2) A submachine gun. The application of the term in the second sense was introduced after World War II from the German and Russian words for the submachine gun, *Maschinenpistole* (machine-pistol) and *pistolyet-pulemyot* (pistol–machine gun), so-called because the submachine gun ordinarily uses pistol-type ammunition. It is called "machine carbine" by the British.

machinist—U.S. Navy warrant officer.

machinist's mate—U.S. Navy specialty rating, chief and first, second, and third class.

magazine—1) A structure or compartment for storing supplies, particularly ammunition or explosives. 2) A sometimes detachable part of a gun or firearm that holds ammunition ready for insertion into the chamber.

magazine gun—A breech-loading weapon with a magazine tube or other container in the stock or in front of the trigger for carrying cartridges. When a round has been fired, the empty cartridge or shell case is ejected and a full cartridge is moved mechanically to take its place.

Magic—Information derived from Japanese naval and diplomatic codes during World War II by U.S. Army and Navy cryptographers.

Maginot Line—The line of fortifications built by France along its frontier with Germany between 1930 and 1934 as a defense against possible German attack. It consisted of a line of CASEMATEs, with great underground forts called *ouvrages* at 5- to 8-kilometer intervals, a tank barrier constructed from pieces of rail set on end in concrete, and steel posts and barbed wire between tank barrier and casemates. The forts could house 100 to 500 men, the larger forts having both infantry and artillery capability, the smaller infantry alone. Because the Maginot Line was so formidable, Germany avoided it and attacked France through Belgium in May 1940. (French fortifications along the Franco-Belgian frontier were minimal.) The defeat of France was due largely to the positioning of most of its army behind the Maginot Line; these troops were thus not available to block the German thrust around the line. The Germans took advantage of the Maginot Line in 1944, using its fortifications to slow the Allied drive across northeastern France after the July breakout from the Normandy beachhead.

mail—Body armor made of interlinked metal rings, sometimes known as **chain mail**. In medieval Europe, mail was usually made of alternate solid punched rings and open rings with their ends riveted together. In Asian mail armor, the ends of the rings were usually butted together on heavy cloth and thus less strong.

mail coif—See **coif, mail**.

main battery—On a naval vessel, the guns of the largest caliber.

main battle tank—See **tank, main battle**.

main body—1) The principal portion of a military force during movement, after detachment of ADVANCE GUARD, REAR GUARD, and FLANK GUARD. 2) The principal portion of a military force, which consists of several groups or contingents, or from which detachments have been made. See also **body**.

main line of resistance (MLR) — A line close behind the forward edge of a battle position, chosen and prepared for optimum defensive capability and so designated for the purpose of coordinating the fire of all units and supporting weapons, including air and naval gunfire. It defines the forward limits of a series of mutually supporting defensive areas but does not include the areas farther forward (toward the enemy) that are occupied or used by covering or screening forces.

main road—A road capable of serving as the principal ground line of communication to an area or locality. Usually, it is suitable for two-way traffic in any weather at high speeds.

maintenance—1) All action taken to retain matériel in a serviceable condition or to restore it to serviceability. It includes inspecting, testing, servicing, and classifying as to serviceability, repair, rebuilding, and reclamation. 2) All supply and repair activity to keep a force in condition to carry out its mission. 3) The routine work required to keep a facility—plant, building, structure, ground facility, utility system, or other real property—in such condition that it may be continuously used at its original capacity and efficiency.

major—A rank in most armies and in the U.S. Army, Air Force, and Marine Corps, above captain and below lieutenant colonel. See also **commandant**.

major contingency—See **conflict levels of intensity**.

major general—A rank in the U.S. Army, Air Force, and Marine Corps, and in many other nations, between brigadier general and lieutenant general. Some nations, like Russia and Britain, do not have the rank of brigadier general; in such armies, major general is the lowest general officer rank. See also **general**.

major war — See **conflict levels of intensity**.

make safe—The action or actions necessary to interrupt the functioning of a weapon system so as to make it incapable of discharge.

malleolus—An incendiary weapon of classical times. A malleolus could be a burning arrow or flaming tow that had been attached to a javelin and was fired or thrown at an attacker's siegeworks.

mameluke—One of a band of Moslem cavalry soldiers from the 12th to the 16th century who originally were chiefly Turkish and Circassian slaves. The mamelukes were developed into very effective soldiers, particularly horse archers, by the caliphs of Bagdad to fight the Crusaders. In time the mamelukes became so powerful that they took control of Egypt, forming a ruling military caste lasting from the 13th century until the end of the 18th century.

man—*n.* Enlisted person. *v.* To supply with enough crew to operate effectively, as "to man a ship, a gun, a platoon."

man-at-arms—An armored horseman of the Middle Ages.

maneuver—1) A movement to place ships, troops, matériel, or fire in an optimum location with respect to the enemy, especially in the battlefield movement of forces. 2) A tactical exercise carried out at sea, in the air, on the ground, or on a map in imitation of war. 3) The operation of a ship, an aircraft, or a vehicle to cause it to perform desired movements. 4) A principle of war emphasizing the importance of locating forces for optimum strategic and tactical effect in combat.

mangonel—A medieval siege engine that used the torsion principle to catapult large rocks and other missiles. Mangonels were used primarily to batter enemy stone fortifications.

Manhattan Project—To develop the atomic bomb in World War II, a special Engineer District was established in August 1942 under Maj. Gen. Leslie Groves, with the deliberately misleading title of Manhattan District. This command, consolidating work begun in 1939–40 under joint auspices of the War and Navy departments, was responsible for all aspects of the development of atomic bombs until August 1946, when Congress enacted legislation creating the Atomic Energy Commission.

maniple—A subdivision of a Roman legion, consisting of two CENTURIES. The maniple and one of its centuries were commanded by a centurion elected by the legion. He appointed the centurion who commanded the other century.

Mannerheim Line—A Finnish defense line extending across the Karelian Isthmus north of Leningrad. It was an important position because it covered the only area of the Russo-Finnish frontier in which the Russians could concentrate large numbers of troops for offensive operations against Finland. The fortifications—mostly pillboxes—were well integrated with the rugged, wooded terrain of the area and were supplemented by wire, mine, and water obstacles. The line was attacked twice by the Soviets. The first attack, in December 1939, was easily repulsed. The second attack, during mid-February 1940, led to a breakthrough but only after the Soviets had suffered tremendous casualties—losses so heavy that Soviet assault forces had to be regrouped and heavily reinforced before the offensive could be resumed. The fall of the line led to the defeat of Finland, and a Soviet-Finnish peace treaty was signed on 12 March. There is no doubt, however, that, had the line not existed, the Soviets would have defeated Finland in December 1939.

Mannlicher rifle—A bolt-action, 11mm rifle designed by Ferdinand Ritter von Mannlicher in 1884 and adopted by the Austrian army in 1885. Subsequently, Mannlicher designed other successful automatic and repeating weapons.

man-of-war—A warship.

man on horseback—A military leader who presents himself as the savior of his country in a time of crisis.

manpower—The human resources available for participation in a nation's war effort. Military manpower, or personnel, is the proportion of a nation's manpower that is in, or available to, the armed forces.

man space—The factor used to determine the combat capability of vehicles and aircraft based on the requirements of one person with equipment. The person with equipment is assumed to weigh between 225 and 250 pounds and to occupy 13.5 cubic feet of space.

mantelet or **mantlet**—A great wicker or wooden shield, sometimes mounted on wheels, used to shelter outpost guards and operators of siege engines that were within the range of weapons on the walls of the fortification.

mantelet

manuballista—A small crossbow used by the Romans in the 1st or 2nd century A.D.

MAP—See **Military Assistance Program**.

map, controlled—A map with precise horizontal and vertical ground control as a basis. Scale, azimuth, and elevations are accurate and can be relied on for the calculation of firing data.

map exercise—An exercise in which a series of military situations or problems are stated and solved on a map.

map reference code—A code used primarily for encoding grid coordinates and other information pertaining to maps.

maquis/maquisard—From the French word for "bush," the name given to the French underground organization of World War II and to its members.

marauder—1) One who raids in search of plunder. 2) The name "Merrill's Marauders" was given by journalists to the 5307th U.S. Infantry Regiment, a long-range penetration unit commanded by Brig. Gen. Frank D. Merrill that served in Burma in 1944.

Marauder (B-26)—A twin-engine U.S. light bomber manufactured by Martin and used during World War II. After World War II, the B-26 designation was given to the Douglas Invader, which formerly had been called A-26.

U.S. Air Force photo

Marauder (B-26)

march—*n*. 1) An organized movement of troops in column. It may be on foot, on horses, or by motor vehicle. A **forced march** is a march carried out at a rapid pace under duress. 2) A musical composition in regularly accented, usually duple, meter (two beats per measure), to accompany marching troops. *v.* 1) To walk in rhythm with a measured cadence or music. 2) To cause someone to move toward an objective.

march order—An order to a military unit, usually artillery, to take all actions necessary to be ready to move as soon as possible. See also **close station**.

marine—One of a body of troops trained for service at sea and on land, particularly in amphibious operations. Such troops have been used since at least the time of ancient Greece for landing parties and boarding parties. In the naval wars of the 17th century both the British and the Dutch organized bodies of marines for landing and boarding and for fighting from the rigging of their warships. Traditionally, marines aboard warships have been used by naval commanders to maintain order aboard ship. This was particularly important in the 18th century, when crews were composed largely of sailors who had been involuntarily impressed into service and were not readily amenable to discipline.

Marine air-ground task force — Marine forces (ground, air, and service support) organized under a single command and structured to accomplish a specific mission.

marine amphibious unit (MAU) — A U.S. marine air-ground task force built around a battalion landing team and a provisional marine aircraft group usually composed of an attack squadron and a helicopter squadron. The marine amphibious unit usually employs about one-ninth of the combat resources of one marine division/wing team. It is normally commanded by a colonel and is capable of performing combat operations of relatively limited scope. The MAU provides an immediate reaction capability to crisis situations and, when committed, is generally supported from its seabase.

maritime—1) Of or pertaining to naval affairs. 2) Of or pertaining to transoceanic commerce and naval lines of communication.

maritime control area—An area similar to a defensive sea area except that it may be established on the high seas. A maritime control area is normally established only in time of war.

maritime forward-looking infrared (MARFLIR)—A system based on thermal imagery that provides U.S. Coast Guard cutters with a 24-hour infrared system to augment radar and other devices.

maritime strategy—1) The strategy of a nation whose security is—or is perceived to be—primarily dependent on control of at least some portion of the seas of the world. 2) That aspect of a nation's strategy focusing on naval and overseas affairs.

mark—A symbol used to distinguish different types of weapons or other equipment. A newly developed type is designated Mark I (or MK I); and when the original design has been sufficiently modified, it is designated Mark II. In the U.S. Army designations, the numeral is arabic ("Mark 1," "Mark 2," etc.).

Mark 37—The analog computer–based fire control system found on major U.S. warships in World War II.

Mark 45—A rapid-fire 5-inch naval gun, capable of firing 16 to 20 rounds per minute.

Mark 75—A lightweight, rapid-fire 3-inch gun mounted on small combat vessels.

marksman—1) A person who is particularly skilled at firing a gun or other weapon at a target. 2) In the U.S. Army and Marine Corps, a rating of rifle proficiency awarded for specified achievement with a weapon on a range. There are three levels in ascending order of competence—marksman, sharpshooter, and expert.

marksmanship—The skill of firing a weapon so that the projectile hits the target at which the weapon is aimed.

marlinspike or **marlinespike** — A pointed metal tool used to separate the strands of a rope or wire.

marshal—*n.* The highest military rank in some armies and air forces (sometimes called field marshal). In the 13th century the title was given to the commander of an army in England. It apparently derives from the title of *marescalci,* held by the master of the horse of early Frankish kings. In armies with marshals there is usually only one grade or degree. In Britain's Royal Air Force there are four levels: air vice marshal (equivalent in the U.S. Army to major general), air marshal (equivalent to lieutenant general), air chief marshal (equivalent to general), and marshal of the Royal Air Force (equivalent to field marshal). *v.* To undertake the process by which forces and equipment that are to participate in an operation are put in order, so that each force may be ready for action in accordance with an overall plan. In airborne assault operations, marshaling is the process of moving ground units to their billets at or near departure airfields, preparing them for combat, and loading them into aircraft. In an amphibious or airborne operation, marshaling includes grouping together or assembling participating units when feasible or moving them to temporary camps in the vicinity of embarkation points, and completing preparations for combat and for loading.

Martello tower—1) A fortification of masonry with a circular ground plan. These towers were used for coastal defenses in many countries in the late 18th and early 19th centuries. 2) Offshore structures built by the British during World War II for antiaircraft batteries (like the German FLAK TOWER).

martial law—1) An arbitrary law proceeding directly from the military power, having no immediate constitutional or legislative sanction. 2) A condition in which military control and military law are imposed on a civilian population. Martial law is usually imposed during war time or when civil authority has ceased to function or is unable to function effectively. Although such a state is usually temporary, martial law may be continued indefinitely in a military dictatorship or in situations when unrest continues for an extended period. Sometimes called "state of siege."

martinet—A strict disciplinarian. In the 17th century Jean Martinet, inspector general of the French infantry and lieutenant colonel of the king's regiment of foot, created a highly trained army for Louis XIV through intensive drilling and training; and his name has been given to strict military taskmasters ever since.

Martini-Henry rifle — A .45-caliber (11.4mm) breech-loading, rifled infantry weapon adopted by the British army in 1871. The breech mechanism was developed by Friedrich von Martini, an Austrian, from the American Peabody action. The barrel was designed by Alexander Henry, an Edinburgh gunsmith. The act of lowering the trigger guard opened the breech, ejected the fired cartridge case, and recocked the firing pin.

mascle—1) A quadrangular device between the chevrons and the arcs of certain sergeants' sleeve insignia (first sergeants in the U.S. Army). Also called a "lozenge" because of its shape. 2) In 13th-century LAMELLAR ARMOR, one of the overlapping steel plates.

mask—*n.* A hill or other natural feature of the terrain or an artificial structure that conceals and thus protects an individual or a force from its enemy, visually or by screening the force from enemy fire, or both. *v.* To conceal one's position or protect it from enemy fire.

mass—*n.* 1) The military formation in which units are spaced at less than normal distances and intervals. 2) The concentration of means at the critical time and place to the maximum degree permitted by the situation. 3) A principle of war in which proper application of mass, in conjunction with the other principles of war, permits application of optimum strength of a force on the decisive point or points on the battlefield. Mass is essentially a combination of manpower and firepower and does not depend on numbers alone; the effectiveness of mass may be increased by superior weapons, tactics, and morale. *v.* To concentrate or bring together, as "to mass the fire of all batteries."

mass bombing—Bombing with a large number of aircraft.

mass destruction, weapons of — See **weapons of mass destruction**.

massed fire—See **fire, massed**.

massing of fire—1) The fire of the batteries of two or more ships directed against a single target. 2) Fire from a number of weapons, directed against a single target. See also **fire, massed**.

massive ordnance air burst (MOAB) — A powerful conventional bomb (21,000 lbs.) that relies on the satellite positioning system to hit the target, in contrast to the "DAISY CUT-TER," which is dropped directly over the target. Referred to informally as the "mother of all bombs."

massive retaliation—1) A large-scale response to an attack, possibly involving nuclear weapons. 2) A short-lived U.S. nuclear deterrent policy, announced by Secretary of State John Foster Dulles in 1954, that called for U.S. response to Communist nation provocations with whatever actions the United States deemed appropriate to its interests, whether or not those responses matched the provocations in geographical location or scale of weapons. By implication, U.S. nuclear superiority was to be used to deter all levels of aggression.

master—A rank in the 19th-century U.S. Navy above that of ensign and below that of lieutenant, subsequently changed to lieutenant, junior grade.

master-at-arms—A petty officer, usually a chief, who is responsible for the maintenance of order and discipline in a ship or naval shore station, including the custody of prisoners. Originally, the master-at-arms was charged with the care of and instruction in the use of small arms.

master gunner—1) The head of a gun crew on a naval vessel. 2) Formerly, the senior gunnery specialist on a warship.

master key fire—In naval gunnery, the firing of guns by a common firing circuit controlled by a firing key at a distant station.

master sergeant—The highest noncommissioned rank in the U.S. Army, Air Force, and Marine Corps.

mast for requests—A period set aside by the executive officer of a naval ship or station during which members of the crew may present requests.

Matador—A ground-launched cruise missile. The first missile deployed by the U.S. Air Force, it was introduced into combat units in the 1950s.

matchlock—1) A device using a match to ignite the priming powder in a weapon. Invented in the late 14th or early 15th century and used in Europe as late as the mid-19th century, the matchlock was a pivoted lever called a SERPENTINE because of its shape. To the free end of the serpentine the soldier clipped the glowing end of the match, which, by a triggering arrangement, was brought in touch with the priming powder. It was a great advance over earlier devices and many variations appeared. It was most commonly used on muskets. 2) A MUSKET or ARQUEBUS equipped with such a lock.

matchlock arquebus—An ARQUEBUS with a MATCHLOCK, used in combination with the pike in the 15th century in the West and in combination with the sword by the Turks.

matchlock musket—A weapon developed in Spain and first used as a defensive position weapon in the Italian Wars (1530–40). It had a longer barrel and fired a heavier ball than the MATCHLOCK ARQUEBUS and could pierce armor and—in sufficient numbers or mass—stop a cavalry charge. A very heavy weapon at first, it was gradually modified until it replaced the arquebus. Loading the musket required some 90 different steps. Gustavus Adolphus simplified this in a lighter musket by issuing measured powder charges wrapped in paper with the ball attached. See also **matchlock**.

match, quick—A cord impregnated with a highly flammable mixture, such as alcohol mixed with black powder. Used as a fuze for flares.

match, slow—The means most commonly used for igniting the charge in small arms and artillery pieces before 1700. Although the match might be made of other combustible material, it was usually a braided cotton cord of three strands that had been soaked in a solution of saltpeter and treated with lye and lead acetate to make it burn only 4 or 5 inches an hour. To ignite an artillery piece the match was held in a LINSTOCK.

mate—1) In earlier times in the British Royal Navy and until the late 19th century in the U.S. Navy, a rank between midshipman and lieutenant. 2) In naval ratings, distinguishing the assistant to a warrant rating, such as boatswain's mate, carpenter's mate, aerographer's mate. In most cases there are two or three classes of mate.

matériel—1) Things of all kinds required for the equipment, maintenance, operation, and support of military activities, both combatant and noncombatant. 2) In a restricted sense, those things used in combat or logistic support operations, such as weapons, motor vehicles, airplanes, component parts of machines, and special-purpose clothing, as distinguished from items of ordinary use, such as uniforms, bedding, and housekeeping equipment.

MAU—See **marine amphibious unit**.

Mauser rifle—A rifle invented in 1871 by Peter Paul Mauser, a German weapons manufacturer. A single-shot clip-fed magazine rifle with a sliding bolt, the Mauser was the regular German army rifle in World Wars I and II and was widely used in other armies as well. It fired projectiles from smokeless powder cartridges, approximately .30 caliber, at a muzzle velocity up to 2,800 feet per second.

Maverick (AGM-65) — An air-to-surface missile designed for use against small, hard targets such as tanks, armored vehicles, and field fortifications. In OPERATION DESERT STORM in 1991, Mavericks, often fired from F-16s and A-10s, played an important role in the destruction of Iraq's ground forces.

Maxim machine gun — A belt-fed, recoil-operated weapon invented by Hiram Maxim in 1884; within 30 years it was used by every major power. Whereas earlier automatic guns had several barrels, the Maxim had one. Cartridges were loaded in a fabric belt; and by using the power of the barrel's recoil the gun loaded itself, fired, and ejected the spent shell. A metal jacket around the barrel containing water prevented overheating from the gun's high rate of fire. British colonial forces first used Maxim guns in the Matabele War of 1893–94. In World War I it was one of the three determinants of the battlefield stalemate (the other two were barbed wire and high-explosive artillery fire).

maximum effective range—See **range**.

maximum range—See **range**.

Mayday—The international distress signal used by ships and aircraft. From the French: *(Venez) m'aider,* "Come, help me."

MBT—See **tank, main battle**.

M-day—The term used to designate the day on which mobilization is to begin.

meaconing—A means of receiving radio beacon signals and rebroadcasting them on the same frequency so as to confuse an enemy's navigation.

mechanize—To equip a ground unit with trucks, tanks, armored personnel vehicles, or other means of transport. It differs from MOTORIZE by the inclusion of armored vehicles.

mechanized cavalry—See **cavalry**.

mechanized division — A combined-arms ground force of DIVISION type and size, the principal combat components of which are approximately equally divided between tank-equipped armored units and motorized infantry units that can be mounted in trucks, armored personnel carriers, or both.

Medaille Militaire—A French military decoration established by Napoleon III in 1852 honoring distinguished conduct in combat.

medal—Any of many metal devices that have a distinctive design, inscription, or both, and are usually hung from a distinctively colored ribbon, commemorating an action, an achievement, or an event, frequently awarded with some recognition. Medals are ranked in the United States and other nations according to the reasons for which they are given (the highest U.S. award being the MEDAL OF HONOR) and worn with the highest at the right of the top row. U.S. medals are worn only with dress uniforms. They are represented on work uniforms by bands of the ribbons accompanying the medals.

Medal of Honor—A decoration awarded in the name of Congress to persons who, while in the U.S. armed services and engaged in conflict with an enemy of the United States, have distinguished themselves conspicuously by gallantry and bravery at the risk of life above and beyond the call of duty. This is the highest U.S. decoration. There are two slightly different versions of the decoration, one for the Army and Air Force, and one for the Navy and Marine Corps; but in both the principal feature of the medal proper is a five-pointed bronze star featuring different likenesses of Minerva. The ribbon for both is pale blue with a pattern of 13 white stars just above the medal. The ribbon worn on the dress uniform is the same pale-blue color with five white stars. ("Congressional" is not a part of the name.)

medium artillery—See **artillery**.

medium-range bomber—See **bomber**.

meeting engagement — A combat action that occurs when two opposing forces, advancing toward each other, usually not fully deployed for battle, engage each other at an unexpected time or place.

melee—1) In ancient and medieval battles, fighting in which the soldiers, having first thrown their javelins or fired their arrows, fought hand-to-hand with their opponents, using swords, clubs, spears, or other weapons. 2) Any fighting on land or sea characterized by great confusion.

mention in dispatches—To recognize bravery or outstanding performance in the British services. The origin of the term was the British custom for a commander in chief to include in his dispatches to London the names of officers who had distinguished themselves in battle or campaign.

mercenary—A soldier who hires himself out for pay to fight in the army of another nation. There probably have been mercenaries as long as there have been wars, but they were particularly prevalent in western Europe in the 13th and 14th centuries after the end of the Hundred Years' War. Mercenaries and mercenary units were important elements in most European armies until the end of the 18th century.

merlon—See **battlements**.

mess—*n.* 1) A place where food is prepared and served; also called, on a base, a mess hall. 2) The occasion of a meal served at such a place, or the eating of such a meal, as in "they showed up at mess." 3) A group of persons who eat together regularly. 4) Particularly in the navy, a special food-related organization, or installation, such as OFFICERS' MESS, coffee mess, and wine mess. *v.* To eat a meal.

message center—A communications office within a military organization charged with the responsibility for acceptance, preparation for transmission, receipt, and delivery of messages.

message precedence — Designations indicating the relative order or priority that is assigned to a message of one precedence designation in respect to all other precedence designators. It establishes the relative importance or urgency of messages.

Messerschmitt 109—The most effective and versatile German fighter of World War II. Later versions could reach a speed of 428 miles per hour and a rate of climb of nearly 4,000 feet per minute.

Messerschmitt 262—The first operational jet fighter in World War II. Powered by two engines, it had a top speed of 540 miles per hour, more than 100 miles an hour faster than propeller fighters of the day. It did not reach front-line German squadrons until July 1944, however, and as a result had limited effect on the Allied air war against Germany.

U.S. Air Force photo

Messerschmitt 262

mess jacket—A short, semiformal uniform jacket worn with evening dress.

mess kit—1) Equipment for eating in the field, either for an individual soldier or for an OFFICERS' MESS. 2) In British usage, uniform evening dress including the mess jacket.

mess sergeant—A noncommissioned officer responsible for the operation of a mess.

MGM-13—See **Mace**.

MGM-29A—See **Sergeant**.

MGM-31A—See **Pershing**.

MGM-51—See **Shillelagh**.

MI5—The British security service responsible for counterespionage activities in the United Kingdom.

MIA—See **missing in action**.

midshipman—1) Originally, a young naval cadet in the British and later the U.S. Navy. The name derived from his battle station, which was amidships or abreast of the main-mast. The midshipmen served a sort of apprenticeship aboard sailing vessels before receiving a commission. 2) In the U.S. Navy and Coast Guard, a student at the service academy (Annapolis or New London), training to be an officer. 3) In the British Royal Navy and others that follow the Royal Navy pattern, a noncommissioned officer below the rank of sublieutenant.

midwatch—See **watch**.

MiG—A line of Soviet fighter aircraft named for the designers, Arten Mikoyan and Mikhail Gurevich. The lowercase "i" represents the Russian word for "and."

MiG-25 (Foxbat)—A Soviet interceptor, introduced in 1964. Designed for high altitudes, the MiG-25 was capable of speeds up to 3.2 Mach; for most of the 1960s, it was the fastest aircraft in the world.

MiG-29 (Fulcrum)—A Soviet multimission fighter/attack aircraft first flown in 1979. It has a top speed of Mach 2.3, and in its fighter configuration carries six air-to-air missiles and a six-barrel, 30mm cannon. Instrumentation includes advanced radar and a laser rangefinder.

Mike—Letter of NATO phonetic alphabets. See also **alphabet, phonetic.**

mil—A unit of angular measurement used in gunnery and the launching of bombs and guided missiles, equal to 1/6400 of a circle.

militarism—The belief that a country's military efficiency is the supreme objective of the state and that all other considerations are subordinate to it. Militarism is often associated with Prussia in the late 19th century and with Japan in the early 20th century.

military—Pertaining to armed services of all branches—army, navy, marine corps, air force. Also used to refer only to the army, particularly in contradistinction to "naval."

Military Assistance Advisory Group (MAAG)—A joint service group, normally under the military command of the commander of a unified command and representing the Secretary of Defense, which was established during the Truman administration to administer the U.S. military assistance planning and programming in a host country.

Military Assistance Program (MAP)—The U.S. program for providing military assistance under the Foreign Assistance Act of 1961. It includes the furnishing of defense matériel and services through grant aid or military sales to eligible allies, as specified by Congress.

military attaché—See **attaché, military**.

military commission—A court convened under military authority to try nonmilitary personnel accused of violating the laws of war or other statutes.

military decoration — See **decoration, military**.

military government—The form of administration by which an occupying power exercises executive, legislative, and judicial authority over occupied territory.

military justice—See **justice, military**.

military operation—1) An action or series of actions, either combat or noncombat, conducted by a military organization. 2) In a restricted sense, an operation involving, or primarily involving, combat personnel against an enemy, as distinguished from a logistical operation.

military police—The organization within an army that carries out police functions. It corresponds to the navy's shore patrol. Its personnel are frequently referred to as MPs.

Military Sealift Command—An operating command of the Navy Department, responsible for meeting the sealift requirements of all U.S. armed forces.

military strategy—The science of employing the armed forces of a nation to achieve its policy objectives by the application of force or the threat of force.

militia—1) Part-time military or paramilitary formations that are organized and trained to serve in defense of a nation in time of emergency. 2) Members of such formations. **Naval militia** are trained for naval duties. See also **reserve components**.

milk run—A routine mission or flight, one presenting little danger or difficulty. The metaphor derives from the daily delivery of milk to a neighborhood.

Mills bomb—A pineapple-shaped hand grenade developed by Sir William Mills and used by the British army in World War I. Although it could be fired by a mortarlike launcher, it was usually thrown by a soldier, who first removed a pin, which released a lever, which activated a 4- to 5-second fuze.

MIM-23—See **Hawk**.

MIM-72—See **Chaparral**.

MIM-104—See **Patriot**.

mine—*n.* 1) A tunnel dug under an enemy position in order to gain entrance to a fortification or the area behind the front lines or in order to lay explosives. The most extensive use of such mines was at Messines Ridge in World War I, where the Allies dug a series of mines and destroyed sections of the ridge, destroying and exposing German positions. 2) An explosive or other material, normally encased, designed to destroy or damage vehicles, boats, or aircraft, or designed to kill or otherwise incapacitate personnel. It may be detonated by the action of its victim, by the passage of time or by controlled means. LAND MINEs are used by ground forces primarily to delay an attacker or defend a position by destroying or damaging tanks (**antitank mines**) or people (**antipersonnel mines**). **Underwater** or **naval mines** are laid at sea to protect harbors, destroy enemy shipping, or blockade an enemy's ports. See also **countermine**. *v.* To build or lay a mine. Land mines played an important role in some World War I engagements; but in World War II both sides used them extensively, notably

in the desert in North Africa, where they were easily buried. Mines differ in design, sensitivity, and method of detonation. A minefield must be at least partially cleared before an enemy can safely cross it. Clearing is generally accomplished with magnetic mine detectors (ineffective against mines encased in wood, cardboard, or plastic) or with tanks or other vehicles fitted with flails far enough in advance to detonate the mine without destroying the vehicle. An important development in mine warfare in the late 20th century was the introduction of SCATTERABLE MINES. Underwater mines may be floating, unanchored, below the surface, or anchored. A convention that was approved at the Hague Peace Conference of 1907 forbade the use of unanchored mines unless they become harmless within an hour after those who lay them cease to control them. The conference also forbade the laying of anchored mines that do not become harmless within an hour of breaking loose from their moorings, and defined other precautions for the protection of commercial shipping. Like land mines, naval mines differ in design, sensitivity, and method of detonation. To counteract those that are detonated by a ship's magnetic field, almost all vessels in World War II were DEGAUSSED.

minefield lane—A marked lane, unmined, or cleared of mines, leading through a minefield.

minelayer—1) A naval vessel that lays underwater mines. 2) A mechanical device that lays land mines.

minesweeper—A naval vessel equipped to search for mines and destroy them or render them harmless. Minesweepers are used to sweep up mines laid by friendly powers, as well as enemy mines, to protect commercial shipping.

mine warfare—The strategic and tactical use of mines and their countermeasures.

minié ball—See **ball, minié**.

minimum range—See **range**.

minion—A 16th-century artillery piece, with a 3.3-inch bore, which fired a projectile weighing 6 pounds. Some 6.5 feet in length, the minion, also known as a "demisaker," weighed 1,000 pounds. Its maximum range was 2,500 yards; point-blank range was 450 yards.

minor contingency—See **conflict levels of intensity**.

minor hostilities—See **conflict levels of intensity**.

minuteman—An armed civilian or militiaman in the American colonies, originally in Massachusetts, before the American Revolution, who was pledged to join his unit and fight at a minute's notice when called to service.

Minuteman (LGM-30)—A solid-propellant ICBM that became operational in 1963. Improved versions, Minuteman II and Minuteman III, remained in the U.S. inventory into the 1980s.

miquelet—A 16th-century device to fire a weapon that used a spring mechanism to hold a match.

MIRV—Multiple independently targetable reentry vehicle, which is a single missile, or booster, equipped with several nuclear warheads that can be armed separately and sent against different targets.

misfire—*n.* Failure of a round of ammunition, the propelling charge of a rocket, or other explosive to fire on ignition. *v.* To fail to fire, or to fire improperly. See also **hang fire**.

missile—Any object that is propelled at a target. The term includes rocks thrown by hand, arrows fired by a bow, bullets from a gun, depth charges dropped from a ship, electronically complex rockets, and all other objects launched by whatever means toward a physical objective. Modern arsenals, in addition to artillery weapons, contain ballistic missiles and rockets of various types.

missile, air-launched cruise — A CRUISE MISSILE launched from an aircraft in flight.

missile, air-to-air—A missile launched from an aircraft against an enemy aircraft or missile.

missile, air-to-surface—A missile launched from an aircraft against a surface target.

missile, antiballistic (ABM)—A defensive missile designed to intercept and destroy incoming nuclear missiles.

missile, ballistic—1) Any missile or projectile that does not rely on aerodynamic surfaces to produce lift and consequently follows a ballistic trajectory when thrust is terminated. 2) In modern usage, a ballistic missile is one (other than a rocket, which provides its own thrust during all or most of its flight) that is not fired from a gun tube. Ballistic missiles in this sense do not include small arms or cannon projectiles. They are usually free-standing and get their initial thrust from a very brief episode of rocket fire. Ballistic missiles are variously classified by range, including the following: **medium range**, a range of 600 to 1,500 nautical miles; **intermediate range**, or **mid-range**, a range of 1,500 to 3,000 nautical miles; and **intercontinental**, a range of 3,000 or more nautical miles.

missile, cruise—A low-altitude, pilotless jet aircraft that can carry nuclear warheads and use terrain-following radar, which makes it highly accurate over long ranges. The major portion of its flight path to its target is conducted at approximately constant velocity. It is hard to shoot down because its small size and low altitude make it difficult for defensive radar to follow its flight. Types of cruise missiles are as follows: **air-launched cruise missile (ALCM)**, which can be launched from an aircraft, like the B-52 bomber; **ground-launched cruise missile (GLCM)**, which can be launched from a land-based mobile launcher; and **sea-launched cruise missile (SLCM)**, which can be launched from a surface vessel or from a submerged or surfaced submarine.

Missile Defense Agency—A U.S. Defense Department organization established in 2002 to carry out research on missile defense.

missile, guided—See **guided missile**.

missile launcher—A weapon or structure that launches ballistic, cruise, or guided missiles.

missile, surface-to-air (SAM) — A missile launched from the ground against an aircraft or missile.

missile, surface-to-surface — A surface-launched missile designed to attack a target on the surface. In land warfare such a missile is used as an artillery weapon.

missing in action (MIA) — A category of personnel casualty whose whereabouts following a combat action is unknown, whether through becoming separated from his or her unit, being captured by the enemy, being wounded or killed and unidentified, or desertion.

mission—1) The objective; the task, together with the purpose, which clearly indicates the action to be taken. 2) In common usage, especially when applied to lower military units, a duty assigned to an individual or unit; a task. 3) The dispatching of one or more aircraft to accomplish a particular task. 4) A group or a detachment of officers, or officers and enlisted personnel, serving in a friendly country for the purpose of providing training or support, or performing some other function of interest to both nations and their armed forces. Often called a **military mission.**

mission creep—The tendency within military and other bureaucracies to outline a mission and then add secondary objectives that significantly enlarge the scope of the mission.

mission effectiveness — The ability of a unit or a formation to accomplish an assigned mission.

mission-type order—1) An order issued to a lower unit that includes an explanation of accomplishment of the total mission assigned to the higher headquarters. A concept pioneered by the German army, particularly since the time of the elder von Moltke (c. 1860), and called *Auftragstaktik.* 2) An order to a unit to perform a mission without specifying how it is to be accomplished.

U.S. Air Force photo

Mitchell (B-25)

Mitchell (B-25) — A twin-engine medium bomber that saw extensive use in World War II. It had a top speed of 315 miles per hour and could carry 3,000 pounds of bombs over a range of 1,500 miles. A modified version of the B-25 was used in the raid against Tokyo led by Gen. James Doolittle on 18 April 1942.

mitrailleuse—An early type of machine gun, used by the French army during the Franco-Prussian War (1870–71). Invented in 1851 and adopted by the French army in 1867, the mitrailleuse had 31 rifled barrels in a single jacket; the barrels were loaded from a plate inserted at the breech and could be fired simultaneously or in sequence. A well-trained crew could fire 12 rounds per minute. It was not a success, however, and was soon abandoned. The name means literally "grapeshot shooter."

MLF—See **Moro Liberation Front**.

MLR—See **main line of resistance**.

MOAB—See **massive ordnance air burst**.

moat—A ditch, usually filled with water, surrounding a fortification and providing extra protection against attack.

moat

mobile—*adj.* Readily movable from one place to another, whether by its own power or aboard a vehicle.

mobile artillery—See artillery.

mobile defense—See **defense**.

mobility—The ability of military units or items of equipment to move as units from place to place, including the ability to support them logistically during and after movement. STRATEGIC MOBILITY is the capability of large military units for movement in or between theaters of operation. TACTICAL MOBILITY is the capability of any military unit for movement or maneuver on the battlefield or in the presence of the enemy.

mobilization—1) The act of preparing for war or other emergencies by assembling and organizing national resources. 2) The process by which the armed forces or a part of them are brought to a state of readiness for war or other national emergency. This includes assembling and organizing personnel, supplies, and matériel for active military service. See also **industrial mobilization**.

mobilization base—The total of all resources that are available to meet anticipated wartime needs. Such resources include the human and material resources and services required for the support of essential military, civilian, and survival activities.

model—1) A small, realistic representation of a real item of equipment, a system, or a situation, usually to scale. 2) A variation of a weapon, piece of equipment, or other item, distinguished by later changes in the characteristics or appearance of the same basic item. See also **mark.** 3) An abstract representation of a real entity or situation by something else that has the relevant features or properties of the original. There are five basic types of such models: a) verbal, b) analytic or mathematical, c) diagrammatic representation, d) analog simulations, and e) digital simulations. In practice, the words "model" and "simulation" are used interchangeably. Also called "simulation mode." See also **war game** and **simulation**.

model, aggregated—A simulation model in which many detailed, discrete elements of a process are combined and examined as an entity. Thus, a model that treats a DIVISION as an entity in theater-level combat has aggregated platoons, companies, battalions, brigades, and supporting weapons into the division.

model, analytical — A simulation model composed of sets of mathematical equations as models of all the basic events and activities in the process being described, and an overall assumed mathematical structure of the process into which the event or activity descriptions are integrated.

model, combat—A simulation model used to describe the basic combat processes of firepower, mobility, intelligence, logistics, and command-control in order to estimate the results (numbers of casualties and survivors, resource expenditures, terrain controlled, etc.) of battles and wars. Most modern combat models are operated by means of a computer program; thus they are often called COMPUTER MODELS.

model, computer (computerized) — A computer program or series of programs designed to simulate the logic of actions or interactions within an environment or a context and to provide the results for subsequent analysis. A computer model is usually designed to run without human involvement for a predetermined period of time or until a set of predetermined conditions are satisfied. A **computer-assisted model** performs the same kind of logical calculations as a computer model but is designed to be responsive to periodic human intervention and decision-making.

model, deterministic—A simulation model that excludes chance variables so that the output of the model is entirely determined by the input. Thus, unlike in a STOCHASTIC MODEL, any given set of inputs should always give exactly the same answer.

model input—The mathematical data entered into a model in order to generate model outputs.

model output—The numerical values or results generated by a simulation model.

model, probabilistic—A simulation model that contains at least one chance variable so that the output of the model is not uniquely determined by the input.

model, research—An analytical model, usually in the form of complex and comprehensive equations or algorithms, used for investigating combat or decision processes or new concepts.

model, stochastic—A computer model designed so that random variables will be introduced during its operation to simulate the effects of chance on the simulated operation. Thus repetitions of the operation of the model with the same inputs will almost always give different answers. If run sufficiently often with the same inputs, however, averaged results should approximate those of a deterministic model. See also **model, deterministic**.

Molotov cocktail—An improvised hand grenade consisting of a bottle filled with alcohol, gasoline, or other flammable liquid and stoppered with a combustible material such as a piece of cloth, which is lighted when the bottle is thrown. Named for Vyacheslav M. Molotov, the Soviet foreign minister during World War II, such grenades were widely used by partisans and other irregulars in World War II; and they continue to be a common weapon for use by people without access to regular weapons.

momentum—The property of continuing forward movement of a military force, as a result of previous success in combat, which is presumed to provide an additive or multiplicative bonus to its combat capability.

Momsen Lung (submarine escape lung)—A breathing apparatus developed in the late 1920s by U.S. Navy Lieut. "Swede" Momsen, Chief Gunner Tibbals, and civilian Frank Hobson to enable crews to escape to the surface from a sunken submarine. The device was an oblong rubber bag that cleaned carbon dioxide from the air that men exhaled, enriched it with oxygen, and recycled it. Besides providing oxygen for the ascent, the lung was also designed to allow submariners to rise slowly to the surface and thus avoid the "bends." The Momsen Lung, however, saved few lives and was replaced by other devices, including a revised version of a Momsen-designed diving bell, which rescued 33 survivors from the sunken USS *Squalus* in 1939, and development of the free ascent method, in which submariners sunk at any depth up to 300 feet learned to fill their lungs with air before leaving the vessel and then to exhale on the way up. The air in the lungs expands as the pressure decreases. See also **deep submergence rescue vehicle (DSRV)**.

Mongoose, Operation—A covert operation, ordered by President Kennedy in November 1961, to initiate actions against Cuba designed to harass the Castro regime and, if possible, bring about its overthrow. During the year it operated, the Mongoose committee approved a number of actions against the Cuban economic infrastructure and considered means of assassinating Castro. The Cuban missile crisis in October 1962 so raised the stakes in Cuba that Operation Mongoose effectively ended.

monitor—A type of IRONCLAD warship developed by the Union in the American Civil War for use in the harbors and rivers of the South. Like the original *Monitor*, which fought the *Merrimack* in 1862, monitors had a low, flat deck and one or more gun turrets that revolved so that the guns could be trained on a target regardless of the bearing of the ship.

Montoneros—Adherents of the Movimiento Peronista Montonero, an Argentine guerrilla group formed in 1970 to promote the populist policies of the exiled dictator Juan Domingo Peron. Although not avowedly Marxist, the group sought a socialist revolution in Argentina.

mop up—To free an area of the last remnants of an enemy. To capture or destroy the remnants of an enemy in an area that has been surrounded or isolated, or through which other units have passed without eliminating all active resistance.

moral—*adj.* The behavioral, nonmaterial, or nonphysical considerations affecting military forces and combat. In the military sense, the word is unrelated to morality and has only incidental relationship to the concept of MORALE. "The moral is to the physical as three is to one," an approximate rendering of a Napoleonic concept, indicated his belief that the capabilities, performance, and motivation of soldiers and commanders were more important than weapons or other physical entities. See also **Square Law**.

morale—1) The state of a person's mental attitude or feeling in respect to what the person is, does, or is going to do, as determined by the presence or absence of such psychological factors as confidence in the person's leaders, recognition of a spirit of sacrifice in others, feeling of comradeship for associates, physical comfort, and hope. 2) A state of mind or feeling attributed to a group of individuals or to an organization.

morion—A helmet without a faceplate, worn in the 16th and 17th centuries, particularly by archers and musketeers because of the broader vision it afforded. The morion has a crest and a wide brim that comes to a high point in front and back. It is still worn by the Swiss guard at the Vatican.

morning report—The daily record or log of certain military units, usually of company size, giving daily strength and status of personnel assigned.

morning star—A type of MACE or war club common in medieval European armies of the 14th century and the first half of the 15th century, after which it fell into disuse. The haft of the infantry version was about 5 feet long and was surmounted by a sphere studded with iron spikes, from which the weapon derived its name. Morning stars used by horsemen had shorter hafts, usually about 2 feet long. A variant type of the weapon had the spiked ball attached to the haft by a chain. Another, not uncommon, name for this weapon was HOLY-WATER SPRINKLER.

Moro Liberation Front (MLF)—A group of Philippine revolutionaries seeking autonomy for Muslims on the island of Mindanao and other parts of the southern Philippines.

mortar—A muzzle-loading weapon that fires shells at relatively short range with a high trajectory. Named for their resemblance to a pharmacist's mortar, such weapons have been in use since at least the 15th century. Mortars are normally infantry weapons that are light, easy to disassemble and carry from one area to another, and particularly effective for lobbing shells over a hill or other obstruction. Rifled or smoothbore, they have been made in many sizes, including very large siege mortars. The largest mortar in general use today is 160mm.

A 16th-century mortar.

mortar

mortar vessel—A successor to the BOMB KETCH in the early days of steam, the mortar vessel was a gunboat mounting mortars, usually of large caliber. The vessel's great extra beam enabled it to resist the nearly perpendicular force of the recoil of the huge weapon, which was mounted amidships on a massive bed.

mosaic (aerial photo) — An assembly of overlapping vertical photographs that have been matched to form a continuous photographic representation of the earth's surface. It is a useful supplement to a standard cartographer's map.

mosaic, controlled—An air-photo mosaic that, because key terrain features are related to each other by survey or by measurements from a standard cartographic map, can be used as a substitute for a map. It often has superimposed grid lines with the same designations as standard map grid lines. A controlled mosaic can be used effectively as an artillery firing chart.

"mothballs, in"—Descriptive of a ship that has been taken out of active service and had its guns and other gear protected in various ways from deterioration in order to preserve it for possible recommissioning. Such ships, said to be "mothballed" or "in mothballs," are moored together in various ports, generally in or near a navy yard.

motorize—To equip a unit or formation with complete motor transportation that enables all of its personnel, weapons, and equipment to be moved at the same time without assistance from other sources. Motorization does not encompass armored vehicles, but a motorized unit may include some armored equipment or armored components. Motorization is distinct from mechanization (see **mechanize**).

motorized division — Also often called a motorized infantry division, or motorized rifle division, it is a combined-arms ground force of DIVISION type and size. Its principal combat components are infantry units that are usually mounted in trucks or sometimes in armored personnel carriers.

motor torpedo boat—Commonly called PT boat (for "patrol torpedo"), a very fast boat built in large numbers in World War II and used effectively for both combat and noncombat operations. The boats were 60 to 100 feet long and equipped with two to four torpedo tubes, machine guns, antiaircraft guns, depth charges, and smoke-making apparatus. One of the most famous was PT-109, on which President John F. Kennedy served. They were also called "mosquito boats" and, by the Germans, "E-boats."

mound—1) Any pile of earth or other material built up to protect or conceal troops or equipment. 2) A small hill or other natural elevation. 3) The basis for a siege technique whereby weapons could be elevated to overlook the defender's wall. Extension of the mound to the edge of a besieged city or fortification permitted an attack without need for scaling the defensive works. This technique was a favorite of Alexander the Great.

mount—*v.* 1) To make all preparations for launching an operation, including assembling troops and equipment, moving and embarking them in ships, aircraft, or vehicles. 2) Of guns, to be furnished with, especially ships and aircraft. 3) Of guns, to put in position. 4) Of a guard, to assume responsibility for a guard system. *n.* A carriage or a stand on which a weapon is placed.

mountain troops—Troops trained to fight in mountainous areas, particularly in snow conditions. For example, U.S. mountain troops were used in Italy in World War II, and as many as possible were recruited from among men who were experienced skiers.

mounted—1) On horseback. 2) On vehicles. 3) Fixed upon (as guns on a tank).

mounted troops—1) Troops that move on horseback. 2) Prior to World War II, troop units or branches of the U.S. Army normally equipped with horses, such as cavalry and field artillery.

movement—A change in the location of troops, ships, or aircraft for tactical or strategic purposes.

movement control—1) The planning, routing, scheduling, and control of personnel and supply movements over lines of communication. 2) An organization responsible for these functions.

movement order—An order issued by a commander covering the details for a move of his or her command.

MRBM—Medium-range ballistic missile. See **missile, ballistic**.

MRE—Meals ready to eat (i.e., field rations in the modern U.S. armed forces).

mufti—Civilian dress worn by military personnel when off duty.

Mujahideen—The term, in Arabic, means "one who struggles for the sake of God." It is a general designation for Muslim fighters but is especially associated with Afghan fighters who resisted Soviet aggression in the Soviet-Afghan War.

Mulberry—Term for an artifical port built off the Normandy beachhead in 1944 with floating caissons and a line of old vessels sunk to form a breakwater.

muleteer—A muledriver, also known as a mule "skinner."

multiple independently targetable reentry vehicle—See **MIRV**.

multiple-launch rocket system (MLRS)—A mobile system of rocket launchers on the chassis of a Bradley fighting vehicle. The MLRS launcher unit consists of 12 rockets packaged in two 6-rocket pods.

multiplier, force—See **force multiplier**.

munition—Usually used in the plural. In a broad sense, any and all supplies and equipment required to conduct offensive and defensive war, including guns, machines, ammunition, transport, and fuel, but excluding personnel and any supplies and equipment used for purposes other than direct military operations.

Munroe effect—The focusing of a detonation into a powerful, high-velocity, narrow cone or stream of fire, resulting from a concavity in the face of the explosive. The direction of the stream of fire is the central axis of the concavity, perpendicular to the face of the explosive charge. The effect was discovered by the American chemist Charles E. Munroe. See also **hollow charge, shaped charge**.

mural crown—A crown or circlet of gold awarded in Roman times to the soldier who first climbed a wall of a place under siege and planted a standard there. The mural crown was often crenelated to resemble a battlement.

mural hook—A long, heavy bar or lever suspended from a high vertical frame to knock down the upper parapets of a wall. The device was invented by Alexander the Great's engineer, Diades.

musette bag—1) A small bag with a shoulder strap in which personal items can be carried. 2) An officer's field bag.

musket—Any of the smoothbore shoulder guns that evolved from the ARQUEBUS in the late 16th century and were replaced by the rifle in the mid-19th century. The original musket was larger and more awkward to handle than the arquebus, and, like its predecessor, was muzzle-loaded. Its advantages over the arquebus were its greater range and accuracy and the greater penetrating power of its bullet. The size and weight of the early musket meant that it had to be supported by a forked rest, which also helped increase accuracy. The earliest musket was 6 or 7 feet long and weighed up to 25 pounds. The Spanish army standardized its bullets to weigh 10 to the pound in 1565. About 1620, Gustavus Adolphus lightened the musket to about 11 pounds and reduced the weight of the ball to 14 to the pound. He also increased the rate of fire by issuing measured powder charges wrapped in paper with the ball attached. Its awkwardness decreased with substitution of the FLINTLOCK for the MATCHLOCK.

musketeer—A soldier armed with a musket.

musketoon—1) A short musket with a very wide bore, sometimes bell-mouthed. 2) A soldier armed with such a weapon.

musketry—1) The firing of infantry small arms, particularly muskets or, in modern times, rifles, including modern automatic weapons. 2) The capability of an infantry unit to fire its small arms.

"mustang"—Slang expression for a U.S. Navy officer who began service in the Navy as an enlisted man.

mustard gas—Dichloroethyl sulfide, an oily liquid that causes irritation and blistering and may cause death. Because of its high volatility and lethal and noxious properties, it was the most effective chemical weapon used in combat in World War I.

muster—*v.* 1) To assemble the members of a unit for roll call, inspection, and review, or to pass along information or orders. 2) To enroll. *n.* 1) The assembly of members of a military unit for such purposes. 2) The roll of members, also known as the **muster roll.**

mutiny—A refusal by service personnel to obey orders or otherwise to do their duty, or the creation of violence or disturbance with intent to override lawful authority.

mutually assured destruction (MAD)— A strategic concept that argues that if each of two contending powers possesses nuclear weapons, neither will use them because of the risk of nuclear retaliation.

mutual support—The support that units render each other against an enemy because of the synergism of their assigned tasks, their position relative to each other and to the enemy, and their inherent capabilities.

muzzle—The end of the barrel of a gun from which the bullet or projectile emerges. Early weapons were all **muzzle-loaders,** that is, the powder and bullet were loaded from that end. Of modern weapons, MORTARs are the principal type of muzzle-loader.

muzzle brake—A device attached to the muzzle of a weapon that uses escaping gas to reduce recoil.

muzzle-loader—See **muzzle.**

muzzle velocity—The speed at which a projectile is traveling at the instant it leaves the weapon. Muzzle velocity depends on the weight of the charge, the weight of the projectile, the amount and quality of the propellant, and other factors. Muzzle velocity is one of the fundamental ballistic properties determining a projectile's range and power.

N

Nan—Letter of old phonetic alphabet. See also **alphabet, phonetic**.

napalm—A powder (the aluminum soap of naphthenic and palmitic acids) that is mixed with gasoline to thicken it, thereby slowing the rate at which it burns and increasing the ways it can be used. Napalm was developed in 1942 for use in flamethrowers, for which pure gasoline had proved problematic because it burned too fast and could not be thrown very far. Napalm is also used in bombs and other devices.

Napoleon gun—A smoothbore bronze gun-howitzer of the early 19th century. A 12-pounder, it was served by five or six men and fired a ball of about 4.5 inches in diameter as far as a mile, accurately within a half mile. Two rounds of shell or solid shot or four rounds of canister per minute could be delivered by an efficient crew. In the American Civil War it was the favorite piece for Federals and Confederates alike, but it was already obsolete in Europe.

narcoterrorism — Terrorism designed to further the activities of drug traffickers, often directed against judges, elected officials, and law enforcement agents. It may include assassinations, extortion, hijackings, bombings, and kidnapping.

nasal—The portion of a helmet that protects the nose and upper part of the face.

National Command Authorities (NCA)—The President and the Secretary of Defense or their duly deputized alternates or successors.

national defense area — An area established on nonfederal land for military purposes and controlled by the U.S. Defense Department. Such an area may be created only in the event of an emergency.

national emergency—A condition declared by the President or the Congress by virtue of powers vested in them that authorizes the implementation of certain emergency actions in the national interest.

national guard—1) The designation of MILITIA units or military reserves of certain nations. 2) In the U.S. armed forces, the militia units of the several states of the United States, controlled by them under federal direction and subject to call in federal as well as local emergencies. The first American use of the name "National Guard" occurred on 16 August 1824, when the 7th Regiment New York Militia took the name in honor of the Marquis de Lafayette, who was visiting in New York at the time, and of the French Garde Nationale, which he had commanded in Paris in 1789. The name was gradually adopted by all the states. National Guard units have served in all the major wars in which the United States has been involved.

national intelligence estimate—A strategic estimate of the capabilities and probable course of action of a nation, coalition, or group. It is generally a product of the Central

Intelligence Agency, with input from other elements of the intelligence community.

national objectives — The fundamental aims, goals, or purposes of a nation toward which its policies are directed and the efforts and resources of a nation are applied.

national policy—A broad course of action or a statement of guidance adopted by the government at the national level in pursuit of national objectives.

National Security Council (NSC)—An executive branch body designed to assist the President in all areas of national security policy. The President, the Vice President, the Secretary of Defense, and the Secretary of State are statutory members. Other organizations that regularly participate in NSC deliberations include CIA and the Joint Chiefs of Staff.

national security interests — A collective term to broadly define essential national objectives above and beyond defense. National security interests may include the maintenance of domestic institutions, fostering of economic well-being, and support for the vital interests of certain allies.

national strategy—See **strategy, national.**

"nation at war"—See **"nation in arms."**

"nation in arms"—The concept, introduced by Revolutionary France in 1792, of complete mobilization of a nation's resources, including manpower, for prosecution of a war.

NATO (North Atlantic Treaty Organization)—An alliance of several nations for collective defense and the preservation of peace and security against aggression, established in 1949. The signatory nations to the NATO treaty are the United States, Britain, France, Canada, Italy, Belgium, Luxemburg, the Netherlands, Norway, Denmark, Portugal, and Iceland. Greece, Turkey, West Germany, and Spain were admitted as member nations after the treaty's original ratification. In 1999, the Czech Republic, Hungary, and Poland were admitted. In 2002, Russia became formally affiliated through the NATO-Russia Council.

nautical chart—See **chart.**

naval base—1) A base primarily for support of forces afloat that is contiguous to a port or an anchorage and consists of activities or facilities for which the navy has operating responsibilities, together with internal lines of communication and the minimum surrounding area necessary for local security. 2) An installation that supports land-based units of the naval air force, more accurately called a naval air base or naval air station.

naval campaign—An operation or a connected series of operations conducted by naval forces, including surface, subsurface, air, and amphibious forces, for the purpose of gaining, extending, or maintaining control of the sea.

naval district—See **district, naval.**

naval gunfire operations center — The agency established in a fleet or task force to control the execution of plans for the employment of naval gunfire, to process requests for naval gunfire support, and to allot ships to forward observers. The center's ideal location is in the same ship as the Arms Coordination Center of a fleet or task force.

naval militia—See **militia.**

naval mine—See **mine.**

naval stores—Any articles or commodities used by a naval ship or station, such as equipment, consumable supplies, clothing, petroleum, oils and lubricants, medical supplies, and ammunition.

navy—All of a nation's warships and naval aircraft and their administrative and support structure, including personnel and equipment, whose purposes are to maintain control of the sea in a nation's areas of dominance and to defend a nation's territory from attacks by sea and by air.

"Navy Regs"—Slang for U.S. Navy Regulations, which are compiled for the organization and functioning of the navy.

navy yard—A naval shore establishment that provides a variety of important services to fleets. The largest navy yards have complete facilities for building, refitting, modernizing, repairing, docking, storing, and providing logistic support for ships. Only a few yards of any naval power are so equipped, however. Most yards provide some of these services—generally refitting, modernizing, and repairing—and most specialize in providing limited services to a particular class of warships.

NBC—1) NONBATTLE CASUALTY. 2) Collective abbreviation for nuclear, biological, and chemical, as in "NBC warfare." See also **CBR**.

Nebelwerfer—A six-tube rocket launcher used by the German army in World War II. The tubes were fired separately in a total of 10 seconds and could be reloaded in 90. The Nebelwerfer was used for short-range bombardments and for the laying of smoke screens. The range was 7,300 yards with high explosives and 7,750 with smoke shells.

needle gun—A bolt-action gun invented by the Prussian gunmaker Johann Nikolaus Dreyse in 1829 and used by the Prussian army from 1848 to 1871. In the needle gun, a long, sharp firing pin is pushed through the powder at the back of the cartridge to strike the fulminate primer at the base of the bullet.

need to know—Reason to see classified information. A criterion used in security procedures requiring the custodians of classified information to establish strictly, prior to disclosure, that the intended recipient *must* have access to the information in order to perform his or her official duties.

neutrality—1) The status of a country that refrains from taking part in a war between other powers. 2) The condition of immunity from attack, invasion, or use by belligerent powers given to an area, a country, or a waterway.

neutralization fire—Fire delivered to prevent or interrupt effective hostile activity, particularly movement or the firing of weapons.

neutralize—As pertains to military operations, to render ineffective or unusable for a critical period of time.

neutron bomb (neutron warhead) — A TACTICAL NUCLEAR WEAPON, more often a missile warhead than a bomb, designed to achieve its lethal effects primarily by radiation rather than by blast. Proponents of the weapon believe that by thus reducing collateral damage, a neutron weapon is both more humane and more effective than is a standard tactical nuclear weapon.

New Model Army—The army organized by Oliver Cromwell in 1645. Having long felt the need for major military reform, Cromwell had urged Parliament to adopt a "frame or model of the whole militia," a proposal accepted by the Commons and the Lords that provided for a standing army of 22,000. This force was to be raised by impressment and supported by taxation. The 12 regiments of infantry totaled about 14,000 men, and the cavalry's 11 regiments totaled about 6,600 men plus 1,000 dragoons. Artillery, a stepchild of the British weapons family, underwent some reorganization and expansion, largely on the basis of Continental experience. For the first time, red garb became the general uniform for a British army. Most significant, the traditional aversion of the local militia to campaigns beyond their home territories was bypassed through the creation of this mobile professional force.

"nickeling mission"—Slang in World War II for an air mission for the purpose of dropping propaganda leaflets, which were called "nickels."

no-fire line—A line short of which artillery or ships do not fire on targets except at the request of the supported commander, but beyond which they may fire at any time without danger to friendly troops.

no man's land—A term that originated in World War I for the land between the two opposing entrenched armies.

nonbattle casualty (NBC)—A person who has not become a casualty in combat, but who is lost to his or her organization by reason of disease or injury, or by reason of being missing where the absence does not appear to be voluntary or due to enemy action or to being interned. See also **casualty**.

noncombatant—A person not normally engaged in or assigned to combat duties.

noncommissioned officer (NCO)—An enlisted member of the armed forces who holds a rank or rating in which he or she exercises authority by appointment rather than by commission or warrant. In the U.S. Army the noncommissioned officers are corporal, sergeant, sergeant first class, technical sergeant, first sergeant, and master sergeant. In the Navy, noncommissioned officers are called petty officers. See also **officer** and **petty officer**.

nonrated—1) In the U.S. Air Force, not having a currently effective aeronautical rating. 2) In the U.S. Navy, referring to enlisted personnel who have not yet attained a specialty rating.

Norden bombsight—A device invented by C. L. Norden in the 1920s and used in a 1931 version by American bombers in World War II. See also **bombsight**.

Nordenfelt gun—A gun having up to 12 barrels, developed from an 1873 design by Helge Palmerantz and financed by Thorsten Nordenfelt, both of Sweden. The barrels were in a horizontal row, with individual locks; cartridges were fed by gravity from a magazine that sat above the carrier block.

Nordenfelt gun

normal barrage—See **barrage**.

normal zone of fire—The area within the ZONE OF FIRE for which an artillery unit is normally responsible and within which its fire is normally directed.

North American Air Defense Command (NORAD)—A joint U.S.-Canadian air force command responsible for detecting aircraft and space vehicles deemed a threat to the North American continent. See also **Distant Early Warning line**.

North Atlantic Treaty Organization—See **NATO**.

November—Letter of NATO phonetic alphabet. See also **alphabet, phonetic**.

November 17 Organization—A Greek leftist group that engages in terrorism to disengage Greece from NATO and expel the U.S. and NATO presence from Greece. The group was responsible for the assassinations of a CIA station chief in 1975 and a U.S. military attaché in 1983.

nuclear incident—An unexpected event involving a nuclear weapon, facility, or component that raises the possibility of a nuclear explosion or radioactive contamination.

nuclear parity—The condition that exists when opposing forces possess nuclear offensive and defensive systems of approximately equal effectiveness.

nuclear safety line—A geographical line selected to follow well-defined topographical features if possible and used to delineate the level of protective measures, degree of damage or risk to friendly troops, or possible limits to which the effects of friendly tactical nuclear weapons may be permitted to extend.

nuclear survivability—The capability of a system to operate during or after exposure to a nuclear environment. It may be achieved by a number of methods, including redundancy, reconstitution, and hardening.

nuclear threshold — Level of violence beneath which military operations can be conducted without causing nuclear war.

nuclear weapon—A device in which the explosion results from the energy released by reactions involving atomic nuclei, either fission or fusion or both.

nuclear weapon degradation—The deterioration of a nuclear warhead to such an extent that the probable nuclear yield is reduced.

nuclear yield—The energy released in the detonation of a nuclear weapon, measured in terms of the kilotons or megatons of trinitrotoluene (TNT) required to produce the same energy release. Yields are categorized as **very low**, less than 1 kiloton; **low**, 1 kiloton to 10 kilotons; **medium**, 10 to 50 kilotons; **high**, 50 to 500 kilotons; and **very high**, over 500 kilotons.

numerus—See **bandon**.

O

objective—1) A goal to be obtained that, when defined and understood, gives direction to an operation or a series of operations. Sometimes used in such phrases as "national objectives" or "strategic objectives." 2) A place to be reached, especially a target or target area, or destination. 3) A principle stating that success in war or battle requires that the goal to be achieved should guide and determine every action taken in the conduct of the war or battle.

oblique order—1) A formation of troops in which all are facing 45 degrees from the direction in which they would face in normal marching order. Such a formation is ordinarily part of a drill routine. 2) A tactical procedure for bringing a part of an army into contact with a portion of an enemy army while the remainder of the attacker, being echeloned to the rear, threatens to engage the remainder of the defender's force. First used by Epaminonidas of Thebes to deploy pike at the Battle of Leuctra, 371 B.C.; most skillfully employed by Frederick the Great at the Battle of Leuthen, 1757. See also **phalanx** and **pike**.

Oboe—Letter of old phonetic alphabet. See also **alphabet, phonetic**.

observation—The watching of an action or activity, usually of the enemy. The two principal forms of observation in combat are ground observation and aerial observation. See also **observe**.

observation post—A position selected or located primarily for the purpose of observation. Often abbreviated as **OP**. An aircraft intended primarily for observation is called an "air observation post."

observe—To employ visual means (eyes or vision enhancement equipment) to gain maximum information about a military situation and, particularly, to ascertain the movements and positions of a hostile military force.

observed fire—Fire for which the points of impact or burst can be seen by an observer. The fire can thus be controlled and adjusted on the basis of observation. Observed fire can be both AREA FIRE and PRECISION FIRE. See also **fire**.

observed fire procedures — Standardized procedures employed in adjusting indirect fire on a target.

observer—1) A person whose mission is to observe general activity. Neutral nations often send observers to learn about military developments in belligerent armies in wartime. 2) A person whose mission is to observe fire. See also **forward observer** and **observation post**.

obstacle—Any obstruction that stops, delays, or diverts movement. Obstacles may be natural (e.g., deserts, rivers, swamps, or mountains) or artificial (e.g., barbed-wire entanglements, pits, concrete, or metal antimechanized devices). Obstacles may also be fixed or portable, and may be issued readymade or constructed in the field.

181

obturate—To close up the breech of a gun so that the gas generated in firing cannot escape.

occupied territory—Territory of a nation held by foreign armed forces.

OD—See **officer of the day** and **olive drab**.

Oerlikon—Any of various Swiss-developed 20mm automatic aircraft or antiaircraft guns, firing greased ammunition and manufactured—or licensed—by the Oerlikon arms manufactory near Zürich.

offensive—1) The state or condition of a person or military force that is attacking; an attitude of attack. 2) An attack, especially a large-scale or sustained attack. 3) A principle of war embodying the thesis that success in war requires offensive action to achieve objectives and to exploit the advantages of initiative, maneuver, and surprise.

offensive à outrance—Attack at all times, at all costs, and under any circumstances. This doctrine of warfare was developed in the French army before World War I by Col. Louis L. de Grandmaison, a disciple of Gen. Ferdinand Foch, who also stressed the importance of the offensive, but with less fanaticism.

offensive grenade—See **grenade**.

officer—A person who, by virtue of rank, exerts authority over other members of the armed services. There are three principal classes of military officer: **commissioned officer**, **warrant officer**, and **noncommissioned officer**. A commissioned officer holds a document (commission) from the duly constituted government (in the United States, from the President), appointing the person as an officer and awarding a rank. A warrant officer holds a warrant of rank, issued by proper authority, and typically wears a uniform identical, or similar, to that of a commissioned officer; the warrant officer's duties are usually administrative, rather than operational. A **noncommissioned officer** is appointed to his or her rank by an officer of the unit or formation in which the noncommissioned officer serves. See also **company-grade; field grade; flag officer; general; line; staff;** and **warrant officer**.

officer in charge—1) The officer temporarily commanding a unit or facility in the absence of a commanding officer. 2) The officer responsible for an office or an activity.

officer of the day (OD) — The officer in a military command who has initial responsibility for handling all internal security problems that may arise during his or her 24-hour tour of duty as well as for overseeing the performance of the interior guard during the period.

officer of the deck—The naval officer on a warship who, during a prescribed period (generally 24 hours in port, or regular watch period underway), has initial responsibility for the operation of the ship and the carrying on of ship routine. This duty is performed by a line officer; and during that officer's watch everyone on board ship, except the captain and the executive officer, is subject to the officer of the deck's orders.

"officers' country"—Slang for that portion of a ship or naval shore station that is designated for the use of commissioned officers only, as working quarters or living space.

"off limits"—Not to be entered, patronized, or used by military personnel.

offset bombing — Any aiming procedure that employs a reference or aiming point other than the actual target.

offshore patrol—A naval defense force operating in the outer areas of navigable coastal waters. It is a part of the naval local defense forces and consists of naval ships and aircraft operating outside those areas assigned to the INSHORE PATROL.

"Oka"—"Cherry Blossom," the Japanese code name for the human-guided (i.e., suicide) rocket bomb called "Baka" ("Fool") by the U.S. Navy.

OKH—*Oberkommando des Heeres.* High command of the German army in World War II. It included the German army general staff.

OKL—*Oberkommando der Luftwaffe.* High command of the German air force in World War II.

OKW — *Oberkommando der Wehrmacht.* High command of the German armed forces in World War II. The staff reported directly to

Hitler. Most of its officers were from the army general staff.

"Old Contemptibles"—Nickname of the first contingent of the British Expeditionary Force (BEF) in 1914. Originally coined by the troops in response to the supposed reference by Kaiser Wilhelm II to them as that "contemptible little army."

"Old Guard"—The elite veterans of Napoleon's Imperial Guard.

"Old Ironsides"—The frigate USS *Constitution*. A 44-gun American frigate active in the Barbary Wars and the War of 1812.

U.S. Navy photo

"Old Ironsides"

olive drab (OD)—1) A standard olive-green color used for U.S. Army uniforms and equipment since the late 19th century. 2) Material of this color.

onager—Developed about the 3rd century A.D. and popularly known as the "Roman onager," it was a torsion-driven catapult, consisting of a stout, heavy, rectangular frame, with an upright throwing bar and two solidly braced uprights with a heavy crossbeam on top. The base of the throwing arm was thrust through the twists of a horizontal skein of heavy cord stretched between the two sides of the frame just behind the uprights. At rest, this cord held the throwing arm tightly against the crossbeam. The top, or end, of the throwing arm usually had the shape of a ladle or had a leather pouch attached to it. In firing, the arm was cranked back to a near-horizontal position by a windlass; then a rock or other missile was inserted into the receptacle at the end of the arm and a trigger mechanism was released. The throwing arm returned with great force to a vertical position and hit the crossbeam. The force of iner-

tia could hurl the 40- to 60-pound rock about 450 yards. Roman soldiers called this engine "onager" (wild ass) because of the tendency of the rear end of the frame to lift or buck when the throwing arm hit the crossbeam.

on berth—A ship that is properly moored to a quay, pier, or buoy or at anchor and available for loading and unloading.

onset—A violent attack or assault, especially the assault of an army or a body of troops on an enemy or a fort.

"on the double"—An expression, generally attached to an order or a command, indicating that the mission should be accomplished rapidly, in double time, that is, at the run.

"on the warpath"—To go to battle. The term appears to have been used first by author James Fenimore Cooper in *The Deerslayer*.

"on the way"—A message to an air artillery observer alerting him or her that a round has been fired and will soon be observable.

OP—Abbreviation for OBSERVATION POST.

open flank—See **flank**.

open order—A formation of troops deployed as for combat, in contrast to close-order formations for drill and marching.

"open skies"—A colloquial term to describe various Cold War treaties that permitted reconnaissance flights of previously denied areas. The concept was launched under the Eisenhower administration but was never embraced by the Soviet Union, whose adherence was essential to any meaningful treaty. By the end of the 1990s, the widespread employment of spy satellites by the United States had made the treaties militarily meaningless.

operation—A military action or the carrying out of a strategic, tactical, service, training, or administrative military mission.

operational—1) Ready and fit for action, referring to troops, installations, naval vessels, weapons, and equipment. 2) Having to do with operations, as a directive or an order.

operational art—See **operations**.

operational chain of command — See **chain of command**.

operational effectiveness—The overall degree of mission accomplishment of a system when operated by representative personnel in the environment envisaged for the system.

operational maneuver group — A large WARSAW PACT formation designed to carry out a Soviet doctrinal concept of DEEP PENETRATION. The force—probably a tank army with two or three tank divisions and one or two motorized rifle divisions, supported by substantial tactical air units—was expected to be prepared to exploit a breakthrough by front-line, probably FIRST ECHELON, forces. The anticipated mission was a rapid and deep strike into the NATO rear area, to create maximum destruction and disruption of NATO defensive operations. It represented an updating of the Soviet mobile group of World War II. Although it did not fit the definition of a SECOND ECHELON force, it was considered by NATO to fall into the category of a FOLLOW-ON FORCES ATTACK. **operational necessity**—A characteristic of certain wartime activity in which a given mission is recognized as likely to have some negative consequences, including loss of life and damage to property, but in which these consequences must be accepted in view of the promised results of the mission.

operational priority—A category of precedence reserved for messages requiring expeditious action by the addressee. See also **precedence**.

operational research—See **operations research**.

operation map—A map showing the location and strength of friendly forces involved in an operation. It may also indicate predicted movements and location of enemy forces.

operation order—A directive, usually formal, issued by a commander to subordinates for the purpose of effecting the coordinated execution of an operation. In the U.S. Army it is usually in five paragraphs that set forth a) the situation, b) the mission, c) the commander's decision, d) the plan of action, and e) the details of the method of execution. Thus, coordinated action by the whole command is ensured. Also called **operations order**.

operation plan—A plan for operations extending over a considerable space and time and usually based on stated assumptions. It may cover a single operation or a series of connected operations to be carried out simultaneously or in succession. It is the form of directive employed by higher echelons of command in order to permit subordinate commanders to prepare their supporting plans or orders. The designation "plan" is often used instead of "order" in preparing for operations well in advance. An operation plan may be put into effect at a prescribed time, or on signal, and then becomes the OPERATION ORDER.

operations—1) The process of carrying on combat, including movement, supply, attack, defense, and maneuvers needed to gain the objectives of any battle or campaign. 2) A conceptual division of the process of waging war, involving combat activities between those of TACTICS and those of STRATEGY. Originally devised by the Germans during World War I to distinguish between the performance of battlefield activities (tactics) and multifront or multitheater aspects of waging war (strategy). As envisioned by the Germans, operations were just above the lower boundary of strategy, and pertained to control of the activities of large ground forces—usually armies or army groups—in a discrete theater of combat. The Soviet armed forces adopted the concept of operations during World War II but treated it much more rigidly than the Germans, viewing it as restricted to activities of armies and army groups and as a distinct form of activity lying between tactics and strategy. They called it **operational art**. This concept, closer to the Soviet than the German pattern, was adopted by the U.S. Army in 1982.

operations analysis—See **operations research**.

operations research—The analytical study of military problems, undertaken to provide responsible commanders and staff agencies with a scientific or mathematical basis for improving military operations. Also known as **operational research** and **operations analysis**.

opposing forces (op-for)—See **aggressor force**.

orb—Formerly in military tactics, the forming of a number of soldiers in a circular defense, generally six deep. This defensive configuration was considered by the French

Marshal de Puysegur, in his *Art of War* (1749), to be particularly strong because the enemy could expect no part of the circular formation to be weaker than any other.

order—1) A communication, written, oral, or by signal, that conveys instructions from a superior to a subordinate. In a broad sense, the terms "order" and "command" are synonymous. 2) With "arms," as in "order arms," the drill command to rest the rifle butt on the ground against the right foot with the barrel perpendicular to the ground, or leaning slightly to the rear, while standing at attention.

orderly—An enlisted man or woman in personal attendance on one or more officers. 2) A person assigned to a specific task to keep things in order, such as a latrine orderly or a medical orderly.

orderly book—1) The record of activities of a unit or a guard. Similar to the log of a naval vessel. 2) An official record of attendance or use.

orderly room—A room in a barracks used as the office of a company or other unit of similar size.

order of battle—A statement of identification, strength, command structure, and disposition of the personnel, units, and equipment of any military force.

order of march—The sequence in which the elements of a military force move from one location to another.

ordinary, in—Used formerly of naval vessels not in actual use, which must be roofed over, with their masts and running gear stowed ashore. The ships were formed in divisions, with a lieutenant in command, and a line-of-battle ship, called a "guardship of ordinary," responsible for the several divisions in a port. Ships similarly stored in modern times are said to be in MOTHBALLS or "mothballed."

ordnance—Collective term for all military weapons, ammunition, explosives, combat vehicles, and battle matériel, together with the necessary maintenance tools and equipment.

organic—Assigned to and forming an essential part of a military organization. Organic parts of a unit are those listed in its table of organization for the army, air force, and ma-

rines and those assigned to the administrative organizations of the operating forces of the navy.

organization—A group of people with responsibilities, authorities, and relationships defined for the purpose of effectively accomplishing a mission.

orientation—A training program for recruits or troops reporting to a new command to introduce them to the organization, functions, procedures, and other aspects of the command.

oriflamme—The red or orange-red silk banner of the Abbey of St. Denis in France. Early kings of France used this banner as their STANDARD in combat.

Orion (P-3)—A four-engine, turboprop, long-range, land-based antisubmarine aircraft. It carries a variety of weapons and radar and can be used for search, patrol, hunter-killer, and convoy escort operations.

Lockheed Aircraft Corporation photo

Orion (P-3)

Oscar—Letter of NATO phonetic alphabet. See also **alphabet, phonetic**.

Oslo Accords—Agreements reached in September 1993 between Israeli and Palestinian negotiators, which provided, among other things, for a Palestinian Authority to administer portions of Gaza and the West Bank. See also **Palestine Liberation Organization**.

Osprey (V-22) — A hybrid helicopter-airplane capable, by rotating its two engines, of near-vertical takeoff. The aircraft was temporarily grounded in 2000 after two disastrous crashes.

other ranks—British term for "soldiers." See also **enlisted personnel**.

"Out"—A signal communication transmission indicator signifying the end of a message, with no response expected. See also **"Over."**

outflank—In ground combat, to maneuver an attacking force around and behind the flank of the opposing force. Thus, a tactical advantage might be gained because the opponent will be forced to divert strength from the front line to defend the flank and rear.

outline plan—A preliminary plan that outlines the salient features or principles of a course of action prior to the initiation of detailed planning.

outpost—1) A military post, base, station, or other installation located far from its national homeland, having the primary responsibility of guarding the nation against surprise attack or of protecting a territory or possession. 2) A detachment of guards or sentries posted outside a stationary military force to protect it against surprise by the enemy.

outpost line of resistance—The outer line of defense of a defensive position or zone. Usually held by a COVERING FORCE.

outrank—To be senior because of higher rank or more time in grade than others. Sometimes shortened to "rank."

outwing—To extend the flanks of a combat force in action in order to gain an advantageous position against the right or left flank of an enemy.

outworks—A smaller fortification built beyond (i.e., closer to a potential attacker than) the main defense structure.

OV-10—See **Bronco.**

over—In naval gunnery, an overrange salvo or shot.

"Over"—A signal communications transmission indicator signifying the end of an element of a message and requesting a response from the party at the other end. Its use with the word OUT—as in "Over and Out"—is improper procedure.

overhead fire — Fire over the heads of friendly troops.

overkill—The provision of more resources or fire power than what is reasonably required to achieve an objective.

overlay—A drawing or a printing on a sheet of translucent material that is keyed to a map or chart, so that it may be placed accurately above it, and shows deployments of forces or equipment.

Overlord, Operation—Code word for the Allied invasion of France across the English Channel in June 1944.

overseas bar—A stripe worn on the sleeve for each 6 months of overseas duty that had been served between 7 December 1941 and 2 September 1946. Popularly called a "Hershey bar," for the former head of the Selective Service, Gen. Lewis B. Hershey.

overseas cap—A visorless uniform cap of the same material as the uniform suit, which, when not on the head, folds flat from side to side so that it can fit in a pocket or under a belt. Such caps were generally optional for wear by all services in World War II.

over-the-horizon radar—A radar system that makes use of atmospheric reflection and refraction to extend its range beyond the line of sight.

over the top—An expression used in World War I for the movement out of the trenches toward the enemy lines as an attack began.

P

P-3—See **Orion**.

pace—1) The regulated marching speed of a military column. For QUICK TIME this is 120 steps per minute; for DOUBLE TIME, 180 steps per minute. 2) A step in marching; for quick time in the U.S. Army, the length of stride is 30 inches. For double time it is 36 inches.

pacification—Any program or series of programs designed to influence and modify popular attitudes in a war zone. Pacification programs were implemented on a large scale by U.S. forces in Vietnam with limited success.

pack—1) A container designed to carry items of equipment on the back of a soldier or an animal. Sometimes called a KNAPSACK. 2) The packaged equipment carried by soldiers on their backs; the infantry soldier's pack generally contains SHELTER HALF, blanket, underwear, socks, toilet articles, and the like. 3) Submarines working together on an operation (e.g., the German "wolf packs" of World War II).

Packard Commission—A blue-ribbon commission on defense management that, in 1986, made a number of significant recommendations with respect to the Joint Chiefs of Staff, the defense command structure, and the defense procurement process.

pack transportation—The personnel, animals, and equipment used for the transportation of matériel and supplies loaded on pack animals (generally horses and mules).

padding—Extraneous text added to a cipher message to conceal its beginning, end, or total length.

Paladin (M-109)—A self-propelled 155mm howitzer system.

pale—A fence or other barrier designed to protect a populated area. From it comes the term "beyond the pale," referring to something beyond the limits of safety or propriety.

Palestine Liberation Organization (PLO)—The umbrella organization of major Palestinian groups that considers itself, and is generally recognized by the Arab world, as the sole legitimate representative of the Palestinian people. When founded in 1964 the PLO openly advocated driving the Israelis "into the sea," but in the 1990s it assumed a more moderate posture. The PLO is the dominant organization in the Palestinian Authority, created in 1993 to administer autonomous areas of Gaza and the West Bank.

palintonon—A type of BALLISTA with the guide beams on an inclined plane. It is estimated that some versions were as large as 10 yards long, 5 yards high, and 4 yards wide, and could fire stones weighing up to 8 pounds as far as 300 yards.

palisade—*n.* A fence made of stakes placed close together to form a defensive barrier.
v. To construct such a fence.

palisade gun—See **tarasnice**.

pan—A shallow receptacle that holds the powder in a matchlock, a flintlock, or other gunpowder weapon.

pandour—One of the lightly armed border troops used in the early 18th century for defense of the Austrian frontier against the Turks, and by Maria Theresa in the War of the Austrian Succession.

pannel—A carriage on which mortars and their beds used to be conveyed on a march.

Panther—A German tank of World War II, the Panther was introduced in 1942. It weighed 45 tons, had a five-man crew, and mounted a 75mm gun. About 5,500 were built, but they were plagued with mechanical problems. (See also **PZKW**.)

panzer—In German, armor or armored. The word was originally used for body armor, but since World War II, in English and German, "panzer" has been used primarily to refer to German tanks.

panzer grenadier—*n*. An infantryman in a German unit composed of both infantry and armored elements (i.e., a mechanized unit). *adj*. Descriptive term for such a unit.

Papa—Letter of NATO phonetic alphabet. See also **alphabet, phonetic**.

parachute troops—See **paratroops**.

parade—*n*. 1) A ceremonial procession of marching personnel, sometimes interspersed with vehicles. 2) The area, more formally called the **parade ground**, where troops march in review. *v*. To cause to march, as to "parade the troops" or "parade the colors."

parafrag—A fragmentation bomb that is carried down by parachute and is designed to explode above the ground.

parallel—A trench; usually one of a series dug approximately parallel to the fortification being attacked, so that each new trench line would bring the attackers closer to their objective. This aspect of siege warfare was developed in the 17th century by the Marquis de Vauban.

parallel chains of command—An arrangement for amphibious operations in which corresponding navy and ground commanders are established at each level to facilitate integrated execution of an operation.

parallel sheaf of fire—See **sheaf of fire**.

paramilitary force—A force or group that is distinct from a country's standing professional forces, but resembles them in such respects as organization, equipment, training, or mission.

paramilitary operation—1) An operation undertaken by a paramilitary force. 2) An operation that provides covert assistance to a friendly government or military organization.

parapet—A defensive wall of earth or stone.

paratroops—Troops carried into battle by aircraft and dropped by parachute, as distinguished from airborne infantry, who are flown to battle but may be landed from aircraft or helicopter. Paratroops are a special category of troops within airborne forces. Also called **paratroopers.**

paravane—A naval mine defense device. It is a type of water kite that is towed from the FOREFOOT of a vessel, riding out to one side at the end of a wire rope usually 56 yards long, to deflect mines that may be moored in the path of the vessel and to cut the mooring lines so that the mine rises safely to the surface.

"pariah states"—See **"rogue states."**

Paris Gun—The designation of any of three long-range 210mm German guns used to bombard Paris from 23 March to 7 August 1918. Most of the several emplacements were in the St. Gobain Wood near Laon, 70 miles from Paris. The Paris Gun, *Pariskanonen* in German, designed by a team of Krupp engineers, had a barrel almost 120 feet long and could fire a 275-pound projectile to a range of approximately 80 miles. When the guns' first shells landed on Paris, it was thought that they had been dropped from German bombers. In all, the Paris Guns fired 203 shells against the city but did not produce the panic and population exodus the Germans had hoped to achieve. The advance of the Allied armies in August 1918 ended the shelling.

park, artillery—1) The area where artillery pieces and vehicles are stored and serviced. 2) The artillery so stored.

parley—A meeting of representatives of opposing forces to discuss terms for ending or suspending combat. Before the 20th century, the side wishing to have a parley announced it by bugle or drum, and fighting was usually halted during the parley.

parole—*n.* 1) A password. 2) Status of a person released from confinement or arrest upon his or her acceptance of terms for such release. 3) Status of a prisoner of war released upon agreement of the opposing side and his or her acceptance of the terms. *v.* The act of releasing a person from arrest or confinement.

parry—To prevent a weapon or a projectile from hitting its target, used especially of thrusting weapons, like swords, spears, and lances.

partisan—*n.* 1) A spear with a two-edged blade and a lug curving out from the base of the blade at either side. It was developed in the 15th century and is still carried ceremonially by the British Yeomen of the Guard at the Tower of London. The French name for this weapon is *langue de boeuf.* In 15th-century England, this became *langedebeve.* 2) A member of an irregular or guerrilla group operating within occupied territory to harass and inflict damage on the occupying forces. *adj.* The form of activity conducted by partisans. See also **guerrilla** and **guerrilla warfare**.

partridge—A very large bombard, formerly used in sieges and in defensive works.

partridge mortar — A weapon developed near the beginning of the 18th century. It had a central bore for firing a standard 110mm mortar shell, surrounded by 13 smaller bores that, arranged in a circular pattern, fired smaller grenades or bombs almost simultaneously. It was used by the French in 1702 at Bouchain and in 1708 at Lille.

party—A small group performing a specific task, such as an INSPECTION PARTY, a BOARDING PARTY, or a SHORE PARTY.

pass—1) A short tactical movement, usually a dive, by an aircraft over a target, either air or ground. 2) A card or a certificate that permits a person to enter a gate, a door, or other area requiring control. 3) Temporary release from duty, certified by written permission or pass.

passed midshipman—In the 19th century in the U.S. and British navies, a midshipman who had passed his examination and was a candidate for the rank of lieutenant.

pass in review—To march in formation before a commander or reviewing dignitaries.

passive—In defensive activities, passivity describes any or all noncombatant measures taken to defend an area or an installation against a ground or air attack or airborne assault, including the use of cover, concealment, dispersion, and the like.

passive defense—Measures taken to reduce the likely effects of enemy action without taking the military initiative.

passive homing guidance — A system of missile guidance in which a missile is guided by radiation from its target.

passport—A document giving a ship permission to leave port in time of war or to pass through restricted waters. It is issued officially, especially to commercial vessels belonging to neutral nations.

password—A secret word or distinctive sound used for friendly identification in reply to a challenge.

patch—1) An embroidered cloth badge worn on a uniform sleeve indicating the wearer's rank or unit. 2) Before the invention of the cartridge, a piece of cloth or leather that was greased and then wrapped around a ball or a bullet so that the projectile fit more tightly inside the barrel of a gun. The infantryman carried a number of patches in a **patch box**, which was cut into the butt of his weapon or carried on his belt.

patch box—See **patch**.

paterero—See **pedrero**.

pathfinder—1) A specialized military team, dropped or airlanded in advance of a main force, whose mission is to mark a drop zone or a landing zone and to operate navigational aids to guide incoming aircraft. 2) The aircraft carrying such a team. 3) A radar device used for navigating or homing to an objective when visibility precludes accurate visual navigation. 4) An aircraft—usually one of several—leading a World War II bombing mission, particularly for the British Royal Air Force Bomber Command. A pathfinder's mission was to designate the target for the main body of following aircraft on the raid or mission by dropping bombs or flares or both.

Patriot (MIM-104)—A surface-to-air missile system for defense against aircraft and short-range ballistic missiles. A Patriot battery includes a phased-array radar and up to eight launchers, each of which holds four missiles with 200-pound warheads. Their effective range is about 30 miles. The Patriot system was employed against Iraqi Scud missiles in the GULF WAR, but the overall success rate is a matter of dispute.

patrol—1) A detachment of ground, sea, or air forces dispatched by a larger unit to gather information or carry out a destructive, harassing, mopping up, surveillance, or security mission. 2) The checking of an area, usually on a periodic basis, by moving from one point to another to see whether a normal condition has been disrupted. 3) The person, vehicle, or vessel that performs such a check. See also **inshore patrol** and **offshore patrol**.

patrol aircraft—U.S. Navy maritime reconnaissance aircraft.

patrol, fighting—A tactical unit sent out from the main body to engage in independent combat activity; a detachment assigned to protect the front, flank, or rear of the main body.

patrol, offensive—A patrol with an offensive mission.

patrol wing—A U.S. Navy organization, later changed to **fleet air wing**.

pattern bombing—The systematic covering of a target area with aerial bombs uniformly distributed according to plan.

pavise—A large shield carried by medieval infantrymen, particularly by crossbowmen. The frame was usually covered by hide or painted canvas. Some pavises were large enough to cover the whole body and could be set upright to protect the bearer as he fired or loaded his weapon. Crossbowmen sometimes wore pavises on their backs and turned around for protection.

Pax Americana—An expression sometimes employed to characterize the global military domination enjoyed by the United States following the collapse of the Soviet Union in 1991. The term derives from Pax Romana, a metaphor used to characterize the dominant position of the Roman Empire at its zenith, and from Pax Britannica, used to refer to the peace imposed by Britain upon hostile nations in the 19th century.

pay clerk—U.S. Navy warrant officer.

PB4Y—See **Liberator**.

peacekeeping—Military operations undertaken with the consent of all major powers to a dispute and designed to implement a ceasefire, a truce, or other such agreement.

peacekeeping force—A military force established with the consent of all the major powers to a dispute for the purpose of implementing a ceasefire, a truce, or other such agreement. Contemporary forces of this type are usually set up by the United Nations and have been used several times in the Balkans, the Middle East, and Africa.

"Peacemaker"—An experimental 12-inch naval gun mounted on an early U.S. Navy steam sloop, the *Princeton*. In a demonstration on the Potomac River in February 1844, the "Peacemaker" exploded, killing the Secretary of State and the Secretary of the Navy and endangering President John Tyler.

pedrero—A 16th-century mortar-type weapon that fired a stone projectile—*pedrero* means "stone mortar" in Spanish—rather than a heavier iron projectile. Despite its thin walls, the pedrero could fire a stone cannonball almost as far as a cannon, with a maximum range of 2,500 yards. Pedreros varied greatly, but a typical one weighed 3,000 pounds, was 9 feet long with a 10-inch bore, and fired a 30-pound projectile. Also known as a **perrier**, derived from the French word *pierrier*, and as *petrera* or *paterero*, derived from the Latin for "rock" or "stone." See also **trebuchet**.

peep—See **jeep**.

pelta—See **peltast**.

peltast—A lightly armed, javelin-throwing infantryman of ancient times who carried a **pelta**, a light, skin-covered wicker shield, crescent-shaped, circular, or oval. The first peltasts were Thracians, who proved so successful that similar troops were introduced into Greek armies. They were cheaper to arm than HOPLITEs and, because lightly armed, they could move more quickly.

penetrate—1) To break through a defense. 2) To force a way into a target or other substance. Said of a shell, a bomb, or other projectile, and also of rays and radioactive dust.

penetration—1) A form of offensive maneuver that seeks to break through an enemy's defensive position, widen the gap created, and destroy the continuity of his positions. 2) The depth to which a projectile or a force has advanced after entering its target.

pennant—1) A flag. Also known as **pennon**, the term is most frequently used for small flags. 2) A small, long, narrow flag, flown on a ship for use as a signal or identification. 3) Such a flag carried on a lance.

Pennsylvania rifle — An 18th- and 19th-century muzzle-loading weapon that was first made by German settlers in Pennsylvania. Later, the weapon came to be known as a KENTUCKY RIFLE.

Pentagon—A large, low, five-sided, five-floor building on the Virginia side of the Potomac River just outside Washington, D.C., in which are housed the principal executive offices of the Department of Defense, including those for the military departments of the Army, the Navy, and the Air Force. The Pentagon was completed on 15 January 1943. It contains 17.5 miles of corridors. It is often personified, as in "the Pentagon says" or "the Pentagon ordered," to refer to defense policy or the U.S. defense community. Approximately 23,000 military and civilian employees work in the Pentagon. See also **World Trade Center and Pentagon, attacks on, 2001**.

U.S. Department of Defense photo

Pentagon

penteconter—A 50-oared galley.

penthouse—1) A shedlike structure for the protection of a gun and its carriage from the weather. 2) A shelter used to protect weapons and troops from hostile fire in ancient and medieval siege operations.

pentomic division—The name given to the standard U.S. infantry division during the late 1950s and early 1960s, replacing the TRIANGULAR DIVISION of World War II and the Korean War. Its principal maneuver elements were five BATTLE GROUPS, larger than the standard battalion and smaller than the standard brigade or regiment. Experimental in nature, the pentomic division was soon replaced by an updated version of the older triangular division. See also **division**.

percussion cap—A device containing a material that explodes on being struck and is used to ignite powder or other explosive material. The first caps were developed about 1814 after the Scottish Rev. Alexander Forsyth's discovery in 1807 of this property in a mercuric fulminate. The caps were small cylindrical cups that resembled a tall hat and were variously made of iron, pewter, and copper. The cap was partially filled with the fulminate, which was, in turn, held in place by a covering of tin foil and shellac. The cap fitted over a tube protruding perpendicularly from the rear end of the barrel of a gun. When struck with a hammer, the fulminate exploded, producing a spark that fired the powder in the gun. Adoption of this device greatly increased the effectiveness of handguns, permitting them to be fired in wet weather, thus altering the tactics of warfare. Percussion caps of various types were used until early in the 20th century.

perimeter defense—An all-around defensive system of field fortifications and weapons to protect an area or locality.

periscope—An optical instrument consisting of a system of mirrors and lenses arranged so that a person can observe objects from a position below the viewing lens. Although periscopes have been employed in trench warfare, they are most often associated with submarines.

permanent fortifications — Fortifications of a lasting, elaborate nature, usually erected in time of peace and constructed of hard materials like stone, masonry, and concrete. Modern examples include the French MAGINOT LINE, the German WEST WALL, and the Finnish MANNERHEIM LINE, all erected in the 1930s for the defense of frontiers. See also **fortification**.

permanent rank—A rank that does not cease with a change of duty or a change of circumstances, as opposed to temporary rank.

perrier—See **pedrero** and **trebuchet**.

Pershing (MGM-31A)—A mobile, solid-propellant, surface-to-surface missile with a nuclear warhead capability. It is designed to support ground forces in the manner of long-range artillery.

personnel—1) Individuals, usually members of the armed services. 2) Collectively, the people of the armed forces. 3) A staff function, activity, or division concerned with military individuals and policies relating to them.

personnel carriers — Armored vehicles, tracked or wheeled, designed primarily to transport infantry into combat, but usually having no provisions for permitting a majority of the transported personnel to engage the enemy while fully enclosed.

petard—An explosive device, often in the shape of a small bell, designed to be detonated against a gate or a wall in order to force a passage through.

Peter—Letter of old phonetic alphabet See also **alphabet, phonetic**.

petrary—See **trebuchet**.

petronel—A 15th-century firearm designed for use by a mounted man, steadying it against the breast (whence the French name *poitrinal*) and a rest attached to the bow of the saddle.

petty officer—A noncommissioned naval OFFICER.

phalanx—An ancient formation of infantry in which soldiers stood so closely together that their shields overlapped, with spears projecting forward, the spears of those soldiers in the rear ranks sometimes resting on the shoulders of the men in front. Such a formation was used in Sumeria as early as the 3rd millenium B.C. The Greeks used it from

about the 7th century B.C. The phalanx, with a depth of 8 to 24 ranks, was greatly improved by Philip II of Macedon and by Alexander the Great. In battle the normal deployment was a long, solid line with narrow intervals through which the PSILOI could pass. Battle was waged on the flattest ground available. However, the Macedonian phalanxes of Philip and Alexander, 16 men deep, were so well trained that they could perform complex maneuvers even in rugged terrain.

Phalanx—A short-range weapon system designed to defend against antiship cruise missiles. Consisting of a radar-controlled 20mm gun, the Phalanx is seen as a "last chance" against antiship missiles that have eluded other fleet defenses.

Phantom II (F-4) — The principal all-weather multipurpose fighter flown by the U.S. Air Force, Navy, and Marines during the 1960s and 1970s. Initially developed as a carrier-based aircraft, the Phantom served in fighter-interceptor, fighter-escort, reconnaissance, and attack modes as well. McDonnell Douglas produced more than 5,000 Phantoms for U.S. and other services between 1958 and 1979.

McDonnell Douglas Corporation photo

Phantom II

pharmacist—U.S. Navy warrant officer.

pharmacist's mate — U.S. Navy enlisted specialty, chief and first, second, and third class. See also **hospital corpsman**.

phase line—A line used for control and coordination of military operations, often a terrain feature extending across the zone of action or an imaginary line connecting two prominent terrain features.

Phoenix (AIM-54A)—A long-range air-to-air missile with electronic guidance. It has a range in excess of 100 miles and can be carried in clusters of up to six missiles on the F-14 TOMCAT.

phosgene—A poisonous gas (carbonyl chloride) harmful to the lungs. Colorless and extremely heavy, it smells like new-cut hay or corn. It was introduced in World War I and generally supplanted chlorine as a gas.

photographer—U.S. Navy warrant officer.

photographer's mate—U.S. Navy enlisted specialty rating, chief and first, second, and third class.

photographic interpretation—The extraction of intelligence from photographs of a target area. Photographs may be taken by aircraft, satellites, surface vessels, or personnel on the ground.

PIAT (projector, infantry, antitank) — A British World War II–vintage individual antitank weapon that was fired from the shoulder. Spring-operated, it fired a 3-pound projectile that could penetrate 4-inch armor at a distance of 50 yards.

pickelhaube—German term used for the ceremonial spiked helmet of World War I vintage.

picker—A small, pointed brass wire, formerly supplied to every infantry soldier to use in cleaning the vent hole of his musket.

picket—1) A pointed stake that, generally used with others, provides a defensive barrier. 2) A group of persons detached from a main party and serving as a line of outposts to guard the others from surprise attack. 3) A radar beacon set up in a peripheral area. 4) A ship that patrols an outer defense point to obtain early warning. 5) Aircraft posted around a sensitive area to provide early warning of the approach of enemy aircraft, to track them, and to control friendly aircraft sent to intercept.

"picklebarrel bombing"—1) Slang expression indicating the bombing of a very small target. 2) Highly accurate bombing.

piece—A general term applied to any weapon, individual or crew-served.

piecemeal attack—A maneuver in which units of a command enter into battle in small increments, as they become available on the battlefield. See also **attack**.

pierrier—See **pedrero**.

"pig's head"—A Roman tactic in which the 10 MANIPLEs of a legion were formed into a wedge—four, three, two, and one maniple from back to front—as a device to break through an enemy's ranks.

pike—A long spear, used by infantry for offensive and defensive purposes from ancient times until the late 17th century. See also **oblique order** and **phalanx**.

pikeman — A soldier, usually an infantryman, armed with a PIKE.

pillage—See **looting**.

pillbox—A small, low fortification that houses machine guns, antitank weapons, and other weapons together with the crew to fire them. A pillbox is usually made of concrete, steel, or filled sandbags.

pikeman

pilot officer — A commissioned rank in the British Royal Air Force and other air forces, corresponding to second lieutenant in the U.S. Air Force.

pilum—A Roman javelin, developed in the 3rd century B.C. There were many types, partly because javelins were made by hand, and partly because of technical innovations. In the 2nd century the Romans seem to have standardized a light pilum that was easily handled and capable of great penetration of hard-surfaced objects. It was basically a 7-foot-long weapon made half of metal and half of wood—a 4.5-foot wood shaft into which was inlaid (with a 2-foot overlap) a 4.5-foot iron rod. Marius made one of the two pins that bound the wooden shaft and metal rod together of wood, so that the shaft would break off in an enemy's shield. Caesar and others made the iron rod of soft metal and the tip hard; thus the tip would penetrate and the shaft would bend so that the javelin could not be easily withdrawn. By the 1st century B.C. the pilum was as important a legionary weapon as the sword.

pincer movement—A type of double envelopment in which two columns drive on each side of an enemy position and converge at its rear to isolate and destroy it.

pinfire cartridge—A cartridge developed by the French gunsmith B. Houllier in 1846. It consisted of a metal case in which a small percussion cap was mounted sideways in the base. A pin protruded through the case; and when struck by a hammer, it drove into the cap, exploding and detonating the charge, thereby propelling the bullet. This was the first completely self-contained ammunition for small arms and was the prototype of the center-fire and rim-fire cartridges.

pintle—An upright pin on the rear of a towing vehicle that serves as a coupling device for a trailer or other vehicle being towed. For example, the trail of a gun carriage attaches to the pintle of the LIMBER or PRIME MOVER.

pioneer—Formerly, pioneers were soldiers in European armies detailed from the different companies of a regiment and furnished with saws, felling axes, spades, mattocks, and billhooks for construction tasks, clearing of obstacles, and the like. The term is still used in the British army for a member of units corresponding to engineer units in the U.S. Army.

pipe—To deliver an order or other message by the musical notes of a boatswain's pipe. Piping aboard, for example, is one of the honors rendered when important persons come aboard.

pipe clay—A clay used for making tobacco pipes. Because of its white color, pipe clay, in its powdery form, was frequently used to brighten the white portions of uniforms, such as the belting.

pistol—A small firearm, one that is often fired with one hand. The origin of the name is uncertain, but it is thought to have derived from the city of Pistoia, Italy, where the weapon may have been developed. However, it is also claimed that the first handguns had a bore the diameter of the ancient coin called a *pistole*. In early times people armed with pistols were called "pistoleers."

pitched battle—1) A battle or, loosely, any form of combat that is highly intense. 2) A battle of forces in close contact, using carefully planned tactics.

pivot gun—A gun, usually of long range and high muzzle velocity, mounted on the bow or poop deck of a warship or armed merchantman, capable of 360-degree traverse. See also **swivel gun**.

plain langauge—Unencoded, used for messages not converted to coded form.

plan—The scheme or proposed method for accomplishing a mission or attaining an objective. A plan for a military operation is usually formulated on the basis of an ESTIMATE OF THE SITUATION, and in turn is the basis for an OPERATION ORDER.

plan, contingency—A plan for a major contingency that can be reasonably anticipated by a national or regional command. A contingency plan is usually related to a geographic region or to one of the principal geographic subareas of a command. There are usually a number of such plans for different possible situations and different areas.

plashing—An obstacle similar to ABATIS, in which trees and limbs of trees were intertwined to form a thick hedge. It differed from abatis in that it was more hastily prepared and the tree trunks were not embedded in the ground. See also **zareba**.

plate armor—Armor in the form of solid sheets of metal, normally shaped to the contour of whatever it protects. Plate armor of bronze was used for body armor at least as early as the 15th century B.C.; but it was not until the 13th century A.D., long after bronze armor had been abandoned, that medieval European armorers began producing plate armor of iron. At first, these iron plates, covering vital and vulnerable areas such as the shoulders and thighs, were worn under the CHAIN MAIL that had been the armor commonly used since Byzantine times. By the middle of the 13th century, however, plate armor was replacing chain mail, and in the next century whole suits of plate armor had been developed. The armor built into or added to ships, aircraft, tanks, and other items of military equipment is also known as plate armor. See also **armor**.

platform—1) The flat base on which a gun is mounted. 2) In the U.S. armed forces, "platform" is used as a generic term to describe any vehicle—aircraft, ship, or motor vehicle—capable of mounting a weapon.

platform wagon—A wagon used for transporting heavy ordnance.

platoon—The next-to-smallest unit in a modern military organization. Composed of 25 to 50 troops and usually divided into squads or sections, platoons are the smallest unit commanded by a commissioned officer (second lieutenant or ensign), although they are often commanded by noncommissioned officers. Two to four platoons form a company. The term "platoon" was used in the 17th century to refer to a group of musketeers who fired their weapons together.

plunging fire—Fire that strikes a target at an angle greater than 45 degrees from the horizontal. This can be direct fire from a superior elevation, but is usually high-angle fire from a gun or a howitzer at an elevation greater than 45 degrees, or fire from a mortar. Plunging fire is more likely to be INDIRECT FIRE than DIRECT FIRE. See also **angles of fire**.

pocket battleship — A lightly armored, diesel-powered warship of which three were built for the German navy prior to World War II. They were designed to comply within the limits of 10,000-ton displacement set for the German navy by the Versailles Treaty, but actual displacement was about 12,000 tons. They carried six 11-inch guns and, by refueling from supply ships, were able to stay at sea for extended periods.

"poilu"—A World War I slang term for a French soldier, particularly one in the front line. The origin is not clear, although the word means "hairy" in French and may have been applied because of the unshaven appearance of many of these soldiers in prolonged combat.

point-blank—Directly in front of the target. Point-blank implies that a target is so close that it is not necessary to allow for the drop in the trajectory of a projectile and that it is almost impossible to miss it.

point-blank range—The distance to that point where an artillery projectile, fired from a level or horizontal bore, first strikes the ground in front of the cannon.

point d'appui—A position, usually fortified and often containing supplies, from which a military force can operate as a base for maneuver in order to apply pressure against an enemy.

point defense—Defense of positions or areas that are critical or important to the security or viability of a force, such as a dominating ridge, an artillery emplacement, or the force commander's headquarters.

point fuze—A fuze at the forward end or point of a shell. See also **fuze**.

point target—A target so small that it requires a highly accurate placement of ordnance, usually by PRECISION FIRE to neutralize or destroy it.

poitrinal—See **petronel**.

POL—Abbreviation for a class or category of automotive-related supplies: petroleum, oil, and lubricants.

Polaris (UGM-27)—The first of the U.S. nuclear submarines capable of launching ballistic missiles from underwater. The missiles, also called Polaris, were first deployed in 1960. They were capable of carrying a nuclear warhead and had ranges of 1,200 to 2,500 nautical miles. See also **submarine, guided-missile**.

pole-ax—A medieval weapon consisting of a long shaft with a head in the form of an ax or a combined ax, pick, and hammer.

pom-pom—1) A rack of light antiaircraft cannon, usually mounted in fours, as on a ship. 2) An automatic cannon. The term was first applied to an automatic cannon used by the Boers in the Boer War, because it sounded like the beating of a drum.

poniard—A dagger, particularly one with a blade that has a triangular or square cross section.

pole-ax

ponton—A floating structure, either a boat or similar to a boat, that serves to support something, such as a dock or a bridge. Can be spelled **pontoon**, but "pon-ton" is the correct pronunciation.

ponton bridge—A bridge built over pontons placed at intervals, parallel to the current of a stream, and connected by planks or other material to afford a temporary means of crossing. Pontons serve both to provide buoyancy and to connect the horizontal members of the bridge. The parts of such bridges are carried by forces anticipating a river crossing and can be assembled quickly.

U.S. Army photo

ponton bridge

ponton carriage—The truck or trailer on which a ponton is carried.

pontonnier—French term for the engineer responsible for pontons.

pontoon—See **ponton**.

Popular Front for the Liberation of Palestine (PFLP)—An organization of Palestinians, formed in 1968, that seeks the destruction of Israel and the establishment of a Palestinian state. It was expelled from the **Palestine Liberation Organization** in 1983.

port arms—Drill command for infantry soldiers to hold their rifles in a diagonal position in front of the chest.

portcullis—In a fort, a grille constructed of iron or wood that is suspended above the gateway and, in case of attack, can be lowered more quickly than the gate can be closed.

portfire—Another name for the artilleryman's LINSTOCK, a long, forked stick, which, before about 1800, held the SLOW-MATCH the gunner used to ignite the charge in an artillery piece.

port of embarkation—The port, sea or air, where military personnel board ships or air-craft for transport to a combat area or to an overseas assignment.

port-piece—A small breech-loading cannon designed to be fired at close range.

Poseidon (UGM-73)—An early class of U.S. nuclear submarines capable of launching ballistic missiles from underwater. The last Poseidon submarine was decommissioned in 1992. See also **submarine, guided-missile**.

position defense—The type of defense in which the bulk of a defending force is disposed in selected tactical localities where the decisive battle is to be fought. Principal reliance is placed on the ability of the forces in the defended localities to maintain their positions and to control the terrain between them. This defense can be successful only if a mobile reserve is available to add depth and to restore the battle position by counterattack.

Posse Comitatus Act—Legislation enacted in 1878 that denied search, seizure, or arrest powers to U.S. military personnel. It was amended in 1981 and 1991 to permit increased Defense Department support of drug interdiction and other law enforcement activity. The terrorist attacks of 11 September 2001 stimulated renewed discussion of greater military involvement in domestic law enforcement.

post—*n.* 1) A military base, including the grounds and buildings. 2) An assigned or designated position or station. *v.* 1) To assign to a military organization. 2) To assign an individual (usually a sentinel) to his or her designated position or station.

postern—In a fort or castle, a back or side entrance door or gate, where entrance or exit could be inconspicuous, including that of defenders mounting a surprise attack on a fortification's besiegers.

post exchange—A retail store at a U.S. post or installation, operated for military personnel and their dependents under the supervision of the commander. Sometimes called **PX**, also BASE EXCHANGE.

posttraumatic stress disorder — Many American combatants in the Vietnam War complained of a psychological disorder marked by emotional numbness, recurring nightmares, periodic panic attacks, and depression. The symptoms were similar to those associated with shell shock in World War I and "battle fatigue" in World War II. In 1980 the American Psychiatric Association labeled the symptoms "posttraumatic stress disorder."

posture, military—1) The disposition, strength, and condition of readiness of military forces as these factors affect capabilities. 2) The particular position of, or attitude assumed by, an organized force or nation from which it can act or react immediately, as in **posture of offense**, or from which it may be unable to react, as in **posture of unawareness**. 3) The state of preparedness of a defending force, as in HASTY DEFENSE, PREPARED DEFENSE, FORTIFIED DEFENSE.

pot de fer—From the French meaning "iron jug," it was a name given to early cannon because of their bottlelike shape. The earliest pot de fer is shown in an illuminated manuscript of 1326–27.

pott—A broad-brimmed helmet used by pikemen in the 17th century.

pounce—To attack an enemy aircraft from above, taking the enemy by surprise.

POW—See **prisoner of war**.

powder—A dry explosive or explosive propellant whose form may be very fine particles or larger pieces. See also **black powder, gunpowder, smokeless powder**.

powder monkey—In sailing vessels, the name given to a young boy who carried cartridges from the MAGAZINE to the guns.

power, military—The capability to use military force effectively in support of national policy.

power projection—The ability of a nation to apply some or all of the instruments of national power, including the military, outside its immediate area.

Praetorian Guard—Elite personal corps of guards of the Roman emperors, abolished by the Emperor Constantine in A.D. 312. The Praetorian Guard was in many instances the military force employed by rebellious leaders to overthrow the reigning emperor.

prawn—A 16th-century armored war cart. Guns protruding from the front were thought to resemble the feelers of a prawn.

prearranged fire—See **fire, prearranged**.

precedence—1) Priority in rank and preference in privileges, or in position in ceremonies, based on rank and length of service. In the U.S. armed forces, the order of precedence is Army, Navy, Air Force, Marines, Coast Guard. 2) An indication in the heading of a military message or dispatch that indicates its degree of priority or the speed with which the dispatch is to be handled. See also **message precedence**.

precision bombing—1) In a restricted sense, horizontal bombing done with the appropriate precision instruments and equipment so as to strike a target of comparatively small bulk or area. 2) In a general sense, any type of bombing against a small or restricted target. In sense 1, precision bombing is usually a strategic operation and is executed either to destroy a target with a minimum expenditure of force or to hit a target near other areas or installations not considered desirable to hit. When the term is used in sense 2, it is usually applied to tactical attacks by dive bombers or fighter-bombers against tanks or other identifiable targets.

precision fire—Artillery fire so conducted that the CENTER OF IMPACT is placed precisely on a target. This method is used for precise registration of a gun or battery on a BASE POINT or CHECKPOINT, as well as for the physical destruction of individual targets, such as immobilized tanks, pillboxes, or other structures to be destroyed by long-range fire. Precision fire *must* be observed.

Predator—A type of unmanned aerial reconnaissance vehicle that was employed effectively in Afghanistan in 2002. Videos taken by Predators and relayed by orbiting communications satellites provided near real-time imagery of targets and terrain. Some Predators were equipped with air-to-surface missiles and used against the Taliban. See also **unmanned aerial vehicle (UAV)**.

preemptive war/strike—An attack against a possible enemy to seize the military initiative and perhaps prevent any attack. An early example was Britain's action, in 1587, in attacking ships in Spanish harbors a year before the Spanish Armada sailed for England.

preparation fire—Fire delivered on a target preparatory to an assault.

prepared defense—See **defense**.

preposition—To place military personnel, equipment, or supplies at or near their point of planned use to reduce reaction time during the initial phase of a military operation.

present arms—1) A form of salute by a soldier armed with a rifle; the rifle is brought to a vertical position in front of the body, muzzle up, trigger side forward, and butt off the ground. 2) The command for a salute by a unit whether or not the troops are armed with rifles. See also **honors** and **salute**.

presidio—Spanish term for a garrisoned post. In the United States, specifically army posts in San Francisco and Monterey, Calif.

press gang—A military detail whose mission was to force men into military service, particularly but not exclusively into naval service. Press gangs are now obsolete, but until well into the 19th century they were a major source of manpower for armies and navies. See also **impressment**.

preventive war—A war initiated by a nation in the belief that military conflict, although possibly not imminent, is inevitable and that to delay action would involve greater risk to the national interest. See also **preemptive war/strike**.

prime—To insert a small amount of explosive, or "primer," in a weapon as a detonator for the main explosive charge. The primer is the highly explosive material, or a device containing a highly explosive material, that causes the detonation of a weapon's main explosive charge. An important early type was the Maynard tape primer, invented in 1845 by Dr. Edward Maynard, an American dentist. Consisting of small pellets of fulminate (usually of mercury) sealed between two narrow strips of paper, it greatly assisted in the conversion of FLINTLOCKS to percussion and was used in the U.S. government's 1855-model pistol-carbines, rifle-muskets, and rifles.

prime mover—A vehicle, including heavy construction equipment, possessing military characteristics, designed primarily for towing heavy, wheeled weapons, and frequently providing facilities for the transportation of the crew and ammunition.

priming pan—A shallow pan in the lock mechanism of a MATCHLOCK or FLINTLOCK gun that holds a small quantity of priming powder.

princeps—A Roman soldier who wore full armor, carried two javelins, and fought in the second line of the Roman legion. (*pl.*, **principes.**)

principle of war—A principle or axiom considered fundamental for conducting war successfully. Principles have been variously stated by Clausewitz, Jomini, Douhet, and other writers on the subject. Modern versions of the principles of war, as understood in the British and American armed forces, are based on a formulation by British theorist J. F. C. Fuller in 1920. The simple summations of these principles usually include the following: objective, offensive, unity of command, surprise, mass or concentration, economy of force, security, maneuver, and simplicity. The principles are interdependent, although some analysts subdivide these principles, call them by different names, or conceive of them in fewer or greater numbers.

priority—A category of precedence reserved for messages that require expeditious action by the addressee or provide essential information for the conduct of operations in progress when routine precedence will not suffice. See also **precedence**.

priority national intelligence objectives—A guide for intelligence collection, compiled annually by the intelligence community and endorsed by the National Security Council. The objectives are designed to be sufficiently specific to influence the allocation of resources but not so specific as to constitute collection requirements.

prisoner of war (POW)—A detained person as defined in Articles 4 and 5 of the 1949 Geneva Convention. Prisoners of war are persons who, while engaged in combat under orders of their government, are captured by the enemy. A prisoner of war may fall into one of the following categories: a) a member of the armed forces, organized militia, or volunteer corps; b) a person who accompanies the armed forces without being a member thereof; c) a member of a merchant ship or civilian aircraft crew; or d) an individual who, on the approach of the enemy, spontaneously takes up arms to resist the invader. A prisoner of war is entitled to the combatant's privilege of immunity from the municipal law of the capturing power for warlike acts that do not constitute breaches of the laws of war.

private—The basic, initial military rank of enlisted or conscripted soldiers in most armies (derived from the term "private soldier"). See also **private first class** and **seaman**.

privateer—1) A privately owned vessel commissioned by a nation at war to attack and seize enemy vessels as a means of destroying enemy commerce. Privateers operated from ancient times into the 19th century, when the practice was abolished by the 1856 Declaration of Paris. 2) Member of the crew of a privateer. See also **letter of marque and reprisal**.

private first class—In the U.S. Army, an enlisted man or woman ranking immediately above private and below corporal, corresponding to airman second class in the Air Force.

prize crew—A crew put aboard a captured vessel to take it into port.

prize law, naval—Law applied by a prize court, in accordance with custom and conventional international law, to determine the ownership of ships and goods captured at sea, and related questions. Naval prize law is determined by **prize courts.**

probable error—The error in range, deflection, or radius that a weapon may be expected to exceed as often as not. In other words, half of the rounds fired from a gun at a given, fixed setting will be between the target and a line drawn at the distance of the probable error from the target. The other half will be farther from the target than that line. Horizontal error of weapons making a nearly vertical approach to a target is usually described in terms of CIRCULAR ERROR PROBABLE.

procurement—In a broad sense, the process of acquiring personnel, matériel, services, or property from outside a military service by means authorized in pertinent laws, regula-

tions, or directives. Procurement is not the same as production. See also **production, military**.

production, military—The conversion of raw materials into weapons or equipment or components thereof through a series of manufacturing processes. It includes functions of production engineering, quality assurance, and the determination of resource requirements.

projectile—An object projected by an applied exterior force and continuing in motion by virtue of its own inertia (e.g., a rock, bullet, bomb, shell, or grenade). See also **ballistics**.

promote—1) To elevate a person to a higher rank. 2) To appoint a person to a more important position, especially one leading to or entailing an elevation in rank.

propaganda—Any information, ideas, doctrines, or special appeals in support of national objectives designed to influence the opinions, emotions, attitudes, or behavior of any specified group in order to benefit the sponsor, either directly or indirectly. Types of propaganda include the following: **black propaganda**—Propaganda that purports to emanate from a source other than the true one. **white propaganda**—Propaganda disseminated and acknowledged by the sponsor or by an accredited agency thereof. See also **armed propaganda** and **psychological warfare**.

propaganda bomb—See **bomb**.

propellant—An explosive charge for propelling a bullet, shell, or other projectile; also, a fuel, either solid or liquid, for propelling a rocket or missile.

proportionality—The concept that the magnitude and extent of any military retaliation should be governed in part by the act that precipitates it; that is, that a minor border violation does not justify a major military operation against the offender.

protected flank—See **flank**.

proving ground—An area where military weapons and equipment are tested to determine their capabilities for combat performance.

provost guards — A detail of soldiers assigned to guard duty, usually over prisoners, under a PROVOST MARSHAL.

provost marshal—1) A staff officer at command or subordinate level who advises on, and exercises supervision and inspection over, the maintenance of discipline, enforcement of security, and the confinement of prisoners. 2) In the U.S. Navy, an officer who has responsibility for prisoners who are to go before a court-martial.

Prowler (EA-6B) — A twin-turbojet, four-person, all-weather, electronic-warfare aircraft designed to operate from carriers. It carries a wide assortment of computer-controlled jamming equipment.

proximity fuze—A fuze for a projectile designed to activate the explosive charge when close to or at the target. Also called an **influence fuze**, the proximity fuze may incorporate photoelectric cells, radar devices, or other devices as activating elements. See also **variable-time fuze** and **fuze**.

psiloi—Lightly armed Greek foot soldiers. Psiloi generally came from the lower classes of society and many were mercenaries.

psychological warfare—The planned use of propaganda and other psychological actions having the primary purpose of influencing the opinions, emotions, attitudes, and behavior of hostile foreign groups in such a way as to support the achievement of national objectives. Psychological warfare may complement armed warfare and be pursued concurrently, or it may be used to exploit armed events before or after they occur.

PT boat—See **motor torpedo boat**.

Pueblo incident—On 23 January 1968, a U.S. Navy intelligence collection vessel, *Pueblo*, was boarded and captured by North Korean naval forces some 12 miles off the North Korean coast. One American sailor was killed in the seizure. The 83 survivors were interrogated, beaten, and forced to write confessions. The Americans were released 11 months later, after the United States apologized and acknowledged that the *Pueblo* had been in North Korean waters.

pulsejet—A jet engine that contains neither a compressor nor a turbine. Equipped with valves in front that open and close, it takes in air to create thrust in rapid periodic bursts rather than continuously. Pulsejets powered the German V-1 cruise missiles in World War II.

punji stake—A sharp stake concealed in high grass or foliage so as to gash the feet and legs of enemy soldiers. Although the term is Indian in origin and is associated with Britain's colonial wars in Asia, punji stakes were also employed in the Vietnam War.

pursuit—An offensive action designed to maintain pressure on, catch, cut off, or annihilate a withdrawing hostile force attempting to escape, usually after having suffered a defeat in battle.

puttee—1) A leather, canvas, or other cloth gaiter covering the lower leg. 2) A strip of cloth wound spirally around the leg from ankle to just below the knee, usually called "leggings" in the U.S. Army.

PX—See **post exchange**.

Pyrrhic victory—A victory in which the side that attains its immediate objective in a battle suffers such heavy losses that the victory is virtually worthless. The name derives from the battles at Heraclea (280 B.C.) and Asculum (279 B.C.), in which Pyrrhus, the king of Epirus, defeated the Romans but suffered extremely heavy losses.

PZKW—Basic designation (abbreviation of *Panzerkraftwagon*) for German tanks in World War II.

Q

Q clearance—A clearance granted by the U.S. Atomic Energy Commission (later the Department of Energy) to persons needing access to specially restricted data related to nuclear energy and particularly to nuclear weapons.

Q-ship—A decoy merchant ship with flotation cargo and hidden deck armament designed to lure a submarine to the surface where it can be disabled or sunk. Q-ships were used extensively by the British in World War I. Also called "decoy ship."

quadrant—An area, usually within an arc of about 90 degrees, assigned to a unit or an individual for surveillance, defense, or control.

quadrant, gunner's—A device to indicate the elevation of the barrel or tube of a cannon (the angle with respect to horizontal). See also **quadrant elevation.**

quadrant elevation—The angle between the level (horizontal) base of the trajectory of a cannon and the axis of the bore when laid. It is the algebraic sum of the elevation, angle of site, and complementary angle of site. See also **elevation** and **site, angle of.**

quadrireme—A galley of ancient times that had four banks of oars on each side. See also **bireme** and **trireme.**

Quaker gun—A wooden log cut and finished to resemble an artillery piece in order to deceive an enemy. Quaker guns were mounted on ships and in forts. In 1861, during the American Civil War, the Confederates mounted logs painted black in their fortifications at Centreville, Va. To Union observers, the Quaker guns resembled cannon, and the Confederate fortifications were judged much stronger than they actually were.

quarrel—A short, heavy arrow or bolt fired from a crossbow. See also **crossbow.**

quarter—*n.* 1) The sparing of an enemy's life. 2) An assigned or proper station; specifically, the position at which officers and crew aboard ship or in shore stations are posted during battle. Usually used in the plural. 3) Housing for military personnel, such as barracks. *v.* To provide shelter.

quarter bill—A list assigning officers and crew to stations during naval action.

quarter cannon or **quarto cannon**—See **cannon.**

quarterdeck—The name for the part of a ship's upper deck—generally the after part—that is reserved for the use of officers. From ancient times the quarterdeck was the station of the ship's commanding officer, from which he conducted official and ceremonial functions. On Roman galleys, an altar was located between the sternpost and the tiller; on this altar was placed a helmet symbolizing the emperor's authority, and sacrifices were offered before a battle. Roman seamen coming aboard a vessel faced aft and saluted the authority represented by altar and helmet. On a modern warship, the national ensign is flown at the stern when a ship is at anchor, and the custom of saluting the quarterdeck persists as a gesture of respect.

quarter guard—A British term for the contingent that guards a force or military post.

quartermaster—1) In the U.S. and other armies and the U.S. Marine Corps, an officer with responsibility for supplying food, clothing, and equipment. The **Quartermaster Corps**, which serves this function, is the equivalent of the Supply Corps in the Navy.

2) In the U.S. and other navies, a petty officer with responsibility for navigation of a naval vessel. Quartermaster derives from the Latin *quartarius magister*, master of the deck from which the Roman TRIREME was steered.

Quartermaster Corps—See **quartermaster**.

quartermaster general—1) In the Prussian army, a senior officer of the general staff. 2) In pre-20th-century British and American armies, the officer responsible for the supply of the army, under the army commander or commander in chief.

quarters—1) Lodgings or accommodations for military personnel. 2) The structure or shelter affording such lodgings or accommodations, or the place where they are located.

3) An assigned station on a warship. 4) The mustering of all sailors in a division aboard ship for inspection, usually held in the morning and followed by drill. See also **general quarters**.

quarters, winter—A camp set up by a campaigning army for housing during the months when snow and cold made fighting difficult or impossible. With some notable exceptions, this practice was followed from ancient times until the invention of the railroad and, especially, of all-weather roads for automobiles and trucks, which facilitated winter travel, making possible the provision of supplies to a mobile army.

quarter staff—A long wooden staff used in hand-to-hand combat before the introduction of gunpowder.

quasi war—A term that is sometimes applied to a state of tension between two countries and is marked by occasional armed clashes but without a formal declaration of war by either side. As such, it represents a step up from a COLD WAR, but is smaller in scope than a LIMITED WAR. The term has been applied to seizures of U.S. ships by France during the Napoleonic Wars and to repeated border clashes between India and Pakistan in the late 20th and early 21st centuries.

Quebec—Letter of NATO phonetic alphabet. See also **alphabet, phonetic**.

Queen—Letter of old phonetic alphabet. See also **alphabet, phonetic**.

Quicklook—A fixed-wing, electronic intelligence collection and radio direction-finding aircraft.

quick-match—See **match, quick**.

quick time—The standard marching cadence of foot soldiers on the march or at drill or in parade. In the U.S. Army this is 120 steps, each 30 inches in length, per minute.

quillon—The bar at the base of the handle of a sword or dagger that prevents the hand from sliding onto the blade.

quincunx—See **checkerboard formation**.

quinquireme—An ancient galley with five banks of oars. See also **bireme** and **trireme**.

quintain—In medieval times, a target, often a half-length figure designed to look like a Moor, with a shield in one hand and a lance or sword in the other. The quintain was set vertically on a post past which a horseman would ride, attempting to spear the quintain with his lance as he passed. Unless he hit it squarely the figure would rotate and hit him.

quoin (gunnery)—A block in the shape of a wedge placed under the breech of a gun to hold the barrel at a selected elevation, set by a QUADRANT.

R

rabinet—A kind of early cannon. Also given as ROBINET. See also **esmeril**.

radar—A term derived from RAdio Detection And Ranging. Radar was developed just before World War II by scientists on both sides of that conflict, although much credit belongs to British scientist Robert Watson-Watt. In 1940 the detection of approaching German bombers by a series of radar stations on the coast of England enabled British fighters and other defenses to meet the attacks and was a significant factor in the Battle of Britain.

radar countermeasures—See **electronic countermeasures**.

radar imagery—Imagery produced by recording radar waves reflected from a target.

radarman — U.S. Navy specialty rating, chief and first, second, and third class.

radar picket — A ship or an aircraft equipped with early warning radar, stationed on patrol at a distance from the force protected so as to extend the range of radar detection.

radeau—A large, unwieldy, bargelike gunboat, driven by sail, such as those constructed during the American Revolution for service on inland waters. One radeau, the British *Thunderer*, was part of Sir Guy Carleton's squadron that defeated the American squadron of Gen. Benedict Arnold at the Battle of Valcour Island on Lake Champlain in 1776. *Thunderer* mounted 14 guns and had a crew of 300 men.

radiation sickness — An illness resulting from excessive exposure to ionizing radiation. The earliest symptoms, nausea and diarrhea, may be followed by loss of hair and teeth, hemorrhage, inflammation of the mouth and throat, destruction of white blood cells, and general lethargy.

radioactive decay—The decrease in the radiation intensity of any radioactive substance over time.

U.S. Navy photo
The USS *Thomas*.

radar picket

radio deception—The employment of radio to deceive the enemy. Radio deception includes sending false dispatches, using deceptive headings, and employing enemy call signs. See also **electronic deception**.

radio electrician — U.S. Navy warrant officer.

radioman—U.S. Navy specialty rating, chief and first, second, and third class.

radio recognition—The determination by radio of the identity or the friendly or enemy character of an otherwise unidentified person or entity.

radio silence—A period during which all or certain radio equipment capable of transmission is kept inoperative. Radio silence may be imposed for all equipment for all frequencies or may apply to only certain types and designated frequency bands.

radius of action—The maximum distance a ship, an aircraft, or a vehicle can travel away from its base with normal combat load and return without refueling, allowing for all safety and operating factors.

raid—An operation, usually small-scale, involving a swift penetration of hostile territory to secure information, seize hostages, confuse the enemy, destroy his installations, or carry out some other specific task. It ends with a planned withdrawal upon completion of the assigned mission.

railhead—The section of a railroad where supplies are unloaded. Also, the position on a railroad line where military supplies, usually for front-line forces, are unloaded for delivery by other means.

raise a blockade—To cause a blockade to be broken up by dispersing the ships, one's own, voluntarily, or the enemy's, by force.

raise a siege—To abandon the attempt to take a place by besieging it, or to cause the attempt to take a place by siege to be abandoned.

rake—To sweep a target, especially the length of a ship or a column of troops, with gun or cannon fire; thus **raking fire**. See also **enfilade**.

raker—A gun so placed on a ship as to RAKE the enemy's ship.

rally—1) To achieve order and to halt or slow a retreat, particularly in a unit that has crumbled in the face of enemy attack. 2) To assemble a group or a force for some purpose.

rally point — A point at which, or over which, aircraft reassemble and re-form after making an attack.

ram—A device protruding from the bow of a warship with which to damage an enemy vessel. Rams were used on ancient and medieval vessels, particularly on rowed galleys, which came into direct contact with each other in battle. Rams were again introduced into the design of some ironclad warships in the late 19th century.

rammer—A device to push home shot or powder in a gunpowder weapon. Originally, it was used with muzzle-loading firearms and cannon to push the powder charge, the wad, and the shot to the base of the gun, at which point the weapon could be ignited and fired. The rammer was a wooden cylinder the size of the bore on the end of a stick or staff, which often was marked to indicate when the elements were in place. A hydraulic device is used with modern breech-loading cannon using SEPARATE-LOADING AMMUNITION to set the projectile and powder charge in the chamber before firing. See also **ramrod**.

rammerman—The member of a gun crew who handles the rammer; the rammerman also handles the sponge used to assure that all sparks in a tube are extinguished after firing.

ramp—See **apron**.

rampart—A wall or an earthen embankment comprising the main defensive work of a permanent or field fortification. A rampart is usually surmounted by a PARAPET.

ramrod—1) A rod, originally of wood and later of metal, that drove home the charge in a muzzle-loading firearm. Because they were long and thin, wooden ramrods tended to break frequently. 2) A metal rod used to clean the barrel of a firearm. In the early 18th century, according to some historians, Frederick William I of Prussia introduced an iron ramrod to replace the fragile wooden ramrod. The new implement permitted an increase in the average rate of fire of the Prussian infantry from two to at least three shots a minute. See also **rammer**.

randing (webbing) of gabions — See **gabion**.

random shot—A shot fired at no particular object.

range—1) The distance between any given point and an object or a target. 2) The maximum distance to which a ship, an aircraft, or a land vehicle can travel before requiring refueling. 3) The maximum distance (**maximum range**) a weapon may fire its projectile. The **maximum effective range** is the maximum distance at which a weapon may be expected to deliver its destructive charge with the accuracy needed to inflict prescribed damage. The **minimum range** is the shortest distance to which a gun can fire effectively from a given position. 4) An area equipped with targets for practice firing. Also called a "firing range."

range deviation—The distance that a projectile's point of impact is short of, or beyond, the target, measured along the gun-target line or along a line parallel to the gun-target line.

rangers—1) A rapidly deployable light infantry designed to conduct direct operations in cooperation with special operations units of other services. 2) The British equivalent of the ranger is the COMMANDO. The first such unit was Rogers's Rangers, a bush-fighting unit formed by the American colonist Robert Rogers to fight against the French and the Indians in North America during the French and Indian War. Rogers's Rangers were revived by Rogers during the American Revolution and fought on the British side as a Loyalist unit. Another such unit was the Queen's Rangers. Irregular light troops in 18th-century European armies, like the PANDOURs of Austria-Hungary, were equivalent to the North American rangers.

range table—A table showing the relationship between the range of a cannon and the elevation settings. See also **firing tables**.

ranging—1) The process of establishing the distance of a target. The term usually describes the process of adjusting weapon fire. Types of ranging can also include echo, intermittent, manual, navigational, explosive echo, optical, and radar. 2) Old term for disposing troops in proper order for an engagement, a march, or a maneuver.

rank—*n.* 1) The status of a person as determined by the grade to which he or she belongs. 2) The relative status of a person within a grade. 3) The grade to which a person belongs. 4) A line of persons, side by side. 5) *pl.* As in "in the ranks": in military service, especially, as an enlisted person. *v.* To be senior in rank to.

rank and file—A collective term for an army's soldiers, derived from military formations, which consist of ranks (lines of individuals) and files (columns of individuals).

rapid fire—Shots fired in rapid succession.

rapier—A long, slender sword. In the 16th and 17th centuries, a rapier had two cutting edges as well as a sharp point. In the 18th century, however, the rapier's utility for cutting was recognized as less important than its importance as a thrusting weapon, and rapiers no longer had cutting edges.

rappel—*n.* The beat of a drum to call soldiers to arms. *v.* To climb or descend a cliff or a wall with a rappelling rope.

Raptor (F-22)—The designated successor to the EAGLE (F-15) as the U.S. Air Force's air superiority fighter. It combines "stealth" design with state-of-the-art avionics and high maneuverability. The first flight of the Raptor prototype took place in September 1997.

rated—1) In the U.S. Navy, the term refers to an enlisted person above the grade of seaman first class. 2) In the U.S. Air Force and air contingents of the Navy and Marine Corps, it refers to a person, officer or enlisted, with a currently effective aeronautical rating, usually as a pilot.

rate of advance—The average distance in miles or kilometers that a force or unit engaged in combat moves forward in a given period of time, usually days or hours. The advance may be opposed or unopposed.

rate of attrition—See **attrition**.

rate of fire—The number of rounds fired per weapon per unit of time (usually a minute).

rate of march—The average distance in miles or kilometers that a unit travels in an administrative (as opposed to combat) movement in a given period of time, including all scheduled or unscheduled halts. It is usually expressed in miles or kilometers per hour.

rating—1) British term for a navy enlisted man. 2) In the U.S. Navy, "rating" is the equivalent for enlisted personnel, "rank" for officers.

rating badge—The device worn by naval enlisted personnel on the sleeve indicating the wearer's specialty and rating.

ratio—A mathematical or numerical comparison of two entities, as in **force ratio**, **strength ratio**, and **power ratio**.

ration—1) An allowance of provisions for one person for one day. 2) A monetary equivalent for such an allowance. 3) The provisions, especially food, in the amount of this allowance. 4) *pl.* Any provision issued in whatever amount, as in a "can of rations." *v.* 1) To provide food. 2) To limit the amount of provision of any kind of supply.

ravelin—An outwork located on the far side of the ditch or moat of a fortification between two BASTIONs, built in the shape of an arrowhead, facing away from the fortification, with an opening toward the wall. Ravelins served many defensive purposes, including the protection of the ground in front of the main fortification.

raven—See **corvus**.

raw troops — Inexperienced or untrained soldiers.

Razon—A 1,000-pound bomb with movable control surfaces in the tail adjusted by radio signals to control its range and azimuth, developed during World War II.

readiness, operational—The capability of a unit, ship, weapon system, or equipment to perform the missions or functions for which it is organized or designed.

ready reserve—The portion of the U.S. military reserve component that may be called to active duty immediately in an emergency declared by the Congress, proclaimed by the President, or otherwise authorized by law.

real time—A term applied to data or information that has been delayed only by the time required for electronic communication.

rear admiral—1) A naval rank between captain (or commodore when such rank is in use) and vice admiral. 2) An officer of that rank. See also **flag rank**.

rear area—An operational area immediately behind the FORWARD AREA containing administrative and service establishments, communications, and other support elements. The communications zone lies within this area. See also **area**.

rear echelon—That ECHELON of a headquarters or of a unit that is located farther from the front than the forward, or main, echelon. A rear echelon is not necessarily in an operational area.

rear guard—A security detachment that protects the rear of a column from hostile forces. During a withdrawal, it delays the enemy by offering armed resistance, destroying bridges, and blocking roads.

recce—(pronounced re-kee) Short for RECONNAISSANCE.

receiving ship—A vessel whose primary purpose is the processing of personnel rather than service at sea.

recognition signal—A signal sent out over airwaves or visibly displayed to enable a person, a body of troops, a ship, or an aircraft to be recognized by those acquainted with the signal.

recoil—*n.* 1) The backward movement of a gun when it is fired. Recoil is caused by the backward pressure of the propellant gases. 2) The distance that a gun or a part travels in this backward movement. 3) The force of this movement as exerted against something else, as in, "The recoil of the gun was felt throughout the plane." *v.* 1) To move rapidly backward, as a gun does upon being fired. 2) To move backward rapidly as a result of some other action, usually hostile.

recoilless rifle—A light, crew-served infantry cannon introduced in World War II, with holes in the breechblock that permit the propellant gases to escape. Recoilless rifles are light in weight (because they have no recoil mechanism) and have lower muzzle velocity and shorter range than other guns or howitzers of the same caliber (because part of the propellant gas pressure is used to prevent recoil). They are often used as antitank weapons, fired from either a ground mount or a vehicle.

U.S. Army photo

recoiless rifle

reconnaissance—A mission undertaken to obtain, by visual observation or other detection methods, information about the activities and resources of an enemy or a potential enemy, or to secure data concerning meteorological, hydrographic, or geographic characteristics of a particular area.

reconnaissance, aerial — Reconnaissance undertaken with an airplane or other aircraft to secure information about the enemy, or about the terrain or weather, by visual observation, aerial photography, or electronic methods.

reconnaissance, contact — Aerial reconnaissance used in a fast-changing tactical situation—as in an amphibious invasion or the isolation of a unit—in order to keep commanders informed, provide assistance where needed, and minimize the danger of shelling or bombing friendly forces.

reconnaissance in force—An offensive operation, larger and more deliberate than a RAID, designed to discover or test the enemy's strength or to obtain other information.

reconnaissance patrol — A small patrol used to gain information about the enemy, preferably without his knowledge.

reconnaissance vehicles — Armored vehicles, tracked or wheeled, designed primarily to scout or conduct reconnaissance.

reconnoiter—To make a reconnaissance of an area, a place, an airspace, or the like.

recovery—1) In air operations, the phase of a mission that involves the return of an aircraft to base. 2) In naval mine warfare, the salvage of a mine as nearly intact as possible in order to study it. 3) In amphibious reconnaissance, the extraction of a landed force or its linkup with friendly forces. 4) In evasion and recovery operations, the return of evaders to friendly control.

recruit—*n.* An enlisted person newly entered in military or naval service, especially such a person who has voluntarily entered. *v.* 1) To strengthen or fill up a military or naval organization or reserve with new personnel, especially through voluntary enlistment. 2) To induce a person to enter voluntarily into active military or naval service or into a reserve component.

redan—A simple type of field fortification consisting of two parapets joined to form a salient angle facing the enemy. Redans are open at the rear. Another name for the redan is FLÈCHE.

Red Army Faction—The Red Army Faction, also known as the "Baader-Meinhof Gang," was a group of German anarchistic leftist terrorists who were active between 1972 and 1998. Their activities included bombing, kidnapping, and aircraft hijacking. Evidence uncovered since German reunification has confirmed that the group received training and other support from East Germany. The group was formed when Andreas Baader, who had been imprisoned in 1968 for firebombing a Frankfurt department store, escaped in 1970 with the help of left-wing journalist Ulrike Meinhof. After terrorist training in the Middle East, they engaged in further bombings and kidnappings until they were captured in 1972. A few years later, both committed suicide.

redeployment—The transfer of a unit, an individual, or supplies deployed in one area to another area or to another location within the area or to the ZONE OF THE INTERIOR for the purpose of further employment.

Redeye (FIM-43) — A man-portable, shoulder-fired, air defense weapon developed for the U.S. Army and Marine Corps in the late 1950s. Called "Redeye" because of the infrared homing device in the nose, it is the predecessor of the STINGER.

red-hot shot—A cannonball heated to redness to be fired by a cannon at a ship, a wooden structure, or another combustible target.

redoubt—A small earthwork, generally outside a main fortification and usually covering the approaches to the areas most likely to be attacked.

reduced charge—A charge of powder for a cannon that is less than the maximum charge for which the weapon is designed. See also **semifixed ammunition**.

reentrant—An angular feature, either manmade, as a fortification, or natural, as a terrain feature (usually a DEFILE or draw) pointing inward or refused from the front.

reflex bow—See **bow**.

refuse a flank—The act of swinging back away from the enemy, usually in successive echelons (each facing front, toward the enemy), the elements of a wing or a flank of an army or other force, which refrains from fighting when the remainder of the battle line is engaged. The purpose is to freeze in place the opposing portion of the enemy force through the obvious threat of sending the refused flank or wing into action, while the other flank or wing is carrying out a decisive attack. See also **echelon**.

regiment—A military unit, particularly of infantry, cavalry, or artillery, that can be either administrative or operational. The origin of the modern regiment may be found in the permanent (usually regional) infantry formations established by French monarchs in the later Middle Ages. Since the late 18th century a regiment, commanded by a colonel, has usually been an operational unit of two or more battalions, and has functioned most often as a component of a division. In the modern U.S. Army, until the mid-1960s, infantry regiments consisted of three battalions, in strengths varying from about 1,500 to 3,000 troops. Artillery regiments (until World War II) consisted of two or three battalions of three gun batteries each, about 1,000 to 1,500 troops, and 24 to 36 guns. In World War I the standard U.S. division consisted of two infantry brigades of two regiments each, and an artillery brigade of one medium and two light regiments. In World War II the standard U.S. division consisted of three infantry regiments and four artillery battalions (three light and one medium). In the early 20th century, the British army adopted a regimental system, with the regiment only an administrative unit, located regionally, and separate battalions being combined into brigades, which in turn were combined into divisions. See also **battalion, brigade, division**.

regimental combat team — See **combat team, regimental**.

regimental landing team—A U.S. task organization for an amphibious landing, comprising a Marine or Army infantry regiment reinforced by those elements required by its combat function ashore, such as engineers and communications personnel.

regimentals—1) The military uniform and insignia worn by a certain regiment. 2) In general, dress or semidress military uniform.

registration—Also known as **registration fire**, precision artillery fire at a registration point or checkpoint to determine the exact settings for range and deflection in order to place the center of impact of fire on the target. From these data the settings for other guns can be calculated so that the centers of impact of their fire can be trained on these points, and, by transfer and calculations from a map or chart, on nearby targets.

regular Army (Navy, Air Force, Marine Corps, Coast Guard) — In the United States, the portion of the armed services that is permanently on active duty in the armed forces, not including the reserve elements.

reinforce—To strengthen by the addition of units, personnel, ships, aircraft, or military equipment.

Reiter—A German mercenary heavy cavalryman of the 16th and 17th centuries, who usually wore black armor and accoutrements and was called *Schwarzreiter*—black rider— or *Reiter* for short. *Reiters* were usually armed with a brace of WHEELLOCK PISTOLS, although originally they were armed with a boar spear and a sword. The early *Reiters* wore CHAIN MAIL; this was replaced by a breastplate, an open helmet, and heavy, thigh-length leather boots. In combat, the *Reiters* advanced at a slow trot in a line of small, dense columns, each several ranks deep, and fired their pistols one rank at a time, in a maneuver called a CARACOLE. The reiters were the cavalry equivalent of the LANDSKNECHT.

relief—1) Replacement of an individual or a unit at a duty post. 2) Inequalities in the height of land features, represented on maps by contours or other means.

relief in place — A combat operation in which all or part of a unit is replaced in a combat area by an incoming unit, to which the combat responsibilities and assigned zone of operations of the replaced elements are transferred. The replaced elements are withdrawn before the incoming unit resumes operations.

relieve—1) To rescue or reestablish contact with a force that is besieged or cut off by the enemy. 2) To take the place of a person or unit at a duty station or post.

remote control—Control from a distance over the operation of an aircraft, a gun, or other piece of equipment, especially using electrical or electronic apparatus.

remotely piloted vehicle (RPV)—See **unmanned aerial vehicle (UAV)**.

remount—A horse that replaces another in a mounted (cavalry or horse-drawn) unit or that is available as such replacement. Generally applied to all new horses delivered to a unit; mounted units have throughout history carried extra horses with them when moving from one area to another.

rendezvous—*n.* 1) A prearranged meeting at a given time and place, from which to begin an action or phase of operation, or to which to return after an operation. 2) A place, a point, or a spot on the ground, on the sea, or in the air where such a meeting occurs, or is planned to occur; a rendezvous point. *v.* To meet at an appointed time and place. See also **rally point**.

repeating firearm—A firearm that may be fired several times without having to be reloaded.

replacement—An individual, a unit, or an item of equipment, or a group of individuals, units, or items of equipment, assigned to a combat unit or force to bring it to or toward its authorized strength after it has incurred losses of personnel or equipment or both.

report—Any transmission or presentation of data or information, whether in oral, tabular, graphic, narrative, questionnaire, punch-card, or other form, regardless of the method of transmission. There can be many kinds of reports: periodic, after-action, morning (daily, by company-size units), and so on.

reprisal—1) In international law, the resorting to force short of war to redress a grievance. 2) In war, a retaliatory act, usually of the same kind or degree as that committed by the enemy.

requirement, operational — Whatever is needed in order for a unit or a force to be able to carry out the mission assigned to it as part of a tactical concept.

requisition—*n.* An authoritative demand or request, especially for personnel, supplies, or services authorized but not made available without specific request. *v.* 1) To make such a demand or request. 2) To demand or require services from an invaded or conquered nation or region.

reserve—1) The portion of a force that is held out of combat in anticipation of its being used later to influence the outcome of a battle, an engagement, or an operation. Such a reserve held out by an army is called the **army reserve** (or the **army's reserve**); that held out by a corps is the **corps reserve**, and so forth. 2) A military organization of people not on active duty but holding ratings or commissions and available to be called to active duty when needed. Members of a reserve may attend regular training meetings and serve periodically for short periods of active duty. 3) A member of such an organization.

reserve army—1) A military force organized or designated as an army not committed to battle. 2) An army held in reserve that is a component of a theater or army group. 3) A force organized and active in the interior of a nation from which replacements or reserves can be sent to the support of forces engaged in combat, as in Germany in World War II.

reserve components — Nonregular military forces of the nature of a MILITIA, available to augment the regular forces in time of war or emergency. In the United States the reserve components include the Army National Guard, Army Reserve (formerly the Army Reserve Corps), Naval Reserve, Air National Guard, and Marine Corps Reserve.

Reserve Corps—Former designation of one of the principal RESERVE COMPONENTS of the U.S. Army.

reserve, general—See **general reserve**.

reserves, floating—See **floating reserves**.

reservist—A member of a military reserve component, in contradistinction to a "regular."

resistance movement — An organized effort by some portion of the civil population of a country or a region to resist the legally established government or an occupying power, and, at a minimum, to disrupt civil order and stability or, at a maximum, overthrow or displace the legal authority.

rest—A device on which to place a hand weapon for carrying or for aiming. On medieval armor, a rest for bearing the weight of the lance was found on the side of a breastplate. The early MATCHLOCK MUSKET, because of its weight and awkwardness, required a rest in the form of a stick with a fork or curved top to steady it on the ground when being fired.

restricted—1) Limited in access or use to a specified class of people. 2) A former security classification for the protection of information, documents, or material. In U.S. military security classifications, the term was used for material not sensitive enough to require a classification of "confidential" (the lowest grade of classification) or "secret."

restricted data—All data concerning a) the design, manufacture, or use of nuclear weapons; b) the production of special nuclear material; or c) the use of special nuclear material in the production of energy, but not including data declassified or removed from the restricted data category.

resupply—1) To furnish a force, an organization, or the like with supplies, or to replenish supplies or equipment that have been consumed, lost, destroyed, or damaged. 2) To supply by air a force, unit, or the like that is cut off from its normal supply force.

retire—*n.* Movement to the rear by a force that is not engaged to avoid contact with a hostile force that is approaching from the front or flank. *v.* 1) To make such a movement. 2) To leave active duty after a certain number of years of service, or to change status from active duty to civil or reserve status.

retirement—1) A retrograde movement in which a force out of contact moves away from the enemy. 2) The status of a military person who has retired.

retreat—*n.* 1) A term imprecisely used for a RETROGRADE MOVEMENT of a force in the face of an enemy attack or threatened attack. 2) The signal to a force to make such a movement. 3) A bugle call played at the lowering of the colors at sunset. *v.* To move to the rear in the face of an enemy attack or threatened attack.

retrograde movement—A movement of a command to the rear, or away from the enemy. It may be forced or voluntary. Types of retrograde movement include WITHDRAWAL, RETIREMENT, and DELAY or DELAYING ACTION. The term RETREAT is sometimes used as synonymous with "retrograde movement."

reveille—1) A signal, usually a bugle call or other music, for rousing personnel at a military post at the start of day. 2) The bugle call sounded for this purpose. 3) A ceremony held in early morning, usually attended by all personnel.

reverse slope—The slope of a terrain feature that falls away from the enemy, that is, the back slope of a hill from the point of view of one who faces the hill.

revetment—Reinforcement of an earthern wall with hard material (wood, sandbags, or concrete). It usually applies to the side of a trench but can apply to any earthen wall for the purpose of protecting aircraft, gun emplacements, storage areas, or other material or places against bombing, shelling, or strafing attacks. The term is sometimes applied to a barricade against explosives. Types of revetment include **demi, fascine**, GABION, **leaning, rectangular**, and **solid**.

review—1) A formal inspection of a military unit or organization, during which the unit marches in parade formation past the inspecting or reviewing official or party. 2) A ceremony to honor a person or persons or to honor an event, to include a march past the person or persons being honored.

revolt—1) The use of military force in a violent effort to overthrow a constituted government or authority. In such a conflict the opposing forces are often classified as "rebels" (those endeavoring to overthrow the government) and "loyalists" (government forces). If the governing authority is indigenous, this is a common form of CIVIL WAR. 2) The acts undertaken by a rebel or a group of rebels who attempt to bring about a REVOLUTION.

revolution—A successful revolt.

Revolutionary Armed Forces of Colombia (FARC)—A guerrilla force dedicated to creating a Marxist-Leninist revolution in Colombia. FARC is considered to be the best-equipped and most effective guerrilla group in South America, and has engaged in numerous acts of terrorism, including bombings and kidnappings.

revolver—A handgun with a rotating cylinder in which several rounds of ammunition can be placed, each in its separate chamber. As each round is fired, the next automatically moves into line with the barrel.

ribaud—A crossbow mounted on a cart. Some ribauds had steel arms and fired 2-foot iron bolts 500 yards.

ricochet—To skip, bounce, or fly off at an angle after striking an object or surface. Usually applied to a projectile from firearms or cannon.

ricochet fire—A form of antipersonnel artillery fire, so directed that the projectiles (equipped with delay fuze) will ricochet off the ground, then explode in the air to provide a wider lethal area of shell fragmentation than would result from point detonation.

rifle—*n.* A gunpowder weapon with spiral grooves cut into the surface of its bore so that the projectile will leave the weapon with a spinning motion that provides greater accuracy and stability to its flight. Although modern cannon and small handguns usually have rifled barrels, the term "rifle" is most commonly used in reference to a firearm fired from the shoulder. Such rifles were originally developed for hunting in Europe and were not rapidly adopted as military firearms because it took more time and expense to produce such precision weapons (in comparison with the smoothbore musket) and it took longer to load them than to load the musket. A typical late-20th-century military rifle is a magazine-fed, gas-operated, air-cooled, semiautomatic, shoulder-type weapon designed for semiautomatic fire but convertible to auto-

matic fire. It usually fires a round between 5.5mm and 7.62mm (about .22 to .30 caliber in inches). *v.* To cut these spiral grooves in a gun barrel.

rifle grenade—See **grenade**.

rifleman—A man armed with a rifle. In the American Revolution, the Continental Congress called for the raising of six companies of expert riflemen from Pennsylvania and two each from Maryland and Virginia. Riflemen served as scouts or sharpshooters, and for similar special or elite duties, since the musket continued to be the weapon of the majority of troops.

rifle-musket—The standard infantry small-arm weapon in the mid-19th century, after the introduction of the conoidal bullet revolutionized weapons and infantry combat.

rifle pit—A hole or a short trench with a mound of earth in front of it to protect one or two soldiers. The connection of several rifle pits by digging between them creates a trench or trench line. See also **foxhole**.

right face—*n.* 1) A 90-degree change of stationary position to the right while at attention. 2) The command to make this change. *v.* 1) To execute such a change in position. 2) In the imperative, the command to do it. See also **face**.

rimfire—1) Of a cartridge, having the primer in the rim of the base. 2) Of a firearm, using rimfire cartridges.

riposte—A blow or attack in response to a hostile blow or attack.

riverine area—An inland or coastal area comprising both land and water, characterized by limited land lines of communication and extensive water routes for surface transportation and communications.

riverine operations—Military operations conducted by forces organized to exploit and to cope with the unique characteristics of a riverine area. Joint riverine operations combine land, naval, and air operations, as appropriate to the nature of the specific riverine area. The operations on the rivers in the West in the American Civil War were classic riverine operations.

road space—The length of roadway allocated to or actually occupied by a column of troops or vehicles on a route, expressed in miles or kilometers.

robinet—See **rabinet**.

rocket—A device that is propelled by the ejection of gases or other material formed by chemical action within the device itself. Although the origin of rockets is obscure, it seems likely that they were developed in the 13th century in China, where the first gunpowder weapons may have been rockets. Various methods of propulsion and various designs were tried in succeeding centuries, but it was not until the 18th century that rockets were used seriously as weapons. Hyder Ali and his son, Tipu Sahib, fighting the British in India, first used rockets with impressive combat results. With the invention of the CONGREVE ROCKET, at the beginning of the 19th century, rocket corps appeared in European armies. Most rockets were propelled by black powder, although other propellants were experimented with, until Robert H. Goddard successfully launched the first liquid-propellant rocket in 1926. Since then, many propellants, solid and liquid, have been developed; and rockets have been developed for many purposes, from the hand-held bazooka of World War II to the interstellar vehicles of the late 20th and early 21st centuries.

rocket launcher—A device for launching rockets. Rocket launchers use rails, posts, tubes, or other devices to carry and guide the rocket. Rocket launchers can be wheel-mounted, motorized, aircraft mounted, and, in the case of the bazooka, designed to be carried and fired by an individual.

"Rocks and Shoals"—Navy slang for the ARTICLES FOR THE GOVERNMENT OF THE NAVY, because of the consequences provided therein for those who "suffered any vessel of the Navy to be stranded upon rocks and shoals. . . ."

"Roger"—A signal communications transmission indicator, signifying understanding or agreement with the other party's previous transmission. See also **"Affirmative."**

2) Letter of the old phonetic alphabet. See also **alphabet, phonetic**.

"rogue states"—So-called outlaw nations as defined by the U.S. State Department. The term is perhaps derived from "rogue elephant," an animal so vicious as to be expelled from the herd. At various times, Libya, Iran, Iraq, and North Korea have been characterized as rogue states. Also called "pariah states."

rolling airframe missile (RAM) — A joint venture between the United States and Germany, the RAM is designed as a high-firepower defense system against antiship missiles. It uses the infrared seeking of the STINGER missile and carries a 25-pound warhead.

rolling barrage—See **barrage**.

rolling fire—Musket fire by a line of soldiers in quick succession from one end of the line to the other.

Rolling Thunder, Operation — The U.S. bombing campaign against selected targets in North Vietnam. The raids began in March 1965 to persuade the North Vietnamese to cease their support of the war in the south. Initially limited to targets south of the 20th parallel, the campaign expanded to include much of the North Vietnamese economic infrastructure.

Romeo—Letter of NATO phonetic alphabet. See also **alphabet, phonetic**.

romper—In World War II terminology, a ship that chose to leave a protected convoy in the belief that its speed would enable it to outrun any U-boat.

rotating band (bouralet)—The projecting ring or ridge on the body of an artillery projectile that is forced into the grooves of the cannon bore and causes it to rotate.

round—A single bullet, shell, missile, or other projectile, including its propelling charge (and its case, in fixed or semifixed ammunition). Originally, a general discharge of firearms by a body of troops, all of whom fired their weapons once. A round of cartridges was a supply giving one cartridge to each soldier. See also **ammunition**.

round ship—A broad-beamed cargo ship of the pregunpowder era, called on to serve as a warship during time of war.

rout—*n.* 1) The disorderly and hasty departure of a defeated force from the combat area. 2) A defeat so massive that the defeated force flees in disorder. *v.* To inflict an overwhelming defeat that causes the enemy to flee in disarray.

route—The prescribed course to be traveled from a specific point of origin to a specific destination.

route march—An organized movement of troops in column by road or cross-country. The troops move in **route order,** or **route step**—that is, they are not required to march in cadence nor, generally, in silence, and are permitted to carry their weapons at will, provided safety precautions are strictly observed. Route marches are usually conducted away from the immediate presence of the enemy; their purpose generally is to assemble the elements of a command expeditiously while conserving the comfort of the troops.

Royal Military College, Sandhurst—A British military college founded in 1801 to train officers for the infantry and cavalry.

ruffle—A continuous drumbeat on a military drum. Ruffles are commonly heard combined with a bugle fanfare, in a combination known as **ruffles and flourishes,** played to announce the arrival of an important person, notably the President of the United States.

rules of engagement—Directives promulgated by the U.S. Department of Defense which delineate the circumstances and limitations under which U.S. forces will initiate or continue combat engagement with other forces encountered.

rules of war—See **laws of war** and **jus belli**.

ruse de guerre—Strategem of war intended to mislead or deceive an enemy.

S

S-3—See **Viking**.

SA-7—A Russian-made, man-portable, surface-to-air missile capable of hitting aircraft up to an altitude of 13,000 feet.

saber or **sabre** — A sword with a single-edged, slightly curved blade, with a curved hand guard, designed for cutting rather than thrusting; it was the standard horse cavalry weapon. Also worn by most officers, up to the middle of the 20th century, for ceremonial purposes.

sabot—In artillery, 1) a support or container around a projectile that permits it to be fired in a gun of larger caliber. 2) An aluminum case or jacket fitting around the steel core of certain armor-piercing ammunition. In sense 1, the sabot is of a size to fill the larger bore and falls from the projectile in flight. The sabot may sometimes incorporate a rocket motor for giving additional velocity or range to the projectile. Originally borrowed (c. 1600) from the French term for a wooden shoe, the word "sabot" has been in military use since about 1850.

sabotage—*n.* An act with an intent a) to injure, interfere with, or obstruct the national defense of a country by willfully injuring or destroying any national defense or war material, premises, or utilities, or b) to disrupt normal processes or procedures. *v.* To commit such an act.

sabretache—A pouch or case made of leather, worn by cavalrymen, suspended from the saber belt.

saddler—One who makes, repairs, or sells saddles. Every mounted company-size unit of the U.S. Army before World War II had a saddler as a military specialist.

safe conduct—A guarantee of passage without hindrance through a military or combat zone, honored by one or both belligerents.

safeguard—A means of protection, specifically, a) a convoy or an escort; b) a pass, safe conduct; c) a precautionary measure or stipulation; d) a technical contrivance to prevent accident.

Safeguard—An early missile defense system designed to protect Washington, D.C., and Grand Forks Air Force Base, N.D. Under the terms of SALT I, it was deactivated on 1 October 1975, one day after it had become operational.

safe house (intelligence) — Innocuous-appearing premises established by an intelligence organization as a secure base for its clandestine operations.

sagittarius—A Roman bowman, named for his weapon, the *sagitta*, or arrow. See also **veles**.

sailor—An enlisted man or woman serving in a navy. Also called a SEAMAN.

saker—A small cannon used in the 16th century that fired a ball weighing about 3.5 pounds. The name may derive from a species of falcon commonly called "saker" (Latin *falco, sacrer*). See also **cannon**.

salient—1) A portion of a battle line that projects into enemy-held territory. 2) A part of a fortification that projects outward toward enemy territory.

sally—A sudden charge of forces from a defended position for the purpose of attacking the enemy, especially an attack against an investing force by besieged troops. An opening in a fortification through which troops can issue is a **sally port**. Such gates are often in the rear of the fortification.

sally port—See **sally**.

salted weapon—A nuclear weapon that has, in addition to its normal components, a capability to capture neutrons at the time of the explosion and produce radiation in excess of the usual radioactive debris.

salute—1) In a general sense, a greeting or a sign of courtesy passed between parties, as by gesturing with the hand, firing a cannon, dipping a flag, or dipping an aircraft wing. 2) Among military personnel, an outward sign, mark, or act of courtesy, respect, or honor given in a specific and prescribed manner, specifically, the hand salute.

salvage—*n.* 1) Property that has some value in excess of its basic material content but is in such poor condition that there is no reasonable prospect of its being used for any purpose and its repair or rehabilitation is impracticable. 2) The recovery of disabled ships from underwater or the surface. 3) The saving or rescuing of condemned, discarded, or abandoned property, and of materials contained therein for reuse, refabrication, and scrapping. *v.* To save or rescue such material.

salvo—1) In naval gunfire, a method of fire in which a number of weapons are fired at the same target simultaneously. 2) In close air support/air interdiction operations, a method of delivery in which all ordnance of a specific type is discharged simultaneously. 3) In artillery fire, the discharge of all pieces in a battery or larger unit in quick sequence with a uniform time interval between rounds. See also **volley**.

SAM—See **missile, surface-to-air**.

Sam Browne belt—A uniform belt with a diagonal strap from the left waist across the right shoulder, worn with the dress uniform by officers of the U.S. and British armies from World War I until World War II. The belt was used by American officers when in field or parade uniform to carry personal weapons, such as saber or pistol, cartridge box, canteen, and first aid kit. The belt originated as a sword belt, invented by British Gen. Sir Samuel James Browne in the late 19th century, to help carry the weight of his sword, which he could not support because he had lost his left arm.

Sam-D—An army air defense surface-to-air missile system designed to replace the Nike Hercules and HAWK systems.

samurai—The military aristocracy of feudal Japan and its warrior members. Many of the practices and formalities of the samurai survived into World War II, including the ritual death that many Japanese officers chose over surrender.

sanctuary—1) A place of refuge for dissidents or fighters. In the Middle Ages, churches and monasteries were regarded as sanctuaries beyond the reach of civil authorities. 2) A remote, inaccessible region used as a base of operations by insurgents.

Sandinistas—A Marxist political-military movement in Nicaragua that took power in 1979 and attempted to create a Marxist state. It had close ties to Cuba and to the POPULAR FRONT FOR THE LIBERATION OF PALESTINE. The Sandinistas were defeated in elections held in 1990 but remained a strong political force.

sanitize (intelligence)—To modify a report or other document in such a manner as to prevent identification of its source or of the means by which it was acquired.

sap—1) A trench, usually in the form of a zigzag, dug toward an enemy's defensive position. A **single sap** is a trench from which the dirt is thrown to one side for added protection. In a **double sap** the dirt is used to form PARAPETs on both sides. If built under fire, two GABIONs are used side by side for protection, pushed forward as the work advances, and the sap is called a **flying sap**. If the gabion is on a roller, it is called a **sap roller.** 2) A tunnel dug under an enemy position in order to place a mine and destroy the fortification. See also **approaches**.

sapper or **sapeur**—One who builds a SAP, or, more commonly, in the British army, a military engineer.

sap roller—See **sap**.

sarissa—A spear, introduced by Philip of Macedon and used by the Macedonian heavy infantry and cavalry during the 3rd and 4th centuries B.C. Under Philip and Alexander, sarissas were 13 to 14 feet long; later, they were as long as 20 feet. The men in the first lines of a PHALANX—Polybius says the first five ranks—held their sarissas pointing forward, so that an enemy faced a wall bristling with sharp-pointed weapons. Spearmen in the rear ranks held their sarissas upright, to help ward off missiles.

saturation bombing—Intense bombing intended to leave no place in a given area free from destructive effects.

saucissons or **saucisses**—Large FASCINES.

scabbard—A sheath for a sword, dagger, or other cut or thrust weapon.

scalade—Climbing over a fortified wall or rampart with the help of ladders, especially during an attack.

scale—v. To climb a wall, a cliff, or other obstruction. n. The ratio of distance represented on a map to actual distances.

scale armor—See **armor** and **lamellar armor**.

scarp—The side of a ditch or a moat that is next to the wall.

scatterable mines—Mines constructed so that they can be laid quickly and in large numbers by artillery fire, by a mechanical minelayer, or even by airdrop. Because of their number and their unconcealed but unexpected appearance along enemy movements routes, they are difficult for troops to avoid, and they delay troop movements until they are cleared. In particular, they make all night movements hazardous. Scatterable mines are one of the most important developments in post–World War II weapons.

scatter bomb—Any bomb, such as a fragmentation bomb, that scatters its effect over a wide area. However, the term is usually applied to bombs that propel submunitions, small bombs or mines that are carried inside the larger bomb.

scattered drop—A drop of either ordnance or personnel in a pattern that was not intended.

scenario—A narrative description of an event or events—actual or hypothetical—usually as an element of an analysis of the event or of matters related to the event. Often the basis for analysis by means of a COMBAT MODEL.

scheduled fire—Prearranged artillery fire, particularly used during PREPARATION FIRES, that provides for a series of artillery concentrations by batteries, battalions, or several battalions on different targets at times related to the attack plans of the supported maneuver elements. See also **fire, prearranged**.

schiltron—Medieval Scottish formation of PIKEMEN, similar to a PHALANX.

Schwarzreiter—See **Reiter**.

Schwerpunkt—A German term (literally, "point of strength") referring to that geographical point on a battlefield at which maximum force is employed to achieve an objective; an expression of the combination of the principles of objective, offensive, and mass (or concentration).

scimitar—A Middle Eastern saber with a strongly curved blade and a single cutting edge on the outside. The scimitar was generally used by Muslim soldiers.

scissoring—A flight technique by escort fighters in which their patterns continually crisscross each other above or below the formation they are escorting.

scorched-earth policy — The practice of devastating the infrastructure and economic resources of an area soon to be left to an advancing enemy. Although the practice is as old as warfare itself, the term first came into use in the mid-20th century.

scorpion—An ancient catapult similar to the ONAGER.

scout—*n.* A person, a unit, a ship, or an aircraft sent out from an armed force, sometimes in secret, to ascertain what lies ahead in the way of terrain or enemy forces. *v.* To search for information about the enemy or the land ahead; to make a RECONNAISSANCE.

scouting force—A contingent of naval vessels, usually small and fast, whose function is to search ahead of and around the main body to obtain information about the enemy.

scramasax—A broad, double-edged dagger about 18 inches long, used by medieval Franks and Saxons.

scramble—*v.* Of aircraft, to take off as quickly as possible, generally to intercept approaching hostile aircraft. *n.* The whole action involved in getting interceptor aircraft into the air in the shortest time possible.

screen—*n.* Anything used to protect or shield a country or friendly force from hostile attack, interference, or observation. *v.* To use forces to protect other forces or to prevent an enemy from gaining information about forces or activities.

screw-gun—A British artillery piece, usually a HOWITZER for mountain warfare, designed to be transported in separate pieces by pack animals. Because the barrel weight of a cannon even as small as 3-inch caliber was too great for one pack mule or horse, the howitzer was made so that the barrel came in two parts that could be screwed together when the piece was assembled. The British 3.7-inch screw-gun was used in mountain warfare in World War II.

"scrub"—1) A slang expression meaning to cancel a plan, a mission, or an operation, especially after a long wait. 2) To wash a person out, dismiss him or her from training.

Scud—NATO code name for a Soviet-designed ballistic missile that was made available to several Arab states in modified form. The original Scud, descended from the German V-2, carried a 2,000-pound conventional warhead and had a range of about 120 miles.

scuppers—Drains on a ship's deck that carry off accumulations of water.

scutatus—A Byzantine heavy infantryman, known as scutatus from the shield (SCUTUM), that he carried. Scutati wore helmets, MAIL shirts, gauntlets, greaves (or knee-length boots), and surcoats. They carried a lance, a shield, a sword, and sometimes an ax. Uniform appearance was achieved by color of surcoat, helmet tuft, and shield.

scuttle—To deliberately sink a ship to avoid its falling into enemy hands.

"scuttlebutt"—Originally a cask of fresh water, later a water cooler, used by the crew of a ship for drinking. Because the crew gathered around the scuttlebutt and talked, the term came to be a slang expression meaning "unofficial reports and rumors."

scutum—A large, rectangular, curved Roman shield, made of wood, leather-covered and iron-edged, and often having in the middle a knob with which the LEGIONARY was expert in pushing and striking his enemy.

Seabee—Member of a naval construction battalion (CB). Established in World War II, such battalions were composed of men with expertise in various construction specialties, in order to build naval bases on islands in the Pacific.

seaborne—Carried on a ship or ships. Of an air assault, launched from a ship or ships.

Sea Cobra (AH-1J)—A single-rotor, light attack helicopter armed with a variety of machine guns, rockets, and antitank missiles.

sea echelon—In an amphibious operation, the portion of the assault fleet that remains outside the immediate landing area but on call.

U.S. Department of Defense photo

Scud

sea frontier—In the U.S. Navy, the command of a coastal frontier, including the coastal zone and adjacent sea areas.

Sea King (H-3)—A single-rotor, medium-lift helicopter used for air/sea rescue and cargo transport in support of carrier operations. Some versions are equipped for antisubmarine operations.

Sea Knight (H-46)—A twin-rotor, medium-lift helicopter for cargo and personnel transport.

SEAL team (sea-air-land team) — A U.S. Navy force organized, trained, and equipped to conduct special operations in maritime and riverine environments.

sea lord—One of six high-ranking British naval officers who served on, or were commissioners or members of, the 10-man BOARD OF ADMIRALTY. The First Sea Lord was the chief of the naval staff and the senior officer of the Royal Navy. The Second Sea Lord was chief of naval personnel. The Third Sea Lord, the controller, was responsible for equipment, ordnance, and research. The Fourth Sea Lord was concerned with supplies and transport. The Fifth Sea Lord was responsible for naval aviation. The Sixth Sea Lord was the vice chief of the naval staff.

seaman—In the U.S. Navy, a nonrated enlisted man. The lowest grade is the apprentice seaman, or seaman third class. The next two grades are seaman second class and seaman first class, above which is the lowest grade of petty officer. See also **private**.

seaman's branch—In the U.S. Navy, sailors working on and above decks, as boatswain's mates, fire controlmen, gunner's mates, quartermasters, signalmen, torpedoman's mates, turret captains, minemen, and coxswains. Men with these ratings formerly wore their rating badges on their right sleeves. All other ratings wore their badges on their left sleeves. See also **"black gang."**

sea pay—A special pay allowance received by personnel assigned to ships.

seapower—1) The power that arises from a nation's ability to put ships to sea and to exercise control over significant sea and ocean areas. 2) An instance of this power as it exists in a particular nation, especially with reference to its adaptation to national policy and naval support thereof.

sear—The part of the lockwork of a firearm that engages the hammer or striker to hold it in a cocked position.

search and destroy—A military operation designed to destroy enemy formations and facilities but not to hold ground.

search and rescue—The use of aircraft, surface craft, submarines, and other special equipment in the search for or rescue of personnel.

Sea Sprite (H-2)—A single-rotor, light helicopter used for air/sea rescue, cargo transport, and antisubmarine operations.

Sea Stallion (CH-53) — A single-rotor, heavy-lift helicopter used for both cargo and personnel, with a range of approximately 650 miles. A version equipped for mine countermeasures is designated RH-53.

Sikorsky Aircraft photo

Sea Stallion

sea supremacy—The degree of superiority at sea that renders an opposing force incapable of effective interference.

second—1) To support a person or a unit in combat. 2) In British usage (with emphasis on the second syllable), to attach a military person temporarily to some unit other than his or her own or to assign some temporary duty.

secondary armament — In ships with armament of various sizes, the guns next largest to those of the main battery.

secondary attack (holding attack)— An attack of only moderate intensity, designed to fix the enemy in position, forcing him to commit his reserves prematurely in a sector other than that in which the main attack will take place.

secondary battery—On a warship, all guns except MAIN BATTERY and antiaircraft guns.

second echelon—In Soviet army doctrine as displayed in World War II, the portion of a command that is not part of the FIRST ECHELON but FOLLOW-ON FORCES. The second echelon is not considered to be a reserve and is always given a specific mission to perform in following up on the anticipated success of the first echelon. If the first echelon fails to accomplish its mission, and thus does not create the conditions for the second echelon to perform its assigned task, the second echelon can be used as a reserve and be committed to reinforce the first echelon and help it accomplish its mission. Like the first echelon, the second echelon at one level of command may be part of either the first or the second echelon of a higher echelon of command.

second in command — An officer whose rank and responsibilities are next in importance to those of a commanding officer, whose duties the second in command performs in the absence of the commanding officer. See also **deputy** and **executive officer**.

second lieutenant—1) The lowest commissioned rank in the U.S. Army, Air Force, and Marine Corps, comparable to an ensign in the Navy. 2) An officer holding that rank.

second line—1) Of aircraft, having officially recognized limitations for combat or other military use but employed in an emergency and in situations for which first-line aircraft are not available. 2) In ground combat, that portion of a force that supports the first line of troops and follows it into battle.

second strike — Nuclear counterattack by the victim of a FIRST STRIKE.

secret—A U.S. government SECURITY CLASSIFICATION of material whose unauthorized disclosure would endanger security, seriously injure the interests or prestige of the United States, or be of great advantage to a foreign nation.

section—1) As applied to ships or naval aircraft, a tactical subdivision of a DIVISION. It is normally one-half of a division in the case of ships, or two aircraft. 2) A subdivision of an office, installation, territory, works, or organization, especially a major subdivision of a staff. 3) A tactical unit of the U.S. Army and Marine Corps. A section is smaller than a PLATOON and larger than a SQUAD; and in some organizations, the section, rather than the squad, is the basic tactical unit.

sector—1) An operational area for attack or defense, designated by boundaries within which a unit operates and for which it is responsible. 2) One of the subdivisions of a coastal frontier.

sector of fire—An area, limited by boundaries, assigned to a unit or to a weapon to cover by fire.

secure—*v.* To gain possession of a position or terrain feature, with or without force, and to make dispositions to prevent its destruction or loss by enemy action. *adj.* 1) An indication that everything is as it should be under the circumstances. 2) Protected against access by unauthorized personnel, as "a secure area for discussion or use of classified material."

security—1) Measures taken by a command to protect itself from espionage, observation, sabotage, annoyance, or surprise. 2) A principle of war emphasizing the vital importance of such measures. 3) A condition that results from the establishment of protective measures to ensure a state of inviolability from hostile acts or influences. 4) With respect to classified matter, it is the condition that prevents unauthorized persons from having access to official information safeguarded in the interest of national defense. 5) Protection of supplies or supply establishments against fire, theft, sabotage, or enemy attack.

security, communications—Measures designed a) to deny to unauthorized persons information of value that might be derived from the possession and study of telecommunications or b) to mislead unauthorized persons in their interpretations of the results of such a study.

security classification — A category or a grade assigned to defense information or material to indicate both the degree of danger to national security that would result from its unauthorized disclosure and the standard of protection required to guard against unauthorized disclosure. The normal security classifications in the U.S. armed forces, in ascending order of sensitivity, are **confidential, secret,** and **top secret**.

security clearance—A clearance given by an investigative authority, permitting access to CLASSIFIED INFORMATION and material up to a specified level of classification, provided there is a NEED TO KNOW.

selected reserve—Those units and individuals of the ready reserve designated as so essential to initial wartime missions that they are considered to be in active status.

selective service—see **conscription**.

self-bow—See **bow**.

self-defense, right of—The traditional justification for military action against a supposed aggressor. Although nations that subscribe to the UN charter renounce the right to initiate war, under Article 51 they retain the right to defend themselves against attack and to defend other signatory nations that are under attack.

self-propelled—1) Of a gun, mounted on a vehicle with its own motive power. 2) Of a missile, propelled by fuel carried within the missile itself. 3) Of a military unit, having self-propelled guns. 4) Of a vehicle, having its own means of mobility.

self-propelled artillery—See **artillery**.

semaphore—A system of transmitting messages by moving hand-held signal flags, or other signaling devices, into various positions.

semiautomatic—1) The capability of a weapon to be fired either in the single-shot or automatic modes. 2) Using part of the force of an exploding cartridge to extract the empty case and insert the next round in the chamber, but requiring a separate pull on the trigger to fire each round.

semifixed ammunition — Ammunition in which the cartridge case is not permanently attached to the PROJECTILE. This permits the withdrawal of a powder packet or packets before firing, in order to fire the weapon at less than full charge. See also **ammunition,**

fixed; reduced charge; and **separate-loading ammunition**.

seniority—A higher rank or position. One military person has seniority over others by holding a higher rank or having held the same rank longer than another. The person is said to be **senior** to these subordinates.

sensing—An observation of the fall of shot with respect to the target.

sensitive compartmented information (intelligence) — Material bearing special control indicators and requiring special handling within the intelligence community.

sensor—A device that detects such things as terrain configuration, the presence of military targets, and other natural and manmade objects and activities by means of energy emitted or reflected by such targets or objects. The energy may be nuclear, electromagnetic (including the visible and invisible portions of the spectrum), chemical, biological, thermal, or mechanical, including sound, blast, and earth vibration.

sentinel—A person posted as a guard to protect something or some area, as to give warning of an approaching enemy. Also known as "sentry."

sentry—See **sentinel**.

Sentry (E-3)—An AWACS aircraft capable of providing all-weather command, control, and communications for battlefield commmanders. A modified Boeing 707, the Sentry mounts radar with a range of more than 250 miles, as well as an identification friend or foe (IFF) subsystem.

separate-loading ammunition— Ammunition in which the PROJECTILE and CHARGE are loaded into a gun separately. See also **ammunition, (fixed** and **semifixed)**.

separation—The process of leaving military service to return to civilian life.

sepoy—An Indian soldier serving in British forces.

September 11, 2001 attacks — See **World Trade Center and Pentagon attacks, 2001**.

sergeant—An enlisted rank of noncommissioned officers in various military services, including the U.S. Army, Air Force, and Marine Corps. There are several grades of sergeant. In the U.S. Army these are, in ascending order, sergeant, staff sergeant, technical sergeant, senior master sergeant, and chief master sergeant.

Sergeant (MGM-29A)—A mobile, solid-propellant, surface-to-surface missile designed for targets up to a range of 75 nautical miles.

sergeant, color—See **color sergeant**.

sergeant, flight—See **flight sergeant**.

sergeant major—A designation for the chief administrative noncommissioned officer of a unit headquarters, who is also normally the senior noncommissioned officer of the unit. The sergeant major usually assists the adjutant.

sergeant-major-general—1) In the 16th century, the senior administrative officer of an army under operational command of a monarch or his lieutenant general. 2) Commander of the militia, by election, in the Massachusetts Bay Colony.

sergeant of the guard — The senior noncommissioned officer of a guard detachment.

serial—A number of aircraft under one commander, engaged in conveying a unit or a subunit to the same objective.

serial number—1) The number given a member of the service upon entry to military service. The same serial number identifies a service member throughout his or her career.

2) Designation of a unit of march when a large military force moves by road. 3) The number assigned to a piece of military equipment for identification and control.

serpentine—1) A cannon used from the 15th through the 17th century. A typical English serpentine—the name was metaphorical, referring to the weapon's deadliness, not its shape—had a caliber of 7 inches and fired a 42-pound shot. 2) The S-shaped arm that held the match of the MATCHLOCK and pivoted to touch the lighted end to the primer in the PRIMING PAN.

service ammunition—Ammunition intended for combat rather than for training purposes.

service dress—The normal uniform worn by service personnel except for special duty requirements. Also simply called **dress.**

serviceman, servicewoman—A person in the armed services.

service medal—A medal recognizing participation in a war, a campaign, or a special operation. It is distinguished from a DECORATION by being automatically awarded to anyone who participated. (The term "medal" is sometimes used for both service medals and decorations.)

service, military—1) Collectively, the armed forces of a nation. 2) One of the separate branches of the armed forces. 3) Formal participation in military activity in the armed forces.

service practice—The training process of firing ammunition in order to increase proficiency. Generally applied to artillery.

service ribbon—A ribbon worn on the uniform to represent a service medal.

service star—1) A small metal star worn in the U.S. services on a campaign or war ribbon, representing a clasp on the ribbon holding the medal and signifying membership in a unit that participated in a war campaign or a separate battle of the campaign. Each bronze star is a symbol of one battle or campaign, each silver one represents five. 2) When worn on a decoration ribbon, the stars represent additional awards of the same decoration.

service stripe—In the U.S. armed forces, a diagonal stripe representing 3 years of active service worn by enlisted persons on the left sleeve of the uniform, except for Navy ratings, who wear them on the right. Also known as "hash marks."

service test—A test of an item, a system, matériel, or technique conducted under simulated or actual operational conditions to determine whether specified military requirements or characteristics are satisfied.

service troops—The units designed to fulfill supply, maintenance, transportation, evacuation, hospitalization, and other services required by air and ground combat units.

service unit—A noncombat army unit. This includes supply, medical, and engineer units.

set-piece battle—The conduct of a battle by a military force in accordance with carefully prepared plans, which have usually been repeatedly rehearsed before the battle.

shakedown—The cruise of a newly commissioned or overhauled ship to check its machinery and to train its crew as a working unit.

shako—A military dress hat made of leather or other stiff material, cylindrical in shape, with a short visor, a chin strip, and a plume.

shaped charge—An explosive charge one side of which is so hollowed as to cause a focusing of the blast energy into a high-velocity jet of flame that will penetrate armor. It is sometimes called a HOLLOW CHARGE or BEEHIVE-SHAPED CHARGE. See also **Munroe effect**.

Sharps rifle — A .50-caliber BREECH-LOADING rifle with a vertically sliding BREECH-BLOCK, invented by Christian Sharps in 1848. It was in use for about 45 years and was a major infantry weapon of the American Civil War.

sheaf, converged—The lateral distribution of fire of two or more artillery pieces so that the planes of fire intersect at a given point.

sheaf of fire—Designates the planes of fire of the trajectories of two or more artillery pieces in order to achieve a desired pattern of bursts in the target area. Sheafs of artillery batteries are normally parallel, unless some other effect is desired. See also **sheaf, converged**; **sheaf, open**; and **sheaf, parallel**.

sheaf, open—1) The lateral distribution of the fire of two or more pieces so that adjoining points of impact or points of burst are separated by the maximum effective width of burst of the type of shell used. 2) Term used in a call for fire to indicate that the observer desires a wider sheaf than the one being employed.

sheaf, parallel—A sheaf in which the planes of fire of all pieces are parallel. See also **sheaf of fire**.

sheaf, width of — A field artillery term meaning the lateral angle between the shell bursts at the sides of the sheaf (called "flank bursts"). The comparable naval gunfire term is "deflection pattern."

shell—*n.* A projectile, usually of iron or steel, containing a high-explosive, chemical, or nuclear charge. A high-explosive shell is designed either to carry the explosive charge for destructive effect against an object or to scatter shell fragments for antipersonnel effect. *v.* To fire shells at a target.

shell case—A cylindrical case of metal or cardboard that contains charge, primer, and shot.

shell fragment—A piece of jagged metal resulting from the explosion that tears apart the case or shell of a high-explosive projectile. The explosion propels the fragments with lethal force in a roughly circular or oblong area around the point of impact. During World War I some military doctors, unaware of the difference between SHRAPNEL and a high-explosive shell, referred to shell fragments and the wounds they caused as "shrapnel" and "shrapnel wounds."

shell shock — See **fatigue, combat** and **posttraumatic stress disorder**.

shelter half—One of the halves of a shelter tent.

Sherman (M-4)—This medium tank, introduced in 1941, was the standard U.S. tank in World War II. Although it went through many modifications, most versions weighed some 33 tons and mounted a 75mm gun.

shield—A protective device for the body, used by warriors since antiquity, carried on the non-weapon-bearing forearm and maneuvered to fend off blows or missiles or set on the ground. Shields were carried by most soldiers before the introduction of gunpowder reduced both the incidence of close-encounter warfare and the effectiveness of the shield. Over the centuries, shields were made of many materials, including leather, wood, and metal, and in many shapes and sizes, from the small circular shield to full-length rectangular shields that covered the entire body. Still in use on artillery pieces and antitank guns is a thin, bulletproof metal sheet designed to protect gunners from small-arms fire and shell fragments, commonly known as a **gun shield.**

shield-wall—A circular or square formation, similar to a PHALANX, used by several Germanic tribes of the early Middle Ages, in which warriors maintained a defensive position, usually against hostile cavalry, by putting together the shields of the front ranks to form a kind of wall across the front or around the formation.

Shillelagh (MGM-51)—A missile system mounted on a main battle tank or other vehicle for use against enemy armor, troops, and field fortifications.

U.S. Army photo
A Shillelagh missile fired from a Sheriden light tank.

Shillelagh

Shining Path (Sendero Luminoso) — A Maoist guerrilla movement in Peru that sought to create a Marxist state there. Founded in 1969, it was one of the most violent, as well as one of the most xenophobic, of Latin American insurgencies, for its leaders had little contact with other leftist movements. Although the movement had as many as 8,000 active adherents in 1990, counterinsurgency actions by the government in the 1990s sharply reduced the Shining Path in numbers and influence.

ship of the line—In the days of sail, a warship that was large enough and had enough guns to form part of the principal battle line, originally so called in the British Royal Navy. During the 18th and early 19th centuries, the typical ship of the line carried 74 or more guns; a few of the largest carried 100 guns.

ship's armor—See **armor**.

ship's clerk—A U.S. Navy warrant officer whose duties are administrative. Senior to him or her is the chief ship's clerk.

ship's company—All the personnel assigned to duty aboard a naval vessel (often also used on naval shore stations), as opposed to others carried aboard, such as naval aviation personnel on an aircraft carrier, observers, or personnel being transported from one place to another. See also **company**.

"shipshape"—A term used to signify that a vessel or portion of a vessel is neat in appearance and in good working order.

ship's service—A service aboard ship and at U.S. naval shore stations that includes such facilities as a store that sells items unavailable in the ship's store or canteen, laundry, barber shop, tailor shop, shoe repair shop, and photography shop. All items are sold at slight profit and the proceeds put in the ship's or station's welfare fund. (Comparable to POST EXCHANGE and **base exchange** in the U.S. Army and Air Force.)

ship's store—A store on a ship or naval shore station that carries personal items for sale to all personnel. Also known as the CANTEEN.

ship-to-shore movement—The portion of the assault phase of an amphibious operation that includes the deployment of the landing force from the assault shipping to designated landing areas.

shock action—Military action employing SHOCK TACTICS.

"shock and awe"—A strategic concept long associated with military operations but especially so with the 2003 Gulf War. It focuses on the psychological destruction of the enemy's will to fight rather than the physical destruction of his military forces. Chinese military writer Sun Tzu (c. 500 B.C.) and Prussian strategist Clausewitz (19th century) were earlier advocates of similar tactics. Many of the precision-guided weapons employed in the 2003 Gulf War were designed to "shock and awe." See also **massive ordnance air bust**.

shock tactics—Tactics, especially of cavalry or armor, in which the physical overrunning of the opponent is contemplated or attempted. "Shock" implies both the physical imposition of force on an enemy and the psychological effect on the enemy of the threat of being overrun.

shock troops—In the German army, a term for troops selected and trained to lead attacks; elite troops. See also **storm troops**.

shock wave—The pulse formed by the blast from an explosion. Can apply to any explosion, high-explosive or nuclear in origin.

SHORAN—A short-range electronic navigation system used in precision bombing. It uses transmissions from two or more fixed stations to measure distance from the stations.

shore fire-control party—A unit specially trained for control of naval gunfire in support of troops ashore, consisting of a spotting team to adjust fire and a naval gunfire liaison team to perform liaison functions for the ground-unit commander.

shore party—1) A group of people going ashore from a naval vessel for whatever reason. 2) A task organization of the LANDING FORCE formed to facilitate the landing and movement off the beaches of troops, equipment, and supplies; to evacuate casualties and prisoners of war; and to facilitate the beaching, retraction, and salvaging of landing ships and craft. It comprises elements of both the naval and landing forces.

shore patrol—The section of the U.S. Navy that carries out police functions on shore; it corresponds to the U.S. Army's military police.

short-range attack missile (SRAM) (AGM-69)—An air-to-surface missile that is armed with a nuclear warhead and launched from a B-52 or other aircraft. The missile permits the carrier aircraft to attack a target from outside enemy defenses.

short-range ballistic missile (SRBM)—See **missile, ballistic.**

short takeoff and vertical landing aircraft (STOVL)—Fixed-wing aircraft capable of clearing a 15-meter obstacle within 450 meters on takeoff and of landing vertically.

shot—1) The inert material (such as a pellet or a bullet) discharged from a firearm. 2) A solid projectile, as opposed to a SHELL.

shot locker—A strongly built compartment in a ship's hold for containing SHOT.

shoulder—*n.* 1) In a fortification, the angles formed by the front and side walls. 2) The angle between the general front line and the side of a salient. *v.* To lay against the shoulder, as in "shoulder arms."

shoulder belt—A belt supported by one or more suspenders over the shoulder or shoulders, on which various items of equipment are carried (such as small arms, ammunition, canteen, and first aid kit). Can be made of webbing or leather. In leather, it is usually called a SAM BROWNE BELT.

shoulder board—An insignia of rank worn by military officers on the shoulder of their uniform blouse, coat, or shirt. The board is a stiff material covered with cloth, and is attached to the shoulder of the uniform through loops or buttons or both.

shoulder patch—A cloth insignia worn by military personnel just below the shoulder seam (either right or left) of the uniform. Shoulder patches usually indicate the unit to which a person belongs or has belonged.

show of force—The marshaling or deployment of substantial military forces to demonstrate to potential adversaries (and potential allies) a readiness or willingness to fight. A show of force is usually intended as a DETERRENCE.

shrapnel—1) A projectile invented by British Gen. Sir Henry Shrapnel in the late 18th century. It had an outer case within which were metal balls as submunitions, equipped with a fuze designed to cause the projectile to explode in midair and scatter the balls with great destructive force on enemy personnel. 2) The material scattered by a shrapnel shell. 3) A designation of SHELL FRAGMENTS that is technically incorrect but commonly used.

Shrike (AGM-45) — An air-launched, anti-radiation missile designed to home in on and destroy radar emitters.

shuttle bombing—Bombing of objectives using two bases. By this method, a bomber formation strikes its target, flies on to its second base, reloads, and again bombs a target on the return to its home base.

sick bay—The medical treatment center of a ship or naval shore station.

sick call—1) A call on drum, bugle, or trumpet announcing that sick personnel should go to a medical facility. 2) The period during which sick personnel may seek treatment at a medical facility.

side arm—An individual weapon that is carried at the side or the waist. Side arms include such weapons as swords, bayonets, daggers, and pistols.

side boys — Nonrated enlisted personnel aboard a U.S. Navy warship whose duty it was to fall in at the gangway in appropriate numbers whenever naval etiquette called for it to be tended, as it usually was when an officer or civilian dignitary came aboard or left the ship. The side was tended by from two to eight "boys," depending on the rank of the person being honored.

Sidewinder (AIM-9)—A 200-pound, supersonic, solid-propellant, air-to-air missile with a heat-seeking homer and a conventional warhead. Introduced in the 1950s, the Sidewinder is the most widely used air-to-air missile in the West, with more than 110,000 missiles produced for nearly 30 nations.

siege—1) The process of besieging a fortress or town. 2) The activities of a besieging force in the process of a siege.

siege artillery—Artillery whose purpose is to breach the walls of a fortress or town that is under siege or to drop projectiles on targets within them. Siege artillery includes not only guns but also, in ancient and medieval times, the whole array of catapults, arms, towers, and other devices.

siegecraft—The art of conducting sieges.

siege gun—See **siege artillery**.

siege tactics—See **siegecraft**.

siege towers—Movable structures, usually built slightly higher than the walls of a besieged fortification, with which to raise archers and missile-throwing machines to a level from which they could fire at defenders on the top of the walls or fire over the walls into the enclosure. Such towers were always constructed on the spot, although prefabricated portions were sometimes carried in the SIEGE TRAIN. They were used from earliest times until about the mid-15th century, when gunpowder weapons made them both unnecessary and too vulnerable.

siege train—The equipment for conducting a siege, carried on wagons and carts with an attacking army.

siege works—The engineering field fortifications used in the process of conducting a siege, particularly the SAPs and PARALLELs used to bring the attacking forces and their siege cannon close enough to the defender's fortifications for effective fire.

Siegfried Line—1) Allied nickname during World War II for the German West Wall fortified zone, which protected Germany's western frontier from the Swiss border to Ostend on the English Channel. 2) German designation, properly given as Siegfried Position, for a deep, fortified zone that General Hindenburg ordered constructed behind the German front lines on the Western Front in the fall of 1916. Between February and April 1917 the German armies withdrew to this line, which was shorter and more defensible than the salient position they had previously occupied. The Allies called the Siegfried Position the HINDENBURG LINE.

Sierra—Letter of NATO phonetic alphabet. See also **alphabet, phonetic**.

sight—*n.* 1) Actual visual contact, contrasted with radar or sonar or other contact in which the object is not actually seen. 2) A device on a weapon by which the person firing it determines where to aim. *v.* 1) To see. 2) To look at a target in order to establish the point at which to aim.

signal—*n.* 1) A message transmitted from one military unit to another by whatever means. 2) Any transmitted electrical impulse. *v.* To send a message.

signal communications — The transmission of messages between military headquarters and units. Usually refers to electric and electronic transmissions.

signal flag—1) Any flag that is flown or used to convey a message. 2) Usually refers specifically to the set of flags of various shapes and colors used for signaling at sea. (At night, lights are used instead.) 3) Flags for signaling on land, by Morse code or SEMAPHORE.

signalman—1) U.S. Navy specialty rating; chief and first, second, and third class. 2) In the Army, a person using signal flags.

signals—See **signal communications**.

signals intelligence (SIGINT) — Intelligence derived from communications, including radio transmissions and land lines.

significant local war—See **conflict levels of intensity**.

simplicity—A principle of war emphasizing that success in war depends, in part, on the use of organizations, lines of communication, plans, and operations that are relatively free of complexity.

simulated rank—A status given a civilian in terms of a military rank.

simulation—1) A representation of a combat situation, usually by means of a computer program. 2) A kind of combat mode. See also **model** and **simulation, computer**.

simulation, computer—An analytical technique using mathematical and logical models to represent and study the behavior of actual or hypothetical events, processes, or systems. It offers opportunities to test theories and proposed modifications in systems and processes; to study organizations and structures; to examine past, present, and future events; and to represent the use of forces that are impractical to mobilize in peacetime.

"simultaneity"—The strategic concept of using massive force simultaneously on many fronts as in the 2003 Gulf War, in contrast to the sequencing of attacks in the Gulf War of 1991, when 38 days of heavy bombing preceded the opening of the ground war.

single fire—1) One ship firing alone at a single target. 2) Firing an automatic or semiautomatic small arm in such a way that only one round is fired for each pull of the trigger.

Single Integrated Operational Plan (SIOP)—A highly sensitive master plan, produced by the Joint Chiefs of Staff, detailing the U.S. response in the event of attack.

single sap—See **sap**.

site, angle of—The vertical angle from a horizontal plane that is formed whenever a target is higher or lower than the gun or guns that are firing at the target. If the target is higher than the guns, a positive angle of site is created, and a round fired at the elevation corresponding to the range to the target would strike the ground in front of the target. If the target is lower than the guns, there is a negative angle of site, and a round fired at an elevation corresponding to the range would strike the ground beyond the target. Thus, in order to have the round strike at or near the target, a positive angle of site has to be added to the range elevation, or a negative angle of site has to be subtracted. By this process the trajectory is considered to pivot around the gun and to be tilted up or down by the magnitude of the angle of site. Because the trajectory is not really so rigid as this concept implies, when the angle of site is large, a compensating value, called **complementary angle of site** and found in firing tables, is applied. See also **quadrant elevation**.

situation map—A map showing the tactical or administrative situation of a military organization at a particular time. In combat, situation maps in unit command posts are constantly updated as new information is received.

situation report—A report giving the status of a unit or formation at a given time.

six-bell hammocks — The hammocks belonging to members of a ship's crew who had night watches and were allowed to sleep until 7:00 A.M.

skip bombing—A method of aerial bombing in which the bomb is released from such a low altitude that its forward motion causes it to slide or glance along the surface of the water or ground and strike the target at or above water or ground level.

skirmish—An encounter in which few soldiers are involved, usually lasting a short time. A skirmish may be isolated or occur as part of a larger engagement or battle.

skirmisher—A lightly armed or specially trained soldier whose purpose is to engage in small actions, often in front of the main body or on the edges of the battlefield. Skirmishers have been used throughout the recorded history of warfare.

skirmishing order—See **open order**.

skirmish line—A line of soldiers preceding an attacking force, or deployed in front of a defending force, prepared to engage enemy skirmishers or units and prevent them from surprising the main body.

Skyhawk (A-4)—A single-engine, turbojet, attack aircraft designed to operate from carriers and short runways. It is capable of delivering either nuclear or conventional weapons.

SLAM-ER—See **standoff land attack missile—expanded response**.

U.S. Navy photo

Skyhawk (A-4)

slant range—The line of visual distance between two points that are at different elevations.

SLCM (submarine-launched cruise missile)—See **missile, cruise**.

sleeper (intelligence)—A spy who is placed in a target area but not immediately activated.

sleigh—1) A vehicle on runners used for conveying loads, especially over snow and ice. 2) The portion of a gun carriage on which the barrel slides in recoil and returns to battery from recoil.

slice—An average logistic planning factor used to obtain estimates of requirements for personnel and matériel. A personnel slice generally consists of the total strength of the stated combatant element, plus its proportionate share of supporting and higher headquarters personnel and equipment.

sling—A device used by ancient warriors for hurling rocks or other projectiles at an enemy. A sling was usually a rectangular piece of leather or hide with a thong or cord attached to each end. The SLINGER set a rock or other missile in the sling and, holding it by the cords, whirled it rapidly around above his head. By loosing one cord at the proper moment, he released the missile with considerable force. David slew Goliath with such a sling. Projectiles included sun-baked clay balls and, during the Roman republic, pellets of lead in acorn shape. Not to be confused with a child's slingshot.

slinger—One who uses a sling. From prehistoric times into the medieval period, slingers were an element of all combat forces. Famous in Roman times, Balearic slingers were equipped with long-, medium-, and short-range slings and organized into special auxiliary army units. Slingers, often recruited from mountainous regions, formed part of the mercenaries in the service of the French crown in the Middle Ages. They are specifically mentioned in action during the Battle of Navarrete (1367).

slit trench—A narrow trench in which one or more soldiers may take refuge in combat or during an air attack. See also **foxhole** and **trench**.

sloop—A modern naval vessal smaller than a destroyer, used as a convoy escort, in antisubmarine operations, and as minesweepers.

sloop-of-war—A small warship of the 17th, 18th, and early 19th centuries. Smaller than a frigate, it was usually brig- or square-rigged but could also be schooner- or fore-and-aft-rigged, with one, two, or three masts.

small arms—Individual and small-caliber (less than 12mm) crew-served weapons that are not a part of another weapon system. Examples are pistol, rifles, shotguns, submachine guns, and light machine guns. Machine guns mounted on tanks are not considered small arms.

small stores—Personal items and clothing issued to enlisted naval personnel.

small wars—A general term used for wars of less than major importance; usually armed conflicts such as colonial wars, punitive expeditions, and the like, that are not likely to precipitate international crises. See also **conflict levels of intensity**.

U.S. Army photo

"smart" munitions

"smart" munitions—Ordnance that is guided to its target by laser or other technology, becoming in effect a guided weapon. See also **joint direct attack munition**.

smoke grenade—See **grenade**.

smokeless powder—A nitrocellulose propellant that burns increasingly explosively under pressure but produces very little smoke. Introduced in about 1885, smokeless powder permitted gunners to continue to see their targets, which formerly had been quickly obscured by the smoke of black powder. Its widespread adoption marked a significant increase in the lethality of weapons, which also became less vulnerable to countermeasures because their concealment was not betrayed by smoke.

smoke screen—A cloud of smoke used to mask either friendly or enemy installations or maneuvers. Smoke screens may be generated on the ground by use of smoke shells, smoke grenades, or smoke pots. At sea, smoke screens are usually formed from warships' smokestacks by burning smoke-producing fuel.

smoke tank—A tank on an aircraft from which an in-flight smoke screen can be laid down.

smoking lamp—A lamp aboard ship that, when lit, indicated that smoking was permitted. Now only an expression, the smoking lamp was lit when there was little hazard of fire or when smoking might not have been considered disrespectful. Thus, the smoking lamp was out during religious services and when ammunition or fuel oil was being taken aboard.

smoothbore—Said of guns, small arms, or cannon, when the bore or interior surface of the barrel or tube is smooth, not rifled. Prior to about 1850, most small arms were smoothbores; the transition from smoothbore to rifled artillery cannon was made between 1865 and 1885. With the exception of GRAPESHOT and CANISTER, smoothbore artillery guns usually fired only spherical projectiles with a diameter smaller than that of the bore. With the exception of shotgun-type rounds, the same was true of smoothbore small arms. Some modern high-velocity tank guns are smoothbore.

snafu—A term originating in World War II and referring to any confused, chaotic situation. The acronym is derived from "situation normal, all fucked (or fouled) up."

snaphance lock (snaphaunce)—A type of flintlock, invented in the 16th century, in which a piece of flint was held by an S-shaped cock. The cock pivoted to strike a piece of steel (the battery or frizzen) on the other side of the PAN, producing a spark that fired the powder in the pan, which, in turn, ignited the charge in the gun chamber.

snaplock rifle, Swedish — A 16th-century Swedish gun lock, distinguished from the MATCHLOCK in that the match was touched to the powder in the PAN by a spring mechanism rather than by manual means.

snipe—To fire a rifle from a concealed position at individual soldiers. The person detailed for this duty is a **sniper**.

sniper—See **snipe**.

sniperscope—A telescopic sight used to enable snipers to fire accurately at long range.

snorkel—1) A retractable air-intake tube on a submarine that permits the intake of air and the escape of gases so that the vessel can stay submerged for long periods. The device (*Schnorchel*) was introduced by the Germans in World War II. 2) A tube attached to the exhaust pipe of a tank to permit the vehicle to cross rivers even when completely submersed, a technique and device exploited by Soviet forces in the post–World War II era.

SOFA—See **status-of-forces agreement**.

soften—1) To weaken the resistance of an enemy by an attack or a series of attacks in preparation for a major assault. 2) To bomb or strafe enemy positions in preparation for another attack or assault. 3) To shell an enemy-held position or area with artillery or naval guns in preparation for an attack or assault. Often **soften up**. See also **preparation fire**.

soldier—1) In a general sense, any person in an army or ground combat force. 2) An enlisted person in an army, as distinguished from an officer.

solid square—A body of troops in which the ranks and files are equal in number.

sonar—A method or system, analogous to RADAR, in which high-frequency sound waves are emitted underwater, so as to be reflected back by objects. Sonar is used by ships for detecting underwater objects, such as submarines or mines. The term is derived from Sound Navigation And Ranging. See also **ASDIC**.

sonarman—U.S. Navy enlisted specialty rating chief and first, second, and third class.

sonobuoy—A buoy containing an acoustic receiver and radio transmitters; it is dropped into the water from a ship or aircraft to detect and transmit underwater sounds, especially the noise of a submerged submarine.

SOP—See **standard operating procedure**.

sortie—*n.* 1) A sudden attack made from a defensive position. In this sense, it is sometimes called a SALLY. 2) An aircraft airborne on a mission against the enemy or in direct support of such a mission. *v.* To depart from a port or an anchorage with an implication of departure for operations or maneuver.

sound surveillance system (SOSUS) — A seafloor acoustic detection system for monitoring submarines. The U.S. Navy operates SOSUS arrays in parts of both the Atlantic and Pacific oceans. SOSUS is used to detect transiting submarines and, in wartime, would be used to direct antisubmarine forces to underwater targets.

Soviet-Afghan War—The conflict between Soviet and Afghan forces that began in 1979 and ended with the withdrawal of Soviet forces in 1989. It began as an effort by the Soviet Union to sustain a satellite regime in Kabul but took on an international dimension when the United States undertook to finance and equip the Afghan insurgents. In contrast to other LIMITED WARs, religion played a key role, with the Afghan resistance treating it as a JIHAD.

SPADATS (space detection and tracking system)—A system for detecting and tracking space vehicles from the earth. It has two main elements: a) the U.S. Navy's space surveillance system (**SPASUR**), which consists of high-powered transmitters and receivers extending across the southern United States, and b) the U.S. Air Force's **SPACETRACK** network of radars, cameras,

and communications worldwide. Both are part of the NORTH AMERICAN AIR DEFENSE COMMAND (NORAD).

spahi—1) A member of a Turkish cavalry corps. 2) A member of an Algerian or Moroccan cavalry corps in the French army.

Spanish square (tercio) — A 16th-century formation developed by the Spaniards, consisting of several COLUNELAs, eventually standardized at three, with just over 3,000 soldiers in total. It is not clear whether the name *tercio* came from the three colunelas or from the fact that the square comprised about one-third of the infantry component of the average Spanish field army. Like the ancient Roman LEGION and the modern DIVISION, it became the basic combat unit of Spain's army, large and diverse enough to fight independent actions on its own. By the time this formation had become standardized, the SWORD-AND-BUCKLER TROOPS and HALBERDIERS had been eliminated, leaving PIKEMEN and ARQUEBUSIERS as the components of the tercio, which dominated European battlefields for the remainder of the century.

SPAR—See **Women in the Coast Guard**.

Sparrow (AIM-7)—An air-to-air solid-propellant missile with electronic-controlled homing. It has a cylindrical body with four midbody wings and four tail fins. The ship-launched version is designated as **Sea Sparrow**.

Raytheon Corporation photo

Sparrow

Spartan—A nuclear surface-to-air guided missile formerly deployed as part of the SAFEGUARD ballistic missile defense system. It was designed to intercept incoming missiles above the earth's atmosphere.

sparum—A kind of dart with a triangular point fired by a crossbow.

SPASUR—See **SPADATS**.

spatha—A long cutting sword of the Roman Empire cavalry and of Germanic tribal cavalry of the Roman era.

spear—Any stick with a pointed head used as a thrusting or throwing weapon. The man armed with such a weapon is a "spearman."

spearhead—*n.* Any force that precedes others in an attack. *v.* To lead an attack; to provide the drive for launching an attack; to take the lead in an undertaking.

special court-martial — See **court-martial**.

special force—Any military force trained for unusual or unconventional operations. The U.S. Army's Special Forces consist of personnel with cross-training in basic and specialized military skills. They are organized into small, multipurpose detachments with the mission to train, organize, supply, direct, and control indigenous forces in guerrilla warfare and counterinsurgency operations and to conduct their own unconventional warfare, special reconnaissance, and counterterrorism operations.

special orders—Orders issued by a headquarters that apply to a particular person or situation and do not have the general application of GENERAL ORDERS.

special operations—Operations conducted by specially trained and equipped units to achieve military, political, or intelligence objectives by unconventional means in hostile or politically sensitive areas. Special operations—the specifics of which are rarely described in detail—are usually characterized by a high level of secrecy and by independence from local support.

special-purpose vehicle—A vehicle incorporating a special chassis and designed to meet a special requirement (e.g., an amphibious vehicle).

special staff—All staff officers having duties at a headquarters and not included in the general, coordinating staff group or in the commander's personal staff group. The special staff includes certain technical specialists and heads of services (e.g., quartermaster officer, ordnance officer, transportation officer).

specialty mark—The device on a naval enlisted person's rating badge that indicates his or her specialty.

specified command—An operational U.S. force of major size and importance that has a broad, continuing mission and is established by the President through the Secretary of Defense with the advice and assistance of the Joint Chiefs of Staff. It can be composed of elements from one service or two or more services. The Strategic Air Command is an example.

spectrum of conflict—The conceptual portrayal, usually in diagrammatic form, of the various types of violent hostility, from least violent to most violent.

Spencer rifle—A repeating rifle invented by Christopher M. Spencer in 1860 and used by Union forces in the American Civil War. It had a tubular magazine in the butt that held seven cartridges. By releasing the trigger guard the rifleman inserted a cartridge in the chamber and expelled the empty cartridge case from the preceding shot. The same device was also incorporated in a carbine, with which Union cavalry was also armed.

Library of Congress photo

Spencer rifle

spike—1) To drive a spike or similar object into the vent of a MUZZLE-LOADING cannon so that the gun is useless. 2) The term is often used for any action to disarm artillery pieces, such as removing the BREECHBLOCK or removing the firing pin.

spin—An aerial maneuver or performance, either controlled or uncontrolled, in which an airplane makes a vertical descent with its nose pointed sharply, or slightly, downward, while revolving about the line of descent in any of various "attitudes." An attitude is a flyer's term for an aircraft's position as determined by the inclination of the axes to a specific frame of reference; unless otherwise specified, the frame of reference is fixed to the earth.

spin stabilization—The directional stability of a projectile imparted by the spinning of the body about its axis of symmetry. The spin is usually imparted by rifling in the tube of the weapon that fires the projectile.

Spirit (B-2)—A multirole intercontinental bomber capable of delivering either nuclear or conventional munitions. Its low-observability or "stealth" characteristics allow it to penetrate radar defenses at high altitudes. The B-2's range is approximately 6,000 nautical miles.

Spitfire—A low-wing fighter of the Royal Air Force with a single in-line engine. Used throughout World War II, the Spitfire had the speed, rate of climb, maneuverability, and firepower that made it one of the most effective fighters of its day. It played a key role in turning back the Germans in the Battle of Britain (1940). In its long operational use it underwent numerous modifications, and some Spitfires were used by the U.S. Army Air Force.

spoiling attack—A tactical maneuver employed to impair or interfere with an anticipated hostile attack while it is being prepared by the enemy. Usually employed by mobile defending units that attack enemy assembly positions in front of the defender's main line of resistance or battle position.

spoils—Whatever the victor takes from the vanquished in time of war. Among ancient Greeks, the general got the largest share, with the rest divided evenly among his troops. Spoils taken by Roman legions belonged to the republic.

sponge—A device for cleaning the bore of cannon, usually consisting of lambskin mounted on a wooden cylinder on a long stick, sometimes on the same stick with the rammer on the other end, which just fitted the gun bore. After the gun had been fired, the wet sponge was swabbed around inside the barrel to make sure there were no sparks remaining. A sponge is used to clean the chamber of modern weapons firing separate-loading ammunition after each round is fired.

spontoon—A short pike that was used by boarding parties in the 17th century and became a badge of rank of infantry officers in

England and in the U.S. Continental Army, where it was called a "half-pike," "feather staff," or "leading staff." Various forms appeared, but the characteristic one of the 17th to the mid-19th century had a broad blade with a rounded base and was heavily decorated with insignia.

spot—1) To determine by observation deviations of gunfire from the target for the purpose of supplying necessary information for the correction of fire. 2) To place in a proper location.

spotter—1) A person who observes and reports on naval gunfire and often designates targets. 2) A person in an aircraft who looks for people, other aircraft, troops, artillery hits, or other objects.

Springfield rifle—1) A .30-caliber U.S. Army rifle, first manufactured at the armory in Springfield, Mass., in 1903. Breech-loading and magazine-fed, with bolt action, it was the most accurate infantry weapon of the early 20th century. It was the U.S. Army's chief arm from World War I until the beginning of World War II, although it underwent some modification in the intervening decades. 2) In the Civil War, the same armory had given its name to a rifle-musket that was the standard weapon on both sides of that conflict. It was a .58-caliber muzzle-loader. An 1873 model was the carbine used by the U.S. Cavalry at the time of the Battle of Little Bighorn. Its caliber was .45 inch.

spy—One who acts clandestinely to obtain information from one side in a conflict, or in anticipation of a conflict, and passes it to the other side.

squad — In a military organization, the smallest personnel unit. In the U.S. Army, for example, a platoon generally consists of three or four squads, each with about 8 to 15 soldiers.

squadron—1) A naval organization consisting of two or more divisions of ships, generally of the same type. In use since the late 16th century, the term originally indicated a number of ships that a single flag officer could command. 2) The basic administrative aviation unit of the U.S. Army, Navy, Marine Corps, and Air Force. 3) A basic administrative cavalry unit (horse or armored), comparable to an infantry BATTALION, with two to four TROOPS and administrative and supporting elements.

squadron leader—1) The pilot in command of a SQUADRON of aircraft. 2) A commissioned rank in the British Royal Air Force and other air forces, corresponding to major in the U.S. Air Force.

square—A body of troops forming a square or rectangle, with several ranks on each side. A square may be hollow or solid. **Hollow squares** have a hollow space or gap in ranks and files in the center. **Solid squares** have the ranks and files equal in length or no gap in ranks and files. Squares were formerly offensive and defensive tactical formations (e.g., SPANISH SQUARE); but with the advent of LINEAR TACTICS in the 17th century, they were largely abandoned as offensive formations and retained only for defense, particularly against cavalry, because they had no flanks that cavalry could attack. The improved accuracy of rifled weapons in the mid-19th century rendered square formations obsolete because the massed troops were an easy target for such weapons.

Square Law—1) One of the two LANCHESTER EQUATIONS. 2) A relationship between physical factors or considerations in war and moral or behavioral factors, as shown in history. Because of this relationship, the effect of human behavioral considerations is judged to be much more important (by an exponential factor of two) than physical considerations. In other words, instead of the relationship suggested by Napoleon—"The moral is to the physical as three is to one"—the new Square Law indicates, "The moral is the equivalent of the physical squared."

squib—A small pyrotechnic device that may be used to fire an igniter, as in a rocket, or for similar purposes. Not to be confused with a detonator, which explodes.

Squid—A British World War II antisubmarine weapon that fired three contact depth charges that would explode close to a submarine and either sink it or force it to the surface.

SR-71—See **Blackbird**.

stability—1) In the context of the balance of power, a high probability that no single nation will become dominant, that most nations will continue to survive, and that large-scale war will not occur. 2) In the context of strategic nuclear forces, usually a low probability of nuclear war.

staff—1) The group of officers assigned to the headquarters of a military command to assist with plans and administration but having no authority to command. Staff of large organizations are usually divided into two major elements: the GENERAL STAFF and the SPECIAL STAFF. 2) A long pole or stick that could be used as a striking or thrusting weapon or could bear a cutting device or other weapon at the end.

staff, allied—A staff or headquarters composed of officers of two or more allied nations working together.

staff, combined—A multinational, multiservice staff.

staff estimates—Assessments of courses of action by various staff elements that serve as a basis for action.

staff sergeant — In the U.S. Army, Air Force, and Marine Corps, a noncommissioned officer. In the Army, a staff sergeant is above a sergeant and below a sergeant first class. In the Air Force the staff sergeant is between an airman first class and a technical sergeant. In the Marine Corps the staff sergeant is between a sergeant and a gunnery sergeant.

staff sling—A simple weapon used in ancient and medieval warfare consisting of a SLING attached to the end of a wooden staff. The use of the staff allowed the slinger to project the missile with greater force and attain greater ranges.

stage—1) To process, in a specified area, troops that are in transit from one locality to another. 2) The part of a missile or propulsion system that separates from the missile at burnout or cutoff. Stages are numbered chronologically in order of burning.

staging area—1) In amphibious or airborne expeditions, a general locality between the mounting area and the objective of the operation through which the expedition or parts of it pass after mounting, for refueling, regrouping of ships, exercise, inspection, or redistribution of troops. 2) In other operations, a general locality, containing accommodations for troops, established for the concentration of troop units and transient personnel between movements over the lines of communication.

stalemate—A situation in which neither of two opposing combatants holds a clear advantage and neither is capable of mounting the effort required to achieve a major victory.

stand (of arms)—A rack for storing small arms, usually rifles.

standard—A flag, a banner, or other device that identifies an individual, an office, a unit, a nation, or a place.

Standard ARM (antiradiation missile) (AGM-78) — An air-launched missile designed to home in on and destroy radar emitters. Originally developed for the U.S. Navy, the AGM-78 was used extensively by the U.S. Air Force during the Vietnam War to destroy North Vietnamese radars controlling antiaircraft defenses.

standard bearer—The person who carries a standard (in a modern military unit it is a **color bearer**).

standardization—1) Use of identical weapons for the sake of economy and flexibility within any large military force, particularly in an alliance of military forces of different nations. 2) The process by which the Department of Defense achieves the closest practicable cooperation among the services and defense agencies for the most efficient use of research, development, and production resources and encourages on the broadest possible basis the use of common or compatible a) operational, administrative, and logistic procedures; b) technical procedures and criteria; c) supplies, components, or weapons and equipment; and d) tactical doctrine with corresponding organizational compatibility.

standard operating procedure (SOP)— A set of instructions covering those features of operations that lend themselves to a definite or standardized procedure without loss of effectiveness. This facilitates rapid, coordinated action in the event of emergency or confusion of battle. The procedure is applicable unless proscribed in a particular case. Thus, the flexibility needed in special situations is retained.

standby—The command that soldiers or matériel be prepared for action without further notice.

stand down—To relax an alert status.

standing army—See **army**.

standing barrage — High-density artillery fire—frontal or flank—fired on call on a preselected line to form a barrier obstructing enemy movement. Usually an element of final protective fire. See also **barrage** and **fire, final protective**.

standing order—An order within a command that remains effective until it is withdrawn or countermanded.

standoff land attack missile–expanded response (SLAM-ER)—A U.S. Navy over-the-horizon air-to-ground missile with improved target acquisition technology. An earlier version was successfully used by F-18 and A-6 aircraft in OPERATION DESERT STORM.

star fort — A fort with several bastions, whose ground plan resembles a star.

Starlifter (C-141)—A large cargo transport powered by four turbofan engines, capable of intercontinental missions with heavy payloads.

U.S. Air Force photo

Starlifter (C-141)

star rank—In the U.S. Army, Air Force, and Marine Corps, the rank of brigadier general and higher, comparable to flag rank in the Navy.

star shell—See **illuminating shell**.

start line—1) A line designed to coordinate the departure of attack or scouting elements; a jump-off line. 2) A marked offshore coordinating line to help assault craft to land on designated beaches at scheduled times. See also **line of departure**.

station—*n.* 1) A general term meaning any military or naval shore installation, location, activity, function or group of functions. 2) A particular kind of activity or function to which other activities or individuals may come for a special service, often of a technical nature (e.g., an aid station). 3) An assigned or prescribed position in a naval formation or cruising disposition or an assigned area in an approach, contact, or battle disposition. 4) Any place of duty or post or position in the field to which an individual, or group of individuals, or a unit may be assigned. *v.* 1) To assign to a billet or post. 2) To place in a specific position for a specific purpose, as a guard at the gate.

status-of-forces agreement (SOFA) — An agreement between allied nations governing the legal status of foreign troops in an allied nation.

stay-behind (intelligence)—An agent or organization designed to be activated and exploited if its base area were to be occupied by hostile forces.

Stealth (F-117)—A single-seat, twin-engine attack aircraft manufactured by Lockheed, the F-117 is the first combat aircraft to embody low-observable technology so as to neutralize enemy radar. First flown in 1981, the Stealth saw extensive service in the Gulf War, where it enjoyed considerable success employing 500-pound laser-guided bombs.

sterilize—1) To remove classified or otherwise sensitive material from a document. 2) To remove from a document material that can identify it as emanating from the sponsoring nation or organization.

stick—1) Missiles or bombs fired quickly, one after another, or released separately at predetermined intervals from a single aircraft.

2) The number of parachutists who jump from one aperture or door of an aircraft during one run over a drop zone.

stiffness—A measure of the tendency of a ship to return to an upright position after inclining away from it because of sea conditions.

stiletto—A small, pointed dagger; the word is a diminutive of the Italian word for dagger, *stilo*. It is thought to have been first used in Italy. The stiletto blade is triangular or sometimes square in section and useful only for stabbing.

Stinger (FIM-92A)—A lightweight, shoulder-fired, air defense missile with a range of up to 10,000 feet. The successor to the RED-EYE weapon system, the Stinger is a "FIRE AND FORGET" weapon employing a passive infrared seeker and proportional navigation system. Stingers were used to good effect by the Afghans in their war against the Soviet Union.

stirrup—A device attached to a saddle that holds the foot of a horseman. The origin of the stirrup is unknown, although it seems to have come from eastern Asia early in the Christian era. Its introduction enabled the mounted horseman to maintain his seat and control his horse while wielding a weapon to an extent hitherto impossible. It significantly increased the lethality of the lance by putting the total weight of horse and rider behind its impact and the lethality of the bow and the sword by giving the horseman a secure mounting from which to use them. It was the principal reason for the predominance of cavalry in warfare for about 1,000 years.

U.S. Department of Defense photo

Stealth (F-117)

stock—1) The portion of a hand or shoulder-fired weapon, usually of wood, to which the barrel and the other parts of the weapon are attached. 2) The portion of a rapid-fire weapon that connects the shoulder piece and the slide.

stockade—1) A fortification, one commonly built in American colonial and pioneer days, consisting of posts or stakes driven close together upright into the ground. 2) An area so enclosed and used for a prison; the term is now often applied to any military prison within a fenced area.

Stockholm syndrome—Derived from a hostage-holding incident in a Stockholm bank in 1973, after which it was noted that the released hostages had developed affection and a protective attitude toward their erstwhile captors.

Stokes mortar—A type of mortar invented by F. W. C. Stokes in 1915 and used by the Allies in World War I. Often called a "trench mortar." The cartridge, with a firing pin at its tail end, was dropped into the barrel and immediately fired. It was the prototype for most modern mortars.

stone bow—A crossbow designed for throwing stones.

stone mortar — A mortar used to throw stones about 150 to 250 yards or 6-pound shells 50 to 150 yards. The stones were put in a basket fitted to the bore, and the basket was placed on a wooden bottom covering the chamber. See also **pedrero**.

storekeeper—In the U.S. Navy, a specialty with four ratings: chief and first, second, and third class.

stores, military—Arms, ammunition, clothing, provisions, and other items pertaining to an army.

storm—*n.* A violent assault on a fortified place *v.* To assault, particularly a fortified place.

storm troops—In the German army, an elite body trained to be hardhitting and efficient. See also **shock troops**.

straddle—A naval gunnery term describing a situation in which several rounds of a salvo or a volley have fallen on each side (over and short) of a target. See also **bracket**.

stradiots—Light cavalry, originally Albanians, introduced by the Venetians into their wars in northern Italy late in the 15th century. Similar cavalry were promptly adopted by the French. The stradiots were lightly armored and carried bows or lances.

strafe—1) To rake a body of troops or other persons with gunfire or rocket fire from a flying aircraft at close range. 2) To attack a roadway, a rail yard, a factory, or other installation with bullets, shells, or rockets fired from a low-flying airplane.

straggle—1) To fall behind a moving body of troops, ships, or aircraft. 2) To fall back individually to the rear in combat, without command. 3) To return late to duty. One who straggles is a **straggler**.

straggler line—A line designated by a force commander in a combat situation where stragglers are to be apprehended, collected, and returned to their units.

stratagem—Any action or maneuver whose purpose is to deceive or surprise an enemy.

strategic—1) Of, or pertaining to, strategy. 2) Often used to refer to long-range air attacks against the industry or population of an enemy nation. See also **strategic air warfare**.

Strategic Air Command — See **strategic air force**.

strategic air force—An air force organized and equipped to carry out long-range air operations deep into the heartland of an enemy nation.

strategic airlift—The sustained air transportation of personnel and cargo between theaters, to provide long-range logistic support for a military effort.

strategic air warfare — Air combat and supporting operations designed to effect the progressive destruction of the enemy's war-making capacity. Vital targets may include key manufacturing systems, sources of raw material, critical material, stockpiles, power systems, transportation systems, communications facilities, concentrations of uncommitted elements of enemy armed forces, and key agricultural areas.

strategic concept—1) A concept related to STRATEGY or strategic affairs. 2) The course of action accepted as a result of an estimate of the strategic situation. It is a statement of what is to be done expressed in broad terms sufficiently flexible to permit its use in framing the basic undertakings that stem from the strategic concept.

strategic envelopment — See **turning movement**.

strategic flank—That flank of a military force that, if turned (meaning that the attacking force has passed around the flank), would expose the force's base or line of communications. See also **flank**.

strategic map — A map of medium scale (1/200,000 or smaller,) used for the planning of large-scale operations, including the movement, concentration, and supply of troops.

strategic material—Any material required for essential uses in a war emergency, the procurement of which in adequate quantity, quality, or time is sufficiently uncertain that prior stockpiling is required.

strategic mobility—1) The capability to deploy and sustain military forces worldwide in support of national strategy. 2) The capability of a unit, a command, a force, or a thing that enables it to be readily moved long distances in advance of engagement with hostile forces. See also **mobility**.

strategic reserve—The quantity of matériel that is placed in a particular geographic location for strategic reasons or in anticipation of major interruptions in a supply distribution system.

strategic vulnerability — The susceptibility of key elements of a country's power to damage by another nation or force. Strategic vulnerability may encompass political, economic, and other nonmilitary factors as well as vulnerability to hostile military action.

strategos—A high-ranking Byzantine officer whose command was a THEMA, equivalent to a modern army corps. A strategos was usually the military governor of the province or THEME from which his troops were drawn or where they were based.

strategy—In war or peace, the planning and management of a nation's total available resources—economic, social, political, and military—in order to achieve the goals of national policy, and in wartime, to maximize the likelihood of victory. Such planning and management are the responsibilities of the highest levels of national and military authority. In a strict or military sense, strategy is the art and science of planning and directing military movements and operations so as to achieve victory. Clausewitz defined strategy as "the use of engagements to attain the object of war." And Henri de Jomini defined it as "the art of getting the armed forces into the field of battle," comprising "all the operations embraced in the theater of war in general." See also **strategy, national** and **strategy, military**.

strategy, military—The art and science of developing and employing in war military resources and forces for the purpose of providing maximum support to national policy in order to increase the likelihood and favorable consequences of victory. Science predominates over art in military strategy.

strategy, national—The art and science of developing and using political, economic, psychological, social, and military resources as necessary during war and peace to afford the maximum support to national policies, and in the event of war, to increase the likelihood and favorable consequences of victory. Art predominates over science in national strategy.

Stratofortress (B-52) — An all-weather intercontinental heavy bomber powered by eight turbojet engines. Long a mainstay of the U.S. Air Force, it is capable of delivering nuclear or conventional ordnance and air-to-surface missiles.

U.S. Army photo

Stratofortress (B-52)

Stratotanker (KC-135) — A multipurpose aerial tanker-transport powered by four turbojet engines. It is designed for high-altitude refueling of bombers and fighters.

strength—The number, particularly of personnel or units, in a military force. Effective strength is the number of personnel fit for combat duty.

strike—*n.* An attack intended to inflict damage on, seize, or destroy an objective. *v.* 1) To attack. 2) In the U.S. Navy, of an unrated seaman, to study and work toward making a rating in an enlisted specialty.

strike force—A force composed of appropriate units necessary to conduct strikes, attack, or assault operations.

striker—1) A firing pin or a projection on the hammer of a firearm that strikes the primer in a fuze or a round of ammunition. 2) A soldier or airman who does extra-duty work for an officer for extra pay. See also **orderly.** 3) A naval seaman who is studying for a rating in a specialty.

strike the colors—To lower the flag in surrender.

stripe—1) Indication of rank worn by naval officers on their lower sleeves and on SHOULDER BOARDs. The warrant officer wears a broken half stripe (0.25 inch), commissioned warrant officer a broken full stripe (0.50 inch), the ensign a full stripe, and the successive ranks add half stripes or full, up to full admiral, who wears a 2-inch stripe and three full stripes. 2) An indication of length of service. See also **service stripe**.

stronghold—A place of security; a fort or a fortress.

strongpoint—A strongly fortified and heavily armed locality in a defense system, usually supported by auxiliary armed positions.

Stuka (Ju-87)—The workhorse dive-bomber that was introduced into the German air force in 1938; it had a top speed of 240 miles per hour and a payload of approximately 1,300 pounds. The Stuka excelled in ground support during the German offensives of 1940–41, but its lack of speed made it increasingly vulnerable as the war went on. "Stuka" was the acronym for *Sturzkampfflugzeug*, or dive-bomber.

Stuka (Ju-88)—German twin-engine light horizontal and dive-bomber.

subaltern—1) In the British army, a commissioned officer with a rank below captain.

2) More specifically, a second lieutenant, as opposed to a first lieutenant.

subcommand—A command subordinate to another command.

subhadar—Indian army native officer rank.

sublieutenant—Second lieutenant or SUBALTERN.

submachine gun—An automatic or a semiautomatic weapon, lighter than a machine gun and fired from the shoulder or the hip.

submarine—A warship designed for under-the-surface operations with the primary mission of locating and destroying ships, including other submarines. Following the experiments of David Bushnell with a submersible craft during the American Revolution, there was considerable experimentation in the United States and in Europe. Submersible vessels were used without much success in the American Civil War. The submarine did not become a serious naval war vessel until the 20th century. In World Wars I and II, German submarines (U-boats) caused serious damage to Allied shipping. By the end of World War II, diesel-powered submarines with electric batteries, motors, and generators were fully evolved. In the 1950s the use of nuclear power made it possible for subs to travel thousands of miles underwater and stay submerged for months at a time. With the introduction of ballistic missiles that can be launched from below the sea toward land-based targets, the submarine's role in warfare was dramatically broadened.

U.S. Navy photo

The *Nautilus.*

submarine

submarine, attack—A class of submarine that entered service in the 1980s and is designed to seek and destroy enemy submarines as well as surface ships. Among the ordnance carried are TOMAHAWK cruise missiles.

submarine, guided-missile—A submarine with the additional capability of launching guided-missile attacks regardless of surface conditions. Designated as SSG, SSGN, or SSBN; the SSGN and SSBN (a ballistic missile submarine) are nuclear-powered. The three main classes are the POLARIS (6,700 tons), the POSEIDON (8,250 tons), and the TRIDENT (18,700 tons).

submarine pay—An allowance paid to personnel serving on a submarine because of the hazardous nature of the duty.

submunition—Any weapon designed to separate from its parent munition in the course of operation.

SUBROC (WM-44A) — A submarine-launched surface-to-surface rocket designed primarily for antisubmarine warfare. It can be equipped with either a nuclear depth charge or a homing torpedo.

subsistence—1) Food or provisions. 2) A monetary allowance given a military person in lieu of food.

substantive rank—The permanent rank of an officer temporarily serving in a higher rank or grade.

subversion—Actions designed to undermine the political, economic, or psychological strength of a nation or organization.

Sudanese People's Liberation Army (SPLA)—A guerrilla group composed of non-Muslim residents of southern Sudan opposed to the Islamic fundamentalist government in Khartoum.

Sugar—Letter of old phonetic alphabet. See also **alphabet, phonetic**.

suicide bombing—A terrorist act in which the perpetrator delivers a bomb either by carrying it on his or her person or by driving an explosive-laden vehicle into a target. Long before the 2001 attacks on the World Trade Center and the Pentagon, U.S. installations in Lebanon were the target of suicide bombers in trucks.

summary court-martial — See **court-martial**.

superintendent—The title of the commanding officer at each of the U.S. service academies: the U.S. Military Academy at West Point, the U.S. Naval Academy at Annapolis, and the U.S. Air Force Academy at Colorado Springs.

Super Sabre (F-100)—The first operational U.S. aircraft capable of flying faster than the speed of sound. Nearly 3,000 aircraft were produced between 1953 and 1959.

supply — The procurement, distribution, maintenance while in storage, and salvage of supplies, including the determination of kind and quantity of supplies.

supply column—A procession of vehicles carrying food, support equipment, and supplies for a combat force. Also called **supply train**.

support—n. 1) The action of a force that aids, protects, complements, or sustains another force. 2) A unit that helps another unit in battle. For example, aviation, artillery, or naval gunfire may be used as support for infantry or armor. 3) A part of any unit held back at the beginning of an attack as a reserve. 4) An element of a command that assists, protects, or supplies other forces in combat. 5) An element of an ADVANCE GUARD. v. To provide any of the aforementioned kinds of assistance to a combat force.

supporting artillery—Artillery that executes fire missions in support of a specific unit, usually infantry or armor, but remains under the command of the next higher artillery commander. For example, an artillery battalion fires in support of an infantry regiment but is commanded by the commander of the divisional artillery, who is the next higher commander above the artillery battalion commander.

supporting distance — A position close enough to a combat area or a force in combat to make it possible to provide assistance.

supporting fire—Fire delivered by supporting units to assist or protect a unit in combat.

support trenches—A system of trenches, generally perpendicular to the front, facilitating support of forces in front-line trenches. See also **sap**.

support troops—Troops assigned to provide assistance to combat forces.

suppress—To reduce the effectiveness of a military force, and to inhibit its activity, by means of firepower from any weapons but usually artillery or tactical air elements.

supreme commander—1) A commander superior in authority to all other commanders within a theater of war. 2) The commander at the apex of a military establishment. Used as both a specific and a general term.

surface burst—1) An explosion of a projectile on the surface of land or water, usually by means of a point-detonating fuze. 2) For a nuclear weapon, an explosion at the surface, or above the surface, at a height less than the maximum radius of the fireball.

surface-to-air missile (SAM) — See **missile, surface-to-air**.

surgeon general—The senior officer in the medical departments of the U.S. Army, Navy, and Air Force.

surgical strike—To take out a target with little or no collateral damage.

surprise—*v*. To make an attack at a time or place or in a manner unexpected to the enemy. This is an important principle of war. *n*. The reaction of a combatant to an unanticipated attack by the enemy.

surrender—1) To acknowledge defeat by ceasing to fight and overtly yielding to an enemy. 2) To yield an object or a place to one's opponent voluntarily.

surveillance—The systematic observation of air, surface, or subsurface areas by visual, electronic, photographic, or other means for intelligence purposes.

suspension of arms — A short truce or cease-fire agreed between hostile opponents for burying the dead, awaiting instructions from a superior authority, or other purpose.

suspension of hostilities — A truce or a cease-fire by formal or tacit agreement of the opposing forces.

sutler—A person, not part of the military, who sells liquor, food, or other commodities to the army. Prior to the 20th century, sutlers followed behind an army in the field, like CAMP FOLLOWERs, and set up their shops whenever the troops halted.

Swedish feather or **swine feather** — A stake about 5 feet long, with a spike at each end, used by MUSKETEERs to protect themselves against cavalry in the Thirty Years' War and the English Civil War. It was sometimes used also as a musket rest. The device was abandoned because of the weight it added to the musketeer's burden, which, if he wore a helmet, approached 60 pounds.

sweep—The rapid movement of a large force (ground, naval, or air) over or through a relatively large geographical area to assure control of the region, or to demonstrate the ability to dominate it, and to eliminate hostile opposition in the area.

switch trench—A trench at an oblique angle to a main defensive trench through which troops could fall back if driven from part of the main trench.

swivel gun — A gun, particularly a naval gun, that is mounted on a pivot in order to point in whatever direction is required. See also **pivot gun**.

sword—Any of many varieties of a hand weapon that has a long, sharp blade, with one or two cutting edges, is wielded with one hand or two, and is effective for either cutting or thrusting. The sword is longer than the dagger and often is carried in a scabbard hung from a belt at the waist, where it can easily be drawn. One who carries a sword and is skilled in its use is a **swordsman**. Swords in the 20th century are primarily ceremonial symbols of rank.

sword-and-buckler troops—Soldiers of the Middle Ages who were armed with sword and buckler. The Spanish army of the 15th century was feared for its sword-and-buckler troops.

syntagma—In the military system of Macedonia, an organization of about 256 troops, an element of the PHALANX, roughly equivalent to the modern battalion.

T-34—The standard Soviet medium tank of World War II. Most versions weighed about 26 tons, mounted a 76mm gun, and carried a four-man crew. A total of 40,000 T-34s were produced during the war. A later version, mounting an 85mm gun, was designated T-85.

tabard—A cloak or tunic worn by a knight over his armor, or worn by his herald. The knight's coat of arms was blazoned on it.

table of organization and equipment— A table listing authorized numbers of personnel and major equipment in standard units or formations. Often called and written **T/O&E**.

TACAN—An ultra high frequency electronic air navigation system able to provide continuous data to a selected station. The term is derived from Tactical Air Navigation.

tactical air control center—The principal air operations installation (land- or ship-based) from which all aircraft and air warning functions of tactical operations are controlled for a region or major command.

tactical air controller — The officer in charge of all operations of the TACTICAL AIR CONTROL CENTER. The officer controls all aircraft and air warning facilities within his or her area of responsibility under the tactical air commander.

tactical air force — An air force charged with carrying out tactical air operations in co-ordination with ground or naval forces. In the U.S. Air Force, it may be a component of the Tactical Air Command or of a theater air organization. A tactical air force's components normally include fighter-bomber units and troop-carrier groups, and its command resides in an air commander. In World War II, the term was used overseas to designate a numbered air force composed of tactical air commands.

tactical airlift—An airlift that provides immediate movement and delivery of combat troops and supplies directly to the objective areas through air landing, extraction, airdrop, or other delivery techniques. It also provides the air logistic support of all theater forces, including those engaged in combat operations.

tactical air operations—Support of ground forces by combat aircraft. It generally consists of three major components: AIR SUPERIORITY, AIR INTERDICTION, and CLOSE AIR SUPPORT.

tactical air support—Support of ground forces in TACTICAL AIR OPERATIONS.

tactical bombing—Bombing, usually conducted by tactical air units, in support of surface forces.

tactical command ship—A warship, converted from a LIGHT CRUISER and designed to serve as a command ship for a fleet or force commander. Equipped with extensive communications equipment, it is designated in the U.S. Navy as CC.

U.S. Navy photo

The USS *Wright*.

tactical command ship

tactical concept—1) A statement in broad outline that provides a common basis for the development of tactical and logistical doctrine, organization, and operational requirements. Such statements are normally developed for periods from 10 to 20 years ahead of their implementation. 2) A particular notion of how to fight a battle. 3) In military theory, a concept of war or air power that leads to an emphasis on tactical operations as the best means of achieving victory.

tactical control—The detailed and usually local direction and control of movements necessary to accomplish missions or assigned tasks.

tactical flank—The flank of a military force most vulnerable to envelopment. See also **flank**.

tactical headquarters—For large formations, such as an army, the portion of the headquarters concerned with control of combat forces, as distinct from the administrative headquarters.

tactical locality—An area of terrain that, because of its location or features, possesses a tactical significance.

tactical maneuver—MANEUVER at the tactical level, as opposed to a strategic maneuver.

tactical mobility—The capability of a unit, a command, a task force, or the like to be readily moved in support of combat or moved while engaged in combat. For example, airplanes, tanks, motorized infantry, and naval destroyers have tactical mobility.

tactical nuclear weapon—A nuclear weapon of comparatively small yield (usually less than 10 kilotons) designed for battlefield employment rather than STRATEGIC NUCLEAR OPERATIONS.

tactical reserve—A portion of a ground combat force held out of combat by the commander for use where and when needed.

tactical security—All active and passive measures that protect both command and troops against observation, sabotage, and surprise attack, and that give the commander enough time and space for the conduct of the operation.

tactical walk/ride — A training activity, usually at the staff school or war college level, in which instructors accompany students on foot, on horseback, or in vehicles in a study of a hypothetical combat operation on the ground.

tactics—1) As defined by Clausewitz, the use of armed force in battle. 2) As defined by Jomini, the maneuvers of an army on the day of ENGAGEMENT; the army's contents, its concentrations, and the diverse formations used to lead the troops to the attack. 3) The technique of deploying and directing military forces—troops, ships, or aircraft, or combinations of these, and their immediate supporting elements—in coordinated combat activities against the enemy in order to attain the objectives designated by STRATEGY or OPERATIONS.

Taliban—The Islamic fundamentalist group that ruled most of Afghanistan from September 1996 until expelled by U.S.-led forces in 2001–02. The word *Taliban* derives from the Arabic word *talib*, or "seeker."

Tallboy—The largest conventional bomb employed in World War II. The 6-ton Tallboys were used to sink the German battleship *Tirpitz* near Tromse, Norway, in November 1944.

Tamil Tigers—Term applied to a number of Tamil guerrilla organizations in Sri Lanka dedicated to the overthrow of the Singhalese-dominated central government.

tampion—A plug that closes the muzzle of a gun to keep it clean and dry. Also known as **tompion**.

tandem hitch—Arrangement of draft horses in pairs to pull a wagon or other vehicle, particularly relevant to horse-drawn vehicles and horse artillery from the 18th to the 20th century.

Tango—Letter of NATO phonetic alphabet. See also **alphabet, phonetic**.

tank—A tracked fighting vehicle with heavy armor protection designed as the principal assault weapon of armored formations (battle tank) or as a reconnaissance vehicle (reconnaissance tank). Tanks are often designated light, medium, or heavy, according to weight and the weapons they carry: **light tanks** usually weigh 25 tons or less; **medium tanks**, 25 to 50 tons; **heavy tanks** are usually those over 50 tons. Tanks weighing between 50 and 60 tons are now generally designated main battle tanks. Tanks were first used in warfare by the British in World War I. See also **tank, main battle**.

"tank"—1) The secure briefing room in the Pentagon used by the Joint Chiefs of Staff; 2) Any sound-secure room used for sensitive discussions.

tank armor—See **armor**.

tank destroyer (TD)—A highly mobile vehicle, lightly armored and fully tracked or half-tracked, mounting an antitank gun. Used widely in World War II, U.S. Army tank destroyers usually carried a 75mm or 90mm cannon or a 105mm howitzer.

tank, main battle—A tracked vehicle providing heavy armor protection and serving as the principal assault weapon of armored and infantry troops. The main armament is usually a gun of at least 105mm caliber.

tank-retriever/tank-recovery vehicle—A vehicle with a tank chassis whose purpose is to remove repairable tanks from a combat area.

tank trap—Any of various devices, such as steel posts set in concrete, installed or built in a combat area for the purpose of halting or destroying advancing enemy tanks.

taps—A bugle call that signifies the end of the day and is sounded at a military funeral as a last honor for the dead. The original call was made by tapping a drum.

tarasnice—A light cannon, usually of the type mounted on walls of castles or other fortifications, made mobile by being mounted on a gun cart or a wagon, used by the Hussites in the 15th century. It generally consisted of a barrel clamped to a trestle or a tripod. The barrel was usually over a yard long, with a caliber of 40mm to 60mm. Cast in bronze or iron or welded from iron plates, the tarasnice was also called a "palisade gun."

Tare—Letter of old phonetic alphabet. See also **alphabet, phonetic**.

target—Any person, place, or thing that is the objective of a belligerent action. A target may be anything selected for seizure or destruction—a soldier at whom a gun is pointed, a geographical area to be taken, a country against which intelligence operations are directed, or an oil refinery on which bombs are dropped.

target acquisition—The detection, identification, and location of a target in sufficient detail to permit the effective use of weapons.

target analysis—The examination of potential targets to determine their relative importance, the priority they should be accorded, and the best means by which they might be attacked.

target array—A graphic and analytical representation of the enemy forces, personnel, and facilities that are the objectives of an operation.

target designation—Action to indicate the nature and location of a target.

target of opportunity—A target, unexpectedly visible to an observer, that is within range of available weapons and against which fire has not previously been scheduled or requested.

target system—A group of targets so related or associated that their destruction will produce a particular effect desired by the attacker. For example, the target system of an oil refinery would include storage tanks, refining areas, associated rail or transportation facilities, and even workers barracks—in short, all of the industrial and administrative components affecting the functioning of the complex to be attacked.

task force—1) A temporary grouping of units under one commander for the purpose of carrying out a specific operation or mission. 2) A semipermanent organization of units under one commander for the purpose of carrying out or continuing a specific task. 3) A component of a fleet organized for the accomplishment of a specific task or tasks.

task group—A component of a naval task force.

task organization—1) The process of organizing combinations of individuals or units so as to provide responsible commanders with the means with which to accomplish their assigned tasks in any planned action. 2) An organization table pertaining to a specific directive.

tattoo—1) A drumbeat or a bugle call at night, signifying that enlisted personnel should go to their quarters. 2) A display of military exercises offered as entertainment.

taxiarchia—A unit of the Macedonian army with 128 men, part of a PHALANX, the equivalent of a modern company, commanded by a **taxiarch**.

taxis—A component of a Macedonian PHALANX consisting of 100 men, arranged in files, eight or more deep.

TBS—"Talk between ships." Very high frequency, medium-power radio equipment used primarily for operational or administrative communication between ships.

TD—See **tank destroyer**.

TDY—See **temporary duty**.

team—A number of persons associated or organized together to achieve a common end, as in, "The bomber team includes both the air crew and the ground crew."

tear gas—Chemical irritants that inflame the mucous membranes of the eyes and cause tears. Used as toxic agents in World War II, tear gas is now mainly used as a simulated toxic agent for combat training purposes and in instances of civil disorder, usually to disperse crowds.

technical intelligence — Intelligence concerning foreign technological development, performance, and operational capabilities that may have a practical application for military purposes. It is the end product of the processing and collating of technical information.

technical troops—Personnel trained in the operation, use, maintenance, and repair of specialized equipment, weapons, or instruments.

technique—A means of accomplishing a desired procedure.

telenon—A siegecraft device invented by Diades, Alexander the Great's engineer, consisting of a box or a basket large enough to hold several armed men. This was slung from a boom that was attached to a tall mast or vertical frame on which it could be raised or lowered with ropes. By this elevator a group of infantrymen could be hoisted above PARAPET height, swung over any intervening obstacle, such as a moat, and deposited directly onto the enemy's battlements.

Templar—A member of a monastic order of priestly knights (Knights Templars, or Poor Knights of Christ and the Temple of Solomon) established in Jerusalem (1120) during the Crusades to protect Christian pilgrims traveling in the Holy Land. For a time the largest, most important, and wealthiest of the Crusading orders, the Templars were accused of corruption in 1307 and suppressed with the approval of Pope Clement V. The principal leader in the suppression of the Templars was King Philip IV of France.

template (intelligence)—A term referring to a graphic illustration of enemy capabilities, drawn to scale. The most common form is a situation template, depicting how an enemy might place his forces in certain specified circumstances.

temporary duty (TDY) — Duty performed away from a person's regularly assigned duty station, usually for a short period of time.

temporary grade or rank — A grade held by a military person in accordance with a special schedule established during a period of emergency or in special circumstances. In such situations, a person may be in a temporary grade of major, for example, and concurrently in a permanent grade of captain. The schedule of temporary grades is usually established to meet the requirements of an expanded service.

tent—A portable shelter usually of canvas or skins stretched over a supporting framework of poles, ropes, and pegs.

tercio—See **Spanish square**.

terminal ballistics—See **ballistics**.

terminal guidance—1) The guidance applied to a guided missile in the latter stages of its flight to the target. 2) Electronic, mechanical, visual, or other assistance given an aircraft pilot to facilitate landing on or departure from an air landing or air drop facility.

terrain — Ground in its physical or topographical aspects.

terrain corridor—See **corridor**.

terrain exercise—An exercise in which a stated military situation is solved on the ground, the troops being imaginary and the solution usually being in writing.

terrain study/appreciation — An analysis and interpretation of natural and man-made features of an area, their effects on military operations, and the effects of weather and climate on these features.

terror bombing—Aerial bombing of nonmilitary targets designed to inspire fear in the target populace and to undermine morale. Terror bombing was employed by German aircraft in support of Franco during the Spanish Civil War and was used by both sides during World War II.

terrorism—A politically charged word, the definition of which is often in the eye of the beholder. However, it is best defined as the use of violence against noncombatants in pursuit of political or social objectives. Terrorism is usually intended to intimidate a government or group into changing its policy or behavior. Among the methods employed are hostage taking, bombing, hijacking, and assassination. Terrorism differs from GUERRILLA WARFARE in that terrorists normally target nonmilitary targets and make no effort to seize and control territory.

terrorist threat conditions — There are four recognized levels of threat: **Threatcon Alpha** applies when there is a general threat of terrorist activity, the target and nature of which are unpredictable. **Threatcon Bravo** applies when there is a more predictable threat; measures taken under Threatcon Bravo must be capable of being maintained for weeks without affecting operational capabilities. **Threatcon Charlie** applies when a terrorist incident occurs or when intelligence indicates that an incident is imminent. **Threatcon Delta** applies in the immediate area of a terrorist attack or when intelligence is received that an attack against a specific location is likely.

test depth—The depth to which a submarine is tested, either by live test or simulations, to determine the maximum depth at which it can safely operate.

testudo—1) From the Latin for "tortoise," a Roman formation in which soldiers, standing close to each other, formed a continuous protective wall or roof as they approached an enemy fortification by placing their shields so that they overlapped on all sides and over their heads. 2) Any armored siege weapon of Roman times, such as a battering ram, which was housed in a wheeled vehicle of wood covered with wicker and hides.

tête-de-pont—See **bridgehead**.

tetrarchia—In the ancient Greek army, a unit of 64 HOPLITEs, corresponding to a modern platoon.

Teutonic Knights — A monastic order of German priest-knights, established in Jerusalem (1198) as the Knights of St. Mary the Virgin. They soon transferred to Europe to convert the pagan peoples of east central Europe to Christianity. In 1233 they began the conquest and conversion of the Prussians in what was later East Prussia. Settling there, they continued to try to promote Christianity among Slavic peoples to the east, particularly Poles and Lithuanians. Efforts to expand into Russia ended in defeat at the hands of Alexander Nevski at Lake Peipus (1242). They nevertheless continued to dominate the southeast Baltic Sea littoral. The order's decline began with defeat by the Poles and the Lithuanians at Tannenberg (1410). Their rule in Prussia ended in 1525 when they were secularized and became vassals of Poland.

theater of operations—1) A large area in which air, land, and sea operations are carried out in an assigned mission. A theater of operations is usually an area large enough to permit the combat and support activities for several armies or army groups. 2) The military command controlling combat activities in a theater of operations.

theater of war—A geographic region with the airspace above it considered to be inclusive of more than one THEATER OF OPERATIONS, as in the Asian-Pacific theater of war.

thema—A Byzantine military formation, usually consisting of two or three TURMAE, commanded by a STRATEGOS, its troops being usually drawn from a specific THEME.

theme—A province in the Byzantine Empire, originally organized about the 7th century as a politico-military district. Most themes were commanded by "strategoi," military governors. Soldier-farmers in each theme held land; and each family was obligated to provide a mounted soldier, fully equipped, when called on by the STRATEGOS.

theory of combat—The embodiment of a set of fundamental principles governing or explaining military combat. These principles encompass the identification of patterns in the interactions and relationships among combat variables, particularly the major elements of combat and the combat processes through which they operate; the description of combat structures and particular patterns of interactions and relationships of variables that shape or determine the outcome of combat; the expression in quantitative terms of the patterns so identified and described. A theory of combat will provide a basis for the formulation of doctrine and will help military commanders and planners engage successfully in combat at any level. Clausewitz's book *On War* and the writings of J. F. C. Fuller are examples of efforts to propound a theory of combat.

thermite—A mixture of powdered aluminum and an oxide of another metal, usually iron, which produces intense heat upon ignition. Used in incendiary munitions and in welding.

thermonuclear weapon — A weapon in which very high temperatures are used to bring about the fusion of light nuclei such as those of hydrogen isotopes (e.g., deuterium and tritium) with the accompanying release of energy. The high temperatures required are obtained by fission.

thin-skin—Term describng an armored vehicle or vessel with relatively light armor protection; usually protection is sacrificed to permit greater speed or mobility.

threat—1) Any hostile capability. 2) The overall military capability of a potential enemy.

throwing ax—See **ax**.

throw weight—The size of a missile's payload (usually that of nuclear missiles), in terms of kilotons of TNT, that can be delivered from the launcher to the target. It consists of warheads and penetration aids.

Thunderbolt II (A-10)—A twin-engine, subsonic, fighter-bomber designed for close support of ground forces. It can operate from short, unimproved airstrips and is an effective platform for the MAVERICK missile. The Thunderbolt II entered service in 1975 and saw extensive service in the 1991 Gulf War, where it flew more than 8,000 sorties. The original Thunderbolt was a U.S. Army Air Corps single-engine fighter.

Thunderchief (F-105)—This aircraft was in the Tactical Air Force inventory between 1958 and 1975. Initially designed to deliver nuclear payloads, the F-105 was used in Vietnam for conventional bombing.

Tiger—The most powerful German tank of World War II, the Tiger weighed 54 tons, carried a crew of five, and mounted an 88mm gun. Only about 1,350 Tigers were produced. See also **PZKW**.

Tigercat (F7F) — Twin-engine U.S. Navy fighter aircraft of World War II, manufactured by Grumman.

timariot—Feudal Turkish cavalryman. The timariots were lightly armored and armed with lances or bows.

time and space—A consideration affecting military operations and planning, usually with respect to calculating trade-offs of speed and power for one or both opposing military forces; an example would be calculation of the strengths available to either or both sides in the event that alternative operations at different times and different places were to be undertaken.

time bomb—See **bomb**.

timed run—A bomb run in which the moment that bombs are to be released is determined by timing the run from a given point. Used in World War II in BLIND BOMBING.

time fuze—A fuze containing a timing device to regulate the interval before which the fuze will begin to function. Used generally for air bursts over an enemy position. See also **fuze**.

time on target (TOT)—1) Time at which aircraft are scheduled to attack or photograph a target. 2) The actual time at which aircraft carry out their mission. 3) A method of firing on a target in which several artillery units so time their fire as to assure that all projectiles reach the target simultaneously.

time orderly—Aboard a U.S. naval vessel, a marine or a seaman whose duties are to keep the officer of the deck informed of the time, strike the ship's bell if it is manually operated, and inform the officer of the deck when activities are to be carried out.

tirailleur—French term for a SKIRMISHER, a rifleman, or a light infantryman. *Tirailleur* came into use during the Napoleonic era and was used thereafter to denote troops armed with rifles.

TNT — Trinitrotoluene. A highly explosive substance used alone or in combination with other explosives.

TNT equivalent—A measure of the energy released from the detonation of a nuclear weapon, or from the explosion of a given quantity of fissionable or fusionable material, in terms of the amount of TNT that would release the same amount of energy when exploded.

T/O & E—See **table of organization and equipment**.

tocsin—An army alarm drum or bell formerly used as a signal for charging an approaching enemy.

Tokyo Convention — An international convention, concluded in September 1963, that attempted to prevent the hijacking of aircraft by, among other means, requiring the signatories to deny sanctuary to hijackers.

Tokyo subway gas attack—A terrorist incident on 20 March 1995 in which members of the Aum Shinrikyo doomsday cult punctured plastic bags containing a lethal nerve gas, sarin, in the Tokyo subway, killing 12 people and injuring several hundred more.

tomahawk — A North American Indian weapon and tool consisting of an ax-shaped head, usually of stone, attached with leather thongs to a stick.

Tomahawk—A cruise missile that can be launched from the ground, the air, or a ship.

It can carry either a nuclear or a conventional warhead.

Tomcat (F-14)—A twin-turbofan, supersonic, long-range interceptor manufactured by Grumman and designed to operate from aircraft carriers. It first entered service in 1973, replacing the F-4 PHANTOM II. The Tomcat's primary mission is long-range fleet air defense, and for this it carries a variety of air-to-air and air-to-ground missiles.

"tommy"/"Tommy"—A British soldier. Derived from **"Tommy Atkins,"** a name often used on sample forms in Britain.

tompion—See **tampion**.

Tonton Macoutes—A personal bodyguard created in Haiti by dictator Francois "Papa Doc" Duvalier in 1957 to eliminate his enemies and quell political dissent.

tool, entrenching—See **entrenching tool**.

top secret—A security classification used for defense information or material that requires the highest degree of protection. The top secret classification is applied only to information or material whose defense value is paramount and whose unauthorized disclosure could result in grave damage to the nation, such as the compromise of military or defense plans or intelligence operations or the betrayal of scientific or technological developments vital to the national defense.

"top sergeant"—Slang for a first sergeant.

torpedo—1) A self-propelled underwater projectile launched from a submarine, a ship, or an aircraft, with a warhead that detonates on contact with a target, usually a ship, or in the vicinity of a target. 2) An explosive device that detonates in or under water. The term was first used in the War of 1812 for various types of vessels designed to operate submerged, none of which was successful. The modern locomotive torpedo was first used in combat on 29 May 1877 in the action fought between the *Shah,* a British frigate, and the *Huascar,* a Peruvian turret ship. The *Shah* fired an easily evaded Whitehead torpedo at the *Huascar.* 3) An obsolete designation of naval mines, primarily known for their use during the American Civil War. Admiral Farragut's famous dictum "Damn the torpedos" referred to Confederate mines in Mobile Bay in 1864.

torpedo boat—See **motor torpedo boat**.

torpedo bomber—See **bomber**.

torpedoman—U.S. Navy warrant officer.

torpedoman's mate—An enlisted rating in the U.S. Navy.

torpedo net—A heavy steel net employed to close an inner harbor to torpedoes fired from seaward or to protect a single ship at anchor or sailing out of the harbor.

tortoise—See **testudo**.

toss bombing—A method of bombing in which an aircraft flies on a line toward the target and pulls up in a vertical plane, releasing the bomb at an angle that will compensate for the effect of gravity drop on the bomb. The procedure is similar to loft bombing and is unrestricted as to altitude.

TOT—See **time on target**.

total war—A war in which the total military, economic, political, and social resources of a nation are used.

touchhole—The vent of early cannon or other firearms by which fire was applied to the powder of the charge.

touman—An organization of Mongol cavalry, roughly the equivalent of a modern division, consisting of 10,000 men. Each touman in turn was composed of 10 regiments of 1,000 men each, and each regiment of 10 squadrons, each comprising 10 troops of 10 men.

tournament—See **joust**.

towed artillery—See **artillery**.

TOW missile — A crew-portable, tube-launched, wire-command missile designed for use against enemy armor.

town-major—The British unit affairs officer in charge of an occupied district or town; usually a major.

toxic attack—An attack directed at individuals, animals, or crops, using harmful agents of radiological, biological, or chemical origin.

trace—In fortification, the ground plan of a defensive work.

tracer bullet—A bullet containing a pyrotechnic mixture that is ignited by the explod-ing powder charge in the cartridge in order to make the flight of the projectile visible by day and by night. Tracer bullets are inserted at intervals in belts of machine gun ammunition to permit the gunner to follow the trail of fire and thus improve accuracy.

track—*v.* 1) To display or record the successive positions of a moving object; also to lock onto a point of radiation and thereby obtain guidance. 2) To keep a gun properly aimed; also, to continuously aim a target-locating instrument at a moving target. *n.* 1) The actual path of an aircraft above or a ship on the surface of the earth. The course is the path that is planned; the track is the path actually taken. 2) One of the two belts on which a full-track or half-track vehicle runs. 3) A metal part forming a path for a moving object (e.g., the track around the inside of a vehicle for moving a mounted machine gun).

track angle—The angle formed by the track of a torpedo and the course on which the target ship is proceeding.

tractor, armored—1) An early type of tank. Both the British and the French experimented in World War I with ways of combining the mobility of the tractor with some sort of defensive chassis. Two Frenchmen, Col. Eugène Estienne and Eugène Brillié, developed such a vehicle using a small Holt tractor. Called a *char d'assault*, it was placed in production and used in combat sometime after the first British tanks had been introduced. 2) A tractor with armor to protect engine and driver.

trade-off analysis — Comparative analysis of different alternatives, usually of force structure or organization and usually based on the assessment of advantages and disadvantages of the alternatives, to include equal cost constraints or operational performance.

trafficability—Capability of terrain to bear traffic. The term refers to the extent to which the terrain will permit continuous movement of any type of traffic.

traffic analysis — A form of communications intelligence in which the origin and volume of radio intercepts are studied to determine patterns. Even if interceptors cannot read a given code, they can draw inferences from the number of messages, their length, and their apparent addressees.

trail—1) The after-part, or tongue, of a towed gun carriage that rests on the ground when the gun is in position and on the PINTLE of the LIMBER or PRIME MOVER when towed. 2) A term applied to the manner in which a bomb trails behind the aircraft from which it has been released. The trail of a dropped bomb is the path it travels from the point of release to the point of impact relative to the course of the aircraft from which it was dropped.

train—*n.* 1) A seagoing naval service force or group of service elements that provides logistic support (e.g., an organization of naval auxiliary ships or merchant ships attached to a fleet for this purpose); usually called a **fleet train**. 2) The vehicles, matériel, stores of supplies, and operating personnel that accompany and support a land combat force and furnish supply, evacuation, and maintenance services to a land unit. The elements of this train are sometimes identified separately as **ammunition train, artillery train, supply train**, and so on. 3) Bombs dropped in short intervals or sequences. 4) **Powder train**: a line of gunpowder used instead of a fuze to explode a charge. *v.* 1) To instruct and drill in order to make for proficiency in a procedure. 2) To aim a weapon at a target.

train band—1) A body of militia with some training raised in one of several English cities and serving as supplements to the English army in the 16th and 17th centuries. 2) Similar militia units in the English colonies in America.

training—The process of preparing military individuals and units to perform their assigned functions and missions, particularly to prepare for combat and wartime functions. Covering every aspect of military activity, training is the principal occupation of military forces when not actually engaged in combat.

training unit—A military unit whose purpose is to train recruits or specialists in some area of military duty.

trajectory—1) The vertical path traced by a bullet, a shell, a bomb, or other object after it has been fired, thrown, or launched. Also called the **ballistic trajectory**. 2) The vertical path traced through space by a guided missile, rocket, or ballistic missile, under power for the whole distance or a part of it; this is the **nonballistic trajectory**.

transfer—To assign or attach and sometimes to move a person or unit from one place or organization to another, temporarily or permanently.

transfer fire—An artillery technique for bringing accurate fire on a target quickly and without preliminary adjustment. After registration on a base point or checkpoint, one not too far distant (within established transfer limits in range and deflection), fire for effect is transferred to the target to be attacked.

transport—1) A ship or an aircraft used for carrying soldiers from one place to another. Also called a "troopship." 2) The collective noncombat wheeled vehicles of an army or smaller ground force.

trapper—Defensive protection for a horse. Trappers made of mail in Roman times often completely covered the horse.

traverse—*v.* To change deflection by turning a weapon to the right or left on its mount. *n.* 1) A bank of earth or other defensive barrier put into a trench or across a rampart that prevents an enemy from firing down it lengthwise. 2) A lateral trench to block a possible flanking attack or envelopment.

trebuchet—A type of catapult used as a siege weapon, developed in the Middle Ages, apparently in the East, and employed in various forms from the 12th to the 16th century. It consisted of a long spar, pivoting on an upright frame, with one end considerably shorter than the other. Heavy weights were attached to the short end. The long end was drawn back by a winch so that the end, on which a sling or hollow receptable was fitted, was on the ground. A projectile, usually a rock, was inserted; and release of the head caused the weights to descend rapidly, hurling the projectile in a high arc over the walls of a besieged city. A trebuchet with a 50-foot arm and 10-ton counterweight could hurl 200- to 300-pound rocks about 300 yards; in the 14th century, projectiles as large as 1,000 pounds, including putrefying horse carcasses, were heaved into besieged towns and castles. The PEDRERO (also known as PETRARY or PERRIER) was a stone-throwing trebuchet.

trench—A ditch, used by troops for protection, usually dug parallel to the front line, with the excavated dirt piled in front for added protection. In World War I, particularly on the Western Front, troops lived for months in such trenches, with the Allies facing similarly entrenched Germans across an empty area called no-man's-land. Typically, to provide defensive depth, the trenches were dug in three parallel lines, joined at intervals by communication trenches through which soldiers could move from one line to the next. See also **parallel** and **sap**.

trench-knife—A kind of dagger or long knife with a sharp point and double-edged blade used in modern warfare especially by raiding parties for hand-to-hand combat in trenches.

trench mouth—A painful bleeding of the gums resulting from poor oral hygiene and stress, which became endemic in the trenches of World War I.

trench warfare—Static warfare in which neither side has overwhelming superiority and each feels the need to dig in for protection with trench lines extended for great distances to prevent envelopment. The classic example of this combat was in France in World War I.

triangular division — A division in which the principal combat maneuver elements (infantry or armor) are organized into three regiments or brigades. Prior to World War I, divisions of most major countries were SQUARE, consisting of four regiments in two brigades. In 1916 the Germans eliminated one regiment from each of their divisions, thus removing a level of control (the brigade) and facilitating maneuver and control. After the war most nations followed the German example and triangularized their divisions. See also **division**.

triarius—An older soldier in the Roman army. The triarii wore full array, carried large shields and spears, and formed the third (rear) rank of a LEGION, in MANIPLEs of 60 men.

tribune—1) A senior officer of a Roman LEGION. Each legion had six tribunes, two for each combat line. The six tribunes generally rotated in command of the legion. 2) In the Byzantine military organization, the commander of a numerus, or BANDON, of 300 to 400 men.

trick—At sea, a period of duty shorter than the standard 4-hour watch. The trick usually lasts for 2 hours.

tricorne—See **cocked hat**.

Trident (UGM-96)—The successor nuclear submarine to the POSEIDON, capable of carrying a nuclear or conventional payload up to 4,000 nautical miles. See also **submarine, guided missile**.

trigger — A device that, when pulled or pushed, activates another mechanism, as the trigger that causes a gun to fire.

triple concentration—Three ships firing at the same target.

tripwire—1) In World War I, a wire in front of a line of trenches designed to set off an alarm if breached. 2) Any force or mechanism viewed as a first line of defense but recognized as incapable of being held against a determined attack.

trireme—A warship with three banks of oars on each side, the most common war galley used by the ancient Greeks and Romans. Long and narrow, the trireme had space to carry troops for boarding or for transport. The trireme had two masts and sails, but in battle it was propelled exclusively by its 75 to 150 or more oarsmen, who sat on three levels. The trireme had a metal beak that protruded as much as 10 feet at or below the waterline. When this beak was rammed into the side of another vessel, the results were deadly. See also **bireme** and **corvus**.

Trojan horse—A person or object intended to deceive. The term derives from Greek mythology: During their siege of Troy, the Greeks pretended to abandon a hollow wooden horse. When the Trojans took the horse into their city, Greek soldiers who had been concealed inside the horse proceeded to open the gates to the besieging Greeks.

troop—*n.* 1) A small unit of cavalry or armor equivalent to an infantry COMPANY. 2) In the British army, one-half (four guns) of a battery of artillery. See also **troops.** *v.* To assemble the colors and color guards of one or more units, usually as part of a review or parade, as in "troop the colors."

troop basis—An approved list of those military units and individuals (including civilians) required for the performance of a particular mission by numbers, organization, and equipment, and, in the case of larger commands, by deployment.

trooper—A cavalryman.

troops—1) Soldiers or military personnel of any service (but not usually applied to naval personnel afloat). 2) The plural of TROOP.

troopship—A ship (in the U.S. armed forces, usually belonging to the army) that carries troops; also often called a TRANSPORT.

truce—The cessation of active hostilities for a period agreed upon by the belligerents. It is not a partial or a temporary peace; it is only the suspension of military operations to the extent agreed upon by the parties. See also **armistice**.

true airspeed—See **airspeed**.

truncheon—1) A piece of the shaft of a broken spear. 2) A heavy club. 3) A short staff or baton that serves as a symbol of authority.

trunnions—Pins or studs protruding from both sides of a cannon barrel or its recoil mechanism to support it in its carriage and permit it to pivot for elevation.

tuck—See **estec**.

turbojet—A jet engine for which air is supplied by a turbine-driven compressor activated by exhaust gases.

turcopoles—Lightly armed horse bowmen used by the Crusaders against the Moslems. They were mostly soldiers of European descent who had been born in the Crusader states of the Levant.

turma—1) A Roman cavalry organization, consisting of 30 horsemen formed in three SQUADRONs, each headed by a decurion during the republic. In Imperial Rome a decurion commanded a turma. 2) A Byzantine army organization, the equivalent of a modern DIVISION.

turning movement—An enveloping maneuver that passes around the enemy's main forces to strike at a vital point in the rear or to threaten the hostile line of communications. Often called a "strategic envelopment."

turn to—In the U.S. Navy, an order or a signal for work to begin.

turret—1) A small tower, usually part of a larger tower or structure in ancient and medieval fortifications, particularly castles. 2) A heavily armored, rotating gun mount, completely enclosing all of the gun and its crew except for the protruding muzzle; used particularly on warships, tanks, and aircraft but also found in permanent fortifications. The two principal features of such a turret are the protection provided to gun and crew and the capability for all-around fire (usually between 180 and 360 degrees). The first appearance of such a turret was on the USS *Monitor* in 1862. 3) An ancient siege device consisting of a tall structure of wood on wheels, in which attackers could be moved close to the enemy wall and high enough to scale it.

turret captain—A U.S. Navy enlisted specialty.

turret gun—1) Any gun mounted in a turret. 2) On a warship, any gun of 8-inch caliber or larger mounted in a turret or a similar structure.

U.S. Air Force photo

The turret of a Martin B-26 Marauder.

aircraft turret

turtle boat—A Korean armored warship of the late 16th century, designed and employed in battle by Yi Sung Sin, with which he defeated the Japanese under Hideyoshi in 1592 in the Battle of the Yellow Sea and again in 1598 at Chinhae (where Yi was killed), thwarting Japanese efforts to invade and conquer Korea.

two-person rule—A system designed to limit access to nuclear weapons and related matériel. It requires the presence of at least two authorized persons at the site, each of whom is capable of detecting and correcting any unauthorized procedure.

Typhoon—1) A class of Soviet nuclear submarines, first deployed in 1982. The largest submarines ever built, the six boats of the Typhoon class displaced at least 18,500 tons on the surface, and carried two crews totaling some 150 men. They were armed with 20 solid-fuel ballistic missiles with multiple warheads, as well as torpedoes for defense. 2) A single-engine British Royal Air Force fighter aircraft in World War II.

U

U-2—A single-seat, single-engine, high-altitude reconnaissance aircraft, capable of collecting a variety of technical data and imagery. An early version of the U-2 was shot down by a Soviet missile in 1960, precipitating a major diplomatic incident when the pilot, Francis Gary Powers, was captured just before a scheduled summit conference of world leaders in Paris. After this, U-2s were no longer flown over the Soviet Union. In 1962, U-2s flying over Cuba revealed the buildup of Soviet weapons there, precipitating the CUBAN MISSILE CRISIS.

Lockheed Aircraft Corporation photo

U-2

UAV—See **unmanned aerial vehicle**.

U-Boat—A German submarine. From the German word *Unterseeboot*.

UGM-27—See **Polaris**.

UGM-73—See **Poseidon**.

UGM-96—See **Trident**.

UH-1—See **Huey**.

uhlan—A type of cavalry, armed with lances, derived from the Tatars and used in the Polish and Prussian armies. The term "uhlan" was in use from the early 19th century through World War I.

ulanka—A type of coat worn by German and Polish lancers. The ulanka tunic, sometimes called a "spencer," became fashionable in many European armies in the mid-19th century.

Ultra—Code word for Allied communications intelligence from intercepted German radio traffic. Early in the war, British cryptographers, employing a captured German cipher machine, the Enigma, were able to break German codes. Although success was intermittent, the breakthroughs obtained were of great value to the Allies and contributed especially to winning the Battle of the Atlantic against German U-boats.

unclassified matter—Official documents or material that do not require the application of security safeguards, but the disclosure of which may be subject to control for other reasons.

Uncle—Letter of old phonetic alphabet. See also **alphabet, phonetic**.

unconditional surrender—A surrender in which a body of troops or a nation ceases its armed opposition and gives itself up to the authority and control of its enemy without terms or conditions. It need not be effected on the basis of a signed document (e.g., troops on the battlefield can unconditionally surrender by grounding their arms and reversing their colors). Subject to the restrictions of the laws of war, the surrendered troops are subsequently governed by the national authority to which they surrender. The term became widely used in the United States after Gen. U. S. Grant's response to the Confederate offer to surrender on terms at the Battle of Fort Donelson in 1862: "No terms except an unconditional and immediate surrender can be accepted." Hence the nickname "Unconditional Surrender" Grant.

unconventional war—1) A type of warfare that departs from the normal combat operations of organized military forces employing the standard weaponry of the period. Most often the term is applied to the irregular combat activities of PARTISANs or GUERRILLAs against the conventional forces of the national authority or of an occupying power. 2) The term can also refer to warfare conducted with nuclear, chemical, or biological weapons.

underground—1) An organized group of rebels or insurgents that carries on regular or irregular military operations against the forces or authority of a regularly constituted government or of an occupying power. 2) The network to which this group belongs. An underground is a mechanism set up for activities involving evasion and escape in a conventional or UNCONVENTIONAL WAR. See also **fifth column**.

undergunner—An aerial gunner whose station is in the belly of an aircraft.

underwater demolition — The destruction or neutralization of underwater obstacles; this is normally accomplished by underwater demolition teams. See also **frogman**.

underwater mine—See **mine**.

undress uniform—The normal service or working uniform of a military person, as distinct from DRESS UNIFORM or FATIGUES.

unified command—A command that has a broad, continuing mission and contains significant components of two or more military services (e.g., army and air force) but operates under a single commander. Unified commands are so designated by the Secretary of

Defense with the advice of the Joint Chiefs of Staff.

uniform—1) Dress or clothing of a distinctive cut, material, and color worn by the members of a military or other force to distinguish them from citizens in civilian attire. 2) A single suit of this kind.

Uniform—Letter of the NATO alphabet. See also **alphabet, phonetic**.

uniform allowance — A fixed amount of funding for a military person, in addition to normal pay or salary, to cover the cost of buying uniforms and other required equipment.

Uniform Code of Military Justice—A single code of military law established for all of the U.S. armed services by a law enacted 5 May 1950. See also **justice, military** and **law, military**.

unit—1) Any military element whose structure is prescribed by competent authority, such as a TABLE OF ORGANIZATION AND EQUIPMENT; specifically, part of a larger formation or organization. 2) In the U.S. Department of Defense, an organizational entity assigned a unit identification code (UIC) and termed a unit (e.g., a company, battalion, ship, squadron, detachment, or similar formation).

unit loading—The loading of troop units with their equipment and supplies ready for combat or other operations in ships, aircraft, or motor vehicles.

unity of command—A doctrine stating that effectiveness in warfare is best served by investing command, including the authority and responsibility that inhere to such a concept, in a single person at the highest echelon and in a single person at each subordinate level in a chain of command. Unity of command is one of the nine PRINCIPLES OF WAR.

universal military training — A national program requiring a period of military service for every person eligible for such service. It differs from CONSCRIPTION or SELECTIVE SERVICE by being applicable to all persons, male or female, and by the facts that such training is limited in time or scope and that the people being trained are not enrolled in normal military units.

unlimited war—See **total war**.

unmanned aerial vehicle (UAV)— Pilotless aircraft, directed from the ground or from accompanying aircraft, used primarily for reconnaissance but in some cases equipped with ordnance. The GLOBAL HAWK can loiter over a target area for 24 hours, while the PREDATOR specializes in low-altitude reconnaissance and can be equipped with missiles. Bird-size aerial vehicles being designed for surveillance are called **mini-UAVs**. They can transmit aerial photos of enemy troops and equipment, and some can carry microphones to listen for enemy vehicles or devices to detect chemical agents.

unobserved fire—Fire against targets that are not visible to whoever is directing, conducting, or controlling the fire. Unobserved fire is conducted by means of data obtained from maps, firing charts, or the results of earlier observed fire.

unrestricted war—A war in which the participants recognize no conventions or restrictions in their conduct or use of weapons. It differs from UNLIMITED or TOTAL WAR, in which it is presumed that the conventions of international law apply.

upper works—Naval superstructure located on or above the weather deck.

"up to the hilt"—A term that originally meant that a foe had been fully impaled on one's sword. More recently, the term may allude to any situation in which a person or an institution is totally engaged.

urban warfare — The specialized techniques or circumstances affecting armed combat in an urban environment.

urgent priority—A category of message or immediate mission request that is lower than **emergency priority** but takes precedence over **ordinary priority**. Situations of urgent priority would include the falling of enemy artillery or mortar fire on friendly troops or the movement of hostile mechanized units in such force as to threaten a breakthrough.

utility aircraft—An aircraft that is generally noncombat but used for local travel and whatever other purposes are required.

V

V-1—A German flying bomb employed mainly in cross-Channel attacks against targets in England during World War II. The missile was really a small, unmanned, pulse-jet aircraft, the body of which was a bomb, with a relatively crude guidance mechanism; it had a speed of approximately 360 mph and a range of 150 miles. Beginning in June 1944 some 2,000 were launched, chiefly against densely populated London. The designation V-1 is an abbreviation of the German expression *Vergeltungswaffe eins,* meaning "revenge weapon one." The British called the V-1 the "buzz bomb" and the "doodlebug."

V-2—The first ballistic missile used in combat, the German V-2 was liquid-fueled and could carry a 1,650-pound warhead some 225 miles. The Germans are believed to have fired some 3,000 V-2s, mostly at targets in the London area, in 1944 and 1945.

V-22—See **Osprey**.

validate—To confirm the reliability of military simulations or models by testing them against actual experience. See also **verify**.

validate (intelligence)—To confirm that a collection requirement is appropriate for a given program and that the requirement has not been previously satisfied.

Valkyrie (B-70) — An experimental U.S. bomber, designed by Rockwell International in the 1960s, with a speed of more than 2,000 miles per hour and a service altitude of 70,000 feet. The project was cancelled in 1967.

van—The first element or portion of an advancing military formation, such as an army or a fleet.

vanguard—See **advance guard**.

variable-time fuze—A fuze designed to detonate a projectile, a bomb, a mine, or a charge when activated by external influence—usually through a radar device in the fuze—close to the target. Variable-time fuzes are also known as **VT fuzes** and PROXIMITY FUZES. Such fuzes were much more effective than the comparatively less precise and less accurate TIME FUZE.

vectored attack—An attack in which a weapon carrier—air, surface, or subsurface—without visual or other contact with a target is directed, or vectored, to the weapon delivery point by another unit that does have such contact.

vedette—1) An individual sentinel, often mounted, who is placed at some distance ahead of an outpost or other outlying military formation or position in order to provide early word of an advancing enemy. 2) A small craft, sometimes called a **vedette boat,** whose function is to scout an enemy naval force.

vehicle, amphibious — See **amphibious vehicle**.

vehicle, armored fighting—See **armored vehicles**.

vehicle, infantry fighting — See **infantry fighting vehicle (IFV)**.

veles—A SKIRMISHER in the ancient Roman army. These troops were lightly armed, usually carrying a round shield, a sword, and javelins, although some had bows and arrows and others slings. A veles with a javelin was a JACULATOR, one with a bow was a SAGITTARIUS, and one with a sling was a FUNDITOR. There were 50 to 60 velites in the ordinary MANIPLE.

vent—The hole in the breech of a gun where the charge is ignited. It was through the vent of a MUZZLE-LOADING cannon that a spike was driven to render it inoperable. The enemy's guns would be spiked during a raid, and a force's own guns were spiked if they had to be abandoned.

verification—In arms control, any action taken to ascertain compliance with measures previously agreed. It may include inspection and detection by clandestine means.

verify—To check the reliability of military simulations or models by assuring internal consistency and (sometimes) by evaluating the extent to which results appear reasonable to a military specialist. See also **validate**.

Verona, Operation—The code word for a U.S. project, begun during World War II, to decrypt intercepted Soviet espionage communications. The intercepts revealed a major Soviet effort to obtain U.S. military secrets, especially those relating to nuclear weapons.

vertical and/or short takeoff and landing (VSTOL)—The capability of an aircraft to take off and land on a very short runway and climb almost vertically to flight level.

vertical envelopment—A tactical maneuver in which troops, either air-dropped or air-landed, attack the rear or flanks of an enemy force that is already engaged in combat to its front.

Very pistol—A device used to fire Very lights, colored flares, or signals. The cartridge was invented by an American naval officer, Edward W. Very, in 1877. Such lights are used for signaling, particularly distress at sea.

veteran—*n.* 1) One who is experienced in a service, a skill, or an art. 2) A former member of one of the armed forces; a service veteran. *adj.* Experienced.

vexillum—The standard of a Roman LEGION consisting of a spear to which was attached a cloth pennant or ENSIGN or other adornment.

vice admiral—1) The naval rank above rear admiral and below admiral, corresponding to lieutenant general in the other services. 2) A person holding this rank.

Vickers gun—1) A water-cooled heavy machine gun, of .303-inch caliber, which was standard in the British army in both world wars. It operated with a tripod, using ammunition in canvas belts, each with 250 rounds. 2) A small infantry cannon of 1.5-inch (37mm) caliber used just before and during World War I.

Victor—Letter of both old and NATO phonetic alphabets. See also **alphabet, phonetic**.

Victoria Cross—The highest decoration for valor in the British forces. It was created by Queen Victoria in 1856 to reward any person of any rank in the British armed services for extraordinary bravery in battle. The decoration is in the form of a bronze Maltese cross bearing the royal crest (a lion standing on a crown) above a scroll inscribed "For Valour." The 1.5-inch-wide ribbon is a dull crimson. The crosses are made from guns captured from the Russians in the Crimean War, when the Victoria Cross was first awarded.

victory—The unequivocal success of a military force in accomplishing a combat mission at the expense of an enemy. The obverse or antonym of defeat.

Viking (S-3)—A twin-turbojet, antisubmarine aircraft capable of operating off carriers. It is designed to locate and destroy enemy submarines using a variety of conventional or nuclear ordnance.

VIP—Abbreviation for "very important person." The term came into vogue in World War II in reference to distinguished guests who were to receive special treatment. Use of the term has been discouraged by the U.S. armed forces as inherently flip, but "VIP" lives on.

visibility—1) The horizontal distance (in kilometers or miles) at which a man-size object can just be seen against the horizon sky in daylight. 2) The range of clearness in the air or other medium through which one sees.

V-Mail—In World War II, letters sent to and from U.S. service personnel overseas using a microfilm service. A V-Mail letter was first written on a special form, then microfilmed to be sent to its destination, where it was printed and delivered.

volley—1) Simultaneous firing of a group of weapons. (The term is often confused with SALVO.) Early firearms were often discharged in volleys in battle by soldiers in close formation, so that the combined weight of metal striking an enemy unit could compensate for the inaccuracy of the individual weapons. 2) The fire produced by simultaneous discharge of weapons.

voltigeurs—French light infantry of the 18th and 19th centuries.

volunteer—A person who joins a military organization of his or her own volition. Most soldiers before the 18th century either served as a result of feudal or other obligation to some authority in the area in which they lived or were mercenaries who hired themselves out to whatever army would pay them. In 1758, British law permitted the acceptance of volunteers in the militia. The U.S. armed forces have always used volunteers, sometimes in combination with conscripts. In 1973 the U.S. services became all-volunteer.

VSTOL—See **vertical and/or short takeoff and landing**.

VT fuze—See **variable-time fuze**.

Vulcan—A 20mm weapon designed for low-altitude air defense that can also be employed against ground targets.

vulnerability—1) The state or quality of being unprotected and open to attack and injury. This kind of vulnerability can be relative to some standard of readiness or preparedness. 2) A particular shortcoming or weak point in a person, a thing, or a force.

W

WAAC—See **Women's Army Corps**.

WAC—See **Women's Army Corps**.

wad—A piece of cloth, paper, or other soft material put into a MUZZLE-LOADING weapon to keep the powder and the ball in place by reducing the effects of WINDAGE.

WAF—See **Women in the Air Force**.

Wagenburg—A circle of armor-plated wagons that was formed by the 15th-century Hussites into a LAAGER and linked by chains to form a defended position. In the 1420s and 1430s, John Ziska's Hussites moved in columns of such wagons, achieving great success with this formation. The troops were mostly foot soldiers, some armed with handguns and crossbows but most with pikes; and Ziska always avoided an offensive battle in the open. His strategy was to penetrate as far as possible into enemy territory and then select a good defensive position on which to establish a wagon fort. Raids from the wagon base were designed to goad the foe to disastrous attack. In front of this wall of wagons a ditch was dug. BOMBARDS were placed between wagons, possibly on their four-wheeled carts, but more likely on earthen mounds or heavy wooden platforms. Also placed between wagons and firing from the wagon loopholes were handgunners and crossbowmen.

walkie-talkie—A two-way portable voice radio set. Walkie-talkies were first used in combat in World War II.

"wallah"—British army slang for a person associated with a particular function or role, as in **transport wallah**. The term is of Indian origin.

Walleye (AGM-62)—A guided air-to-surface glide bomb for standoff attacks.

war—An armed conflict, or a state of belligerence, between two factions, states, nations, or coalitions. Hostilities between the opponents may be initiated with or without a formal declaration by any of the parties that a state of war exists. A war is fought for a stated political or economic purpose or to resist an enemy's efforts to impose domination. A war can be short—measurable in days—but usually is lengthy, and some have endured for generations. War has been called the most enduring nonbiological function of mankind. See also **conflict levels of intensity**.

war college—An educational institution in which midcareer military officers study the art of war, including such subjects as strategy, staff work, politico-military relations, and operations analysis.

war correspondent—A person employed by one of the communications media and assigned to a theater of combat operations to report on events for publication or broadcast.

war crime—An action that is recognized by a competent tribunal as a violation of established customs of warfare or of international agreements. It may include mistreatment of the civilian population of an occupied territory, the mistreatment of prisoners of war, or the wanton plundering of private property. The Nuremberg trials (1945–46) established that international laws pertaining to warfare are applicable to individuals as well as to sovereign states. There is no codified body of laws or agreements defining war crimes, although regulations are published in the U.S. armed forces to serve, for all practical purposes, as such a codification. The first such regulation in history was published during the American Civil War in 1863 by the U.S. Army as *General Order No. 100; Instructions for the Government of the Armies of the United States in the Field*. It was written by Francis Lieber and approved by President Lincoln. This was a code defining war crimes and regulating the conduct of the Army as a whole; it later became international law when incorporated into the Hague conventions of 1899 and 1907.

wardroom—A space on a ship set aside for its commissioned officers for dining and social purposes.

war game—A simulation of a military operation involving two opposing forces, using rules, data, and procedures designed to depict an actual or an assumed real-life situation. War games may be manual, with all decisions, assessments, and bookkeeping functions performed manually; computer-assisted; or completely computerized. See also **model** and **simulation**.

warhead—The part of a missile, projectile, or torpedo that contains the charge, whether explosive, chemical, or biological.

war horse—A horse that is used in combat, either to be ridden or to pull weapons and military equipment into battle.

warning order—A preliminary notice of an order or action that is to follow. It is designed to give subordinates time to make necessary plans and preparations.

war of attrition—A war in which one or both sides aim to win by destroying, usually over a protracted period of time, as much as possible of the other's irreplaceable resources.

War Office—Office of the British government that was responsible for administering and directing the British army. It functioned under the direction of the War Minister, who was a member of Parliament and a cabinet officer. In 1964 the administrative offices of the British armed services were merged into the Ministry of Defence.

war of liberation—A Soviet term for an internal war in which the rebel or insurgent force attempts to overthrow an established government, especially when the attempt is to establish a Communist regime.

war paint—Any material applied directly to the face or body, usually for camouflage, when going into combat. War paint was used by the North American Indians and by various tribes worldwide.

war party—1) A band of warriors engaged in a formal or informal combat action, often a raid. 2) A political party urging a nation to embark on a war.

war potential—The capacity and capability of a country to conduct a war, especially measured by the resources in manpower, industry, agriculture, and economic strength required to sustain war.

warrant—An official document appointing a member of the armed forces to a rank or a grade between enlisted and commissioned officer. In the U.S. services, commissions are issued by the President, whereas warrants are issued by the military service.

warrant officer — An officer ranking between noncommissioned officers and commissioned officers by virtue of a WARRANT. Depending on service customs and regulations, a warrant officer has all or many of the rights and privileges of a commissioned officer. In the U.S. Navy a warrant officer may be a boatswain, a gunner, a machinist, an electrician, a radio electrician, a carpenter, a pay clerk, or a pharmacist; a **commissioned warrant officer** (who has a commission appointing him or her to that rank) in each specialty is a chief boatswain, a gunner, and so on.

warrior—One who fights or engages in the armed combat activities of a war.

war room—A room or rooms in a military headquarters (usually a major command) in which authorized personnel meet to receive and discuss information about the current military situation.

Warsaw Pact—An alliance of Communist powers formed in Warsaw, Poland, in 1955, for collective defense under a joint military command. Members were Bulgaria, Czechoslovakia, East Germany, Hungary, Poland, Romania, and the Soviet Union. The fall of the Berlin Wall in 1989 led to the end of the Cold War and of the Warsaw Pact as well.

wash out—1) To eliminate a person from a training program. 2) To be eliminated from a training program.

watch—1) A naval term for a period of duty aboard ship, usually 4 hours in duration. Standard navy watches are as follows: **first watch**, 8:00 P.M. to midnight; **midwatch**, midnight to 4:00 A.M.; **morning watch**, 4:00 A.M. to 8:00 A.M.; **forenoon watch**, 8:00 A.M. to noon; **afternoon watch**, noon to 4:00 P.M.; **first dog watch**, 4:00 P.M. to 6:00 P.M.; **second dog watch**, 6:00 P.M. to 8:00 P.M. 2) That portion of a ship's crew on duty during a given watch.

watch, quarters and station bill—The list of assignments of every member of a ship's company.

watchtower—A tower from which a guard or lookout can observe any unexpected activity that threatens the security of the force to which the guard is attached.

watchword—1) A password given in response to a challenge. 2) A word or a phrase used as a rallying cry or a signal.

water tender—U.S. Navy enlisted specialty rating: chief and first, second, and third class.

wave—A formation of forces, landing ships, landing craft, amphibious vehicles, or aircraft, required to beach at or generally reach an assigned objective about the same time. Waves in amphibious warfare can be classified as to type, function, or order as assault wave, boat wave, helicopter wave, numbered wave, on-call wave, and scheduled wave.

WAVES—An acronym formed from the World War II designation "Women Accepted for Voluntary Emergency Service," a branch of the U.S. Naval Reserve for women, established 30 July 1942.

weapon—An instrument of combat, either offensive or defensive, used to destroy, injure, defeat, or threaten an enemy. By extension, any device, method, or circumstance that can be used either directly or indirectly to destroy, injure, or defeat an enemy, such as ra-

dar or the disruption of supply lines, can be termed a "weapon."

weapons carrier—Any vehicle that is used to carry light weapons, such as rifles, mortars, or recoilless weapons, and on which such weapons may be mounted, fixed, or installed.

weapons of mass destruction (WMD)—Nuclear, chemical, or biological weapons that, by their very nature, cause indiscriminate and extensive casualties and property damage.

weapon system—1) A weapon and the components required for its operation. Thus, a warship and all of its embarked personnel, weapons, and stores can constitute a weapon system; similarly, a group of air defense cannon or missiles, plus the radars, communications, and logistic equipment and the personnel assigned to operate the weapons and equipment, constitute a weapon system; so do a group of aircraft, their crews, installed weapons, and base support personnel and equipment. 2) Items that can be used by the U.S. armed forces to carry out combat missions that cost more than $100,000 or for which the eventual total procurement cost is estimated at more than $10 million.

weather gage — In engagements between sailing vessels, the advantage of being upwind, or to windward, of one's opponent. A ship with the weather gage could head directly toward its opponent, who would have to tack into the wind in order to close the distance between the vessels. Various advantages in fighting ship to ship with the weather gage favored an attacker, but there were disadvantages, too, including the difficulty of withdrawing from the battle without passing through or close to the enemy's line.

webbing—A stout, close-woven tape used for reins, straps, etc.

wedge—A triangular piece of wood; a QUOIN.

wedge formation—A tactic used by attacking military forces since the dawn of warfare. An example is that used by German forces in World War II, in which a formation with tanks as a spearhead, followed by a wider formation of motorized divisions, and that followed by a still wider formation of infantry divisions, would strike an enemy line and drive through it like a wedge.

West Wall—A generic term to describe German defenses in Western Europe during World War II. The West Wall consisted not only of the SIEGFRIED LINE, protecting the Saar region, but also of fortifications from the Netherlands to the Swiss border. In contrast to France's MAGINOT LINE, the West Wall was not easily bypassed.

wheel—Of a line of troops, ships, or other military unit, to pivot on one end as the rest of the line swings around in an arc to change direction, while still retaining linear formation.

wheellock—A device for igniting the powder charge of a gun, introduced in the early 16th century. In the wheellock, a small piece of flint or iron pyrites was held in a cock. To produce a spark and ignite the charge, the pyrites were rubbed against a rough-edged or notched steel wheel that was wound up by a keylike device. Because it was much easier to handle, the wheellock rapidly replaced the MATCHLOCK.

Whisky—Letter of NATO phonetic alphabet. See also **alphabet, phonetic**.

white phosphorus (WP)—A white or light-yellow, waxlike, luminous substance (phosphorescent in the dark) used as a filling in projectiles or bombs intended for incendiary or smoke-producing purposes. On ignition it produces a yellow-white flame and dense white smoke. Although WP is poisonous when taken internally, its smoke and fumes are not. When dispersed by a bursting charge, as small particles, it ignites spontaneously on exposure to air and continues to burn on contact.

white propaganda—See **propaganda**.

Whitworth gun—A mid-19th-century gun invented by the Englishman Joseph Whitworth. It had a twisted hexagonal bore and fired a long, six-sided projectile, with each plane slightly skewed. It marked a great advance in accuracy over smoothbore guns. The hexagonal bore was used in both small arms and cannon. However, the Whitworth was used primarily as a target-range weapon rather than on the field of battle.

width of sheaf—See **sheaf, width of**.

Wildcat (F4F)—Single-engine U.S. Navy World War II fighter aircraft, manufactured by Grumman.

William—Letter of old phonetic alphabet. See also **alphabet, phonetic**.

Winchester rifle—A lever-action magazine rifle first produced in 1866 by the Winchester Repeating Arms Company of New Haven, Conn. It looked very much like the HENRY RIFLE, and its mechanism for loading and firing was the same as the Henry's. However, the Winchester was stronger and lighter than the Henry chiefly because of changes in the magazine and the method for filling it. The M1866 Winchester fired .44-caliber rim-fire metallic cartridges at a muzzle velocity of 1,125 feet per second. Subsequent models were improved and more powerful. For example, the M1873, the best known of all lever-action repeaters, fired a .44-caliber center-fire cartridge at a muzzle velocity of 1,325 feet per second. The .45-caliber M1876 model was famous as the gun preferred by most buffalo hunters.

windage—1) The deviation in the course of a projectile caused by wind. 2) The correction that must be made in the sighting of a gun because of the effect of wind on the flight of the projectile. 3) The difference between the bore of a gun and the diameter of the ammunition fired from it.

window—Code word for CHAFF.

wing—1) The portion of a military body, army or navy, that is deployed to the right or left of the main body. 2) A U.S. Air Force unit that is larger than an AIR GROUP, including a primary mission group or its equivalent, and is adaptable to particular requirements and situations. 3) In the U.S. Marine Corps, a balanced air task organization that supports a Marine Corps division. See **group**.

wing commander—1) The commander of a WING. 2) A commissioned rank or person in the British Royal Air Force and other air forces equivalent to lieutenant colonel in the U.S. Air Force.

wings—1) Insignia worn by personnel in any of the services who have completed training and qualified as a pilot, bombardier, gunner, navigator, observer, flight surgeon, balloon pilot, or other aircraft crew member. The device consists of a pair of wings with various symbols between them, depending on the service and the type of qualification. Such insignia may be embroidered but is most commonly a pin. 2) The plural of WING.

wire entanglements—See **barbed wire**.

withdraw—To carry out a WITHDRAWAL.

withdrawal—A retrograde movement in which a military force breaks contact with the enemy in order to conduct an orderly movement to the rear, away from the enemy.

WM44A—See **SUBROC**.

WMD—See **weapons of mass destruction**.

Women in the Air Force (WAF) — The women's branch of the U.S. Air Force, established in June 1948. See also **Women's Army Corps**.

Women in the Coast Guard (SPAR)—The women's reserve of the U.S. Coast Guard, established on 23 November 1942. The name SPARS was derived from the Coast Guard motto, *Semper Paratus*.

Women's Army Corps (WAC) — The women's branch of the U.S. Army in World War II. Originally the Women's Army Auxiliary Corps (WAAC), established 14 May 1942, it was incorporated into the U.S. Army as WAC on 1 July 1943. The WAC included women in the U.S. Army Air Forces until about one year after the U.S. Air Force became a separate service. See also **Women in the Air Force**.

works—A fortification, either temporary or permanent.

World Trade Center and Pentagon attacks, 2001 — On 11 September 2001 teams of suicide bombers hijacked four American domestic airliners, crashing two of them into the north and south towers of the World Trade Center and a third into the Pentagon outside Washington, D.C. The fourth flight crashed in Pennsylvania. Some 2,800 people died at the World Trade Center and another 200 at the Pentagon. The coordinated attacks constituted the worst terrorist incidents ever to take place in the United States.

World Trade Center attack, 1993—On 26 February 1993 a truck containing explosives detonated in a parking lot under the north tower, killing six people and injuring 1,000. The attack, which was determined to have been made by Islamic extremists linked to Osama bin Laden, was the worst terrorist incident in the United States up to that time.

worldwide military command and control system (WWMCCS)—A centrally managed information exchange network consisting of computer systems at geographically remote areas, connected by a wideband communications systems. Updated many times, WWMCCS is said to have performed well during Operation Desert Storm.

worm—An iron probe used to clean the debris from the bore of a cannon.

wound chevron—A U.S. decoration given to men wounded in action in World War I, worn on the left sleeve of the uniform.

wounded in action (WIA)—A battle casualty who has incurred an injury as a result of enemy action. Refers to all battle casualties who receive medical care, including those who may later die of wounds.

WP—See **white phosphorus**.

X

Xray—Letter of both old and NATO phonetic alphabets. See also **alphabet, phonetic**.

Y

Yankee—Letter of NATO phonetic alphabet. See also **alphabet, phonetic**.

yardarm blinker—A signal light on the yardarm of a warship that is used for signaling by Morse or other telegraphic code.

yard craft—Any craft assigned for use by a U.S. naval yard, base, or harbor.

yataghan—A long curved knife or short saber, common in Arab or Muslim regions. The yataghan's notable feature is that it has no hilt crosspiece (i.e., there is no guard at the bottom of the hilt where it joins the blade).

yaw—*n.* The movement of an aircraft, a ship, or a projectile about its vertical axis, measured in degrees. *v.* To turn about the vertical axis.

yeoman—An enlisted rating in the U.S. Navy. A yeoman's duties are secretarial and administrative.

yeomanry—In Great Britain, a volunteer force of cavalry that in 1761 was organized as a home guard. Since 1907 it has been part of the British Territorial Army.

Yeomen of the Guard — Personal bodyguard of the sovereign of England, established in 1485, and the oldest military formation in continuous service in the world. The duties today are largely ceremonial.

Yoke—Letter of old phonetic alphabet. See also **alphabet, phonetic**.

Z

zareba—An obstacle similar to ABATIS used by the British in 19th-century colonial campaigns, in which trees and limbs of trees were entwined to form a thick hedge. It differed from abatis in that it was more hastily prepared, and the tree trunks were not embedded in the ground. See also **plashing**.

Zebra—Letter of old phonetic alphabet. See also **alphabet, phonetic**.

zero—To adjust the sights of a rifle or other small arm so that the projectile hits the target at which it is aimed. See also **boresight**.

Zero (Zeke)—The single-engine Japanese plane (AGM) that was the dominant fighter aircraft in the Pacific in the first year of World War II. Although lightly armored, Zeros were noted for their maneuverability and were employed from both land bases and carriers.

zone fire—Artillery or mortar fire designed to cover an area in which a target is situated or is expected to be situated.

zone of fire—An area within which a particular unit delivers, or is prepared to deliver, fire.

zone of operations—Any surface area or airspace where action, especially offensive action, against an enemy is being conducted or contemplated. The term is used especially in connection with air-ground operations, in which the zone of action for air forces may be far removed from the battle area.

zone of the interior—1) That part of a national territory held intact against the enemy, in which the main manpower, weapons, and equipment resources are generated or reserved for use of the armed forces. 2) The continental United States.

Zouaves—A 19th-century infantry unit in the French army, composed of Berber tribesmen from North Africa and noted for their colorful uniforms and close-order drill. In the American Civil War, several regiments on both sides emulated the Zouaves and fought under that name.

Zulu—Letter of NATO phonetic alphabet. See also **alphabet, phonetic**.

Zulu time—Greenwich mean time.